QUEER EURIPIDES

QUEER EURIPIDES: RE-READINGS IN GREEK TRAGEDY

Edited by Sarah Olsen and Mario Telò

BLOOMSBURY ACADEMIC

LONDON • NEW YORK • OXFORD • NEW DELHI • SYDNEY

BLOOMSBURY ACADEMIC
Bloomsbury Publishing Plc
50 Bedford Square, London, WC1B 3DP, UK
1385 Broadway, New York, NY 10018, USA
29 Earlsfort Terrace, Dublin 2, Ireland

BLOOMSBURY, BLOOMSBURY ACADEMIC and the Diana logo are
trademarks of Bloomsbury Publishing Plc

First published in Great Britain 2022

A catalogue record for this book is available from the British Library.

A catalog record for this book is available from the Library of Congress.

ISBN: HB: 978-1-3502-4962-2
       PB: 978-1-3502-4961-5
       ePDF: 978-1-3502-4964-6
       eBook: 978-1-3502-4963-9

Typeset by RefineCatch Limited, Bungay, Suffolk
Printed and bound in Great Britain

To find out more about our authors and books visit www.bloomsbury.com
and sign up for our newsletters.

CONTENTS

Contents

Part V Reproduction

Part VI Encounters

Part VII Transitions

ACKNOWLEDGMENTS

We are grateful to Georgina Leighton and Alice Wright at Bloomsbury for their enthusiastic interest in this project, to Lily Mac Mahon for shepherding the volume through production, and to our five supportive anonymous referees for their comments and suggestions. We also want to thank the people who joined our contributors in five *Queer Euripides* workshops held online between February and May 2021: Catherine Conybeare, Katie Fleming, Sara Lindheim, Helen Morales, Naomi Weiss, and especially Jack Halberstam. Several of the contributors to this volume participated in the events sponsored in 2020–1 by Queer and the Classical (QATC), and we would like to express our deep gratitude to the QATC organizers for creating space for these conversations.

Unless otherwise indicated, the texts of Aeschylus, Sophocles, and Euripides are cited according to the most recent OCT editions—by Page (1972), Lloyd-Jones and Wilson (1990), and Diggle (1981–94), respectively—and the contributors have used their own translations.

QUEER EURIPIDES: AN INTRODUCTION
Mario Telò and Sarah Olsen

Anarchical, clever, decadent, iconoclastic, ironical, irreverent, pre-postmodern, revolutionary, transgressive: these literary-critical labels, commonly used to define Euripides, expand on the characterization that Aristophanes (especially in *Frogs*) bequeathed to modernity, in particular to Friedrich Nietzsche, Euripides' harshest enemy.[1] The fascination with Euripides disavowed by both Aristophanes and Nietzsche has turned, among modernist, postmodern, and post-postmodern scholars and artists, into an explicit or implicit engagement or even cathexis. Already in antiquity Euripides was the most widely performed and read tragedian, and papyrological discoveries have led scholars to conclude that among his surviving plays—all represented in this volume— his most popular were *Medea, Phoenician Women*, and *Orestes*.[2] We mention this fact because the three plays could not look queerer. In different ways, they emblematize, in their thematic and formal features, some of the interpretive questions and theoretical orientations that are central to this book, which stages a sustained encounter between Euripidean tragedy and queerness—as defined, redefined, or, rather, left undefined in the past three decades of critical theory.[3]

Medea, Phoenician Women, Orestes: the plays that compose the canonical triad (trio, threesome, throuple) of Euripides—often cast as the most uncanonical tragedian— evince an abiding interest in forms of aesthetic and political anti- or non-normativity that we can call *queer* or *genderqueer* (a portmanteau of *transgender* and *queer*).[4] In the definition of Judith Butler, "queer" articulates "a contestation of the terms of sexual legitimacy" and "produc[es] a subject through [a] shaming interpellation" (1993a, 18 and 23). For Lauren Berlant and Michael Warner, "queer" points to "changed possibilities of identity, intelligibility, publics, culture, and sex" (1998, 548). According to José Esteban Muñoz, the term "allows us to see and feel beyond the quagmire of the present" (2009, 1). From Susan Stryker's trans(*) perspective, it encompasses an embodied "motion across a socially imposed boundary from an unchosen starting place" (2008, 1).[5] Before situating the book's concerns and goals in broader and more abstract terms, we wish to introduce its agenda—experiments in re-reading and, to an extent, re-inventing the Euripidean corpus—by exploring some of the concrete ways in which those three plays communicate or resonate with different current conceptualizations of queerness. The initial excursus will provide a sense of this project as a theory and practice of (re-)reading, a demonstration of how we can read Euripides otherwise, but also of how a queer approach can alter the modalities of reading (in) classics as a whole.

A tragic fiasco[6] and one of the foundational texts of Western tragedy, as well as of queer and trans(*) art,[7] *Medea* projects its own agonistic failure through Jason's rejection of Medea as a threatening alterity, a destructive challenge to biological reproduction. In contesting the reduction of womanhood to maternity and materializing the Symbolic's fear of a world without the Child, Medea is the figure of the queer as theorized by Lee Edelman—"those *not* 'fighting for the children,' the side outside the consensus by which all politics confirms the absolute value of reproductive futurism" (2004, 3).[8] As D. A. Miller puts it, "If she can't deprive [Jason] of heterosexuality, then she can … deprive him of his reasons for heterosexuality" (2021, 25). The Black Sea princess is also, to an extent, an icon of the gaga feminism theorized by Jack Halberstam: an intersectional, queer, cis and trans(*) feminism[9] characterized by "a refusal of the mushy sentimentalism that has been siphoned into the category of womanhood"; an "ecstatic embrace of loss of control"; "funky forms of anarchy"; and "an antisentimental fascination with loss, lack, darkness" (2012, xiii, 139, and 143). *Medea*'s agonistic failure cannot be separated from the anarchical undoing of kinship that empowers the eponymous heroine while radically disidentifying her, liberating her from the confinement of gender and of the human subject position itself, as shown by Sarah Nooter in her chapter. For Medea, "now is never" (Miller 2021, 226); her being-in-time is repeatedly undone by an a-temporal impetus—a dynamic we also find in *Hecuba*, as suggested by Karen Bassi and, inflected with destructive anti-sentimentalism, in the twin play *Trojan Women* analyzed by Carla Freccero.[10] It is as though, projected outward, the dramaturgy of *Medea*, which enacts the wild self-undoing of infanticide—a self-cutting expressive of what Halberstam calls the "queer art of failure"[11]—succeeded in causing the play's own failure (a theme that Sean Gurd explores in *Alcestis* from the different perspective of performative impossibility or, to be more precise, performance-as-impossibility). In *Medea*, the dissolution of heteronormative kinship goes along with the negativity of female rivalry—a theme that in other Euripidean plays is colored with campy tinges, as shown by Sarah Olsen—but also with intimations of a strong female homosociality (with the Nurse and the members of the Chorus). Solidarity, friendship, and parenthood form a messy web of attachments, of overcharged yet impalpable intimacies—on the threshold between reparative and anti-reparative—an alternative, expansive kinship laden with quasi-erotic intensities, or an anerotic eroticism, as we also see in *Suppliant Women* (see Mario Telò's chapter).

In *Phoenician Women*, a play destined to become a school text in late antiquity and then to be almost forgotten in modern times,[12] we see a queering of Oedipality. While Oedipus' sons seek to bury their father without killing him, the sexual conjugality between Oedipus and Jocasta in Sophocles becomes, in Euripides, an asexual or hyper-sexual fetishistic care that delays Jocasta's suicide long beyond Oedipus' self-discovery and anticipates the nomadic intimacy of Oedipus and Antigone beyond the play's bounds.[13] Queerness here—as we see in Rosa Andújar's chapter—can provide an apt frame for interpreting unsettling, minoritarian configurations not only of relationality, but also of time and aesthetic form. The longest extant play of Greek tragedy and one of the latest, *Phoenician Women* spirals around an impossible ancestral origin[14]—a movement that, looking ahead to the play's scholastic reception, we can connect with the psychic dynamics behind education, an ostensibly constructive exertion that disavows and sublimates the negativity of the repetition it relies on.[15] Time in the play is truly out of joint, to use a Shakespearean phrase appropriated by Derrida and employed in the discussion of queer temporalities offered in the works of Carla Freccero and Elizabeth Freeman especially; it is permeated by a sense of *à venir*, an impossible future, an ongoing deferral, or even an intrinsic lateness.[16] This out-of-jointness, an aestheticized atmosphere of exhausting protractedness, stems from a proliferation of characters and deaths that are difficult to keep apart. This proliferation, with its queerly ironic negativity, disfigures and disidentifies the Oedipality underlying the play's mythical construction and upsets the normativity of the tragic form—the *muthos*—by subjecting it to a kitschy, hypertrophic de-formation. In a sense, the irony resulting from the exuberant proliferation of doubles and surrogates (which makes the play while twisting time and dramatic form) goes a step further, ironizing itself, generating what Damon Young has called "queer seriousness."[17]

Orestes, famous for its late style—"a platform for alternative and unregimented modes of subjectivity" (Said 2006, 114)—stages the tension between identity and disidentification that is integral to queer studies. The intimate friendship of Orestes and Pylades, which finds one of its most sustained representations in this play,[18] can be read according to the model of *erastês/erômenos*, central to a view of (normative) male-to-male sexual attachments in classical Athens that has had an influential—and problematic—impact in modern times, as Daniel Orrells shows.[19] Alongside this reading, dictated by the implicit normativity of a historicist orientation, the play allows for others. As David Youd shows, beyond the pederastic model, the twisting of poetic form opens up disidentificatory possibilities: not just an eroticized friendship beyond the sexual—a queer intimacy in its own right—but configurations of affective attachment beyond the couple structure, beyond the male homosexual dyad.[20] While the dramatic finale's double heteronormative closure—the parallel marriages of Pylades and Electra and of Orestes and Hermione— conjures, *à la* Eve Sedgwick, the scenario of a twofold homo-hetero triangle (Orestes/ Pylades/Electra; Orestes/Pylades/Hermione) in which the cis female characters become the excluded misfit,[21] the paradigm of the "epistemology of the closet" may not account for all the expressions of queer affectivity contemplated by this play's "closet of masks"[22] and, in particular, for the imagination of polyamorous intimacies, or throuples. This possibility of a relationality beyond the dyadic is suggested, as Youd observes, by the play's metrical form, by triangular resolutions, which intimate the unbounded (or differently bounded) contours of queer bonds, challenging the rhythmical distribution of what might be called the relational sensible. In a further turn, an unsettling metrical anarchy informs the flamboyant, astrophic lyric solo of a "minor" character, the Phrygian slave, admitted into Helen's rooms and fanning her, as in a scene of fin-de-siècle orientalism. In scholarship, the Phrygian is often cast "as a freak, [an] Oriental eunuch who cuts a ridiculous figure as a total coward."[23] We do not need to know whether the Phrygian is literally a eunuch[24]—he is certainly a sex slave victimized by a bio- and necro-political system of racialized social and economic oppression.[25] To an extent, the enterprise of determining the anatomical status of the Phrygian inscribes the biopolitical enforcement that underlies transphobic surveillance.[26] When Orestes says to the Phrygian, "You were neither born as a woman (*gunê pephukas*) nor are you in the count of men (*en andrasin . . . ei* 1528)," we feel the oppressive resonance of a binarist Symbolic, but also the denial of trans(*) realism, of "the constative field of transgender desire,"[27] of the paradox of the transgender experience. This paradox, explored in various ways by the chapters of L. Deihr, Kirk Ormand, and Isabel Ruffell, is described by Caél Keegan as "the impossible possibility of living one life in two genders or the illogical project of seeking to be recognized as a gender one already is" (2020a, 70). Yet in the very astrophic structure of the Phrygian's metrically hybrid monody we can also see the force of trans(*) as "a name for expansive forms of difference . . . uncertain modes of being . . . the disaggregation of identity politics," or perceive the ways in which, for some trans(*) thinkers, "trans* bodies, in their . . . unfinished . . . forms, remind all of us that the body is always under construction" (Halberstam 2018, 4–5 and 135).[28]

Along similar lines, the twenty-one chapters of *Queer Euripides*—covering the surviving corpus of complete plays, including the satyr drama *Cyclops*, the pseudo-Euripidean *Rhesus*, and Aristophanes' *Women at the Thesmophoria* (a comedy on Euripides and Euripidean tragedy)—draw out queer readings of relationality, temporality, feeling, and poetic form, considering queerness both as and beyond sexuality. As Joshua Weiner and Damon Young have observed, "Queer bonds reach beyond sexual self-recognition because we need a theory of queer sociality that cuts across identitarian positions that will remain forever incommensurate" (2011, 227). Which forms of queer relationality, concrete yet abstract, constructive yet corrosive,[29] arise from Euripides' manipulation of time and poetic form? How might we consider the significance of those forms beyond the contextualist considerations of the sexual, affective, and social practices that, on the basis of other literary works, we view as contemporaneous and thus relevant to the production and performance of his plays? How do these relationships twist the subject/object positions and the ever-present boundaries of what we call gender—even when we conceive of it as fluid, unstable, indeterminate? Which modes of resistance are projected by queer kinship—understood as "a set of representational and practical strategies for accommodating all the possible ways one human being's body can be vulnerable and hence dependent upon that of another" (Freeman 2007a, 298)?

*   *   *

Rather than adhering to a single school of thought, this volume aims to showcase multiple ways in which queer theory, intended in the broadest sense, opens up new vantage points on the politics and aesthetics of Euripidean theater, and how, in turn, the corpus of Euripidean tragedy anticipates some of the distinctive concerns of queer theory. Madhavi Menon—the editor of *Shakesqueer: A Queer Companion to the Complete Works of Shakespeare*, the volume that has inspired this one—suggests that "it is not enough simply for Shakespeare to be queered: queer theory, too, needs to be shaken" (2011, 3); we likewise take inspiration from the talking possibilities of Euripides' name.[30] The noun *euripos* describes a narrow strait, a place of flux and rapid reversal, an image that corresponds well with our desire to embrace, rather than resolve, the contestations and disagreements that animate queer theory. Yet lest the *euripos* seems too confining, we would also highlight the resonance between the name "Euripides" and the adjective *eurus*, "wide, far-reaching." We intend to facilitate or accelerate the dialogue of Greek tragedy and queer theory, and also to expand queer theory's purview and extend its range of figurations, expressions, and possibilities. This book is a "narrow strait" (*euripos*) in its specific focus upon the corpus of the ancient playwright Euripides and the interventions of largely self-identified queer theorists, but it is a tumultuous and paradoxically "wide" (*eurus*) one, capacious enough to allow multiple reading modes.

We hope that this image of constriction, even intimacy, paired with tumult and breadth will prove productive for the study of queerness beyond Euripides, as well. While queer and trans (with or without an asterisk) studies have battled and still battle each other,[31] they are also divided within themselves between optimism and pessimism, the reparative and the anti-reparative, the futural and the anti-futural, the utopian and the non-utopian, the civil-rights-oriented and the anarchical, and, with particular reference to transness, between valorization of realism and of disidentification, recognition, and opacity.[32] These approaches are all represented in the book, and the tensions are left unresolved, displayed with no forced attempt at reconciliation, even as the practice of Euripidean reading can point to strategies for preventing the dialectics from calcifying into dichotomies. While we believe that the theoretical notion of queerness, in its various definitions and with its various implications, can provide insights into the interpretation of Greek tragedy as a whole,[33] we wish to suggest that queerness can become an embracing category for reading what ancient and modern critics have called the Euripidean "revolution" or seemingly the opposite, Euripidean "decadence" (a derogatory, classicizing term that we are ready to reclaim).[34] Queer reading—or "queering"[35]—can also help us at once problematize the methodological divide between the analysis of the plays themselves and the study of their receptions, and read genders (including "no-gender") and sexualities not simply as potential bridges between literary imagination and social practices (ancient and modern), but as complex, imaginative anti- or non-normative modes of discursive and embodied becoming materialized in tragic form.

Some of the critical language employed to assess Euripides' generic experimentalism—"comic," "melodramatic," "romantic," "weird"[36]— further points to the need for aesthetic queerness as a hermeneutic category. For example, in criticizing Justina Gregory's attempts to reclaim for tragic orthodoxy Euripidean passages suspected of comic deviation (1999–2000), Donald Mastronarde says that, while Gregory wants us to "to take [them] 'straight,'" her argument "runs the risk of flattening Euripides' art, or rendering it to too 'normal'" (1999–2000a, 18). Referring, in the same passage, to Euripidean "jarring[ness]," "hypertrophy," and "awkwardness," Mastronarde employs categories that speak to queer aesthetics.[37] For Aristophanes and ancient critics, Euripides is "thin," "lean" (*leptos*), the tragedian who put tragedy on a diet with vegetable juices after she became "swollen" (*oidousan*) under the tutelage of his predecessor, the "heavy" Aeschylus (*Frogs* 939–42; cf. 828 *kata-lepto-logêsei*). We suggest re-reading this *thinness*, in spite of its potential normativity, as one kind of *queerness*—like its equally excessive opposite[38]—not simply because it looks ahead to Hellenistic models of dandy intellectualism, affected polish, and "decadent" self-denial, but because of its resonance with some queer theorists' use of "thinness" for "intimacies that dwell in their infirmness" (Kasmani 2019, 49).[39]

We can similarly re-evaluate Ann Michelini's catalog of Euripides' ostensibly defective dramaturgical style, which encompasses "the *clumsiness* of the narrative prologue and the *cheapness* of the divine finale, both of which seem to revive the practices of a more *naive* and *undeveloped* dramaturgy," as well as "formal *rigidity*[,] . . . absurd coincidences[,] and *bizarre* shifts of chance" (1987, 111 [our emphases]). *Undeveloped* conjures queer temporality, as detailed above, while *clumsy*, *naive*, *rigid*, and *bizarre* are expressions both of what Halberstam has called the "queer art of failure"—a theme discussed in several chapters—and of Heather Love's "feeling backward" (2009), as well as the queer non-agentic agencies theorized by Berlant (2011). Even Euripides' characteristic self-consciousness—what Simon Goldhill has called "the self-reflexive and transgressive manipulation of the conventions of genre" (1986, 253)—can be connected with queer reinterpretations of Freudian narcissism as a discomfort with the deceptive sense of wholeness offered by heteronormativity, as the reclaiming of "a relation to the self and the world that is queer in the sense that it complicates, competes with, or belies heterosexual object relations" (Young 2019b, 444). Another topos of Euripidean criticism, the apparent opposite of this self-reflexivity, the so-called "realism,"[40] is an excessive *effet de réel*, often conflated with anti-tragic abjection related to class, which exposes the audience to a dizzy feeling of the paradox of literature, that is, of its inevitable distance from what is called "reality." This sense of literature's alienation from, non-belonging to, reality, which is caused by hyper-realism, parallels the queer's belonging yet non-belonging to the normativity of reality. Euripides' realism can consequently be regarded as "queer realism."[41] In what is allegedly the most realistic play, *Electra*, where the title character appears in a state of social abjection and solipsistic, ragged solitude, we perceive a queer contestation of reproduction, as Melissa Mueller discusses in her chapter—a push, we might say, by the Real, in the Lacanian sense, against the most basic and foundational "reality." A broad range of aesthetic categories allied with queerness (camp, the cute, kitsch, the wild, and others) can help us understand Euripides' peculiarities, his genre troubles—satyrically faced, once again, by Daniel Boyarin—and notorious "formal novelty" and "denaturalization," which, as Victoria Wohl observes, were "more than simply an aesthetic matter" (2015, 6).[42]

This book also integrates elements of reception throughout, rejecting the common structure of the "companion" volume that concludes with the (often selective) consideration of an ancient author, text, or theme in modern times. We have done this in order to both acknowledge the ways in which readings of sexual difference in tragedy are conditioned by the times and contexts in which we read, and also to unsettle the assumption that ancient texts and interpretations must take precedence over modern ones. Rejecting what Kadji Amin has called *endochronology*—a teleologically oriented attempt to create trans-historical continuities and, consequently, a "singular . . . origin point," in queer and trans(*) history (2018, 602)—we embrace creative anachronism, unhistoricism, and hauntology as temporal orientations in our readings of individual plays. (As Oliver Baldwin's chapter shows, *Rhesus*, a non- or hyper-Euripidean play, encapsulates the unhistoricism, the persistent hauntologies that Euripides seems to thrive on.) While we lean away from appropriative gestures and believe that the genealogical desire to find avatars and predecessors is always undermined by gaps and fissures, we programmatically push against historicist contextualism and its ostensible distance from the past it aims to reconstruct. Establishing distinct temporal areas through periodization and thus delineating discrete identities in the name of cultural difference, historicism pre-empts the possibility of porousness between identitarian domains, of unexpected and wayward contacts. In other words, historicist reading can have the effect of interpretive containment, an implicit inscription of normativity and an enforcement of identity.[43] Historicism's apparent detachment entails, in fact, mechanisms of melancholic incorporation, of archival possessiveness, of appropriation of the notionally distant past into the interpreter's mind and body.[44]

We believe that "notwithstanding the illusion of historical situatedness afforded by the ancient Greek idiom, the text is diachronically stratified, hosting multiple contexts shading into each other that have been or will be actualized in experiences of reading" (Telò 2020, 9). To conceive of the interpretive act not as the impossible inhabiting of irreproducible, historically determined cultural codes but as a creative experience, in which the interpreting subject's and the interpreted artwork's temporalities deterritorialize each other, lays the ground for productive forms of queer unhistoricism. In seeking discontinuous, spectral, non-hierarchical connections, such unhistoricism encounters a "shifting web in which proximity and distance, similarity and difference are constantly (re-)negotiated and in which changing desires give rise to moments of communion . . . both in and across time" (Matzner 2016, 192).[45] As Jennifer Doyle and David Getsy observe, "To prompt us to see a material or an object in a different way—against or to the side of its intended use—is a queer tactic" (2013). In response to anxieties about "reading *into*" that this experimental enterprise may raise especially among classicists, we might say that such anxieties evince not only an understandable attachment to the normative, which exerts its own power on all of us, regardless of our intentions, but perhaps also a disavowal of the erotic—the affective excess that informs yet exceeds poetic form—and of other visceral feelings that come through in the gaps of representation. As Ella Haselswerdt shows in her reading of the unstable, perennially-under-suspicion textuality of *Iphigenia in Aulis*,[46] interpretive "escape routes" can emerge from the very uncertainty of the ancient text, and queer reading can unravel philology's normative desire to re-constitute, (re-)create tragic form.

Reconsidering Euripidean relationalities through twisted arrangements of tragic form that yield "unceasing semantic spirals" (Telò 2020, 279) can further help us recover an expansive spectrum of prepositional and disidentificatory conditions (*between, beside, by, toward, within*, etc.); sociabilities, socialities, and sodalities disposed along horizontal or diagonal orientations; and a rhizomatic multiplicity of proximities, adhesions, and adjacencies.[47] How do queer reinventions of the social—interruptions of the "normal" to which the negative, anti-social pressure of sex may or may not contribute—problematize the sense of community and belonging through unsettling affective transactions, dynamics of attachment, or disattachment in the thin space between visibility and opacity, between legitimacy and lawlessness? As Freeman observes, by lingering on the intensive excess and the unruly beyond-time-ness of kinship, queerness makes us (re)discover belonging as "longing" and a sense of "being long" (2007a, 299). Expressing the temporal position of the queer subject, Carolyn Dinshaw has observed, "I am yet another subject of anachronism, experiencing a kind of expanded now in which past, present, and future coincide" (in Freeman et al. 2007, 190). Queering the linear time and hierarchical verticality of heteronormativity, reproduction, and capitalistic production means not only being attuned to "the present's irreducible multiplicity," but also inhabiting the radical possibilities of achrony,[48] suspension, protraction, and stasis. Which affective encounters do Euripides' plays foster between the tragic crises they represent and our current time of crisis? How do they intimate deep, *jouissant* sensations of time's out-of-jointness? A queer approach to Euripides' form, intended in the most capacious sense, seen in its plasticity and potential for de-formation, can open up ways to dis-rupt, dis-able, or "crip" chrononormativities[49] through unpredictable exchanges of virtual and actual; creative juxtapositions and mismatches of chronological registers; and disarticulations of conventional combinations of affect and time: joyful stuckness, ecstatic immobility, energizing crisis, intangible presents, fertile pasts, sterile or wildly emancipatory futures, exuberant backwardness, futural regression, projective presents, achronic punctualities, disjunctive synchronies. These and other possibilities are, explicitly or implicitly, opened up in the chapters of this book, which we hope will mark a new phase of Euripidean and tragedy studies.

As we can infer from Jonathan Goldberg's analysis of Euripides, Proust, Wilde, and Carson, the story of the two versions of *Hippolytus* (another Euripidean "queer failure") disrupts performative chrononormativity and invites us to map the unrequited queer desire of Phaedra for Hippolytus onto Euripides' own fraught relationship with his audience.[50] Going further, we can regard the overdetermined, impossible relationality between the stepmother and Artemis' devotee (asexual? homosexual? a "male lesbian"?) as not simply the target of repression, of a phobic interpellation whose violence is reflected in textual fragmentation, in the loss of the "original," edgier version, but as the realm of an achronic, almost utopian, ancestrality, or a futural regression, materialized in the void of virtualities left by the disappearance of the scandalous first play. These virtualities, however, still come through, in a sense, in the version that we have, in which we are drawn toward minoritarian attachments, queer eroticized proximities (between Artemis and Hippolytus, Aphrodite and Hippolytus, Aphrodite and Phaedra, Phaedra and Artemis, and perhaps even Aphrodite and Artemis) that multiply and problematize the dyadic but also the triangular through affective overlaps and disorienting simultaneities.

The queer (re)readings proposed in this companion volume envision the aesthetic and political potentialities of tragic form in a manner that combines the emancipatory force of critique with post-critique's hermeneutic elevation of "emotion, mood, ... disposition" (Anker and Felski 2017, 11), attachments, and cathexes. In various ways, the chapters pursue "an affective relationship ... with language" (Hamacher 2010, 110)—a queer desire in its own right—demonstrating how "*form informs queerness*, and queerness is best understood as a series of *relations* to form" (Amin, Musser, and Pérez 2017, 228). As Wohl observes, "Euripides' plays reveal the active force of aesthetic form—whether 'beautiful' or 'ugly'— and insist that we ask what form means and what it does" (2015, 135). Subjecting representation to contortions and subversions, Euripidean form, with its micro and macro doings and undoings, lends itself to suggestive, intensive, and perverse readings based on strong or weak impressions, an "aesthetics of … indirection," which may provide "a way of moving beyond identity" (Amin, Musser, and Pérez 2017, 236), personal as well as literary. Alastair Blanshard's reading of *Heracles*— a play famously described by Gilbert Murray as "broken backed"—provides an emblematic illustration of these aesthetic contortions.[51] By heeding the Euripidean queering of form (or the invitation to queer it), we can bring to bear, in Deleuzian terms, minoritarian (that is, fugitive, nomadic) aesthetics, exercising a rebellious interpretive desire whose vitalistic negativity—a wayward affective as well as hermeneutic impetus—is queerer than any outcomes or actualizations.[52]

We believe that, in the face of the racist, xenophobic, and sexist cultural codes embedded in the texts of Greek antiquity (not excluding Euripides), queer anachronism offers opportunities for emancipatory thinking, for altering disciplinary boundaries, and for bridging the gap between scholarship and activism. When Amin, Musser, and Pérez observe that "queer formal practices [can] wrest representation from the heterosexist and racist mishandling of history" (2017, 229), they are operating within a tradition that begins, to an extent, with Sedgwick's model of queer reading as ethical over-reading. As Meridith Kruse points out, "Sedgwick describes how an intense form of close closeness or 'visceral near-identification' with specific textual features, such as 'sentence structure, metrical pattern, [and] rhyme,' enables her … to 'appropriate' the 'resistant power' of a given object for her own use" (2019, 135).[53] Queer reading is a form of ethical appropriation, or, we could even say, activist reading, that draws a reparative energy from relentless interpretive activity and mimeticism while always deferring closural reparation—in line with the suspension and openness of Euripidean finales.[54]

To foster contributors' own modes of ethical over-reading, we have encouraged them to experiment with the format and style of their essays, contemplate the possibility of more personal kinds of writing, stage dialogues with people who queer Greek tragedy outside academia (as in the chapter by Nancy Sorkin Rabinowitz and David Bullen), and reject the constraints of exhaustive (and exhausting) footnoting. As teachers employed in (non-)positions of increasing precarity, many scholars of queerness and antiquity are working from the margins of academia, a place of economic as well as intellectual privilege often shaped by neoliberal logics and even by manifestations of racialized capitalism.[55] At a time when the legal rights of communities of queer and trans(*) people are under assault and subjected to ever more oppressive webs of state surveillance,[56] we want scholarly writing on Greek tragic poetry—where "scholarly" is meant to include and foster (not exclude) creativity and counterintuitive thinking—to reflect and embrace this marginality, use it as a force for pushing against the boundaries and barriers of the field of classical studies.

We agree with Andrea Abi-Karam and Kay Gabriel, who in the introduction of their anthology of radical trans(*) poetry observe (2020, 2):

> We don't hold that poetry is a form of, or replaces, political action. Poetry isn't revolutionary practice; poetry provides a way to inhabit revolutionary practice, to ground ourselves in our relations to ourselves and each other ... We believe that poetry can do things that theory can't, that poetry leaps into what theory tends towards. We think that poetry conjoins and extends the interventions that trans people make into our lives and bodily presence in the world, which always have an aesthetic dimension.

The destabilization of subjectivity as a subjection to subjecthood that is central to many theorizations of queerness is not incompatible with activism, for, as Kara Keeling reminds us, "rather than simply a mode of negativity with the capacity to destroy, 'queer' exists as a generative force that works unpredictably ... within the social, shaking loose surplus and investing it in the creative modes of sociality that may not be recognized as such" (2019, 88). The readings suggested in the individual chapters lean on the contributions of "queer-of-color critique" (Ferguson 2003), which has played a major role in diversifying queer theory and decentering its white, middle-class, cis-gender bias, by demonstrating, for example, that "indigeneity itself functions similarly to queer as a means for interrogating how race, gender and sexuality, labor, possession are produced globally" (Byrd 2020, 107). Patrice Rankine provides an illuminating exemplification in his reading of *Helen* by showing the queering potential brought into the play by the Egyptian enemy of Helen and Menelaus, the indigenous "villain" who wants to foreclose their happy conjugal reunion.

Some contributions to this volume propose creative ways to strengthen the dialogue between queer/trans(*) theory and Marxism, which share the effort to reconceptualize, reinvent—we dare to say, liberate—a subject made other to and from itself by the imperatives of (re)production.[57] (A more Marxist queer theory can push against both homo-normativism and homo-trans-nationalisms.)[58] Responding to the charge of apolitical quietism that Frederic Jameson leveled against poststructuralism—the theoretical space where queer theory developed—Petrus Liu (2020) has drawn out the Marxist implications of Butler's queer theory, specifically her notions of gender and sexuality as technologies of dispossession.[59] In his formulation, "queer theory and Marxism can be both reconceived as materialist theories of social structuration that foreground the constitutive sociality of the self" (40). Trans(*) studies, in "exploring how bodies and body parts are broken down, pieced together, and reanimated for labor under neoliberal mandates," have demonstrated, in particular, how the bodies of workers and gender-non-conforming subjects are wounded by bio- and necro-political strategies for maximizing production.[60] What is the relationship between poetic form, production, and labor? In Aristophanes' *Frogs*, Euripides is presented as rolling his tongue endlessly to gather and breathe out "much labor of lungs" (*pleumonôn polun ponon* 829), a phrase in which the alliteration emphasizes prolongation and exhaustion.[61] In his chapter on

Children of Heracles, Ben Radcliffe invites us to revive Marxist readings in light of queerness beyond historicist contextualism.[62] Within the context of a theory and practice of queer reading that aspires to be a form of critique and social activism in its own right, this volume, we hope, will facilitate further reflection on work (or no-work) in relation to Euripides' queer temporalities and relationalities and the ways in which Euripides' queer aesthetics, materialized in the order and disorder, the consensus and dissensus of tragic form, reflect and contest transcultural dynamics of labor.

In constructing this volume, we deliberately avoided a chronological organization of plays, as well as one that would have segregated *Cyclops*, *Rhesus*, and Aristophanes' *Women at the Thesmophoria* into a distinct section. Within the tumultuous and perhaps twisted strait of *Queer Euripides*, the chapters have been divided into thematic sections that highlight specific methodological and thematic affinities. Yet even within these sections, no single theoretical framework predominates, and we intend these section titles to be suggestive rather than prescriptive. We invite our readers to observe the other points of contact among chapters highlighted by this Introduction, the intimations of thematic bridges and affinities in the passages from one section to another—as well as the cross-references scattered throughout.

Part I ("Temporalities") considers both queer conceptions of time within Euripidean drama itself and the temporal rhythms and disjunctions of reception and interpretation. Daniel Orrells starts us off by considering the reception of Euripides at the turn of the twentieth century, taking up Walter Pater's "Hippolytus Veiled" (1889) as an entry point for the exploration of Euripides' potential, then and now, as a source of queer heritage. Oliver Baldwin then situates *Rhesus*, a "Euripidean" (or *Euripidean) work of uncertain date and authorship, a work of reception folded into the corpus of the "original," within queer understandings of immaturity and belatedness. He demonstrates how the nocturnal setting of the play and the alternative futurity of Rhesus himself contribute to the drama's unsettling unknowability—a quality that makes it both alien to and ideal for this volume on Euripidean queerness. The radical no-futurity of *Trojan Women* is discussed by Carla Freccero in a chapter that locates the queerness of the play—the Euripidean and the recent one, with animal characters, by Anne Carson—in the removal of affect "from the scene of devastation," in the rejection of sentimental mourning, a theme that looks ahead to the topic of the next section.

Part II ("Escape/Refusal") explores how queerness can offer new perspectives on the interpretive and affective "quagmires" (Muñoz 2009, 1) of notoriously challenging and/ or undervalued plays. Ella Haselswerdt, in her chapter, embraces the instability of *Iphigenia in Aulis*, finding queerness in the gaps, fissures, and plural possibilities of the transmitted text. In a critical move that recalls Muñoz's insistence that queerness resides "in the horizon," she highlights aspects of queer, feminine eroticism that come—however distantly, however obliquely —into view, especially at the very moment of Iphigenia's sacrifice. The escape advocated by this play takes the unsettling form of a "perhaps," of a faint self-liberating hope emerging negatively in the interstices of philological hierarchy of (im)possibilities. Patrice Rankine's chapter on *Helen*, attentive to the entanglements between gender, sexuality, and other forms of cultural identity, directs our attention away from the dominant narrative of Helen and Menelaus and toward the "wayward" figure of Theoclymenus. Focusing on Euripides' construction (and queering) of the "Barbarian," he explores how this play unsettles and unravels the cultural norms it might seem to uphold. Ben Radcliffe then attends to queer refusals of normative modes of production in *Children of Heracles*, exposing how the apparent aesthetic failures of the play, embodiments of dissensual "kitsch," are implicated in its articulation of alternative modes of familial and kin relations. Constructions of kinship, labor, and reproduction remain central to Mario Telò's chapter on *Suppliant Women*. Observing the centrality of labor (*ponos*), reproductive and otherwise, to this play, Telò finds in Adrastus a compelling model of ironic disidentification and queer adhesion that, like Derridean hospitality, resists the teleology of productivity.

"Failure" (Part III) builds upon the preceding section, with its thematic proximities to its neighbor enacting the kind of adhesion discussed by Telò. In her chapter on *Medea*, Sarah Nooter finds queerness not only in Medea's violent rejection of normative womanhood but also in the play's representation of touch. Medea and Jason, in deriving both pleasure and pain from the "soft skin" of their children, momentarily inhabit a space of refusal and escape beyond the binaries that otherwise define them. Sean Gurd, drawing upon the work of Halberstam, reads *Alcestis* as a play that prefers failure—a play that carves out a space between celebration and defeat through the distinct (and often circular) logic of failure, through the very impossibility of translating a script into a performance, of animating language with the precarious markers of tone, intonation, modulation. Articulating a kind of meta-failure, Kirk Ormand proposes that Euripides' *Ion*, despite its engagement with notionally queer issues of secrecy and identity, fails to offer a meaningfully queer critique of Athenian politics and imperialism.

The three chapters comprising Part IV, "Relations," explore queer configurations of desire, domesticity, friendship, and hostility. Alastair Blanshard, in a "thoroughly irresponsible" reading that hearkens back to our earlier invocation of queer anachronism, argues that the concept of "homosexual panic" can illuminate the intersection of madness and homosociality in *Heracles*. Sarah Olsen's chapter on *Andromache* complements this approach by focusing instead on relations between women, suggesting that this play exposes the queer intimacy of polygynous marriage and highlighting the queer energy that animates the conflict between Hermione and Andromache, the play's two female protagonists. David Youd concludes this section by considering triangulation and triads from a different angle. Attending to the metrical rhythms of *Orestes*, he reveals how this play deconstructs conjugality as a literary and erotic form.

Part V, "Reproduction," builds on the preceding section's interest in relationality by attending specifically to the dynamics of genealogical and reproductive kinship in Euripidean drama. Karen Bassi takes up the essential ephemerality of tragedy itself in her chapter on *Hecuba*, in which she explores how the figure of the Dead Child exposes the fragility of normative temporal and reproductive order. Bassi's analysis exemplifies a queer resistance to teleological reading and highlights the interplay between fecundity and sterility that animates this play. In Rosa Andújar's account, *Phoenician Women*, with its cyclical representation of time and abiding interest in anti-normative reproductive models, emerges as a version of Oedipal myth well-suited to contemporary understandings of queerness. Looking beyond psychoanalysis, Andújar explores how the play's overdetermined excess contributes to the play's queer construction of time, power, and geneaology. Melissa Mueller explores how Electra, in the play that bears her name, occupies a space beside and beyond (*para-*) normative categories of gender, sexuality, and life. Drawing upon Marquis Bey's conceptualization of Black and trans* paraontology, she traces how Electra relates to yet also resists the identities of girl, woman, and mother, especially through her queer (false) pregnancy.

Part VI, "Encounters," finds queer potential in the interface between Euripidean drama and other genres, forms, and contexts. Nancy Sorkin Rabinowitz and David Bullen offer a dialogue between scholar and artist on By Jove Theatre Company's *The Gentlest Work*, probing the queer potential of Iphigenia and Artemis in *Iphigenia in Tauris* and beyond. A powerful commitment to activism and intersectionality drives their conversation, as they examine the racial connotations of "barbarian" identity in both ancient and modern contexts and stress the connections between racism, colonialism, and certain manifestations of queerness. Their essay opens up the possibility of performance itself as a kind of queer reading, and invites us to encounter Euripidean drama in new and surprising ways. Daniel Boyarin situates Euripides' surviving satyr play, *Cyclops*, in relation to Plato's *Symposium*, arguing that reading the two texts together enables us to see how the satyr play engages in the queering of genre.

The title of the final section, "Transitions," gestures both to key themes of the plays discussed as well as their authors' engagement with theories of crossing, transformation, and transness. Circling back to the prominently queer play that opened the volume, Jonathan Goldberg follows Anne Carson into a meditation on doubling in and around *Hippolytus*, engaging both Euripides' text and its reception by Carson, Racine, and, obliquely, Proust. Goldberg's reading exemplifies the porousness and wayward connections between texts made possible by queer unhistoricism, and his analysis of Carson's identification with Oscar Wilde and its implicit crossing of gender and identity gestures to the ongoing interface between queer and trans(*) theory.[63] L. Deihr, drawing upon Grace Lavery's articulation of "egg theory," reveals how Aristophanes' comedy *Women at the Thesmophoria* represents both the impossibility and the inevitability of gender transition. Deihr's chapter expands the volume's purview to include Aristophanes' engagement with Euripidean aesthetics and encourages us to consider the value of trans-centric queer theory for the study of Greek drama. Isabel Ruffell's chapter on *Bacchae* then offers a model of such analysis. Comparing the violent results of Pentheus' transphobic self-denial with Teiresias' singular escape from Dionysus' wrath, she offers a reading of the play that encourages the embrace of the trans and the queer.

* * *

Queer Euripides, or the portmanteau *Queeripides*, which we originally thought of using as the title of the book, affords us an opportunity to consider how we might scramble fields and subfields, how we might envision alternatives to existing disciplinary and institutional structures of knowledge from the perspective of classics, a field arguably at the center of such structures.[64] Our goal, in the wake of Halberstam's most recent theorization (2020a), is to embrace "wildness" as a queer methodology for Greek tragedy and classics as a whole, to valorize messiness and unruliness instead of restoration and reconstruction. This is not simply a desire to blow up disciplines or to create new disciplinary structures, but, instead, to promote forms of communication and become alert even to productive miscommunication between classicists and queer theorists, and to contemplate possibilities for classicists to disidentify themselves as queer theorists. *Queeripides* responds to the urgent need for creative, "wild" inter-disciplinary and anti-disciplinary interpretive work, which we hope future instantiations will reflect. Rethinking how and why Greek tragedy and its most controversial representative still matter today may become an occasion for turning *inter-* into *anti-* and *anti-* into *inter-*, imposed, inherited sociality into rebellious gestures and agencies, for destroying and building anew, for imagining new shapes of relationality—inclusive, intimate, unbound, and messy, just like the word *Queeripides* itself.

Notes

1. For a survey of the literary-critical assessment of Euripides in antiquity and modernity, see Mastronarde 2010, 1–15; see also Walton 2009 (ch. 11). Mastronarde (2010, 28–43) provides an overview of Euripides' extant plays, with dates, key production details, and plot summaries. Gabriel (2021) supplies an exemplary account of the theoretical positions of Romantic and post-Romantic critics that have constructed the still-operating sense of Euripides' "untimely modernity."

2. See esp. Fassino 2003 and Prauscello 2006, 123.

3. As Menon (2011, 7) observes, "If queerness can be defined, then it is no longer queer . . . Queerness is not a category but the confusion engendered by and despite categorization."

4. For Bey in Aizura et al. (2020, 142), there is a distinction between anti- and non-normativity: the former is "a militant rejection or reactive opposition," while the latter, which Bey identifies with trans* studies, is "a refusal that cares less about opposing the hegemonic on its own terms and much more about subverting the hegemonic by way of living life on another terrain." Dean (2019, 261–2) draws attention to the gay community's reclaiming of the word "queer" during the HIV epidemic: "Queer gave us a rationale for explaining how, even if HIV-positive, we were not thereby pathological. Neither pathological nor normal, we were—and are—queer." Even though we have to resist the "misconception . . . that anything quantifiable as non-normative must . . . be queer" (Dean 2019, 262), the idea of queerness without anti-normativity (see Wiegman and Wilson 2015) seems (almost) inconceivable: see Halberstam 2015.

5. See also Eve Sedgwick's influential definition of "queer" as "the open mesh of possibilities, gaps, overlaps, dissonances and resonances, lapses and excesses of meaning when the constituent elements of anyone's gender, or anyone's sexuality aren't made . . . to signify monolithically" (1993, 8); in the same year, Michael Warner defined queerness as a contestation of the "regimes of the normal" (1993, xxvi). On the use of trans* (with an asterisk), see Tompkins 2014; Bey 2017, 284–6; and Keegan 2020c, 395n1.

6. Euripides' play ranked third in the tragic contest at the Great Dionysia of 431 BC.

7. See, for example, Pier Paolo Pasolini's *Medea* (1969) and Luis Alfaro's *Mojada* (2012); see also Kidd 2002; Billotte 2015; Powers 2018 (ch. 2); and Baldwin 2020.

8. For the relevance of Edelman's position to feminism, see esp. Deutscher (2017, 51), who points out that "to fetishize the figure of the imaginary Child can also be to ... produce, presuppose, *and* render invisible the role of the woman as subordinated to the ends of reproduction and collective futures." For an interpretation of *Medea* in light of death-driven resistance to reproductive futurism, see Telò 2020, 90–113.

9. While a number of prominent theorists have conceptualized trans(*) theory in opposition to queer theory (see esp. Hale 1997; Namaste 2000, 9 and 23; Stryker 2004; and Keegan 2020a) and we do not wish to erase the differences in positions and sensibilities between them, as they correspond to different lived experiences, the contributions in this volume lean toward an approach to queerness that encompasses transness and that is informed by the concerns, contributions, and criticism of trans theorists: for an exemplary negotiation of the trans(*) and the queer, see Love 2014. Chen (2013, 171) observes: "The opposition of *trans* and *queer* suggests a false dichotomy: just as gender and sex are unavoidably linked, so too are trans and queer. They can be considered as independent factors which participate in intersectional spaces." See also Stanley (2015), who always speaks of "trans/gender-non-conforming and queer people" and "trans/queer folks"; for an approach that emphasizes the "kindredness, the concatenation" of queer and trans(*) studies, see also Bey in Aizura et al. 2020, 142.

10. Humphrey (2020) locates an "archaic modernism"—a queer temporality—in Pasolini's film, but, to an extent, this temporality already shapes Euripides' play: see Telò 2020, 90–113.

11. See Halberstam 2011, 135–45, on Yoko Ono's "Cut Piece" (1965) as a kind of queer performance.

12. See esp. Cribiore 2011.

13. See Telò 2020, 82–7.

14. Telò (2020, 68–87) emphasizes the death-driven dimension of this an-archival dynamic; there is also the sense of "feeling backward," along the lines of the model of queerness theorized by Love (2007).

15. On the psychological connection between education and death-driven repetition, see Edelman 2017.

16. See Telò 2020, 68–87; on the Derridean *à venir* as equivalent to the arrival of a lack and a form of lateness, see Gurd and Telò 2022, esp. Telò 2022b; on "time out of joint," see Derrida 1994, 3. On time out of joint and queer spectrality, see Freccero 2006. Freeman (2010, 19) observes that "failures or refusals to inhabit middle- and upper-middle-class habitus"—that is, the position embraced by queers—"appear as ... asynchrony or time out of joint." See also Edelman 2011. A recent special *GLQ* issue (Fiereck, Hoad, and Mupotsa 2020) reflects on how African views of non-conforming sexualities may alter the landscape of the so-called "queer customary."

17. Young (2014) links "queer seriousness" with K. W. F. Schlegel's idea of "real transcendental buffoonery."

18. The homoerotic reading of this relationship is already presupposed in the so-called Iolaus fragment (P. Oxy. 3010, second century CE), which features a Petronian, male homoerotic romance and cites the play's praise of friendship: see Parsons 1971, 56–9. In Mary Kay Gamel's adaptation of the play *Orestes Terrorist*, the homoerotic attachment between Orestes and Pylades is part of a triangular structure involving Electra's infatuation with her brother.

19. See, among others, Halperin 1990; Ormand and Blondell 2015; Davidson 2001; Orrells 2011 and 2015; and Shapiro 2015.

20. On friendship as the scandal of queer relationality, see esp. Foucault 1998, 136; see also Doyle 2007, 329: "The 'queerness' of queer friendship is ... composed of more than the sexual identities of its practitioners."

21. See Sedgwick 1985. As Weiner and Young (2011, 228) remark, "'Queer bonds' name a mode of recognition to the side of this deadly epistemology, a laterally constituted togetherness that persists in the face of homophobia."

22. Sedgwick 1990. Youd brings out the queer potential in the title of Froma Zeitlin's influential article on the play, "The Closet of Masks" (1980).

23. Battezzato 2005, 22. Lenfant (2013) contests the identification of the Phrygian slave as a eunuch.

24. See Handy and Johnson 2015, 714 on the EA (the Eunuch Archive): "The Eunuch Archive should be preserved with other trans* archive collections, as it adds a new area of gender identity that has been largely ignored in past studies of the trans* world."

25. Innuendos are activated by multiple occurrences of words for "sword" (e.g., *xiphos, phasganon*).

26. "As individuals flow through the system of surveillance and control in the airport," Currah and Mulqueen (2011, 577) point out, "transgender people—with their incongruous and unexpected histories, documents, and bodies—often find themselves in the uncomfortable interstices between spatial and temporal registers, between stasis and change, between what," from the police's point of view, "one is and what one says or does." As Stryker and Currah (2018, 161) observe, in relation to state transphobic practice of surveillance, "Without surgery, a gender-variant person could be a cross-dresser, a butch ... or a drag queen, but by definition that person was not a transsexual because they didn't cut their flesh ... That is, genital-altering transsexuals are considered (though not without contestation) to have *really* changed sex, while everyone else who strains against the naturalized pink/blue dichotomy is just dressing up and playing around."

27. Keegan (2020a, 70), referring to Prosser 1998.

28. See also Bey 2017. See Telò 2022a (ch. 4) on Aristophanes' *Women at the Thesmophoria*.

29. Reconsidering the debate on the so-called anti-social thesis in queer theory spurred by Edelman (2004), Weiner and Young (2011, 224) observe that "[the] queer is at once disabled and inventive sociality."

30. It is hopefully clear that we are drawing here upon sonic resonance, not etymological links.

31. See above, note 4. Keegan (2020a, 71) offers a helpful chart of the binaries (!) that have divided queer from trans(*) studies respectively: e.g., "failure" / "recovery," "refusal" / "transitivity," "deconstruction" / "reconstruction," "discourse" / "materiality."

32. The opposition between "reparative" and "anti-reparative" dates back to the foundational and influential essay by Sedgwick (2003, 123–51); see, e.g., Love 2010 and Hanson 2011. Lesjak (2013, 254) points out how Sedgwick conceived of "reparative reading"—that is, a kind of reading that responds to the allegedly aggressive, "paranoid," distant, vertical modes of reading imputed to deconstruction and psychoanalysis— as a complement rather than an alternative. Berlant and Edelman (2014) and (2019) push against the "critical desire to stabilize reparativity as Eve's last (and lasting) bequest"; see also Edelman 2022 on the position of Butler (2018) in the debate. On reparative sentimentalism, see esp. Berlant 2011; Halberstam 2012; Young 2019a; and Stuelke 2021. The opposition between futural and anti-futural and between utopian and anti-utopian is associated with the apparently antithetical positions of Edelman (2004) and Muñoz (2009): see esp. Shahani 2013; Deutscher 2017 (ch. 2); Ruti 2017; and Keeling 2019 (ch. 2). On trans* utopia, see Nirta 2018. On the risk of liberal complacency behind a rights-oriented approach to queerness and transness, see esp. Eng and Puar 2020. Halberstam (2012 and 2015) follows the radical, anarchic anti-normativity of the "undercommons" advocated by Harney and Moten (2013); for an approach to queerness beyond the human subject, see esp. Chen 2012. For a Marxist revision of the

"subject-less" trend in queer theory, see Eng and Puar 2020. On transness as radical disidentification and rejection of identity, see esp. Nelson 2015, 53; Bey 2017; Halberstam 2018; and Preciado 2018 and 2021. On trans realism, see esp. Gabriel 2016 and Lavery 2019 and 2020. On queer and trans* opacity as resistance, see Stanley 2011. For a queer and trans rejection of the liberal logic of inclusion, see Spade 2015.

33. See Telò 2020 (epilogue) for an attempt to formulate a queer theory of Greek tragedy as a whole.

34. For an assessment of the labels "revolution" and "decadence" in the history of Euripidean cricisim, see esp. Gabriel 2021.

35. While queering is a practice of reading grounded in deconstruction and its multiple possibilities for emancipatory thinking, we agree with Freeman (2010, 11) that "what makes queer theory queer as opposed to simply deconstructionist is," among other things, "its insistence on risking a certain vulgar referentiality" and "its understanding of the sexual encounter as precisely the body and the ego's undoing." Menon (2011, 8–9) says that queerness "expands the ambit of the sexual rather than being restricted by it." On the relationship between deconstruction and queerness, Menon remarks that "while deconstruction at first challenged philosophy's claim to transcendence, queer theory has always been interested in the larger lived realities of desire."

36. On some of these labels, see Mastronarde 1999–2000b. See also Gabriel 2021.

37. On the queerness of "awkwardness," see, e.g., Smith-Prei and Stehle 2016. "Awkwardness" is a trait imputed to Euripides in ancient biographies: as Mastronarde (2010, 3) puts it, they say that "he was socially aloof . . . and he composed his plays in a lonely cave." Is this a portrait of what Yergeau (2018) has called "neuroqueerness"?

38. See, e.g., Crawford 2017 and McFarland, Slothouber, and Taylor 2018.

39. On Euripides' and Hellenistic *leptotês*, see Telò, forthcoming. On queer thinness, see also Love 2013.

40. On Euripidean realism, see esp. Goldhill 1986, 251–2.

41. Lavery (2016) uses "queer realism" in reference to Gilbert and Sullivan's *The Mikado*.

42. For an expansive, if problematic, treatment of Euripidean formalism, see Michelini 1987 (ch. 4); cf. Wohl 2015. For an analysis of Michelini's position, see Gabriel 2021, 4–5.

43. Eng, Halberstam, and Muñoz (2005, 3) define queer epistemology as "a continuous deconstruction of the tenets of positivism at the heart of identity politics," the positivism that is inherent in demarcating the boundaries of distinct subjectivities in the name of the cultural pluralism advocated by liberal thinking. Deconstructing identitarian domains is essential to opposing liberal complacency and enacting a radical politics of queer disidentification.

44. For a critique of melancholic historicism, see Best 2018.

45. On queer unhistoricism, see esp. Freccero 2006, 2007, and 2013a and b; cf. Halperin 2015. As Menon (2011, 3) says, referring to the field of Shakespeare studies, "The understanding of scholarly 'expertise' is located squarely in the realm of historical specificity rather than methodological modes of reading and thought." The queer unhistoricism we are practicing is particularly appropriate for Euripides' tragic aesthetics, which, as Gabriel (2021, 3) has observed, is strongly "motivated in response to the uneven rift between an old and a new social world."

46. On *Iphigenia in Aulis* as a terrain of fundamentalist philology, see Gurd 2005.

47. On proximities and adjacencies as practices of queer reading, see Sanyal, Telò, and Young 2022, which provides examples of reading *with* (and, thus, *à la*) Judith Butler.

48. Cf., however, Annamarie Jagose (in Freeman et al. 2007, 191), who warns against "the credentialing of asynchrony, multitemporality, and nonlinearity as if they were automatically in the service of queer political projects and aspirations."

49. On the "cripping" of chrononormativities, see Samuels and Freeman 2021, 251.

50. As is well known, the first, more risqué version of the play featured Phaedra confessing her love to Hippolytus. The surviving *Hippolytus* bears metatextual markers of its performative vicissitudes: see McDermott 2000 and Torrance 2013, 146–51.

51. Blanshard makes a suggestive connection between Murray's description and the term "Broke Back" in the title of Annie Proulx's novel and Ang Lee's film *Broke Back Mountain* (1997; 2005).

52. On the vitalistic negativity of tragic form, its expressions of verbal and visual suspension and interruption, which push against the representational, see Telò 2020. On minoritarian aesthetics, see esp. Deleuze and Guattari 1986; on Deleuze and queer theory, see esp. Colebrook 2009. See also Rosenberg 2014.

53. Kruse (2019, 135) refers to Sedgwick 2003, 3.

54. See Dunn 1996; Wohl 2015, *passim*; and, in a different psychoanalytic vein, Telò 2020.

55. For a radical critique of the contemporary university, see esp. Harney and Moten 2013, and, from the specific perspective of queer people, Brim 2020.

56. As Stanley (2015, 2) observes, "[W]e must pay attention to the ways that the PIC [Prison Industrial Complex] harms trans/gender-non-conforming and queer people and also to how the PIC produces the gender binary and heteronormativity itself."

57. In the introduction to *Transgender Marxism*, Gleeson and O'Rourke (2021, 28) observe, "Our end is not just a more rigorous understanding of our social afflictions, but fuel for the abolition of what has long been intolerable." As Liu (2020, 42) puts it, "The liberal-pluralist language of diversity and inclusion presents a reformist strategy to assimilate the disenfranchised into the national polity in accordance with mainstream views, instead of a transformative strategy that reconfigures relationships of power and expands the field of gender possibilities." See also Alderson 2016.

58. See esp. Duggan 2002 and Puar 2007 and 2017 (ch.1).

59. See Butler 2011, 385 on the relationship between bond and body: "To demarcate the human body through identifying its bounded form is to miss the crucial fact that the body is, in certain ways and even inevitably, unbound."

60. Eng and Puar 2020, 15. Puar (2015) points out how the rhetoric of flexibility and mobility intrinsic to the logic of becoming trans(*) has been appropriated for the rhetoric of capitalistic flexibility. "Becoming is not about trying to make the body more capacitated but about allowing and reading more multiplicity, multiplicities of the impersonal and of the imperceptible"; yet "becoming has become a zone for profit for contemporary capitalism" (63).

61. See Telò 2022a (ch. 2) for a reading of proto-capitalistic labor in *Frogs*. In her version of Euripides' *Heracles* entitled *H of H Playbook* (2021), Anne Carson depicts Heracles as a worker whose madness is a consequence of his "labors," that is, capitalistic frenzy: "The Labours tell me when to go to bed, what to eat, what to wear . . ."

62. For a Marxist approach to Euripides' materialism, see most recently Hall 2018.

63. See above on the complex relationship between queer and trans(*) theory more broadly. Gabriel (2018) offers a critical appraisal of Carson's engagement with transness and the representation of transgender lives.

64. We owe this observation to Jack Halberstam, who participated in an online *Queer Euripides* workshop on February 20, 2021.

PART I
TEMPORALITIES

CHAPTER 1

HIPPOLYTUS—EURIPIDES AND QUEER THEORY AT THE FIN DE SIÈCLE AND NOW

Daniel Orrells

"Queer Euripides" might suggest that Euripides, the Athenian poet, could and should be seen as "queer," that the cultural and sexual conditions of the 1970s to the 2020s might be seen to be present in the late fifth century BC: queer studies might have an ancient heritage. Alternatively, if not used adjectivally, the "queer" in "Queer Euripides" could also be an imperative, which reflects a critical call to "queer" Euripides, that is, to apply the insights and methods of modern queer studies and theory back onto Euripides' texts. Whereas one usage of "queer" proposes the long historical connections between ancient and modern, the other celebrates the potentially disruptive anachronism of projecting modern theory onto classical antiquity.[1] The delicious ambiguity of the title of this book reflects an enduring central question for queer literary studies: its engagement with anachronism and historicity. What does it mean to see "queer" subjects in the past? What might "queer history" look like?

Contemporary queer theory has invested a lot of energy in locating its heritage in the literary and cultural experimentation of the fin de siècle. In *Epistemology of the Closet*, Eve Kosofsky Sedgwick (1990, 91 and 44) famously marked the year 1891 as foundational for Western queer culture in contrast to Michel Foucault's provocative proposal that the homosexual emerged into history in 1870. This question of the relationship between modern, contemporary discourses of sexuality and older, historical modes of desire was itself also a much-debated topic in late-nineteenth-century Britain. Benjamin Jowett, John Addington Symonds, and Walter Pater all examined the historical similarities and differences between Greco-Roman and nineteenth-century masculinities.[2] The reception of Euripides was a crucial aspect for these late-Victorian debates about the history of gender and sexuality. If fin-de-siècle culture has repeatedly been seen as a foundational moment for the origins of the Western queer self, this chapter explores the importance of the fin-de-siècle reception of Euripidean tragedy for contemporary, twenty-first-century debates in queer studies.

This chapter argues that readings of Euripides in the late nineteenth century anticipate and intersect with our own discussions today about the relationship between feminism and queer politics. This is hardly surprising: Euripides' supposedly misogynistic characterization of women was already mocked by Aristophanes in the fifth century,[3] and Satyrus' biography claimed that he hated women. And yet, more modern readers have argued that Euripides' plays provide opportunities for feminist reception. Indeed, Euripides' provocative presentation of the passions of women has shocked and fascinated ancient and modern audiences. Euripidean tragedy, so innovative already in the fifth century, has repeatedly changed and shifted in form, meaning, and political significance. Euripides has continually resisted the efforts of classical scholars and modern writers who have sought to interpret and categorize him and put him in his place. So, with such a complex reception history, can Euripides be queered? How might thinking about "queer Euripides" contribute to larger questions about what it means to look back to the (ancient) past and find a queer heritage?

To explore these questions, we will trace out how the scholarly fascination with the textual fragment in the nineteenth century inspired the fin-de-siècle imagination to fill in the blanks and rewrite the classical text. As we will examine, the textual fragment figured both the disappearance of antiquity and the possibility of contesting scholarly and heteronormative accounts of the ancient world. As we will discover, the fragmentary forms of the classical text were of particular interest to readers and writers from the 1870s onward who sought to critique hegemonic patriarchal norms. Pater's 1889 "Hippolytus Veiled: A Study from Euripides," a text that has barely ever been discussed, will prove a fascinating resource for us today.[4] Pater's version of Euripides' fragmentary play *Hippolytus Veils Himself* begins with a discussion of the difficulties in obtaining secure knowledge about the ancient Greek world, and in particular, its earliest periods of history. It then modulates into a story about the "primitive" family of Hippolytus and his single mother, the Amazon Antiope, who has been deserted by Theseus who has gone to rule Athens and turn it into a modern city. Mother and son survive in precarious thrift but are enriched by mutual care and devotion. The death of Hippolytus and Antiope's lamentation for her son mark the end of the narrative, which mourns the disappearance of alternative modes of living and loving that do not conform to modern, supposedly civilized standards. Reading Pater's fin-de-siècle Euripidean story, which looks back at the ancient past, gives us the opportunity to think about our own queer investments in antiquity.[5]

Textual Fragments and Scholarly Desires

Euripidean tragedy is a "fragmented and chaotic" form (Wohl 2015, 3), which has come to be seen as not only representative of Euripides' historical context in the tumultuous late fifth century, but also as giving voice to the possibility of new modes of aesthetic and political expression in the fourth century and beyond: "Euripides marks both the end of Athens—that's it: that's how the fifth century turned out—and its continuity in new and unexpected shapes" (140). Euripides' ancient fin-de-siècle positioning anticipated his modern nineteenth-century fin-de-siècle receptions. As Sean Gurd has explored, the forms of Euripidean textuality became fascinating case studies of the mutability of the ancient text in the hands of the professional textual critics who sought to stabilize the form and meaning of Euripides' words. The scholarly attempts to fix Euripides' *Iphigenia in Aulis* produced literally new forms of the play as the text became increasingly fragmentary at the hands of the textual critics.[6] The scholarly production of Euripidean fragmentation emerged out of romantic philhellenism as a commentary on "the inaccessibility of the ancient ideal" (Gurd 2005, 114). The textual fragment was both an ancient relic and a modern form. The fascination with the Euripidean fragmentary form culminated in the 1854 publication of the fragments of Euripides' plays by Johann August Nauck. But if this publication and others of fragments of Greek drama in the middle of the nineteenth century sought to preserve decaying ancient remains and erect them into worthy monuments of admiration for classical scholars and students, their romantic fragmentariness would prove profoundly impactful on the decadent imagination of the late nineteenth century.

Indeed, the 1870s and 1880s witnessed a series of questions aimed at these scholarly attempts at the erection of stable, historicized monuments of classical learning, which sought to put ancient texts in their historical place and stop them from shape-shifting and changing. The late nineteenth century became a crucial moment in the modern history of debates about classical scholarship. Friedrich Nietzsche's lectures that mocked the classical profession and his essay on the uses of history interrogated the relationship between the ancient world and its modern scholarly reception.[7] The discovery of Troy contributed to the nineteenth century's fascination with deep time and the prehistorical. The preclassical remains of Troy looked both very old, embedded in geological layers of temporality, *and* very modern, a vision of the collapse of a luxurious, decadent society.[8] In response to these difficult questions, biblical archaeology attempted to reassert ecclesiastical accounts of history, which nevertheless ended up putting the ancient and the modern into connection in new and controversial ways.[9] The professional understanding of the relationship between the modern scholarly gaze and the ancient object under scrutiny had been profoundly disrupted and unsettled. By 1907, Sigmund Freud could pen his essay "Delusion and Dream in Jensen's *Gradiva*," where he explored how a classical archaeologist in Pompeii could fall in love with and marry his scholarly object of analysis. The fragmentariness of the poems of Sappho especially encouraged the eroticization of ancient remains in the closing decades of the nineteenth century. In 1885, all the then-extant fragments, using the correct pronouns, were published in English. The multiple love interests mentioned in the poems, the various renderings, and the fragmentary nature of Sappho's poetic corpus meant that late-Victorian authors were free to develop and enlarge upon the tattered remains in numerous different erotic voices.[10] Romantic Hellenism, rerouted through the decadent sensibility, then, subverted attempts at historicist, objective, professionalized scholarship, and encouraged subjectivizing perspectives, anachronizing receptions of and queer relationships with the ancient world. To quote Gurd again: the "fragmentary quality [of the remains of antiquity] encapsulates the unsettling similarity between critic and corruptor" (2005, 100–1). The fragment put into focus the unstable relationship between ancient passions and modern scholarly desires.

Euripides contributed to this fin-de-siècle questioning of scholarly notions of historicity, temporality, and objectivity. Euripides did not fit in historically: for Nietzsche in his 1872 *Birth of Tragedy*, building on and undoing a generation of German scholarship, Euripides was both the belated Decadent denouement of true tragic grandeur and yet his *Bacchae*, despite being his final play, was important evidence of the

Apollo/Dionysiac opposition at the historical origins of Greek tragedy, which, in turn, was, for Nietzsche, meant to inspire modern, nineteenth-century writers. In the English-speaking world, Euripides was also receiving more attention. John Addington Symonds responded to nineteenth-century critiques of decadent Euripides in his 1873 *Studies of the Greek Poets*. While Nietzsche preferred Dionysus and lamented Euripides' oversophisticated Apolline modernity, Symonds turned to Apollo to cite a line from a speech in John Milton's masque *Comus* in praise of the sensual enjoyment of "divine philosophy" (lines 475–8). From Nietzchean-Dionysiac *kômos* to English-Apolline *Comus*, Symonds's comparison of Euripides' poetry with Apollo's music associates the tragedian with the pinnacle of classical Greek sculpture. The Apollo Belvedere was one of the most admired Greek statues in the world in the nineteenth century because of Johann Joachim Winckelmann's 1764 paean to it. For Symonds, Euripides was not a belated decadent failure but a poet of the classical period. But again, Euripides could not just be slotted back into historical place. Crucially, Winckelmann's veneration of Apollo had been couched in an argument he had traced back to Plato's *Symposium*, that access to philosophy was gained through the contemplation of the beautiful male body. For Symonds, Euripides' poetry was a combination of musical wisdom and sensuous beauty.

The erotic suggestions in Symonds's pedagogical prose on Euripides reflected his interest in blurring the sensual and the scholarly, the personal and the professional, the ancient and the modern. Symonds was deeply skeptical of the historicist training he had received as an undergraduate at Oxford from his tutor, the Regius Professor of Greek, Benjamin Jowett, who had attempted to argue that any mention of pederasty in the Platonic dialogues was merely "a figure of speech." For Symonds, it was impossible for men attracted to other men to have a dispassionate relationship with their study of the ancient Greeks—they could not simply be put into their historical place. Indeed, Symonds's *Studies of the Greek Poets* emerged out of lectures he had given to the male sixth-formers in Clifton College in Bristol, where he had engaged in a passionate affair with one of his students, Norman Moor. The combination of pederasty and pedagogy, beauty and philosophy—a scene of Socratic/Platonic love—resonates throughout Symonds's discussion of Euripidean poetics.[11]

Despite his nods to male pederastic erotics, Symonds's writing about Euripides' *Hippolytus* was especially inspirational to a younger female poet Agnes Mary Frances Robinson, who was guided by Symonds in what Yopie Prins has called a "queer tutelage" (2017, 153 and 162). Robinson was fascinated by Symonds's discussion of Hippolytus and his Amazon mother, "a feminized masculinity born from a masculinized femininity" (Prins 2017, 163), and wrote her own translation of the play in 1881. Prins again: "Indeed, Hippolytus would seem to be one of those adolescent boys that female aesthetes could appropriate from male aestheticism and turn into a trope for desire between women: the male Amazon as Lesbian boy" (167). We should not be surprised if a famous neighbor of Robinson's in London—Walter Pater—would become interested in Euripides' play. Euripides was becoming a modern classic despite the scholarly attempts at putting him in his historical place.

Unveiling Hippolytus

It was in this heady intellectual context that Pater wrote and published his "Hippolytus Veiled: A Study from Euripides." Appearing in the August 1889 issue of *Macmillan's Magazine*, Pater's text reflected the contemporary aesthetic of subjectivizing fragmentation. Like Nietzsche and his critique of professionalized, historicist classical scholarship, Pater was also fascinated with the untimeliness of Euripidean tragedy, which might both give access to a primitive, prehistorical layer of antiquity and also act as a belated, decadent signifier of the loss of the greatness of ancient Greece. And like Symonds, Pater saw in Euripides' *Hippolytus* the possibility of a queer alternative that rejected the hegemonic social-sexual norms of the day. But what is so fascinating about Pater's response to Euripides' play is that he did *not* choose to write a version of the extant *Hippolytus Garland-Bearer* but the fragmentary *Hippolytus Veils Himself*. It is one of the least discussed texts by Pater and those who have explored it have said virtually nothing about Pater's interest in rewriting the fragmentary *Hippolytus*. Before we turn to Pater's text, let us think about the fragment with which he engaged.

The extant play was Euripides' second attempt at writing a tragedy about Hippolytus. His first play—of which we have some forty lines—had supposedly scandalized the audience for its depiction of Phaedra's bold seduction of Hippolytus.[12] The *hypothesis* of Aristophanes of Byzantium states that *Hippolytus Garland-Bearer* was written and performed second in time and that what was "unseemly and reprehensible" in the earlier production had been put right. Euripides' second play portrayed an apparently nobler Phaedra battling against the depredations of Eros, and it won the Athenians' approval and first prize. Ovid, Seneca, and then Racine would also explore the power of desire and female sexuality in successive versions which examined the painful dilemmas of Phaedra's predicament. Pater's "Hippolytus Veiled: A Study from Euripides" offered a radically pointed response to that long tradition, by creatively filling in the gaps between the scrappy fragments of Euripides' first *Hippolytus*, to counter the misogynistic Athenian reception of Euripides' first Phaedra and to imagine a lost urtext about a queer family of masculine femininity and female masculinity, which resisted the pressures of modern imperialist heteronormativity.

If we turn briefly to the fragmentary lines themselves, we can see how they allowed for contesting readings and responses and might have inspired Pater. On the one hand, it is clear to see from these lines how one might find a bolder Phaedra and an expression of the untrustworthiness of women in a world of duplicitous words. And yet, one can also see how Pater might have used these fragments to read against the grain: that women are "harder" and "very hard to fight against" (fragments 429 and 430 Kannicht) becomes in his story a tale about Antiope, Hippolytus' mother, who, despite the annihilation of the Amazons, maintains her traditional religious beliefs and frugal lifestyle; Antiope is someone who strives and toils and, rather than obeying laws, she follows what is necessary in difficult circumstances (see fragments 432 and 433). Antiope does not integrate herself into the modern life of the city. In fragment 444, Phaedra possibly voices a sense of inevitability ("O you deity, how mortal men have no way to avert their inborn or godsent troubles!"), which in Pater's story becomes Antiope's "long forebodings" and "misgivings" about Hippolytus' fate. From Phaedra's disavowal of responsibility in the face of fate to Antiope's presentiment: "Men's mortal fortunes are not in accordance with their piety" (fragment 434). While Theseus might critique Hippolytus' hubris—"I can see that for many people previous success generates arrogance" (fragment 437)—Pater's poor and precarious Hippolytus turning away from the richesses of city life might have been inspired by fragment 438: "Wealth in life, not thrift, generates arrogance." Just as the earlier fragments express the military strength of women and the later ones critique women's untrustworthiness, so with Pater, the fragment becomes a story about the loss of matriarchal power and the rise of patriarchal authority.

Pater's rewriting of a lustful Phaedra to a strong Antiope reflects his cutting-edge work as a classical scholar in the late nineteenth century. Pater was at the forefront of an emergent body of classical scholarship that presented "a different version of antiquity, one defined by worldly, chthonic deities, wilder emotions, and sexual dissidence" (Potolsky 2020, 5). But Pater's interest in the preclassical Greeks also reflected his fascination with periods of transition and uncertainty in ancient Greek culture. While contemporary scholars were arguing for the historical development of mythopoetic thinking in ancient Greece, Pater was interested in how ancient Greek texts might betray a palimpsest of historical mindsets and beliefs, overlayed and entangled with one another. In his 1876 essay "The Myth of Demeter and Persephone," Pater saw different historical layers of mythical thinking—primitive and later—in the *Homeric Hymn to Demeter*: "in his [the hymn-writer's] Demeter, the dramatic person of the mysteries mixes itself with the primitive mythical figure" (Pater 2020, 200). For Pater, the *Homeric Hymn* was a more modern reworking of pre-Homeric myth—not simply a story about the emergence of life from the earth, but also a text that contains within itself the history of the emergence of Greek mythology as it stages the transition from matriarchal authority to patriarchal power. In his essay "The *Bacchanals* of Euripides," written sometime before 1878 but appearing in print in 1889 (the same year as "Hippolytus Veiled"), Pater also took pleasure in staging a violent contest between feminine and masculine power in his description of the ruler Pentheus' death at the hands of Dionysus' female maenad followers.

"Hippolytus Veiled: A Study from Euripides" contributed to this project of questioning the politics of scholarly historicism by rethinking the history of family life. In rewriting the first *Hippolytus* in the late 1880s, Pater self-consciously questioned the relationship between the first and the second, the original and the copy, the ancient and the modern. Just as in his other articles on Greek myth, "Hippolytus Veiled" also questioned scholarly attempts to historicize and periodize the ancient world by focusing on the issues of desire and sexual dissidence. Indeed, right from the very start, Pater's text questions its status.

Despite the intensive attempts of modern scientific archaeology—ironically characterized as emotional or religious by the word "zealous"—ancient Greek culture has been transmitted to us in only fragments and scraps. Pater laments the disappearance of "the early Attic deme-life" of which we possess merely "isolated documents" of "many provincial peculiarities" (2014, 216). "[M]any a relic of primitive religion," "its trade and crafts," would go on to disappear as "Athens, the great deme, absorbed more and more of those achievements, passing away almost completely" with the onset of the Peloponnesian War (216–17). And yet, as Pater goes on, "it was just here that ancient habits clung most tenaciously—that old-fashioned, homely, delightful existence, to which the refugee, pent up in Athens in the years of the Peloponnesian War, looked back so fondly." On the one hand, the ancient, preclassical past is lost to the present, and yet, on the other, it somehow persists. Religious practices of "primitive local variety" lingered on. Pater imagines a "boyish" Thucydides, "that severe historian" (221), characterized as the objective, positivist scholar, who could not help but including "many picturesque touches" in his history—as if his text were a painting—about "the ancient provincial life": "the Attic people are already impressed by the immense antiquity of their occupation of its soil" (220). Pater's historical account is not the standard narrative of progress and development from archaic origins to classical apogee. The "modern" geopolitics of the fifth century BC beget a nostalgia for an older way of life "which this conflict with Sparta was bringing to an end" (221). Pater questions the relationship between the inchoate, the incomplete, and the immature, on the one hand, and the perfected, the complete, and the mature, on the other. His rewriting of the relationship of the first and the second offered him a way to rethink the scholarly narrative of the archaic and the classical. And he pictures a very different sort of "student of fine art" from those scholars who can only see the anticipation of classical greatness in archaic culture. Pater's student is neither a dry-as-dust antiquarian nor a professionalized scholar, but a youth aroused by a passion for what has been lost, a fragmentary and yet absolute beauty. Pater not only subverts the historical relationship between the early and later periods of Greek history, but he also questions the valorization of mature, professional archaeology over youthful enthusiasm. Like Symonds, Pater detects a boyish desire at the heart of institutionalized classical scholarship.

At this point in the text, Pater modulates into the mythical, to tell his story of Hippolytus and sets the scene with Theseus: "'the modern spirit' of his day . . . who thus figures, passably, as mythic shorthand for civilization, making roads and the like, facilitating travel (how usefully!), suppressing various forms of violence, but many innocent things as well . . . He slays the bull of Marathon and many another local tyrant, but also exterminates that delightful creature, the Centaur. The Amazon, whom Plato will reinstate as the type of improved womanhood, has the luck of Phaea, the sow-pig of Crommyon." Theseus was "a type still of progress triumphant through injustice, set on improving things off the face of the earth" (222–3). Just as he opened his text with a meditation on the uncertainties of transition from the archaic to the classical, so in his story, Theseus becomes the symbol of modernization. And yet the past again persists. As he says (223), despite their extermination, Centaurs and Amazons represent "the regret of Athenians," emerging in protest in "the fine art of Greece." For Pater, the sculptures of the Parthenon and the Amazon frieze, the latter being the best preserved of the three sculptural friezes from the tomb of Mausolus of Halicarnassus—both on display at the British Museum—are *not* exemplary achievements of classical Greek art. Rather, they contain messages of "poetic protest," allowing Pater to read these sculptures against the grain. It is not the mature archaeologist who can see this, but "young people's eyes" who perceive classical Greek culture's critique of its own "civilizing" values enshrined on its most famous monuments. Far from being a corpus to be slotted into its historical context or to be timelessly admired, the ancient past recorded in classical Greek art speaks out in protest at the modern age. Just as classical Greek art, for Pater, records the "countercultural" protest against Greek "civilizing" modern values, so Euripides' fragmentary *Hippolytus* will become a "poetic protest" against the modern, late-Victorian family life. The archaic, while ruinous and decaying, will somehow linger on.

Indeed, Theseus' defeat of the Amazons is not total: his sexual relationship with Antiope, the last of the Amazons, produces a son, Hippolytus. They are sequestered away "in one of the doomed decaying villages . . . hidden, yet safe still within the Attic border, as men veil their mistakes or crimes" (224). In Pater's story, Theseus' affair with Antiope is an indiscretion as he is already married to Phaedra. As a single mother, then, Antiope brings up Hippolytus. And yet, there is a proliferation of mothers in the tale. Hippolytus becomes a devote worshipper of Artemis, a "scholar" of "a series of crowded imageries in the devout spirit of earlier days" (227), which were hung on the wall of the recess of the goddess's chapel: "To her, nevertheless, her maternity, her solitude, to this virgin mother . . . he devotes himself" (228). Then, Pater leads into a discussion about the identity of Artemis' own mother: was it Leto or Demeter? Antiope was filled with foreboding about her son's worship of Artemis, herself a "two-sided figure" — "Hecate still counting for him as Artemis goddess of health." Hippolytus, then, grew up in a world of the primitive past, practicing an archaic religion, never really growing up, a boy in a family of multiple mothers (229).

But Theseus "felt a half liking for the boy," an "outcast" (230 and 231), and invited him to "come down to Athens and see the sights," where he might contrast "the elegance of life there" with "the thought of his own rude home." "The boyish driver with the fame of a scholar" became "a victor in the day's race" and "carried home as his prize a glittering new harness." But Theseus could not help but wonder: "Might this creature of an already vanishing world, who for all his hard rearing had a manifest distinction of character, one day become a rival?" Hippolytus elicits much gossip: "At Athens strange stories are told in turn of him, his nights upon the mountains, his dreamy sin, with that hypocritical virgin goddess." The handsome youth attracts Phaedra's attention, who attempts to seduce him. But she receives "indifference" from Hippolytus, leaving her to wonder: "Is he indeed but a child still, this nursling of the forbidding Amazon, of that Amazonian goddess?" (233). There is no misogynistic address against women delivered by Hippolytus in Pater's story. Instead, Phaedra hounds the boy out with "a tempest of insulting speech" and tells Theseus a false tale. The King's "accumulated store of suspicion and dislike" turned "to active hatred" (234). Hippolytus returns home and succumbs to a "strange illness," which again elicits Antiope's "long forebodings". But despite "the curses of the father [and] the step-mother," the boy recovers. And yet, just as Hippolytus sought to compete in a chariot race again, so "those still unsatisfied curses" accompanied him, and like "Adonis, and Icarus, and Hyacinth, and other doomed creatures of immature radiance," he was to die young, "like a child" (235 and 236). His chariot is overturned—was it an earthquake or Poseidon or Aphrodite? the narrator wonders. "[H]is mother watching impassibly, sunk into the condition she had so long anticipated" (236). The story closes, as it had opened, in a more scholarly tone with reference to Ovid (*Metamorphoses* 15.470–552), to record that Hippolytus "flourished still, a little deity, but under a new name and veiled now in old age, in the haunted grove of Aricia," as Virbius (337).

Just as Euripides had challenged the historicism of nineteenth-century classical scholarship, so Antiope and Hippolytus do not fit into their historical moment: they are "poetic protests" against the modern world of Theseus' Athens—they comprise a queer, "primitive" family. Like a male Amazon, Hippolytus is surrounded by too many maternal figures, without a father. In rewriting *Hippolytus Veiled* from a lustful Phaedra to a strong Antiope, the fragmentariness of the Euripidean text, which allowed for multiple potentials, becomes for Pater a story about the fragmentary life, cut short, of Hippolytus, not fully developed and yet fully beautiful, somehow both archaic and classical as well as being the last of his line. Pater's Hippolytus is a protest against the modern, late-nineteenth-century nationalist politics of sexual-social reproduction. This ancient Greek is no exemplar for modern, Victorian masculinity, but is a figure of dissent who rejects modern policies of the healthy and vigorous propagation of the nation-state that was such an important issue in late-Victorian society.

Indeed, the 1880s and 1890s witnessed huge debate about the physical strength of the nation and evinced profound anxieties about immigration and racial "miscegenation." These concerns most often centered on the figure of the "New Woman" and the intrusion of women into the political arena. By the time "Hippolytus Veiled" was reprinted in 1895, the year after Pater's death, there had been a steep rise in studies about motherhood and the child. While some feminists and many male writers emphasized the importance of married life for the production of healthy children, at a time when the Eugenics Movement was gathering pace, many other novelists also reflected upon the unfulfilling and even torturous nature of marriage. Taking its title from Greek myth, one of the most radical of the "New Women" novels of the 1890s, *The Daughters of Danaus* by Mona Caird, was a denunciation of modern motherhood, comparing it to prostitution. It was enthusiastically received by the feminist press, on the one hand, and met with predictable dismay by many others. New discourses on childhood and adolescence were emerging, which expressed anxieties about the "brutish" and "primitive" child. The new discipline of child development exercised a suspicious surveillance over mothers who might exert too much or too little pressure on their progeny, producing either precocious children who grew up too soon or stunted offspring who remained at an immature state. The language of "degeneration" and "arrested development" accompanied the craze for athleticism and physical education, as evolutionary biologists, embryologists, neuroscientists, criminologists, and anthropologists all produced papers arguing for the improvement of criminal and cretinous children and worried about the atavistic regression of the well-reared child. It is hardly surprising that numerous Victorian authors were preoccupied by stories of single parenting.[13]

Pater's tale of Antiope, the single masculine mother, and Hippolytus, the male Amazon who never grew up, is a queer response to these contemporary, late-Victorian discourses about mothering, the child, the emergence of the modern nuclear family and the health of "the race." Pater's Hippolytus joined a line of beautiful but doomed young men in decadent fiction, which celebrated those fin-de siècle discourses of decline and degeneration. Pater's "poetic protest" against the nationalist, imperialist politics of reproduction in the late nineteenth century similarly sought to question the sexual ethics of modern, supposedly civilized society.

The Reception of Euripides and Queer Theory

In a recent discussion of Pater, Dustin Friedman has argued that in late-Victorian "aestheticism is one of queer theory's unacknowledged ancestors" (2019, 5). Fin-de-siècle Decadence, Friedman argues, explored the possibilities of self-fashioning non-normative subjectivities through art in the context of socially normative and hostile discourses. For Friedman, Pater's essay on Winckelmann argued that the engagement with ancient Greek sculpture allowed the German art historian to comprehend the historical distance between antiquity and his own time. While, for Friedman, Pater turned to the world of art to create alternative selfhoods, for Heather Love, on the other hand, Pater is a queer who "embraced backwardnesss in many forms: in celebrations of perversion, in defiant refusals to grow up, in explorations of haunting and memory, and in stubborn attachments to lost objects" (2007, 7). Pater, Love argues, practiced a "politics of refusal" (58), which sought to celebrate the queer resistance to an identity politics of assimilation and normalization.

"Hippolytus Veiled"—considered neither by Friedman nor by Love—offers the possibility of both readings. On the one hand, one might read with Friedman that Hippolytus' intense worship of Artemis provides him with an alternative subjectivity within the autonomous realm of aesthetic experience outside of the norms of city life. Moreover, the story proposes that preclassical antiquity offers a different, non-heteronormative, non-binary model of kinship. On the other hand, with Love, Hippolytus might be seen as an example of "ruined or failed sociality" (22), vulnerable, childish, naive, and politically disinterested. Indeed, we might go further to suggest that Pater's text already marks out Lee Edelman's anti-social, queer negativity in *No Future* (2004). Pater's Hippolytus is a child without a future, a child happy to look back to the past, a child with no desire for social-sexual reproduction, a child whose *jouissance* in aesthetic worship puzzles and raises the suspicions of the city of Athens. But rather than looking back to Pater to locate the ancestor or origins of queer theory like Love and Friedman have done, we might instead see how Pater's reception of Euripides *anticipates and enacts the tensions of contemporary queer-theoretical debate*. Indeed, a central issue in queer theory has revolved around "the (im)possibility of recycling or rejecting the terms of intelligibility" (Honig 2013, 53): what are the stakes of reusing terms like "family" or "kin" for the sake of a queer future or of refusing to resignify, assimilate, and integrate into social-sexual norms? "Hippolytus Veiled" stages a protagonist who does not fit easily into the battle lines recently drawn up by queer politics.

Pater's text should also cause us to think about Antiope, the mother left to lament at the end of the story, and in turn, then, about the relationship between feminist and queer politics, another crucial contemporary debate. In his first attempt to write a history of Greek love, *A Problem in Greek Ethics* (1883), Symonds depicted classical Athens as looking back in awe at the historically irrecoverable early Greek world of manly, virile "Doric love." But by 1891, after the 1885 Labouchere Amendment that had criminalized "gross indecency," Symonds revised his position in *A Problem in Modern Ethics*, to argue that "Doric love" between two masculine adult men should now be seen as a model for modern democratic, socialist politics. For Symonds, like Pater, archaic Greece slid around time.[14] But despite Symonds's politicization of the issue of Victorian homophobia, there were no women involved in his archaic, "Doric" Greek love. Pater's archaic Greece, on the other hand, was populated by Demeter, Artemis, and Antiope.

"Hippolytus Veiled" is so interesting because Pater deliberately omits the misogyny of the extant Euripidean tragedy and presents a strong and independent Antiope who nevertheless ends up doing nothing but mourning. Pater's text anticipates the complexities of queering classical antiquity, and in particular Greek tragedy, in the twentieth-first century, in the context of a debate about the utility of Sophocles' *Antigone* for contemporary feminist and queer politics. Bonnie Honig has recently explored the centrality of Antigone in the turn to a "mortalist humanism." She has traced out the appropriation of the tragic heroine in Judith Butler's works, as "an assertive politics that quests for power in *Antigone's Claim* (2000) gives way in *Precarious Life* (2004) to a lamentation of sovereignty's excesses on behalf of a (post)politics or ethics premised on human commonalities of vulnerability and morality," that is, "a politics that quests for sovereign power to a lamentation of power's excesses" (Honig 2013, 45). While Pater's story can be seen to offer both a depiction of queer kinship and a queer politics of refusing the norm, his movement away from the polis keeps Antiope the mother in her place. How are we to read the end of Pater's story? Is Antiope's lament for the death of an alternative mode of subjectivity that cannot live in the modern world also a political critique of the anti-feminism of the late nineteenth century? In our identification with Antiope in mourning for Hippolytus and a lost queer past, is there also meant to be a politics of mourning as and for Antiope? When we mourn as Antiope, are we meant to be acquiescent or angry? Is Pater's "poetic protest" just lamentation or radical historiography that might ensure that a different mode of loving might live on outside of its historical limits? Pater's text asks us to consider the political stakes of turning back to the past: revolutionary or reactionary or somehow both? Indeed, it is not surprising that Pater's story should elicit such questions: Euripides has continually polarized ancient and modern audiences as misogynist and feminist, patriarchal and transgressive, primitive and (post)modern. If Euripides was so crucial to the fin-de-siècle imagination, which, in turn, has been such a foundational moment for contemporary queer theory, then Pater's reception of Euripidean tragedy makes for a fascinating staging of late-twentieth- and early-twenty-first-century queer-theoretical debates. Reading Pater's

"Hippolytus Veiled" offers us a way to explore the risky pleasures and the pleasurable risks of bringing classical antiquity into dialogue with contemporary debates about looking back and finding a queer heritage in the (ancient) past.

Notes

1. See Introduction.
2. See Dowling 1994 and Orrells 2011 and 2015.
3. See Deihr in this volume.
4. See Ohi 2015 and Østermark-Johansen 2014 and 2017.
5. On queer modes of reading and reception, see also Rabinowitz and Bullen in this volume. See also Introduction.
6. See Haselswerdt in this volume.
7. See Postclassicisms Collective 2020.
8. See Davies 2018.
9. See Goldhill 2021.
10. See Prins 1999 and Orrells 2015.
11. On Jowett, Symonds, and their writings on the pederasty/pedagogy of classical Athens and its projection onto his relationship with Moor, see Orrells 2015, 100–25.
12. Shuttleworth 2010. See Goldberg in this volume.
13. See Bending 2002 and Bowlby 2013, 115–47.
14. On the historical shifts in Symonds's account of Greek love, see Orrells 2015, 100–25.

CHAPTER 2
RHESUS—TRAGIC WILDERNESS IN QUEER TIME
Oliver Baldwin

This chapter on *Rhesus* should perhaps not be in this book. The authorial classification of its fellow chapters may disqualify a play whose Euripidean authorship remains unproven and—perhaps—unprovable. And maybe it should not even be called a tragedy at all, or even Athenian. But perhaps this is precisely the reason why this chapter should be here, occupying textual space and reading time—or not occupying it if skipped. The unfixity and untidiness of the canonical and generic placement and chronology of *Rhesus*, as (non-/other-/post-/early-/pseudo-)Euripidean (?) (pro-satyric/comic/ Homeric/Macedonian/fourth-century) tragedy, may serve to unfix, question, and decenter canonical and generic presumptions and demands, that is, begin to queer Euripides and Greek tragedy as we know it. Highly influenced, in murky and untidy ways, by queer theory's focus on time and temporalities, what follows is an exploration of the openness and wildness of *Rhesus* in the face of authorial hauntologies, chronological mappings, tragic time, generic success, and the demands of discipline. My focus here will be the most salient unfixity of *Rhesus*, time, and how the play, its authorship and text, expectations and classifications of what Euripidean and Greek tragedy must be, reveal that *Rhesus* is always and already queerly positioned in time.

Epic Synchronicities of the (An)achronic *Rhesus*

There is no certainty of when *Rhesus* was staged at the City Dionysia in Athens, the festival in which trilogies of tragedies were performed. The text has come down to us under the name of Euripides, but already in Hellenistic scholarship, as explained in *hypothesis* b (an ancient introduction to the play), some scholars thought it rather to be in Sophocles' style. These unknowns of time and canonical position have opened a great array of theories, theses, judgments, and analyses that attempt to fix *Rhesus*'s temporal and authorial unfixity.

Despite the historical-philological debate about its authorship, ever since, at least, the sixteenth century, there has been some consensus on the work not being fully Euripidean, that it is too imperfect, too messy, too badly executed.[1] These judgments of what is and what is not Euripidean have brought many to assume temporal locations for *Rhesus* either within or without the Euripidean corpus, revealing disciplinary frameworks allied with and co-dependent on other temporal hegemonic normativities, such as colonialism, racism, and heteronormativity. Most supporters of its Euripidean authenticity propose a youthful hand creating the strangeness and imperfection of *Rhesus*, thus subscribing to the notion of temporal distinction and/or progression between infancy, wildness, playfulness, primitivism, and uncertain desire, and mature, tamed, serious, civilized and erotically appropriate adulthood.[2] Accordingly, *Rhesus* is an immature work, a first stab at the greatness of Euripidean tragedy, *prin phusai phrenas* ("before growing his wits"), as Kitto explains (1977, 350), a phase to be outgrown, tamed, disciplined, and superseded. As normative responses to queer experiences insist, it is just a matter of time before normalcy and maturity kick in.[3] Interestingly, although similarities with later Euripidean oddities such as *Orestes* and *Iphigenia in Aulis* have been pointed out by some, the main alternative temporal positionality of *Rhesus* is post-Euripidean, as a work of fourth-century tragedy.[4] This, on closer inspection, betrays the temporal discourse of decline, informed by both the ancient trope of a lost Golden Age, and the melancholic yearnings of the discipline of classics that coincide with (and participate in) the long-established denunciations by many hegemonic powers and knowledge structures of a loss of civilization, morals, and tradition. It transpires that post-Euripidean tragedy is tragedy in decline, unbounded by its formal and generic frameworks, fissuring what we once knew to be proper tragedy. However, in its resistance to firm positionings as either too early or too late, *Rhesus* stands as queer, and queering, in the face of normative chastising and disciplinary temporalities.

If *Rhesus* is detached of its Euripidean authorship, it becomes queer precisely in its otherness, in its uniqueness and in its opening up of other times, places, and voices. For *Rhesus* not to be Euripides', one must assume a historical replacement, either wittingly or unwittingly, of an apparently lost Euripidean text with the one that survives today. This redefines *Rhesus* as standing in for a loss, both masquerading as the object of desire and being haunted by it. But its non-canonical positionality also makes *Rhesus* stand in for another loss, that of tragedies and tragedians lost in/to time, again both masquerading as and haunted by them. These two hauntings ultimately render the author of *Rhesus* a "specter," which haunts critics in turn. The first haunting, that of Euripidean authorship, is what informs pro-Euripidean theses, and perhaps theories of it being created by a namesake or his son, *standing in* for Euripides.[5] The second haunting, that of lost tragic voices, drives claims of a fourth-century origin, opening further possibilities, such as its being written by an actor and/or for a Macedonian audience—or even enjoying a Hellenistic provenance.[6] In this haunting, *Rhesus* opens up new epistemologies away from the canonical fifth-century Athenian voices of Aeschylus, Sophocles, and Euripides; it perhaps allows us to experiment and explore the art and voices of those who have been deemed unworthy, part of a decline, of a post-canonical spectacularization, of thrill-driven imperfection. *Rhesus* may stand in for what has been deemed most queer in Greek tragedy.[7]

Rhesus is the only extant tragedy to adapt an episode of Homeric epic, book 10 of the *Iliad*, the *Doloneia*. The story of the *Doloneia*, recognizable to anyone familiar with the *Iliad*, poses a new authorial haunting on *Rhesus*, evident in the practice of comparing and contrasting it with the Iliadic book. By discussing whether the play is Homerically accurate or tragically sensible, an intertextual reading surfaces that alters the generic specificity of *Rhesus* as tragedy, broadening it into tragic epic or epic tragedy. If we add that the *Doloneia* could be spurious, what commentators may achieve is the comparison and contrast of the pseudo-Euripidean with the pseudo-Homeric. To its temporal and authorial unfixity *Rhesus* must add its own generic unfixity as the tragedy of (pseudo-) Homeric epic.

Rhesus evidences further generic instabilities beyond the epic subject matter. The main points of contention for many are the alleged lack of tragic conventions, as well as the somewhat comedic and farcical elements rendering it a more light-hearted piece than the classification of tragedy allows. Indeed, there are elements that could be read or interpreted as provoking amusement, a smile, or even hilarity. This light-hearted tone has provoked comparisons, for example, with Greek comedy.[8] What to make of this? Is *Rhesus* a comic or funny tragedy? Others have proposed that *Rhesus* may be a pro-satyric play, that is, a light-hearted short play standing in for a satyr play, the drama that followed the tragic trilogy.[9] This not only means that the category of tragedy may not fit *Rhesus*, but, in addition, that *Rhesus* would again be standing in for a loss of temporal significance, in this case as a substitution for a satyr play, a stand-alone piece *after* the tragic trilogy.

Vayos Liapis proposes that the great number of loans and borrowings of other tragic texts points toward a fourth-century imitator, probably an experienced and knowledgeable actor, replicating the greatness of the canonical tragic poets (2012, liii–lxiii). The implication is clear: *Rhesus* is a pastiche of Greek canonical tragedy, further blurring the lines of chronology and genre, placing itself at once as pseudo-Aeschylean/Sophoclean/ Euripidean. If we add the borrowings and adaptations from Homer, Archilochus, and Pindar, as well as its potential pro-satyric nature and possible similarities with Greek comedy, the blurring of generic and chronological distinctions needed for its normative assessment grows exponentially. *Rhesus*—the tragic pastiche, the generic collage—brings disparate authors, texts, genres, and voices into a dramatic artifact that, in its already shifting authorial and chronological unfixities, appears as a queer diffuser of the norms, categories, and presumptions that are used so firmly in attempting to tame its wildness.[10]

Rhesus, as an unfixed and untameable wild cultural artefact, not only resists categorical and chronological exigencies but reveals them to be, to a large extent, a fallacy of normativity in which the positioning of *Rhesus* must respond to the presumed disciplinary frameworks established in neat, ordered, and proper chronologies, genres, and authorship.[11] *Rhesus* stands as the space of the unknown and the unknowable. It reminds us of classics' dependency on the transmission and classification of texts by Hellenistic and later scholars; of our appraisal of certain data over others to fix meaning, chronologies, and categories; of our continued insistence on authorship and context as markers of meaning; of our refutational posturing toward other scholars. In the insistent attempt to find indicative tenses for *Rhesus* ("it *was* written by Euripides"; "it *is* the only fourth-century tragedy we have") what transpires is that the temporal instability of *Rhesus* resides in its constitutive scholarly tense being the conditional, evidencing both the impossibility and the multiplicity of understanding. It also reveals the achronicity of it all: *Rhesus* may or may not be Euripidean and/or fifth-century tragedy, and all critique of tragedy and Greco-Roman antiquity is always out of time and out of tense, always late.

Rhesus, by being the place of the wild, of the unknowable, sheds light on the taming and fixities established by modes of reading and exigencies of academic discipline. The wild and queer *Rhesus* questions the order(ing) of classics.

Rhesus is also a failure, in the sense theorized by Jack Halberstam (2011). To most critics, *Rhesus* is a bad tragedy, for one reason or another: "It is not merely that the play fails as a tragedy; it fails at any level," Kitto despaired (1977, 345). *Rhesus* is either too light-hearted, too epic, not Euripidean enough, an imitation, a sign of immaturity or decadence, or a dramaturgically inconsistent spectacle of fourth-century tragedy, to mention a few. In the analyses of why it is bad we are meant to be reminded of what, conversely, good tragedy is. By analyzing tragic failure, we are instructed on tragic success. But this comparison ultimately reveals the inconsistencies and interests behind each opposing category. For example, if one is to carefully follow the analyses and comparisons that John Parker Poe (2004) makes of *Rhesus*'s oddities—an exercise also practiced partially by other scholars—we discover that they are mostly paralleled in other extant tragedies. The comparison of the failed *Rhesus* with other—successful?—tragedies does not serve to normatively understand the play according to categories, norms, and data; in its comparison, *Rhesus* serves to queer tragedy altogether.

Considering the problems of normative classification, chronology, and genre in fixing the unfixed *Rhesus*, of taming its wildness, of exposing its failure, I believe that perhaps *Rhesus* is pointing us toward another way of reading, one unburdened by the exigencies of discipline, history, and philology. *Rhesus* may participate in Halberstam's *queer art of failure*, initiating a "low theory" for classics, thus proposing "knowledge practices that refuse both the form and the content of traditional canons [which] may lead to unbounded forms of speculation, modes of thinking that ally not with rigor and order but with inspiration and unpredictability" (2011, 10). *Rhesus*'s unstable and polyphonic authorship could invite us to considerations of texts beyond the canon and question its formation and policing. *Rhesus*'s generic wildness could open new paths of reading outside designated categories of generic appropriateness and success. *Rhesus*'s textual pastiche could help us to reconsider transhistorical reading communities in which past, present, and future merge into one same cultural artifact.[12] We may embrace *Rhesus*'s unfixity, wildness, and openness to imagine, read, and explore new possibilities for the Euripidean, tragedy, the pro-satyric, the comic, the epic, textual transmission, fourth-century theater, the losses of ancient voices, or drama outside Athens. *Rhesus*'s queerness questions the rigidities, demands, and expectations of normative classics and opens up a queer futurity of reading, thinking, and understanding as it floats in the queer darkness of achronic time.

In the Dead of Night

Rhesus also floats in its own internal darkness of Trojan night. Among its numerable uniquenesses, *Rhesus* is the only extant tragedy to take place at night, with dawn serving as the closing—or re-opening—note of its action. Although this exceptionality is informed by the night-action of the Iliadic *Doloneia*, night is exploited in *Rhesus* as the internal mechanism for its own queering of time, drama, and action. *Rhesus* thus conjoins its own external queer historical and authorial time with its internal queer night of subterfuge, marauders, truncations, deception, and transformations.

Nighttime action, as much in *Rhesus*, is not that straightforward. Whatever the moment of its composition and performance, *Rhesus* must have been performed in bright daylight, in an outdoor theater and under the—one expects—ever-present sun. I believe that the choice of the *Doloneia* and night was already attempting to alter the perceived time-references of audiences and subvert their senses. Although realism was in no way a goal of Greek drama, to play night tests the imagination of audiences, who can at once believe it is night-in-day and day-in-night. This subversion of temporal and sensorial distinctions may have created a suspension of time, a no-time, a queer sensorial time. Thus, although we will go on to venture into the darkness of/in *Rhesus*, we should have the bright light of the Mediterranean sun ever present in our mind's eye—or even read what follows in the outside, under whatever sun you may have watching over you.

The choice of night also subverts a set of established dramatic relations between Greek tragedy and daylight. Days are often markers of meaningful time in tragedy— "This day will reveal your birth and bring your ruin" (Sophocles, *Oedipus the King* 437). A single day is, in many cases, the unit of time for action.[13] The sun, and its presence, is ubiquitous as a marker of life, since to die means to never see the sun again, a topos repeated even in this most nocturnal of tragedies: "those who suffered worse no longer see the sunlight" (849–50).[14] *Rhesus*'s sunlessness, daylessness, is therefore the place of death, the fleeing of life, the stagnation of action, the time that tragedy fears, expects, and laments but never explores completely. Night is tragedy's queer time. *Rhesus* uses specific compound words to designate its own nocturnal modality of communicating and misunderstanding, such as night-news (*nuktêgoria* 19) or night-debating (*nuktêgoreô* 89). *Rhesus* may be using Phoebus, Apollo's epithet closely associated with solar/light divinity, "the bright one," as the safe-word in the Trojan camp in accordance with its subversive temporal irony—a safe-word bringing death to Dolon and Rhesus, the latter interestingly called "Zeus the light-giver" (355). What in other tragedies is the mark of life, light, is the token of death in *Rhesus*, which also stages Homer's concept of "immortal night" in the *Doloneia* (*Iliad* 10.41 and 142). Night, like day, comes to an end, but while it does not, it is an immortal suspension of time, elsewhere from the measurable passing of daytime, of the knowable time of day. In this unknowable time, markers of time are fused in nowness "stretched out and spanned by a past now and a future now" (Dinshaw 2012, 2). This temporal and cognitive disorientation provokes a world of dark confusion, camp marauders, divine and animalistic transformations, lucid dreams, and the queering of heroism.

The cognitive disorientation of night is an overall theme of *Rhesus*. Nobody understands what is going on. This non-/mis-understanding affects and tricks all senses, and it is both the cause and the effect of either inaction or unexpected action: "Your message is unclear … What are you telling me?" Hector replies to the Chorus (34–8). This lack of communication and understanding, in combination with Hector's impulsivity, creates several moments of frustrated activity and possibilities, further confusing the dramatic action and opening the possibility for the also cognitively disoriented Odysseus and Diomedes to appear onstage: "Is the noise that drops on my ears a delusion?" Odysseus wonders (566). Athena intervenes, both to instruct them to kill the newly arrived Rhesus and to deceive another cognitively disoriented character, Alexander (Paris), by appearing to him as Aphrodite in a scene that is "multiply bizarre" (Liapis 2013, 247). Alexander arrives to warn of intruders, yet his sources seem as confused as everyone else: "One man who did not see them talks of them, and another who saw them after they had arrived can say nothing of them" (658–9). Truth is both unfathomable and unreliable in the queer night of *Rhesus*. Rhesus's charioteer's accusation that the Trojans have killed the Thracians has to rely on logic—who else could have sneaked in unnoticed?—because his senses are hampered both by night and sleep: "Though I am an eye-witness to the catastrophe, I am not able to say how those who are dead met their end or who killed them" (800–2). This eye-witness, however, did in fact encounter the killing of Rhesus in a dream, in which two wolves (Odysseus and Diomedes) snatched Rhesus' horses (780–8). A "night-terror" (*ennuchos . . . phobos* 788) he woke up from as Rhesus was being killed. The night of *Rhesus* distorts, annuls, and disorients all lucid and conscious senses, replacing the normative path of sensorial knowledge with the semi-conscious senses of queer hypnopompic awareness.

The nocturnal cognitive disorientation in *Rhesus* provides fertile ground for cover and infiltration, for roaming without being seen, recognized, or accounted for. Night suspends the Homeric action of war battles, opening space for the surreptitious activities of spies, runaways, and marauders. Night makes the barriers of space, of warring sides, permeable, penetrable, open, a preoccupation often voiced in the play (e.g., 17, 91–2, and 644–5). Thus, Aeneas proposes to send a Trojan spy to the Greek camp, a mission Dolon promises to complete strictly before daylight (223). But Odysseus and Diomedes will keep Dolon in immortal and eternal night, becoming themselves the ultimate spies and marauders. These penetrative and nocturnal tactics are largely deemed unheroic, improper, yet skillfully practiced by Odysseus, having entered Troy twice before, once at night and once disguised (501–9 and 710–21). The unstable and penetrative state of night also brings with it a series of strange, awe-inspiring divine apparitions, those of Rhesus, Athena, and Rhesus' mother, the Muse. It also develops a permeability of the stage, with entrances and exits of characters either out of place, out of time, or, for many, out of logic, such as Aeneas persuading Hector to send a spy, or Alexander's inconsequential appearance, except to justify Athena's divine drag and as the potential reason for a fourth actor.[15] It is even possible that Dolon himself emerges from the assembled Chorus after having stood unacknowledged for over 150 lines.[16] To make sense of the chase scene, Gilbert Murray, in his translation, even materializes a group of Thracians instead of the Trojan guards (1913, 37–40). It seems that in *Rhesus*'s night, anyone can appear onstage in any way—a stage incidentally left completely empty at one point (564). *Rhesus*'s permeable stage ultimately enables *Rhesus*'s generic permeability in the almost-slapstick chase of Odysseus: Chorus: "Do you know where the men have gone?" Odysseus: "I saw them somewhere over here" (689).

The darkness of night also indulges in gendered, ontological, and cross-species transformations, aided by cognitive disorientation and the permeability of space, most importantly the central transformations by Dolon and Athena. The transformation of Athena into Aphrodite to fool Alexander (642–74) has been dismissed as a poor excuse for an exciting spectacle in showing the only divine-to-divine transformation in Greek tragedy[17]—once more *Rhesus* misbehaves, unheeding to the directives of appropriate generic conventions. Yet this transformation has profound queer potential in transgressing the performance of gender and sexual identities. The masculine and virgin Athena plays out the role of Aphrodite, thus performing as the feminine goddess of sex. What is here interesting is that Athena, safe to Greek male eyes in her appearance as non-feminine in her gender and sexual expression, can willingly become genderly and sexually feminine to the extent of fooling Aphrodite's own favorite at Troy. In her nocturnal performing of Aphrodite, Athena queers gender and sex by proving the unfixity of epithetical identities. Athena does this as written and performed—and perhaps watched—by men in ancient Greece, and, perhaps most importantly, within a drama that presents no female mortal characters, breaking the tendency of much of Euripidean extant tragedy once more. In this play of dark and surreptitious male homosociality, the masculine Athena, patron of the heroic couple Odysseus and Diomedes, plays the feminine Aphrodite to fool the Trojan prince, of epic effeminacy (e.g., *Iliad* 3.39–57).[18] Fate would have it that this dramatic queer gender reversal and performance would be replicated in *Rhesus*'s limited performance history, when this very male play was performed by a predominantly female cast in its 2014 production in London by the Fourth Monkey theater company.

In *Rhesus*, Dolon describes his method of infiltration into the Greek camp not as a mere wolf-disguise, but as wolf-imitation, as becoming a wolf himself (208–16):

> I shall fasten a wolfskin round my back and place the beast's gaping jaws over my head. I shall fit the fore-feet to my hands and the hind-legs to my legs and mimic (*mimêsomai*) a wolf's four-footed lope. The enemy will find it hard to penetrate this disguise as I come near to the trenches and the barriers that protect the ships. But when I set foot on an empty stretch of land, I shall walk on two feet. This is the trick (*dolos*) I have devised.

Unlike in the *Doloneia*, where the wolfskin is just camouflage, here Dolon, in his mimicry, in his enactment of Homeric simile, becomes a wolf in his nocturnal infiltration. *Rhesus*'s external canonical and chronological wildness is replicated internally in the appearance of ontologies that roam in the interstices of the human and the non-human, of transbiologies and "animacy."[19] Not only does Dolon become a wolf, but Rhesus, who is compared to both a lion cub (381) and Zeus (355), is closely associated with his magical horses, who gleam at night (617–18). At one point a nightingale's "sorrowful song" is referred to as child-murdering (550), pointing to the filicide Procne, transformed into a nightingale (*Odyssey* 19.518–23). *Rhesus*'s night also provides interspecies permeability. Dolon believes his disguise to be impenetrable or undiscoverable (*dus-euretos* 212), even though he acknowledges the instability of this demarcation: he can also unbecome a wolf at will. The penetrability and unfixity of this nocturnal disguise will be proven precisely in its interception by Odysseus and Diomedes, literally penetrating it in killing Dolon. This is ironically hinted at repeatedly in *Rhesus* through the play on the homophonic similarities between Dolon's name and trickery (*dolos*), not only boastfully proclaimed above, but also in Hector's own word-game with his name (158–60).[20] Yet the word *dolos* is closely associated with Odysseus, as the Muse states (*dolios Odusseus* 894). Dolon's inability to transform not only into a wolf but also into Odysseus, grandson of Autolycus, "the wolf himself," ultimately culminates in Rhesus' death. In donning the wolf disguise, Odysseus and Diomedes can become themselves wolves and as such they appear in the hypnopompic awareness of the Charioteer, who sees in his night-terror a pair of wolves attacking Rhesus' horses. The effectiveness of the ontological transformation from human to animal, as much in this play, can only truly work outside and beyond conscious senses and real time.

A Truncated Force

What Simone Weil (2005) saw as an inescapable *force* that impelled and crushed soldiers in the *Iliad* has been transformed in the night of *Rhesus* into a truncated force, in which action can never be fully taken, in which it is always redirected, halted, interrupted, foreclosed. Night has, after all, suspended Hector's winning progress in battle (52–74), imposing a sense of stagnation on present action. This truncation is most clearly seen in *Rhesus*'s treatment of future and futurity. Hector in his impetus to follow his past success often speaks of the future, as the projection of a nowness to come. Although the Chorus at first encourages this (83), it later warns Hector of its perils: "Beware of the future. The god often reverses things" (332). Indeed, in the night of *Rhesus* temporal progression is halted and future projections reversed. This is best exemplified in the importance and frequency of conditional clauses in *Rhesus*. The future cannot be seen to be determined and clearly approachable, but only mediated by the successful completion of a condition that can result in a number of, not always positive, outcomes. This grammatical instability of knowledge replicates and adds to the scholarly instability on *Rhesus*, as well as the sensorial disorientation, the suspension of nighttime, and the permeability of distinctions discussed. Hector, somewhat surprisingly given his impetus, provides a great number of *ifs* to his deliberations, most of which do not terminate in a desired result, as when worrying for Dolon: "If he is safe, he is approaching the Trojan camp by now" (525–6). Conditional clauses can indeed serve, in the night of *Rhesus*, to open up expectations and actions that are ultimately frustrated and truncated. But conditionals can also open up possibilities for alternate realities in which they were not frustrated, in which actions could in fact favor the Trojans and their allies: if only night had not fallen, Hector complains, he would have beaten the Greeks (59–62); if he were to win victory with Rhesus' help, he would be grateful to the gods (474–6). Conditionals, therefore, also appear as markers of alternative futurities in which those mythically fated to lose could be fated to win. *Rhesus* thus opens the possibility of queer futurities, away from normativities of myth and tradition. It is with this optimism for an alternative outcome that Hector sees impending victory in the arrival of dawn ending *Rhesus*.

The most important alternative and queer futurity in the play is that of Rhesus himself. Rhesus appears onstage out of time in several ways: he is not expected, he is late, and he arrives at night, stunning and scaring the shepherds on Mount Ida (284–316). The Chorus hails his arrival as if a god, with almost erotic delight (342–87). He appears before an unimpressed Hector offering to achieve, on his own, in one day what the Trojans have been unable to do in ten years, and then destroy Greece (443–73). Rhesus thus combines, in his apparition, a nowness of awe, the truncation of Hector's actions, delayed and neglected past commitments, and a fulminating futurity of heroic, semi-divine victory. His ability to end the war in one day, which seems like bragging at first, is confirmed by Athena in the most potent of futurities and conditionals: "If he lives through this night till tomorrow, neither Achilles' nor Ajax' spear could stop him razing the Argive walls" (600–2). But Rhesus will not see the light of day. Rhesus' appearance gives audiences the chance to imagine and project an alternative myth in which the Trojans win and the Greeks are defeated, in which Rhesus becomes Achilles. However, as it transpires, Rhesus cannot survive the queer night of *Rhesus*.

Rhesus' mother informs us, in her lament, that his existence was always already queer and transforms the normative hero into a secretive queer prophet. Rhesus was conceived by the Muse and the river Strymon out of wedlock, and raised by nymphs, thus hiding the dishonor to the Muse's virginity (915–31). Despite fate's decision that he would vanquish the Greeks in one day at Troy, Rhesus' parents tried to prevent him from going to Troy precisely to stop another alternative in his futurity: that he would be killed there (900–1 and 934–5). However, the darkness of night fell upon his eyes. The grieving divinity's response to this, aside from a condemnation of those who have conspired to kill her son, includes a statement of anti-reproductive negativity: "Alas for the suffering of mothers, for human woes! All who take good account of such pain will live without children. They will not give them life and then bury them" (980–2). What makes this statement different from similar ones in Euripides[21] is an air of admiration for those who *actively and consciously* refuse *heterofuturity*, as theorized by Lee Edelman (2004)—a position she might be attempting to replicate by considering her son dead to herself, as quoted below. What the Muse also reveals is that the light-giving hero Rhesus is to have an afterlife in the darkness of a cave as a man-god (*anthrôpodaimôn* 971) and prophet at the mysteries of the queerest of Greek gods, Dionysus, a god for those who understand (*semnos toisin eidosin theos* 973). Rhesus' future will not be one of heroic *kleos* in Iliadic battle, but of mysteric darkness in serving queer Dionysus. Rhesus' queer transformation seems somewhat fitting to a play that has repeatedly insisted on the invalidity of heroic war progression during immortal night, a no-time plagued with other planes of knowledge beyond conscious senses, the penetrability of distinctions between animal, divine, and human, and the instability of grammatical tenses. Rhesus' ultimate futurity is one of queer darkness, mystery, initiation, and devotion, away from his fated glory, truncated in the dead of night, just as *Rhesus*'s darkness, mystery, and unfixity reveal our own inability to know, understand, and analyze its own queer time, authorship, and genre. Rhesus and *Rhesus* exist in queer nocturnal unknowability (967–73):

> To me he will be as a dead man who will never see the light of day—for he will lie concealed in the caves of this silver-bearing land, a man-god, beholding the light, a prophet of Bacchus who lived on rocky Pangaeus, the deity revered by those who understand.

Notes

1. See Fantuzzi 2018 and Burlando 1997, 105–27.
2. See Grube 1961; Ritchie 1964; and Burnett 1985.
3. See Halberstam 2011, 27; Love 2007, 5–7; and Dinshaw 2012, 5.
4. See Kitto 1977, 346; Liapis 2012 and 2013; and Fries 2014. Some early-twentieth-century critics did defend a late Euripidean authorship: see Burlando 1997, 119–20.
5. See Murray 1913, vii, and Fantuzzi 2018, 179–80.
6. See Murray 1913, vi; Burlando 1997, 115; and Liapis 2009 and 2012, lxxi–lxxii.
7. On queer hauntings, see Freccero 2006 and 2013a, and Introduction.
8. See Burnett 1985; Liapis 2013, 244; and Fantuzzi 2018.
9. See Murray 1913 and Roisman 2018.
10. On collage as queer form, see Bassi in this volume.
11. On wildness and queerness, see Halberstam 2020a.
12. See Introduction. On queer failure, see esp. Gurd, Nooter, and Rankine in this volume.
13. See Bassi in this volume.
14. All translations of *Rhesus* are by Morwood (2008).
15. See Battezzato 2000 and Liapis 2012 and 2013, 247–8, 250–2.
16. See Jackson 2020, 59.
17. See, e.g., Grube 1961, 444; Kitto 1977, 340; Burnett 1985, 36–41; Liapis 2012, xxxviii–xli and 2013, 247–9.
18. On *Rhesus*'s tragic all-male concomitant, Sophocles' *Philoctetes*, and homosociality, see Telò 2018.
19. On animacy and its queerness, see esp. Chen 2012.
20. On the *Doloneia* and *Rhesus* as epic and tragedy of *dolos*, see Fantuzzi 2006.
21. See esp. Nooter, Telò, and Mueller in this volume.

CHAPTER 3
TROJAN WOMEN—NO FUTURES
Carla Freccero

In *Trojan Horses*, Page Dubois estranges ancient Greece from the hands of neo-conservatives into which it has fallen. Her list of the "lessons" attributed by such conservatives to the ancient world reveals the degree to which the so-called cradle of democracy has been "straightened out" first to assert Greece's exclusively "Western," proto-Christian and white origins, and second to present timeless lessons that justify conservative ruling ideologies: that war is both necessary and a perduring feature of human nature; and that democracy without strong leadership and pedagogical indoctrination becomes mob rule (DuBois 2001, 53). She concludes, "There is a belief in the human condition, in human nature, which is never historicized ... described without consideration of ... gender difference, and militarism and conservatism are assumed to be appropriate to the universal subject, the white European male. Ancient Greece is fetishized and idolized as the origin of Western civilization, which is in turn considered to be the single source of our contemporary culture" (53–4). Instead, she (re)queers ancient times by focusing on, not epic, but lyric; not the ideality of democracy but the realities of exclusionary citizenship—the non-enfranchisement of women, the enslavement of foreigners and prisoners of war—not war, but love; not xenophobia but cultural diversity; not idealized male homosociality, but "polymorphous eroticism ... pleasure and poetry ... same-sex love" (68). Here queering is tantamount to historicizing, the effect of which is to dislodge a culture and a cultural heritage from normative atemporal sameness with the present (of modern Western, implicitly US culture).[1]

If DuBois's portrait of two Greeces (one conservative, the other "progressive") corresponds to two literary genres—epic and lyric—where does tragedy, and especially Euripidean tragedy, fit in? On the one hand, it is difficult to believe the epic myth of ancient Greece, and fifth-century Athens in particular, upon reading (or watching) the drama of *Trojan Women*.[2] Modern adaptations commonly perform it as a drama protesting the brutalities and abuses of war, militarism, and the traffic in women and/as slaves. But the play defies political categorization; one could even say it rejects the political as such in its refusal to imagine either an alternative or a future that would offer a solution to the devastations of the present.

Indeed, at first glance, *The Women of Troy* seems a queer topic for tragedy; women of a defeated country, the victims of a genocide or ethnic "cleansing," are not tragic, they are the ordinary if pathetic collateral of war. To elevate the perspective of women—whose "theft" and "rape" constitute the founding narratives of so many "civilizations" when such stories are told in the epic strain as the victory of a people and the founding of a new nation—is to narrate history from the position of the losers rather than the victors; it is a people's history and, worse, a history of collaterals, spoils rather than prisoners, objects rather than subjects. No flaw makes for the women's tragic fate, no "lesson" hovers in the air around this drama. Rather, the play insists that in this world there shall be no futurity for these object-subjects, no redemption, no point to any kindness offered, no meaning to symbolic action. In the brushing of history against the grain,[3] *The Women of Troy* queers it, not in order to offer a different, better future, or the vision of a kinder, gentler version of civilization, but to refuse the very possibility of a "future" as such, at all. This is, perhaps, the work "queer" tragedy performs—to dash epic expectations in a drama of futility.

And yet . . . if tragedy is about getting intimate with "grief and rage," as Anne Carson suggests in *Grief Lessons* (2006, 7), it is also, of necessity, a modality of containment, as Nicole Loraux argues in *Mothers in Mourning* (1998). For any polis in the mold of Athens to exist, the sheer destructivity of war must somehow be justified, its resulting grief and rage managed. Death must become, not a biological fact of living mortality, but ontological, essential, a telos that, in retrospect, confers meaning on the incompleteness and insignificance of individual life.[4] Warriors must happily die for the nation; mothers must sacrifice their (selfish) desire to hold on to male children and offer them up for glory. And endless war must be endlessly justified.[5] The women especially must be appeased, even when they are less than warrior-citizens, else they respond in Lysistratan fashion to the call to reproduce fodder for the war machine.

But . . . the women must be appeased *only* in the theater, only through tragedy, where actors lament fulsomely as "men" in the guise of "women." Euripidean tragedy thus is and is not queer. By staging lament, and staging it aesthetically, raising it to the level of tragedy, the grief and rage of citizens are appeased, provided with an outlet, given the opportunity to be expressed without their becoming "political," that is, public, a matter for the city-state to manage and negotiate. It allows male citizen-subjects to "become women," as it were, and thereby to mourn.[6] And so, the tragedy could almost be called, to invoke Marcuse, "repressive desublimation," were one to ignore the fully advanced capitalist element of Marcuse's analysis. This form of containment is surely not queer at all.

*   *   *

In *No Future: Queer Theory and the Death Drive*, Lee Edelman associates queerness with a rejection of the political discourse of reproductive futurism, which offers people the condensed image of the "child" as stand-in for the hope of a better future.[7] It is a form of "cruel optimism," in Lauren Berlant's phrase (2011), insofar as what is on offer is deferral and sacrifice in exchange for a promise that things will get or be better, in exchange, in other words, for hope.[8] In this regard, *Trojan Women* might be thought of as the corrosive and definitive answer to such a discourse: there is no future, not for the Trojans, nor, if the gods and Cassandra are to be believed, for the Greeks, at least not the future that the victors of history would like to claim. The play goes so far as to thematically literalize its refusal of and resistance to this figural futurity by staging, extravagantly, the death of the one subject who could carry the future aspirations of a Trojan city-state, Astyanax, enacting the clear-eyed and cold political wisdom that the heir to one's enemy warrior-leader must be eradicated.[9] Indeed, although the lamentations following the announcement of Astyanax' fate, to be thrown from the battlements, seem to suggest that a young child can do no harm by being left alive, Hecuba has already conceived the thought that decides his fate, for her advice to Andromache is to submit to her new husband and thereby produce a line of sons, like Astyanax, who will rebuild Troy: "[S]ons one day born of your lineage may refound Ilium and it may become a city once again" (704–5).[10] Hecuba's "cruel optimism" is condensed in the line she offers Andromache: "My child, to die is not the same as to be alive. The one is nothing, but in the other there are hopes" (632–3), for Andromache alone lives on as a possible source of a royal line of rulers. Andromache, responding, spells out, instead, the definitive anti-futural rejection of a narrative of hope: "Not to be born is the same, I say, as to die ... For <one who is dead> feels no <more> pain <than those who have never been born> ..." (636–7). As for the (other) "women," ethnic cleansing and slavery will do the job of preventing succession. What better articulation of a kind of death drive that names "what the queer, in the order of the social, is called forth to figure: the negativity opposed to every form of social viability" (Edelman 2004, 9)?

Indeed, for Edelman, queerness is a name for what undoes identity, the social order, the consolidation of futurity, and politics itself. In *The Women of Troy*, it is "women" who mark the place of queerness as the force of this undoing. There are several moments in the play when a kind of political agency threatens to be restored to the women-objects who lament. That agency takes the form of fire. The first coincides with Cassandra's appearance as the one character who does seem to retain some agential intent—if only for a moment—in the play. Talthybius worries, when he sees fire, that the women of Troy are staging a resistance in the form of self-immolation (298–303):

> But what is this? Why is the light of a pine torch gleaming inside? Are the Trojan women burning their tents, since they are about to be led off from this land to Argos, and setting fire to their own bodies from a desire to die? ... In circumstances like these free spirits bridle at misfortune.

In this instance, it is Cassandra brandishing a flaming torch, and Talthybius is not altogether wrong, although he reads as suicide what is, in Cassandra's prophesying, homicidal revenge: "With my marriage I shall destroy those you and I hate most" (405). Finally, when Hecuba is about to be handed over to Odysseus, she also invokes self-immolation: "Come let us rush into the pyre! It is noblest to die together with this land of ours as it burns!" (1282–3). Fire, in these and other instances—for example, when Helen mentions in passing Hecuba's dream portending Troy's destruction, that Alexandros/Paris "fatally resembled a torch" (922–3)—suggests a destructive agency, and in the women's case that agency can only act against the self to deprive the Greeks—whose agential fires reduce Troy to smoke and ashes—of their possessions. As Edelman remarks of Antigone, "Political self-destruction inheres in the only act that counts as one: the act of resisting enslavement to the future in the name of having a life" (2004, 30).

But this is a description of heroic action, and Antigone is a virile woman, a virgin who retains the ability, however brief, to act as subject. Not so the Trojan women. The brief flicker of political agency the drama stages subsides each time, and each time is a reminder of the futility of hope. Coterminous with the city reduced to rubble, the women mark an insistence as remainder, a complete destitution of anything like heroism, a remnant, a trace.

Loraux asks the question, "What does the city fear in female mourning?" (1998, 28), and suggests that it is in part the necessity of a sacrificial relation to the city: the ideal (masculine) citizen-subject curbs his passion and "sublimates" his embodiment for the sake of the polis—an "ideology of death," as Marcuse calls it (2011). The city regulates mourning and it regulates women's relation to mourning, thus confirming a reciprocal relation between the two and establishing a norm: it is effeminate to mourn in the masculine. "If mourning is feminine as such," Loraux reasons, "it is also an opportunity to repress femininity among males" (1998, 19 and 24). "Tragedy," comments Gregory Nagy in the introduction to Loraux's book, "must represent the grief of the Other, not of the Self" (1998, xi).

In a provocative essay on the genealogy of "phallogocentrism"—the symbolic deployment and valorization of the phallus—and its origins in ancient myth, Jean-Joseph Goux suggests that a renunciatory logic founds archaic masculinity and installs the subject as originally masculine in its detachment and abstraction from corporeality. For Goux (1992), metaphysics founds itself on an inaugural split between form (intelligence, spirit) and matter, masculine and feminine, a split that testifies to a renunciation and compensatory reward for what will become the masculine subject/agent of exchange. That reward—originally enacted through an initiation that concretizes both what is lost and what is gained—is transformed into the abstract symbolic power that constitutes the masculine subject (64):

> That in the most elementary and most archaic structures of kinship men are in the position of *agent* of the matrimonial transaction, and women are in the position of *patientes* (or passive objects) of this exchange, cannot but be of signal importance to an archaeology of the "subject" and thus also to a line of thought which seeks to demonstrate the constitution of that subject. It would be, archaically, as a *male subject* . . . that the subject would constitute itself.

Goux argues that, ultimately, the "returns" on such a sacrifice will become completely abstract, and that what remains "is subjection to a universal law, a symbolic order which is the same for all, and to which the subject must submit" (67). But among the initial sacrifices required of the accession to masculine subjectivity is the cutting off of affect, embodiment, and the primal attachment to the mother.

Here in the scene of tragedy, then, the sacrifice, and its costs, are made explicit through the words of women/mothers and a bride: Hecuba, Cassandra, and Andromache all register the logic that sons are born, not to belong to them, but to serve the glory of the polis and, in the context of total civilizational annihilation, they lament that loss. In her extravagant mourning, the tragic mother also mirrors and deflects/absorbs masculine grief; "a mother's sorrow," Loraux reminds us, "is generic, a general sorrow that contains all mourning within itself" (1998, 3). Their words thus "unveil" the phallic contract, demystify it and reveal it to be so much mortal matter, rendering ironic the lofty idealism of symbolic masculine subjectivity and its concomitant values: glory, honor, and the future of the polis. They announce—even as the play enacts—the end of history for Troy. Could this be what the city fears in female mourning? This sort of absolute refusal seems queer indeed in its negational force, its insistence that the future end here.

Formally, as well, *Trojan Women* machinically enacts the repetitive and insistent force of the death drive against the narrativization produced by, for example, historical epic.[11] Edelman comments (2004, 23):

> One way to approach the death drive in terms of the economy of this "chain of natural events" thus shaped by linguistic structures—structures that allow us to produce those "events" through the logic of narrative history—is by reading the play and the place of the death drive in relation to a theory of irony, the queerest of rhetorical devices.

If, as Edelman (following Paul de Man) argues, narrative is the linguistic and temporal unfolding of desire toward a telos—the Symbolic and thus futural mode par excellence—*The Women of Troy* ceaselessly and repetitively interrupts narrative with "the corrosive force of irony" (2004, 23), figured as repeated lamentation that breaks down the blocks of narrative coherence while the play drifts (or crashes) toward the silences of "Troy is no more" (1325).[12] "Irony," writes Edelman, "severs the continuity essential to the very logic of making sense" (2004, 24), a severing the mad Cassandra seems to embody (and promise) in her ironic "celebration" of marriage. Reproductive futurism parodied and ironized into death and destruction.[13]

*   *   *

The simultaneous containment (in the mode of catharsis) and refusal is one of the paradoxes of the text. Another is its status as aesthetic object: in a drama where futurity is declared futile, where what is thematically laid out negates the possibility of "survival," the existence of the text instead seems to fix and "elevate" this negation into an ideal form. Victoria Wohl has noted precisely this conundrum (2018). She writes: "Euripides replaces that ruined city with a sublime city of words." And yet, she argues, he does so in the modality of the trace, there and not there at once, "the smoky trace of a polis that never was" (18). Thus, she writes, "Amidst the smoking rubble of Troy, the play refuses the easy consolation of idealization" (18), an idealization she argues was part of a celebration of abstract dematerialization in fifth-century Athens and that remains the epic ideology of war-mongering nations. To justify widespread destruction, there must be, ideologically, an ideal that persists beyond matter's ruin. But that ideality, that "fantasy screen of futurity" normatively elaborated by narrative temporality is, in *The Women of Troy*, shattered "by irony's always explosive force" (Edelman 2004, 31), figured in the thematic (and diegetically literal) crashing of the towers shortly after Troy becomes dust and dissipating smoke (1320–4):

> *Hecuba* Dust, like smoke winging to the sky, shall take away the sight of my home.
> *Chorus* The land's name shall be wiped out! In one place one thing, in another another vanishes away, and poor Troy is no more!

Wohl comments (32–3):

> Out of this total disintegration, something survives, something beyond both the human and the material, a bare wisp of something that may be nothing … language itself … which, like smoke, endures precisely in its dissipation or dissemination. Dispersed, it persists in the material/human world as an energy, a feeling … And it is in this form, if at all, that Troy's walls and women endure, as a trace, the lingering smell of evaporated smoke. Troy is no longer between two deaths but beyond both death and life, absent and present at once …

This trace or remnant, in the *Troades*, is an inscription belonging neither to the living nor to the dead, but to language, to a figure evoking dissipation, dispersion, dissemination, as Wohl, following Derrida, calls it. It removes Troy and Hecuba from the visible, returning a reader, metaphorically, to other senses. As such, it is not human; it is linguistic, as much the material remnant of things as of people, and it does not lend itself to any narrative future.[14]

It is perhaps no wonder, then, that Rosanna Bruno and Anne Carson transform the drama into a comic populated not by persons, but by animals, plants, and things, each iconically commenting on the singularity of the proper name to which the bits of dialogue are attached (2021). Hecuba is an "ancient, emaciated sled dog of filth"(14), resembling both the she-wolf mother of civilizational foundings and the dog into which she has turned in legend and myth. Talthybius is a raven, eternal messenger of dire tidings. The Chorus are herds of cattle and packs of dogs, while Andromache is a sundered poplar tree with Astyanax as her sapling (as he is also called in the drama). Menelaus is a "cog in the machine" of death, while Helen is fox and mirror, pure narcissistic reflection. Only Cassandra is human, bearer of a futurity promising death and destruction, consumed by a (pseudo-)madness, as though it were the only condition in which the shape of the human might persist. The graphic-linguistic form of the comic offers a literalization of irony's disaggregating interruptive effect on narrative cohesion, with its spatialized blocks of sometimes non-sequential text surrounded and at times overwhelmed by images. Here, too, the figural undoes meaning-making in a particularly ironic way, insofar as the text/image stages the disconnect between tragic narrative and comic juxtaposition at every turn. What better way to refuse a future than to de-sentimentalize and de-idealize both the ideology of death and the lamentations of its victims, to portray the war machine as precisely that, and its players as so much "stuff" to be disposed of—"Troy swallows Troy" (2021, 77)—and yet, somehow, to persist: "We can't go on. We go on" (2021, 77). The invocation of Samuel Beckett's postwar *The Unnamable*—pluralized for the collective "we" of many creatures—comments both on the Greek text and on Bruno/Carson's adaptation (2010, 111):

> I'm all these words, all these strangers, this dust of words, with no ground for their settling, no sky for their dispersing, coming together to say, fleeing one another to say, that I am they, all of them, those that merge, those that part, those that never meet, and nothing else, yes, something else, that I'm something quite different, a quite different thing, a wordless thing in an empty place, a hard shut dry cold black place, where nothing stirs, nothing speaks, and that I listen, and that I seek, like a caged beast born of caged beasts born of caged beasts born of caged beasts born in a cage and dead in a cage, born and then dead, born in a cage and then dead in a cage, in a word like a beast, in one of their words, like such a beast, and that I seek, like such a beast, with my little strength, such a beast, with nothing of its species left but fear and fury, no, the fury is past, nothing but fear.

Words, dust, sky, air, dispersal, nothingness, death, beasts, things, nothing but fear—the lines recall the Greek metaphor, while the absurdist, sardonic energies and animal comparison inspire the adaptation.

The famous ending of *The Unnamable*, echoed by the final lines of the comic, comments on the convergence of "the story" and the speaker, first in words then in silence, and on the predicaments of agency (134–5):

> [Y]ou must go on, I can't go on, you must go on, I'll go on, you must say words, as long as there are any, until they find me, until they say me, strange pain, strange sin, you must go on, perhaps it's done already, perhaps they have said me already, perhaps they have carried me to the threshold of my story, before the door that opens on my story, that would surprise me, if it opens, it will be I, it will be the silence, where I am, I don't know, I'll never know, in the silence you don't know, you must go on, I can't go on, I'll go on.

Beckett's lines stage the (pseudo-)subject vacillating between continuance and cessation, refusing then responding to an (affect-inflected) imperative to continue with agential assent ("I will"). In this, the text salvages some form of subjectivity, however attenuated; the subject is the protagonist/hero of the story, even as he is carried to its threshold by the words that say him.

Carson's text and Bruno's images change the modernist terms of the situation in their comic theater of the absurd. Subjective agency has disappeared from the final lines of Carson's text—"H: '. . . We can't go on. We go on' Ch: 'We go on'" (2021, 77–8)—so that cessation and continuance are described as objective conditions of the "we," a "we" that is, in this space, both collective and not human, encompassing as it does the women, Troy, the cats, the cows, the dogs, the Greeks, the (endless) wars, and, who knows, perhaps the gods as well.

49

Are "we" to hear this as some kind of apostrophic address, warning "us" that we cannot go on this way, and yet we do (at our peril, it would be implied)? Certainly, many modern theatrical adaptations of *Trojan Women* have understood it to carry just such a moral imperative in its depiction of war's devastating and dehumanizing consequences. Even the refusal Edelman associates with the anti-reproductive insistence on *jouissance* in the here and now would confer some heroism on the scene of no future. But the comic demurs and in its demurral refuses either moral injunction, consolation, or, indeed, pathos. It withdraws affect from the scene of devastation. In this it gets at what might be stubbornly queer about the *Troades*, its relentless inability to "believe in" or to advocate a future and to (sentimentally) mourn.

Notes

1. See Introduction on queer unhistoricism.
2. I will be using three titles interchangeably: *The Women of Troy*, *Trojan Women*, and *Troades*.
3. I am referring, of course, to Benjamin 1969b, 257.
4. Marcuse 2011, 124. See Bassi in this volume.
5. See Cavarero 2008 and Rose 2018.
6. For this account, see Zeitlin 1996; for an alternative, see Telò 2020 and Telò in this volume.
7. Edelman 2004. See esp. Bassi in this volume.
8. On the troubles with hope, see Bassi in this volume.
9. In a sense, *Trojan Women* makes us see how the title of Bersani's book *A Future for Astyanax* (1977)—which looks ahead to his later, pathbreaking work in queer theory—can be regarded as a foreshadowing of Edelman's concerns. See also Olsen in this volume.
10. I reproduce, with minimal alterations, the translation of Kovacs 1999.
11. On death-driven aesthetics and tragic form, see Telò 2020.
12. This is, in effect, though framed differently, the argument Wohl (2018) is making. On irony, see Telò in this volume.
13. See Bassi in this volume.
14. See Loraux 1998 on the city-state as the subject of tragedy, and Wohl 2018 on the identification between Troy and the Trojan women.

PART II
ESCAPE/REFUSAL

CHAPTER 4
IPHIGENIA IN AULIS—PERHAPS (NOT)
Ella Haselswerdt

The Horned Doe, or: Becoming Wild

I will place a doe into the loving hands of the Achaeans, a horned one, which, having slaughtered, they will proclaim that they have slaughtered your daughter.

These lines are usually attributed to Artemis, goddess of the hunt, of unweddedness, of wilderness, and of female homosociality.[1] With them, young Iphigenia is liberated from the gruesome fate that myth has demanded of her, and around which Euripides composed his *Iphigenia in Aulis* (*IA*): her throat slit at her father's behest, a perverted sacrifice that would send fair winds, allowing the stalled Greek fleet to sail to Troy, ending the deferral of the most productive mythic complex in the ancient Greek imagination.

In the nick of time, Artemis asserts that she will offer a curious creature to take Iphigenia's place, one that subverts Greek ritual and gendered expectations. On the former, bovines and caprids are by far the most common animals offered in sacrifice to the gods, in accordance with a ritual logic that insists on a fundamental, structural distinction between domesticated and wild animals (Larson 2017). For anthropologists, alimentary sacrifice is closely tied to domestication; raising animals for ritual slaughter, a fate to which the creatures must obediently assent, is a linchpin in situating civilized humans as cosmic intermediaries between animals and gods (Detienne and Vernant 1989). When the girl's fate appears sealed, the Chorus will lament by comparing her to a more traditional sacrificial creature, a heifer. At the moment of her salvation, then, Iphigenia is replaced by—and therefore, in some sense, becomes—an animal who, though subject to the arrow of a hunter, lives her life largely beyond the bounds of human control.

More unusual still is the fact that this deer is genderqueer, her butch antlers revealed by Artemis in a surprise enjambment (*elaphon . . . keroussan* "a deer . . . a female horned one, that is").[2] This is not the only horned doe in the Greek mythic tradition. Pindar in his third Olympian recalls Heracles hunting "a *female* deer with golden horns" (*chrusokerôn elaphon thêleian* 29) that is sacred to Artemis as one of his labors, a creature elsewhere called the Ceryneian hind (but more often referred to as a stag). On most tellings, this particular labor for Heracles is less about strength or courage than it is about patience and deferral. A simple hunt would provide the conflict and action necessary for a discrete, linear plot. Indeed, following Ursula Le Guin, "the hunt" may be the ur-story itself, the source of humanity's collective fascination with masculine narratives that build to a climax of (often violent) action and end with a definitive and satisfactory resolution

(2019).[3] But in this case, killing or harming the animal will incur Artemis' wrath, so Heracles spends a year stalking it over and beyond the known world, evading conflict, meandering into the uncharted wilderness of the snowy north (Pindar, *Olympian Odes* 3.31–2).

The horned doe therefore seems to elude domestication and subjugation to an even greater extent than her normatively gendered counterparts. A similarly deferred and frustrated narrative follows the horned doe into the early modern period. In a twelfth-century Breton lai by Marie de France, the knight Guigemar, a young man on a coming-of-age quest, happens upon and shoots an arrow at a snow-white horned doe. Inexplicably, the arrow ricochets back and injures him. The queer deer speaks, telling him that his wound will not heal until he finds a woman who loves and will suffer terribly for him, and for whom he will suffer in return.[4] Guigemar's encounter with the horned doe distorts the temporality of his body and disrupts the trajectory of his quest. The horned doe, for her part, ranges freely through both space and time, a sort of mystical time traveler, a fugitive subject queering plots that demand a straightforward teleological progression to and through conflict.

The appearance of the horned doe in *IA* similarly sidesteps the plot's seemingly inevitable telos, but the ontological terms of the replacement of the girl with the horned doe are difficult to discern. After the slaughter, the Achaeans will "boast" (*auchêsousi*) that they have killed Iphigenia. Somehow, despite the corpse that must lie before them, they do not perceive the bait and switch. One might posit that the resemblance between the girl and her stunt double is purely superficial; that Artemis uses her divine power to disguise the doe as Iphigenia. But the relationship between the two goes deeper than mere apparent resemblance, or than a veil cast over the doe or over the eyes of the Achaeans. Artemis accepts the horned doe that she provides as commensurate with the girl whose blood she previously demanded, and the replacement, or transformation, does not impact the ethical status of the Achaeans who believe, and even revel in the fact, that they have committed a homicide. A deep affinity exists between the two entities, though they can never exist in the same realm. In some respect, the horned doe becomes Iphigenia, and, reciprocally, Iphigenia becomes the horned doe.

Perhaps we can posit the horned doe and Iphigenia as "queer doubles," a phenomenon elucidated in a study of the films of Hitchcock by Alessandra Soares Brandão and Ramayana Lira de Sousa (2013). The authors argue that queer doubling in the films goes beyond "more traditional definitions of doubles" that "resemble a distorted reflection of the 'real' character," pushing against the binary composition such a formulation entails. Rather, they understand the relationship between the pairings in the Deleuzian terms of "molecular" as opposed to "molar." As they describe it, "Whereas molar structures operate in an 'either/or logic'—thus asserting an invariable self-identity—molecular structures claim for a 'both/and' standpoint that poses a problem to identity ... queers, as expected, would be a 'minority,' a molecular arrangement with the potential to disturb molarity. A minority that does work in the logic of identity, but is undefinable, provisional, open" (22–3). Queer doubles, then, operate on a disruptive molecular level. They do not merely reflect their counterpart back at us, but the entities fundamentally transform one another into each other, making it impossible to reinscribe an original subject with a discrete, molar, identity. The very terms of Iphigenia and her deer double are radically destabilized by the existence of the other, even as they reinforce each other's reciprocal identities. While Iphigenia reinforces the vulnerability that was always already constitutive of the figure of the horned doe, the horned doe reinforces the untameable queer potential, the disruptive wildness that was always already constitutive of the figure of the girl.[5]

Both ancient and modern reception of the play has recognized an affinity between, indeed a blending of the figures of Iphigenia and her sacrificial counterpart. A fourth-century BC red-figure *krater* (see Figure 1) seems to depict the offstage climax of the play, the split second prior to the sacrifice. Iphigenia stands before the altar, head bowed, as Agamemnon raises a knife over her. But Iphigenia is not alone. Situated precisely behind her is a figure of a dappled doe (unhorned here) reared up on its hind legs, assuming a remarkably human posture. Its ears peek up over Iphigenia's head, its snout protrudes in front of her face. Their torsoes seem to fade into one another, and the knee of the creature's left hind leg moves just barely into the foreground, in front of Iphigenia's robes, giving the subtle impression that the creature is straddling the girl. Iphigenia's left foot is slightly lifted with the toe pointed, mirroring the exact angle of the two deer hooves just behind it, evocative of vase images of horses pulling chariots and ranks of marching hoplites, images that stress synchrony of movement, unity of purpose, and the

Figure 1 Apulian volute krater, ca. 370–350 BCE. Photo courtesy of the British Museum.

interchangeability of subjects. And don't the girl's hands look oddly cloven? The painting offers no real direction as to the primacy of one figure over the other. Without the narrative clues provided by the mythic background it would not be at all clear who of the two is coming or going, or that the relationship between them should not be construed as metamorphic rather than transactional.

A 2021 virtual performance by the Barnard/Columbia Ancient Drama Group features an Iphigenia costumed throughout with a headdress fashioned from twigs, arranged in a manner unmistakably evocative of antlers.[6] A Roman fresco of the sacrifice discovered in Pompeii shows Iphigenia doubled, simultaneously struggling for her life on the ground and flying into the sky toward Artemis, clutching the horns of the doe as both of their lower halves fade into the mist of the sky.[7] The duo escapes together, again undermining the transactional model wherein the life of one is given for the other. The play has clearly left its interpreters with the sense that Iphigenia and the creature are neither identical to nor strictly discrete from one another.

Just as these images capture an eternal moment where Iphigenia and the doe simultaneously occupy the same position between life and death, "a world where the living and the dead coexist" (Soares Brandão and Lira de Sousa 2013, 23), in the play the pair stand in an unsteady relationship to time. I want to emphasize here the future tense of Artemis' proclamation in the quoted lines: *enthêsô*, she says, "I *will* place." We hover in the moment somewhere between prophecy and fulfillment. The bestial queer double of Iphigenia is a promised but not yet present escape hatch in a play otherwise marked by a grim, overdetermined fate. The plot of *IA* is a prison. It methodically chews through every indulgence the patriarchy has to offer the girl—the paternal sympathy of Agamemnon, the heroic gallantry of Achilles—all of it revealed to be toothless and useless in the face of the war machine, mobilized as the ultimate expression of masculine squabbling over the ownership of a woman.[8] But when Iphigenia becomes the horned doe, a line of flight, a narrative disruption, emerges. No longer a cow raised for ritual slaughter, or a young girl raised for the rites of marriage, Iphigenia may yet break free of the heteroreproductive structures designed to tame both animals and women. As Soares Brandão and Lira de Sousa write (2013, 23), echoing recent theory on queer temporality (e.g., Muñoz 2009; Freeman 2010 and 2019): "The queer is not here yet. The queer is always coming or, rather, is yet to come. Delayed gratification."[9]

Queer Ticking Time Bomb

Or perhaps the horned doe will not arrive after all. As some readers will have been objecting from the start, the lines discussed above *do not* appear in Euripides' *IA*, at least not integrated into the text of the play as you typically find it sitting on the shelf. Instead, you will likely discover in its place a similar tale of last-minute salvation, with some key differences: now the account is reported as a fait accompli by a messenger rather than a prophecy proclaimed by the more authoritative goddess; the hind is unhorned; and the Achaeans immediately recognize that they have killed a deer, not a human girl. This speech is received with apprehension and skepticism by Clytemenstra in her final lines (1615–18), clearing the way for the bereaved mother's mythically fated revenge plot against her husband to proceed after the close of the play's dramatic action. The fragment cited at this essay's opening was discovered a few hundred years ago in Aelian's second-century AD *On the Nature of Animals* (7.39), biding its time for over a millennium in a bestiary.

Initially, the lines seemed to promise a solution to either one of two major textual problems that have plagued the *IA*.[10] The first being that the play as transmitted, uniquely among the extant plays of Euripides, has no iambic prologue, that is, a prosaic opening address to the audience that describes the setting and sets the expectations for the plot; the second, that due to metrical and other stylistic issues, many editors do not believe that even the ending described in the previous paragraph could have actually been written by Euripides, despite the fact that it was transmitted in the manuscript. Ultimately, though, there is no way to incorporate the stowaway Aelian fragment into the current text without destroying it. If it stands at the beginning of the play, Artemis' proclamation renders the entire dramatic action absurd and improbable. The possessive pronoun ("*your* daughter") suggests that the goddess must be addressing either Agamemnon or Clytemnestra. But if either of these characters know that Iphigenia will be saved, Agamemnon's tortured indecisiveness or, alternatively, Clytemnestra's desperation—the two emotional engines of the play as we understand it—no longer remain plausible. If the fragment were to appear at the end of the play, delivered by the *dea ex machina* in the place of the much-disputed messenger speech, we lose hundreds of lines of Greek and gain just two and a half; furthermore, the entire *Oresteia* is *ex post facto* rendered impossible, as Clytemnestra would be unable to dispute the pronouncement of a god. Yet again, the horned doe intercedes to disturb the trajectory of a plot.

As it turns out, the creature was a queer ticking time bomb, poised to blow an already unstable text to smithereens, the conditional promise of queer liberation ineluctably tied to profound temporal and epistemic disruption. So, the fragment remains unincorporated, in a detached paratextual relationship with the *IA*. Neither of the text nor completely separable from it, the spectral presence of the horned doe and/as Iphigenia reveals the epistemic crises that haunt the play; that haunt philology as a discipline; that haunt restorational orientations toward antiquity more broadly.[11] It is the impossible, excluded Other, a creature whose inconvenient presence can neither be metabolized nor disappeared by traditional disciplinary means. But promise remains in the creature's impossibility and in its marginalized position *beside* (*para-*) the text.[12]

Iphigenia's Body in Pieces, or: Cut/Paste/Run

While the Aelian fragment is a particularly dramatic instance of what are often termed the textual "problems" of the *IA*, the fault lines run much deeper. As Christopher Collard and James Morwood note, "only 200 or so of its 1629 lines have not been suspected or deleted by somebody" (2017, ix), rendering the text a veritable Ship of Theseus. There are a number of explanations for the unruly nature of the play, most of them as banal as the typical effects of the ravages of time and occasional neglect. But there are some peculiarities to this particular text's (mal)formation. Scholiasts tell us that the play was produced in 405 BC shortly after Euripides' death. Most imagine that the posthumous nature of the play invited interventions and interpolations from many hands from the very beginning.[13] Furthermore, I argue that the play's content is deeply implicated in the text's disintegration. If one common hypothesis is true, namely that the first performance ended when Iphigenia walked off the stage to her death, then the various reports of her last-minute salvation were the work of later editors, re-stagers, and interpolators, who could not bear, or thought that an audience would reject, a play with such a disturbing ending. Those who interfered with the text of the *IA* projected either their own horror at the presumed fate of the young girl, or, responding to the presumed horror of an imagined audience, desired an opportunity for her survival, and dismembered and reconstructed the play to make it more palatable. Whatever the reasons may be, the fact remains that what we have received as a play is really an unruly assemblage of fragments held together by sheer force of will, by the prodigious work that translators and interpreters have undertaken of hiding the seams.[14]

The failure of *IA* to cohere in a respectable manner reminds us of the uncomfortable truth that philological practice is always, to some extent, a slow deep art of collaborative cut and paste, the evaluation and arrangement of sources that always represent, at best, a highly mediated view of antiquity, a fact that is elided by the page of clean text presented in modern editions. And no matter how learned the scholar or expansive her imagination, re-formations (and attendant interpretations) of ancient texts will always be limited by a presumed horizon of possibility that will never, and *can* never, be identical to the conceptual apparatus of an "original" author. While all works suffer from this inevitable myopia, perhaps few do more than those of Euripides, whose plays consistently defy expectations of tone, genre, and mythic precedent.

But if we expand our own horizons, and revel in the uncomfortable problems and the distortions, we may find that the text has more to offer us today. That is, while the radical instability of the text stymies historicist analysis, leading to negative valuations, it also offers a plenitude of hermeneutic possibilities that are particularly well-suited to a queer approach. A queer reading demands, in my view, attentiveness to the disruptive power of non-normative desire and potential for collective liberation. In its artificially seamless form, the plot of the play presents a girl with vanishingly few choices available to her. It also presents the brink of a catastrophic war that, despite the hesitations of its primary architect, Agamemnon, will proceed. But one thing that the indeterminacy of the text can tell us is that, if the plot of the *IA* is a prison, it is a prison of our own making.

I posit that the queer potential of the *IA* emerges not in its capacity as the vessel of a unified plot, but rather where rifts emerge, the places where the text breaks down. These were made especially visible in a notational practice developed by James Diggle, for the purposes of his 1994 OCT edition of the *IA*.[15] His sigla integrate into the Greek text itself his evaluation of the probability that any given verse of the play was written by Euripides:

The judgment of the editor concerning the authorship of individual verses is indicated by these signs in the margin:

○ up to ○ perhaps Euripidean
⊖ up to ⊖ perhaps not Euripidean
⊗ up to ⊗ hardly Euripidean
● up to ● not Euripidean[16]

By leaning into these seams, we might be able to start to think of the text in its capacity as a sort of collage.

Collage as an artform is helpful here because it does not seek to disguise the seams between the elements of an assemblage. As Jack Halberstam puts it, collage is "feminist and queer" in that it "precisely references the spaces in between and refuses to respect the boundaries that usually delineate self from other, art object from museum, and the copy from the original, working through a negative destruction of [the image] that nonetheless refuses to relinquish pleasure" (2011, 136). The moments where the text "fails," then, are potential sites of queer meaning.[17]

Invoking the flamboyant and impossible horned doe as a talisman of queer liberation and destruction, I offer this reading as a jailbreak. The creature explodes the teleological narrative structures that constrain and condemn Iphigenia, the logic of the hunt, or of heteroreproductivity, directing us toward the points of disruption where escape routes emerge. One promising seam lies in the wild desires of the Chorus.   ⊗

Queer Choral Escape Routes, or: *Gunaikes* to Watch Out For   ○

There is always something queer about a tragic Chorus. They are paradox and anachrony embodied, simultaneously fundamental to the genre and estranged from it. Both singular and plural, both more and less than a dramatic character, interested in but detached from the tragic action, mortal but deathless in the extant canon, at times they express a distinct point of view, at others they seem to serve as a conduit for the play's affective energies. Sung choral lyric, the Chorus's primary communicative mode, is recursive and ruminative, operating at an odd disjunction with the teleological plot. The tragic Chorus stands at a homohistorical orientation to the unfolding drama.[18] Like collage artists, they make and unmake images, concepts, and narratives by means of surprising juxtaposition.

But the Chorus of *IA* is further queered by an odd whiff of scandal. The dramatic role assigned to them is that of a group of married women (*gunaikes*), who have fled their city unchaperoned to gaze upon the gathering of the Greek fleet at Aulis. It is difficult to overstate how alarming this scenario would have been to a male Athenian audience. Ideally women, in particular married citizen women, stayed home, their freedom of movement strictly circumscribed. The disruptive potential of this Chorus of women on the loose, having traveled a great distance independently and with the exigency only of curiosity, is second only to that of the terrifying Chorus of maenads in the *Bacchae*, who follow the god Dionysus from the East, driven to revel in the pleasures he offers.[19] The

Chalcidian women of *IA* sing of their breathless journey over hills and across rivers, their "cheeks redden[ing] with new-blooming (*neothalei*) shame" (187–8). They describe themselves as on the cusp of erotic awakening, an eyebrow-raising sentiment from women who are supposed to have already been domesticated by marriage.[20]

Multiple signals in the *parodos*, the Chorus's entrance song, direct us to consider the ode alongside Sappho 16, a poem that itself eroticizes a woman's departure from the constraints of heteroreproductivity: just as Helen leaves (*kallipois'* 9) her husband and children, the Chalcidian women leave (*prolipous'* 168) their polis. But while the women initially seem aligned with the normative desires Sappho invokes only to reject ("Some say that a host of cavalry, some an army of footsoldiers, some a host of dark ships is the most beautiful thing on the dark earth" 1–3), even within the song their erotic gaze will begin to overflow the bounds of its object. And there are multiple instances where they express desire in terms so extreme and non-normative, that so exceeds the horizon of expectations, that they create a rupture in the text.

The opening of the ode is marked with Diggle's most optimistic sigil: O "perhaps Euripidean." But now, at line 231, he demotes the text to ⊗, "hardly Euripidean." This disjunction corresponds with a striking assertion by the Chorus of the desire motivating their breathless trip to Aulis. They sing (231–4):

I came to count and to behold[21] their ineffable ships … so that I might fill the womanly (*gunaikeion*) sight of my eyes with seeing, an ash-wood (*meilinon*) pleasure.

Clearly something is amiss in the manuscript. What follows are some theories proposed by editors:

- so that I might fill the womanly sight of my eyes with gentle (*meilichon*) pleasures (Markland)

- so that I might fill the womanly sight of my eyes with delicious ("sweet-to-the-mind" *meliphron'*) pleasure (England)

- so that I might fill my women's eyes with pleasures sweetened with honey (*melichrôn*) (Stockert)

- so that I might fill the womanly sight of my eyes with greedy (*lichnon*) pleasure (Wilamowitz)

- so that I might fill the womanly, greedy (*lichnon*) sight of my eyes with pleasures (Jackson)

- so that I might fill my womanly sight more (*mallon*) with pleasures (Hermann)

Stockert concedes that Wilamowitz's conjecture *lichnon* is "paleographically plausible and supported … with evidence." But like nearly every other commentator, he dismisses it based on an inability to countenance a group of young women in so elevated a genre as tragedy using a word so shocking. The etymology of *lichnos*, from the verb *leichô*, "I lick," gives some sense of its visceral connotations, a semantic complex of gluttony, lasciviousness, desire, and inquisitiveness. As Collard and Morwood put it, "The English word jars here, the Greek one is 'always disapproving' ... it most often implies sexual interest or prurience," citing an example where it refers to "a male ogling women" (2017, 306–7). Diggle finds the sentiment too *putidus* ("disgusting") to impute to Euripides. Despite the generally wanton behavior of the women, their role as *gunaikes* apparently renders this baldly appetetive word unfathomable in their mouths. Most editors, reviewing the options, ultimately print the difficult word † in daggers †, that is, mark it as hopelessly corrupt, its original meaning impossible to recover.[22] The negative valuation that inheres to the † symbols is highlighted by their identification, in philological terminology, as *cruces desperationis*, or "crosses of despair." They are a symbol of last resort, when all attempts to domesticate an unruly bit of text have failed.

But rather than rejecting all of these readings for their failure to meet standards of philological rigor that shrink interpretive horizons, I want to consider what happens when we accept all of them together, as a molecular structure. A luscious stream of affective excesses pours out of a text that is ruptured by an unbridled band of women's defiance of expectations, a swirl of pleasure and:

more / honey-sweet / delicious / gentle / greedy.

In trying to find their way around or through desire, the philologists unwittingly conspired to collectively compose something like a Sappho fragment. Also noteworthy are the variations on the word "pleasure." In some instances, the word is understood as singular, and a predicate for "women's sight." In others, it is plural, and refers to the delectable substances the women feast their eyes on. On some readings, then, the perceptive power itself is a pleasure, whereas in others, the pleasures lie in the objects of perception. This vascillation complicates the hetero- orientation of their gaze. While they admire the hypermasculine bodies of the Greek heroes alongside their gleaming instruments of war, in some respects the pleasure of perception itself, rather than its particular object, is ultimately what overwhelms their expression and the text.

Another textual rupture occurs in the Chorus's following ode. The song is a sort of hymn to marriage and piety. In most respects the ode expresses a view of marital love that is so chaste, so moderate, that it could be interpreted as a palinode or recantation for the erotic excesses of the song we just discussed. They "forbid [Eros] from [their] bedchambers." (552–3); "Let my joy be measured (*metria*)," they dourly intone; "Shame is wisdom" (554–5; 563).

But suddenly, in delineating the gendered bifurcating paths for wife and husband, they seem to sing a discordant note (568–72):

It is a great thing to hunt after virtue: for wives, through secret Kypris (*Kuprin kruptan*), among men, in turn, an infinite order existing within will make the polis grow greater.

Though the wording of the description of the path for virtue for men is strange, the meaning is more or less clear, and in keeping with commonly expressed and performed assumptions about ancient Greek gender roles: virtue for men has to do with their service to the polis, to the public sphere. What the Chorus is trying to say about women, however, is confounding. Like the phrase discussed above, many editors print *Kuprin kruptan* in daggers. Interpreters who accept the text tend to understand it as having the expected reciprocal meaning of managing the private household, the domestic sphere.[23] But *kruptos*—the ancestor of our prefix "crypto"—does not really seem to mean anything like "private" anywhere else; its resonance is something much more like hidden, secret, or concealed. *Kupris* is a cult name of the goddess Aphrodite, who is often invoked as a metonymy for sex. Based only on the text before us, an obvious interpretation —but one too outlandish for interpreters to countenance—is that the Chorus of Chalcidean women is praising illicit sex.

Leaning into this possibility, could this jarring assertion refer to sex between women? It makes sense for non-male homoerotic indulgence to be described as concealed, not so much in the modern idiom of the closet, but in the sense that it is inscrutable and illegible to the culture at large. They will go on to ruefully recount the divine beauty contest and the eventual meeting of Helen and Paris; heterosexual desire leads to war. In the previous scene, the Chorus has witnessed Agamemnon casting aside indecision and vowing to sacrifice his daughter for the war effort. Faced with the real toll of the war, perhaps the shine has begun to wear off. The bloody business of glorifying the polis makes the women turn inward, toward each other.[24]

As the play comes to a close, and Iphigenia is about to depart to her apparent demise, she directs the Chorus to help her raise a song of praise to Artemis. She sings, directing the Chorus to "whirl about" the altar of the goddess, and "to sing together with her (*sun-epaeidet'* 1492)." If the Chorus came to Aulis to marvel at the military forces, they are by now drawn into the feminine sphere, directing their attention and coordinating their actions with Iphigenia and the virgin goddess. But many editors cut the play off before the Chorus is able to sing in response, some practically lamenting that the text in fact continues on.[25] This is precisely where some scholars imagine the first performance would have ended, and modern productions of the play often follow suit. While Diggle awards Iphigenia's song a ⊖, "perhaps not Euripidean," he downgrades the Chorus's response to ⊗ "hardly Euripidean." England calls the verse "a feeble and at times senseless" recapitulation of Iphigenia's.

But continue the manuscript does, and the Chorus's response to Iphigenia's song begins, "Oh, oh! behold her leaving . . .!" (1509–12), as they shift their gaze, so heavily eroticized in the *parodos*, toward the girl. They go on to sing a set of lines marked off by most editors with the now-familiar daggers, lamenting that she will spatter "the goddess's altar with drops of streaming blood, and the beautiful neck of her body." One of the primary "problems" with these lines is temporal. The tenses of the participles are a confusing mishmash of present and past, whereas in Greek the future is required. There is an utter breakdown of the temporality of the sacrifice, a confusion between what has happened, what is happening, and what will happen later.

But ultimately it is a minor phrase and a minor problem that I want to focus on here, a moment where the slightest semantic slippage conjures again the multiplicity of

Iphigenia. In the manuscript, the Chorus sings of the "beautiful neck of her body"; some editors fiddle with the phrase, printing instead "the neck of her beautiful body." But the real oddness here lies in evocation of Iphigenia's "body" at all. Why must the girl's neck be further specified? Is there an aspect of Iphigenia that is, in fact, distinct from her body? As Collard and Morwood put it, "the superfluous 'body' is very strange" (2017 ad loc). By confusing the singularity of her body and confounding the temporality of the sacrifice, the Chorus's fake, feeble, impossible song disaggregates "Iphigenia" from her fate. At the moment when the ultimate dismemberment of Iphigenia's body is imminent, the body is itself multiplied, as though some version of the girl may yet survive.   O

On the Horizon   ●

[STAGE DIRECTIONS]:
Iphigenia † and/as the horned doe † walk[s] off the stage, accompanied by a whirling band of recently converted devotees to Artemis, heading into the wilderness to indulge whatever excessive sensory pleasures they desire free from the critical gaze of the philologist. The fleet stays stalled in the harbor.[26]   ●

Notes

1. For more on Artemis' queerness, see Rabinowitz and Bullen in this volume.

2. The question of whether or not female deer could be horned seems to have been a live one in antiquity. I argue that the poetics of the lines cited indicate that the description of the female deer as horned is neither an error from misunderstanding nor a casual observation, but an intentional surprise gender reveal crafted by the poet.

3. Cf. Umachandran forthcoming.

4. See Freccero 2015. Thanks to Carla Freccero for alerting me to this comparandum.

5. On *parthenoi* (virgins or young girls) and gender trouble see, e.g., Hanson 2007. On wildness and queerness, see Halberstam 2020a. See also Freccero in this volume on Carson's transformation of Trojan women into animals.

6. https://www.youtube.com/watch?v=fMW4g_5jn4E

7. For more on the identification of the figures in the image, see Kahil 1990, 719 and 726.

8. See especially Foley 1982 and 1985; Seaford 1987; and Rabinowitz 1993.

9. See also Radcliffe in this volume.

10. On this, and other matters concerning the history of the text of the *IA*, see esp. Gurd 2005.

11. See Introduction.

12. For generative readings of this relational preposition, see Mueller in this volume; see also, in general, Sedgwick 2003, 8–9.

13. See especially Kovacs 2003.

14. See Ward 2019 on assemblage as metaphor for classical reception.

15. See Gurd 2005, 67–8.

16. Translated from Diggle's Latin in Diggle 1994, 358.

17. On failure, see Gurd in this volume and Introduction.

18. On queer unhistoricism, see Menon 2008, 1–25; Matzner 2016; and Introduction.

19. It may indeed by relevant that *IA* and *Bacchae* are thought to have been produced together as a trilogy (with the lost *Alcmaeon*), meaning that these two Choruses would have been played by the same men on the same day to the same audience. For a discussion of the power and limitations of *Bacchae*'s Chorus of women on the loose as a site of feminist refusal, see Honig 2021, especially 72–100.

20. See Carson 1990, 144–5: "[A] woman's life has no prime, but rather a season of unripe virginity followed by a season of overripe maturity, with the single occasion of defloration as the dividing line."

21. For vision and the Chorus of *IA*, see Weiss 2018 (ch. 5).

22. See, e.g., Kovacs, Diggle, Stockert, Collard and Morwood.

23. But see also Wasdin (2020), who argues that it is an indirect reference to the strange relationship between Iphigenia and Achilles.

24. On the suggestiveness of prepositionality in regard to female homoerotic attachments, see also Telò in this volume.

25. See, e.g., Collard and Morwood 2017, 618–19.

26. I am grateful to Sasha Anemone and Mathura Umachandran, who read early drafts of this essay and gave extraordinarily helpful feedback.

CHAPTER 5
HELEN—QUEERING THE BARBARIAN
Patrice Rankine

Euripides' *Helen*, first performed in 412 BC, builds on the rhetorical device that Helen did not go to Troy, but rather her likeness, an *eidôlon*, did. Although Euripides did not invent the trope of Helen's false image, he put it to good dramatic use, and for any playwright worth their pay, the drama is the thing.[1] I propose in this essay that throughout Euripides' *Helen* the figure of the Barbarian, Theoclymenus, is worth lingering over, worth queering, even if he might seem to be no more than a narrative device. In the play, the audience meets Helen first, and learns that she has been in Egypt for seventeen years, brought there for safe keeping by Hermes, under Hera's direction. Menelaus will arrive to rescue her from this plight, and she will reveal to him the truth about Troy. Everything Helen tells her audience, and the fact that Hera would choose this place and its people, indicates the strength of Egypt as a safe harbor. Yet for the play to work, Euripides must invent the Barbarian Theoclymenus, whose tyrannical rule and insistence on marrying Helen shames his ancestors, described throughout the play as kind and noble. In a play that proposes things are not what they seem, something seems strange.

Three overarching theoretical considerations guide my reading. The first is Toni Morrison's insights about American literature, which she offers in *Playing in the Dark: Whiteness and the Literary Imagination* (1992), where she shows how white American writers used Black people as literary tropes. These writers were not consistently aware of their interest in Black people, but their Black characters stand in for a "denotative and connotative blackness" (6). White characters know themselves in counter-distinction to Blackness, i.e., they play in the dark. Without suggesting any modern racial discourse in Euripides' *Helen*, his Barbarian is analogous to the Black characters Morrison describes in American literature. Euripides' need for a narrative device in Theoclymenus, however, belies the traces he leaves throughout the play of the fuller, more amenable reading of Helen's host. My reading of Euripides' Theoclymenus as a kind of "playing in the dark" is, secondly, an application of Jack Halberstam's notion of indiscipline, where we linger over—and queer—aspects of cultural texts that we have become accustomed to reading in particular ways. As Halberstam puts it, "We have to untrain ourselves so that we can read the struggles and debates back into questions that seem settled and resolved" (2011, 11). In some ways the normalcy of Euripides' use of the Barbarian trope might cause us to gloss over certain aspects of the text. For example, three quarters of *Helen* is spent anticipating the terrible Theoclymenus, but the focus on the threat he purportedly poses shifts attention from the Greeks' behavior, and particularly that of Menelaus. There is evidence throughout the play that allows us to read otherwise, to queer the text.

Thirdly, then, as it pertains to the queering of the text, I am drawn to Rahul Rao (2020), whose study of gay rights movements in Uganda and India situates queerness in gender but also in other dynamics of power. As he puts it, "the sex/gender order blends with a wide range of institutions and ideologies—the family, state, market, 'culture', religion, 'race', biomedical and other regimes of the body" (127). I am not suggesting that Rao's postcolonial categories (e.g., "state," "market," "race") apply anachronistically to the fifth century BC, any more than the "Africanism" of Morrison's critique, the figuration she gives to deployments of denotative and connotative Blackness, would itself apply to the world Euripides creates for Helen.[2] These theoretical considerations, however, enrich a reading of the play through analogy.

Queer and race theorists have been especially adept at noticing wayward aspects of culture, literary and dramatic texts, and at centering marginal voices in ways that are also helpful to our collective understanding. To this end, Halberstam encourages the analyst to linger over even those aspects of culture or knowledge that cannot really be known. In Euripides' *Helen*, Theoclymenus is just such a wayward figure, underdeveloped to an even greater degree than his sister Theonoe.[3] With Theoclymenus, the audience and playwright are playing in the dark. Theoclymenus is presented as a tyrant, a contrast to the Greek leadership. He fails to win Helen, who reunites with Menelaus, and the appearance of the Dioscuri at the end of the play affirms the appropriateness of this conclusion. The theoretical considerations of Morrison, Halberstam, and Rao, however, allow us to linger on, to queer, the Barbarian.[4] Queering Euripides' *Helen* opens an illuminating and disruptive entry point into the play's ordering, which includes man/woman, warrior/civilian, hero/villain, Greek/Barbarian, tyranny/democracy.[5] We might not be able to know exactly what Euripides wanted to convey about war or dramatic narrative, but a queer reading of *Helen* is instructive when we consider the oppositional pull away from Helen and Menelaus' triumph, linguistically, structurally, and in terms of the relationships established and revealed in the play. The dominant perspective of the play accrues from the predominance of Greek characters as the collective voice of the play, e.g., Helen, the Chorus of Greek girls, Teucer, Menelaus, Castor and Polydeuces (Helen's brothers, the Dioscuri). An irrepressible centripetal focal point, however, is the play's setting and its people, i.e., Egypt, its current ruler Theoclymenus, and his sister Theonoe.

"Greek" and "Barbarian" figure throughout Euripides' *Helen*. In "Greek," I recognize two primary registers in Euripides' language, one distinctly Homeric, which is taken as a given across readings of the play, where specific groups, such as the "Achaeans" (e.g., 74), sacked Troy, and a second in which a kind of Hellenism is clearly operative, "Greek" denoting collective cultural acts, and specifically those against a military adversary.[6] The Greek characters, moreover, are unreliable narrators.[7] Unsurprisingly, their accounts tend to be self-serving. Not only do Helen and Menelaus deceive their host, but their actions call into question whether the things they say about their foreign helpers can be trusted. Whatever Euripides' intention, a central tenet of the play supports a narrative strategy of undermining his characters, namely that appearances belie reality, Helen being the premiere case in point. Euripides introduces the Homeric trope of the wooden horse through the bull ostensibly to be sacrificed in commemoration of Menelaus' death, but it is an omen of war.[8]

People, Places, and Dramatic Tropes

Although not the only play with a Barbarian figure, *Helen* emphasizes the setting from its very first word, Nile: "These are the streams of the Nile belonging to the beautiful virgins [the Nymphs], the Nile that wets the fields of Egypt with the dew of white melting snow instead of heavenly rain" (1–3). Helen offers no details about this fictional Egyptian setting or its customs beyond stereotypes, except that it is a strange, desert place, with the Nile replacing rain the Greeks would know for fertilization. Helen is speaking to an audience accustomed to a different set of realities from what she has seen in Egypt.[9] Helen is not quite in league with those who attribute human traits to geography, but she conveys the idea that the audience is witnessing a foreign place with different customs. In the Egypt Helen describes everyone is a slave except one man, the ruler (276). The focal point of her frustration is Theoclymenus. "Greeks" operate in clear contrast to these customs. When he arrives onstage, Menelaus claims to have led a great army "not as a tyrant" using force but as overseeing "willing young men of Greece" (395–6).

To play in the dark, to borrow Morrison's figure, Euripides must rely on clear characterizations of "Greek," then set these against the Barbarian. That is, the Barbarian queers the norms of identification.[10] Helen sets the tone for narrative assumptions throughout the play, even if she gives little actual evidence.

Euripides establishes setting and norms of identification, toggling between a Homeric register and one resonant with his own time,[11] but he deploys these norms for dramatic purposes. Like the Homeric Phaeacians, for example, Euripides' Egyptian sovereign is xenophobic, in this case on guard against some outsider, possibly a Greek, discovering the ruse involving Helen.[12] The old woman, a servant in Theoclymenus' palace, tells Menelaus upon his arrival that his credentials bear no weight in this place.[13] Like the wandering Odysseus of Homeric epic encountering the Cyclops, Menelaus seeks the kindness that Greeks extend to *xenoi*, and yet he will later use the kindness that he expects of others to deceive Theoclymenus. As it pertains to the contemporary context, the playwright needs these Egyptians to be strange in particular ways, but he draws from tropes about non-Athenians that are part of classical norms of identification, such as rule by tyrant, xenophobia, heightened warlikeness. The Barbarian trope is somewhat out of place, however, because of the initial hospitality toward Helen that the plot requires.

Before Theoclymenus' rule, Helen has depended on the kindness of his father Proteus, at whose tomb she sits as a suppliant. The audience learns from Helen that this family has extended every kindness to her. In Euripides' genealogy, Proteus is a descendant of Nereus, a lineage that seems to draw from both Homer and Aeschylus. Hesiod's account of Nereus in *Theogony* is worth citing because it fills out some of the countervailing characterological background (233–6):

Pontus bore Nereus, his eldest offspring, a truthful person and without guile. They call him the old man because he was kind and unerring, and he did not disregard the laws. Rather, he knew kind management and justice.

Although Hesiod makes no mention of Proteus, Euripides builds a genealogy based upon an impeccable family lineage. Helen reports that Proteus was deemed "the most temperate of all men" (47), his home the safest place for her.[14] In addition to the stories of these men, the characterization of Theonoe the prophet extends the family practice of closeness to divinity, serving as a contrast to her brother. She has "tak[en] after her forebear Nereus in the honors" of prophecy (13–15). Theonoe will later be enlisted to deceive her brother, an action that requires her to conform to the Greeks' plot to escape Egypt by sea.

Euripides needs a device to initiate Helen's departure from Egypt once she and Menelaus reunite. Because of Theoclymenus' reportedly insistent desire to marry Helen, he gains a villainous reputation from the perspective of others in the play, in particular Helen, followed by Menelaus. This, however, was not Euripides' only choice. Theonoe, for example, quickly does the Greeks' bidding and betrays her brother, who could simply follow in her path through a triumph of diplomatic persuasion. If he does, however, there is no drama. Theoclymenus' gendered character—he is the warlike tyrant in contrast to his godlike and mild sister—is thinly conceived. Euripides can draw from various "Barbarist" figures, to echo Morrison's (Africanist) idea of playing in the dark. As I suggest later, however, whether deliberately or not the playwright implicates himself in the play's theme of the precariousness of appearances.

Gendered People, Places, and Dramatic Tropes

It should come as no surprise that gender plays an important role in Euripides' *Helen*. The drama has a female titular character, but its resolution involves a conflict between men. The Homeric register of Euripides' *Helen* makes Egypt a second Troy, Theoclymenus a type of Paris,[15] especially given the play's proposition that a different Helen was taken to Troy. Theoclymenus repeats Paris's abduction of Helen. Ironically, the drama stages the real battle over Helen since Troy was based on a false pretense. Menelaus will leave Egypt with the spoils of war, which he did not truly do at Troy, despite what he has come to believe. Euripides' *Helen* culminates in a battle, a "reenactment of the Trojan War" (Juffras 1993, 46), and it is worth drawing attention to the degree to which martial verbal play in the text is gendered as masculine.[16] There are queer possibilities, however, outside of normative Greek masculinity. Gender is militarized in Euripides' *Helen*, but militarized masculinity is not the only possibility at hand for the play's characters.

As it pertains to masculinity, Teucer laments not having died with Ajax, the brother who took his own life after failing to secure Achilles' armor, a prize of war superseding any human plunder. Helen was ostensibly the prize for the Trojan conflict (43–4), a contest between the most outstanding men (*kratistos Hellados* 41). The play's Chorus were *thêrama*, "booty" from a Barbarian ship (193), which suggests some previous piracy.[17] When Menelaus arrives on the scene from his postwar wanderings, he is years removed from the military conflict at Troy, but he has been at risk, outside of peaceable regimes. As it pertains to his precarious situation, he remains militaristic. Whereas Helen and the female Chorus appeal the pity of their hosts (939 and 943), Menelaus chooses war.

Menelaus' appetite for war might seem his only masculine choice, but it is worthwhile to recognize this as not the only option Euripides presents. Helen and Menelaus embody potential dramatic directions that are to an extent gendered, but not entirely. After reuniting, they decide to convince Theonoe to help them escape. In their arguments persuading Theonoe to betray her brother, they present the alternatives of persuasion or force in gaining her cooperation. The persuasion option is a non-starter when it comes to Theoclymenus, given the ongoing, Barbarist characterization of him as also prone to conflict. It is noteworthy, however, that, although claiming democratic principles in contrast to Theoclymenus' Barbarist tyranny, Menelaus tends toward the path of authoritarian violence. He himself presents other available paths, even for Greek men, in his exchange with Theonoe (944–53):

> I would not in the end deign to fall prostrate at the knees of the likes of you nor shed a tear. In doing so we would shame the major calamity that befell Troy, showing ourselves to be cowards—although they say it is of a well-born man in hard times to shed tears. But if this is nobility, I will not choose such nobility in this present misfortune.

Striking in this passage is the idea that Menelaus could enter Egypt on hospitable rather than hostile terms and retain his masculine esteem. Helen came to Egypt as a suppliant, and supplication would be the nobler choice for Menelaus, even as a man. He could appeal to pity, and doing so would not feminize him, even by his own estimation. However, he shows disdain for his host.[18] He goes as far as to suggest that he would forego noble behavior altogether if nobility is submitting oneself in this situation. Instead, he chooses war, even though he knows a peaceable option. In their exchange with Theonoe, Helen asks her to continue the kindness of her ancestors. Menelaus also appeals to Proteus' legacy but quickly threatens conflict (977–9). He refuses to approach Theoclymenus straightforwardly, choosing guile instead and bringing a conflict that doubles the Trojan War despite the Chorus's statement regarding the foolishness of strife (1151–3).

Whereas Menelaus exhibits a militarized mindset resulting from a decade of war and his subsequent struggle simply to survive, in heightening his combativeness Theoclymenus has chosen an unprecedented path for himself and his ancestral legacy. The direction is borne out of the necessity of the drama; it is a path that the play must take as a mechanism to facilitate Helen and Menelaus' departure from Egypt. There is no denying that Theoclymenus enters the drama with hostile intention.[19] As we have seen, however, violence is a departure from his family legacy, the noble pedigree that has been consistently conveyed throughout the play. His family has hosted Helen for seventeen years, and now another stranger, Menelaus, seems to him a hostile intruder. All of this is to say that another possibility is latent in the text, that of a continuation of diplomatic solutions to conflict. This other possibility is present in Theoclymenus' claim to "rebuke myself much because I haven't punished evil people with death" (1171–2). That is, he sees himself as having been too accommodating in the past (a past the audience cannot fully know). By the time of his belated entry into the drama, however, the cruelty of his Barbarism has already been firmly established, even if he presents his hostility as a departure owing to present necessity. Helen uses the language of "helping friends and harming enemies" (1426), but in the hands of the Barbarian "harming enemies" is cruelty. Still, there is a degree of inconsistency to Theoclymenus' characterization, something worth undisciplining, to borrow from Halberstam. In a drama that asserts things are not what they seem, something seems amiss. Theoclymenus fulfills a Barbarist trope but also must demonstrate enough consideration to clothe Menelaus properly, replacing his ragged attire, and to allow Helen to bury her dead husband, the false premise that secures Helen and Menelaus' departure.

The result of Menelaus' militarism and Theoclymenus' Barbarist characterization is that they become worthy masculine adversaries in what amounts to a second Trojan War. Menelaus and Helen's plot to escape Egypt culminates in a final battle on the Phoenician ship that Theoclymenus gives them to bury by sea Menelaus, disguised as a shipwrecked Greek soldier. The Greeks claimed piety as the reason for being outfitted with a ship and attendants. The messenger later reports the destruction that takes place on the ship, a result of Theoclymenus putting the Greeks in charge (1552–3).

The degree to which this battle scene echoes the Homeric description of Troy's fall is another significant aspect of the drama's resolution because it draws attention to Greek deception while allowing the Barbarian a range of emotional reactions, including disappointment, betrayal, and rage. In the *Odyssey*, Demodocus tells the Phaeacians the story of Greek *dolos* (8.509–20), the deception of a wooden horse presented as a peace offering to the Trojans. The Trojans weigh alternatives but decide to offer it as a gift to the gods, bringing it into the city, and the Achaeans rush out of the horse to sack Troy. In the scene in *Helen*, a bull substitutes as the vehicle of deception. The attendants believe that the bull is "a sacrifice for the dead [Menelaus]" (1564). The bull is Menelaus' sacrifice to the gods for safe passage from Egypt for himself and his wife—*damar* (1586), itself an archaizing and militarized usage that reinforces both Homeric and militaristic modes. The messenger reports the recognition of an attendant crying for help: "Someone said, 'This voyage is a trick'" (1589). Helen reinforces the idea that this battle is akin to the *kleos* or "glory" won at Troy (1603). Echoing the report from Troy, "the ship poured out with murder" (1602). If the real Helen is in Egypt, this battle corrects the false premise that led to the fall of Troy.

A degree of pity for what Greek *dolos* does to the enemy is not unusual, as is evident in the description of Troy's fall in Homer's *Odyssey*. In the context of *Helen*, it is worth considering what Euripides is accomplishing beyond his Barbarist representation of Theoclymenus. The character is a plot device but one that raises more questions if we linger on the scene to see Greek *dolos* from the enemy's perspective. We cannot know if this was what Euripides would have us do, but we might undiscipline a reading of Theoclymenus as a straightforward villain. Egypt has served as a host for Helen for almost two decades, and an autonomous political entity fearing that its generosity toward strangers will be to their military disadvantage is also not Barbary. Hosting can be a blessing as well, and in the long run it proves to be for Theoclymenus. Through the *deus ex machina*, Castor reveals that Theoclymenus' marriage to Helen was not fated and asks him simply to let go of any ill-feeling resulting from the turn of events. This outcome, however, comes with significant turmoil and disruption for the host. Conflict, moreover, only follows from the narrative logic by presenting Theoclymenus in Barbarist terms.

Queering the Barbarian

Theoclymenus exists in a context where Helen praises the other Egyptian characters. He, however, "kills every Greek guest he apprehends" (155), anticipating that someone will discover her. To achieve Helen's reputational redemption, Theoclymenus' character becomes a foil to Menelaus. His role in the narrative depends on his Barbarist portrayal. The use of Theoclymenus as a dramatic trope, however, creates an ethical dilemma within the cultural mechanisms established within the play. There is a Homeric dimension to this characterization, examples including Odysseus' encounters with Polyphemus and Alcinous and the Phaeacians, where the poet calls attention to the degree of kindness the host exhibits. A letdown comes at the end of Euripides' *Helen*, the Greeks' trickery and departure creating a messy resolution because of the ambiguity surrounding the hosts—a noble and loyal Theonoe somehow convinced to deceive her brother, an irate Theoclymenus on the brink of harming a sister who has been celebrated throughout the play. The play requires, therefore, the device of the *deus ex machina*, the Dioscuri. Their intervention spares Theonoe and absolves Theoclymenus. He could be viewed as a tyrant in his behavior toward Helen and Theonoe, or his actions follow from helping friends and harming enemies. His vengeance against Thoenoe would at least be justified. Theoclymenus acts as a Barbarian man forcing the issue of marrying his Greek guest, and yet the unfolding drama reveals the Greeks as the killers accomplishing their desired ends through deception.

Categories or norms of identification are mutually reinforcing. In the context of Toni Morrison's literary analyses, for example, whatever the cultural perceptions of certain people (Black people, in the case of the nineteenth and twentieth centuries in the United States), fictional works only need to signal somewhat in those directions both to reinforce those perceptions and to deploy them as literary tropes. Morrison calls this phenomenon "Africanist." Norms of identification affirm that which seems to be, as if this seeming is the only reality. The Morrisonian analogy offers much to consider about the Barbarist trope in Euripides' *Helen*. Barbarians are tyrannical, and Theoclymenus' facilitation of the Greek story line affirms the norms of identification. Euripides needs him to be useful in other ways, however, and this dramatic necessity opens possible interpretations different from how things initially appear. In addition to the narrative contradictions within the drama, the embedding of Euripides' *Helen* within a context of Homeric poetry and its precedents affords the play a degree of queer irony, a kind of palimpsestic depth that upsets its characterizations.[20]

Seeming is Not Being: The *Eidôlon* as Queer Phenomenon

Helen's *eidôlon* meant trust in her appearance was misguided, but the same paradox, that seeming is not being, applies to other characters in the play, including Theoclymenus. The characters each have a double, as if themselves embodying weaker arguments and stronger ones.[21] Not only is Helen's bad reputation reversed, but the Egyptian hosts allow themselves to be duped into helping the Greeks, who are not their friends. The drama's reversal of expectations extends beyond Helen as *eidôlon*.[22]

A few examples, beginning with Helen. When he passes through Egypt early in the play, Teucer marvels at seeing a *mimêma*, a "copy" of Helen. He believes he sees a "murderous image," the *eikô phonion* of a "hated woman." The character of Helen is at the center of a doubling. She seems to be the cause of strife (261), but the *eidôlon* is really the guilty party, not the Helen who stands before Teucer. Helen herself is an *aischron eidos* (263), a "shameful figure," a monster (*teras*) to be taken away in place of the *agalma . . . tou kalou* (262), the "gleam of the good." By the end of the play, it is proposed that Helen was not the cause of the Trojan War, and the *eidôlon* has disappeared, leaving no one to blame except perhaps war itself. Helen first presents the idea of an *eidôlon* early in the play (34), using language that she will later repeat throughout. By the end of the play, Castor presents her as a woman of the most noble *gnômê* (1687), a "disposition" or truth that replaces the previous false impression.

The play is about appearances and reality even beyond Helen. Menelaus, too, is not what he appears. As Teucer reports, Menelaus has disappeared; he is *aphanês* (126). When he manifests, he is a stranger in rags, escaping notice as himself to many characters: the old woman, Helen initially, and Theoclymenus. He appears contrary to the expectation because many believe that he is either dead or missing at sea.

The characters are themselves and their double, their seeming and their being. Theonoe is a trusted prophet who betrays her brother, Theoclymenus, a tyrant who helps his guests even after being said to kill Greeks without exception. As Rao has offered, queerness brings the fundamental questioning of the cultural mechanism that we deem normal. The gender/sex order is but one dimension of a broader social order, even if a significant one. Morrison provided theorization of how literary othering works within this order. Theoclymenus is a Barbarist trope, but Euripides' use makes him an *eidôlon* as well. Like other characters, he is not what he seems to be. I do not subscribe to the idea of *Helen* as a failed tragedy,[23] despite its strange resolution, but lingering on the drama's thin Barbarist premise, if even momentarily, opens us to seeing conflict and the making of enemies in otherwise ways.

The Chorus confirms that the play's final revision is "contrary to expectation" (*aelptôs* 1689):

> The things that seem as they should be are not what end up being the case. To the contrary, god found a way for the things we do not expect. This matter turned out in such a way.

If the premise that things are not what they seem is true of Helen, it is also true across the drama.[24] Tied in with the performance of gender roles, Theoclymenus as *aelptos* is intriguing. To borrow again from Halberstam, a disciplined reading of the play would accept the Barbarist presentation. The audience cannot know for certain propositions that Euripides leaves out. They rely rather on their own experiences, imaginations, and projections. What is this Egypt? What are its customs? Who in their experiences might be like Theoclymenus, and are these non-Athenian people friendly or hostile? Do we have the wherewithal to examine ourselves, as Athenians?[25]

A last consideration might lead closer to what is real, beyond expectations. As Heather Sebo (2014) has noted, Euripides' *Helen* operates on yet another register, beyond the Homeric and contemporary ones. There is a ritual register, a chthonic depth, wherein the Chorus roots the dramatic action in the story of Persephone's abduction to Hades. On this level, Theoclymenus is a type of Hades.[26] The play contains this reading. Teucer immediately represents the palace as akin to Hades' home. Hermes, who transports souls to Hades, has led Helen to this place. If war is the human manifestation of a natural cycle, Helen's return to Sparta is like Persephone's resurrection into the light. Put in terms of gender performativity, "Helen's ultimately marks Menelaus's return to the Greek homosocial" (Jansen 2012, 328). Euripides' commitment to this proposition, namely the prospect of resolution and the peaceful return to normalcy that the *deus ex machina* announces, is unclear. When we queer the text, we leave room for skepticism regarding other possibilities for its interpretation and staging. If the norms of identification that the audience has come to know are not real and true, then they should question everything, including the poet and their own expectations.

Notes

1. This essay is indebted to Hall (1990), who also draws from Edward Said's *Orientalism*.

2. As Morrison puts it, "I use it as a term for the denotative and connotative blackness that African people have come to signify, as well as the entire range of views, assumptions, readings, and misreadings that accompany Eurocentric learning about these people" (1992, 7).

3. On the sketchiness of Euripides' characterization of Theoclymenus, Theonoe, and Egypt, see Bacon 1961 and Hall 1990.

4. My use of "queer" here is consistent with the experimentation with form that Amin, Musser, and Pérez (2017) propose. See Introduction. Readers and viewers come to expect certain things from tropes and genres.

5. See Goldberg and Menon 2005 on categories and historicity, as well as Introduction. Mueller in this volume offers a further meditation on Euripides' interest in unsettling oppositional structures of cultural identity. See also Rabinowitz and Bullen on the "Barbarian."

6. On the premise of a different register in the play, see Segal 1971.

7. On the unreliability of Euripides' characters, see Pippen 1960 and Pucci 2012.

8. Virgil's *Aeneid* offers another theoretical provocation to Euripides' *Helen*, a way of queering the text or of seeing it otherwise. From the perspective of an *other*, in this case a fictional, literary character, Laocoön, the priest of Poseidon who is skeptical about the larger-than-life wooden horse that the various opposing troops have left at the gates of Troy, ostensibly as a peace offering, the enemy, the *Greek*, cannot be trusted. For queer approaches to the relationship between epic and tragedy, see also Andújar and Baldwin in this volume.

9. Another theoretical consideration underlying this reading is Edward Said's orientalism, where England knows of Egypt primarily through a "textual attitude" but no real anthropological exposure (Said 1979, 82). By 412 BC, when Euripides' *Helen* was first staged, the playwright could rely on a consistent set of metaphors and images of the other, the undesirable, or the enemy.

10. On identity as being generated in part through norms of identification and norms of treatment, see Appiah 2014. On norms of association with Egypt in the play, notwithstanding the positive depiction of Nereus and Proteus, see Allan 2008, 55–61. See also Rabinowitz and Bullen in this volume.

11. See Allan 2008, 24–8.

12. Specific translations might press the Egyptian hostility to Greeks a bit beyond what the language allows (e.g., Kovacs 2002a), and this choice has consequences for how we understand what Euripides is ultimately doing.

13. Comparison could also be made to Thucydides' characterization of Sparta as a closed society. Notably, Helen is Spartan, although any negative association is curiously de-emphasized in the play. On Helen's veneration in Sparta, see Allan 2008, 5–6. Religious observance is part of cultural norms, and Menelaus wonders if there is anyone called "Zeus" in Egypt (490–1).

14. See Marshall 2014, 79–95, on the precedent for these characters in Aeschylus' *Proteus*.

15. He can also be read as a type of Cyclops in that character's treatment at the hands of Odysseus.

16. See Allan 2008, 49–55, on normative gender roles in the play.

17. It is unclear how exactly these women came to be captive in Egypt. The story of Persephone is at the center of this plundering, e.g., 175, and the choral ode, 1300ff. I will take this up later by way of conclusion. See also Sebo 2014.

18. The position of the objective pronoun, for example, is emphatic: "I would not fall prostrate to [the likes of] *you*."

19. See, e.g., Marshall 2014.

20. On queer irony, see esp. Freccero and Telò in this volume.

21. On queer doubling, see also Goldberg in this volume.

22. Even Theonoe is part of a play on ideas about appearance and gleam. Helen offers an alternative name for Theonoe, Eidô. Eidô is "the appearance," the *aglaisma*, or "manifest glory," of her mother. See Marshall 2014, 79–95, for more on the naming, which is slightly different in Aeschylus' *Proteus*.

23. A problematic formulation, for which see Allan 2008. On the persistence of the negative view of *Helen*, see Allan 2008, 16–18. See also Juffras (1993), who argues that "Euripides ultimately undercuts the new Helen with which the play begins" (54).

24. See Wohl 2014 on the contrafactual dramaturgy of the play.

25. Hall (1990) advances the idea that the tropes of Barbarism form a critique of the Greeks by the time of later fifth-century plays.

26. See Juffras 1993, 47.

CHAPTER 6
CHILDREN OF HERACLES—QUEER KINSHIP: PROFIT, VIVISECTION, KITSCH
Ben Radcliffe

Even by the experimental standards of Euripidean drama, *Children of Heracles* is a baffling play. It stages the story of how Heracles' orphaned children seek refuge in Athens from their father's implacable enemy, featuring a plot driven by arbitrary reversals of fortune, disorienting shifts in tone and characterization, and miracles that pass almost without comment. Scholars have recently shed light on the political meaning of the play's investment in formal fragmentation and displacement,[1] but there is a kernel of truth in the judgment of older generations of critics who regarded *Children of Heracles* simply as bad: "lifeless," "deprived of tragic resonance," "bear[ing] little trace of dramatic mastery," "a thoroughly bad play."[2]

So bad it's good? There is certainly an undercurrent of schlock, of delightfully failed seriousness, that runs through a narrative full of tear-jerking monologues and self-defeating heroism. These effects suggest that we can understand the badness of *Children of Heracles* not only in terms of artistic failure or as a vehicle for political reflection, but, above all, as a source of perverse pleasure. That is to say, we can situate the play somewhere on the boundary of kitsch, a category of "bad" art that has long been an object of queer appreciation. Much of what is pleasurably bad about *Children of Heracles* has to do with its train of queer characters and scenarios. The star of the show on this count is Iolaus, Heracles' former companion and lover: in old age he becomes the devoted foster parent of Heracles' children, but during the play's penultimate act, he is miraculously transformed by his deified lover into a handsome young man. Iolaus is "queer" in both the narrow sense of the term (he has a sexual history with Heracles) and in a more capacious sense—by raising children who are not his biological progeny and by maintaining a lifelong attachment to Heracles, he engages in forms of care and desire that exist in tension with the norms of the conjugal-procreative family.

In a discussion of queerness and kinship theory, Elizabeth Freeman defines "queer belonging" as the desire "to endure in corporeal form over time, beyond procreation" (2007a, 299). By this measure, Iolaus is one of several characters in *Children of Heracles* who forge bonds of queer kinship that refuse the story line of the traditional family, of the husband and wife who reproduce their aging bodies through the generation of children.[3] This mode of procreation comes under pressure from the antagonist's relentless vendetta, compelling the kin of Heracles to find other ways to "endure in corporeal form over time," including acts of self-sacrifice, memorialization, fosterage, and reverse-aging that bend various gender and kinship norms and break up the play's dramatic consistency.

Nearly all of the incongruities that are supposed to make *Children of Heracles* "bad" are tied to these acts of queer refusal. As a genre, Attic tragedy is constitutively fixated on the vagaries of heterosexual marriage, procreation, and paternity. *Children of Heracles* queers the genre-form—renders it kitsch—precisely by having its central characters subvert this thematic complex and develop alternative forms of kinship. My premise is that the badness and the queerness of *Children of Heracles* are two aspects of a single process: even as audiences are invited to revalue the play as a kitsch alternative to "good" drama, the characters in the play endeavor to compose alternative modes of familial care and desire. I am interested in how these two circuits of fragmentation and recomposition intersect and draw together the valences of *genos*, the Greek term for "genre" that also means "gender," "kin," and "family."[4] The resources of contemporary queer theory are especially fruitful in this line of questioning, for they give us a way of thinking about how a common set of material conditions underlie both the production of artworks and the production of gender and sexuality.

Profit and Kin

Iolaus opens *Children of Heracles* with a monologue that contrasts his own sense of familial duty with the egoistic pursuit of profit. The speech reads on first inspection as a conservative defense of family and community as sites of virtuous social obligations, but Iolaus' oblique language suggests that the interrelations between duty, desire, and selfhood are rather more convoluted (1–11):

> Long ago I formed the following opinion: one man is by birth just to his neighbors, but the man who holds his unfastened desire toward profit is useless to the community and difficult to intercourse with, but he is his own best friend; I know this and learned it through experience. For I, out of reverence and in awe of kinship (*to sungenes*), though I could have dwelled peacefully in Argos, was the one man who had a hand in Heracles' many exertions, while he was among us: but now, since he dwells in heaven, I keep his children safe, holding them under my wings, though I myself am in need of saving.

The abstract opposition in the first verses—the just man against the man who desires profit—immediately maps onto the antagonism between Iolaus and the tormenter of his family, Eurystheus, the king of Argos and Heracles' devoted enemy. Iolaus does not make this equivalence himself: he only posits the moral opposition and says that he developed it through experience (*ou logôi*), literally "not through discourse," a signal that his present moralizing discourse maintains an oblique relation to his implicit knowledge about kinship and desire.

Indeed, Iolaus confesses that, as a young man, he left behind a quiet, domestic life in Argos to accompany his half-uncle Heracles on his famous labors. He thus preferred a passionate attachment to his distant blood-relation over a sense of duty to his "neighbors" in Argos and, ultimately, to the prospect of raising his own biological progeny. Iolaus does not refer explicitly here, or anywhere in the play, to his pederastic relationship with Heracles, which is attested in connection to Iolaus' Theban hero cult and complements the pattern of Heracles' other *erômenoi*, most notably Hylas.[5] The silence at the level of overt discourse (the sexual history is, at it were, *ou logôi*) promotes Iolaus' self-styling as a man driven by a sense of altruism, who followed his uncle only "out of reverence and in awe of kinship." But this overloaded phrase intimates the intensity of Iolaus' feelings, and the word for "kinship" here, *sungenes*, also means "alike" and "same;" indeed, in Aristophanes' famous account of sexuality in Plato's *Symposium*, *sungenes* denotes the "same sex" in same-sex desire (*to sungenes aspazomenos* 192b; cf. *to sungenes sebôn* at *Children of Heracles* 6).[6]

Iolaus' monologue underscores the ways in which the logic of kinship can exceed itself, engendering passions and attachments that transform the possibilities of familial care. In the play's final act, Eurystheus is defeated by the allied armies and, under questioning, reframes his antagonism in terms of the ethical distinction that Iolaus posits in the prologue. He initially opposed Heracles out of a kind of divine madness ("Hera made me suffer this disease" 990), but after Heracles' death, Eurystheus sustained his monomaniacal effort to extirpate the Heraclids, representing it as a rational measure to secure his own family's safety, since the former would inherit their father's enmity (1002). The ethics of kinship become particularly tangled here. Eurystheus admits that he chose to advance the interests of his lineal descendants at the expense of his collateral kin (987). Heracles is his distant cousin via descent from Zeus, and Eurystheus uses precisely the same term to describe his relation to Heracles (*sungenes* 988) that Iolaus uses for this purpose in the prologue. The ostensible difference between Eurystheus and Iolaus thus belies their kindred nature on the level of desire: both style themselves as passionate defenders of family and friends, but they pursue these passions along eccentric, diverging trajectories that (as we will see) engender unconventional configurations of familial care and belonging.

Either character, in this sense, could fit the description of the man in Iolaus' maxim "who holds his unfastened desire toward profit," if by "profit" we understand a certain excess over what is given or established. This suggestive expression is worth quoting in Greek and examining more closely (4):

ho d' es to kerdos lêm' ekhôn aneimenon

To Greek ears, the juxtaposition of *kerdos* ("profit") and *lêma* ("desire") would have sounded perplexing, because only the doubling of the letter *mu* differentiates *lêma* from its near homophone *lêmma* ("profit"), which is itself a synonym for *kerdos*. The verse thus almost means, "holding his profit [*lêmma*] toward profit [*kerdos*]." One *mu* becomes two: profit engenders profit, kin beget kin, like desires like.[7] This tautological logic marks the point at which familial duty (*to defend one's kin, the same lineage*) converges formally with Iolaus' queer desire (*to desire the kindred, the same sex*) and Eurystheus' desire for profit (*gain engenders gain*). In other words, the very notion of kinship harbors collateral lineages that split away from, and sometimes rehybridize with, the ideal of the conjugal-procreative family. Iolaus' biography dramatizes this tangled lineation: his same-sex relationship with Heracles realized a certain devotion to kinship even as it directed him on a trajectory away from life of a settled, child-rearing patriarch that he might have led in Argos; and in old age, through devotion to the memory of Heracles, Iolaus becomes the guardian of a parentless family seeking refuge in a foreign state, hounded by Eurystheus in his effort to secure his own family's advantage.

Eurystheus undergoes a parallel transformation: in the play's final scene, he has been captured by the victorious Heraclids, and Alcmene (Heracles' mother) insists on executing him. To placate her more conscientious Athenian allies, she proposes to hand over Eurystheus' corpse to his kin (1023–4), but Eurystheus turns his impending death against the Heraclids, proposing instead to donate his corpse to Athens and establish a hero cult that will protect the city from a prophesied invasion by the descendants of the Heraclids (i.e., the Spartans in the Archidamian War).[8] Eurystheus prefers to bring *kerdos* (1043) to his adopted city as a foreign resident instead of being buried by and among his own kin. *Kerdos* supplements and finally supplants the bonds of consanguinity, engendering forms of voluntary care and belonging that outlive Eurystheus' body.

Queer Kinship

As a concept and a social practice, kinship is often associated with a conservative vision of the family organized around marriage, biological descent, and heterosexual gender norms. But a variety of other relationships can be identified or analogized with kin relations, including friendship, caregiving, mentorship, and pedagogy. Queer theorists have broadened the notion of kinship to explore the ways in which sexual minorities form "families of choice" that engage in the work of social reproduction traditionally associated with the heterosexual family.[9] In its most inclusive sense, kinship is based on the possibility that relations of intimacy and care can endure over time, beyond a single generation. This formulation stresses kinship's corporeal dimensions: as Freeman writes, kinship in its various forms "accommodat[es] all the possible ways one human being's body can be vulnerable and hence dependent upon that of another, and for mobilizing all the possible resources one body has for taking care of another" (2007a, 298). The need for mutual care in the face of corporeal vulnerability is precisely what Iolaus understands as the basis of his role as foster parent ("I keep his children safe, holding them under my wings, though I myself am in need of saving" 10–11).

If kinship negotiates the corporeal dimensions of care and vulnerability, it also complicates the notion of the body as a stable, self-present referent. What exactly *of* the body is supposed to pass among and between generations of kin? Beyond genetic inheritance between parents and children, there are other kinds of inheritances—learned styles, habits, dispositions, and affects—that are acculturated but also deeply ingrained in the body as a kind of second nature. Freeman's formula for queer belonging quoted above ("to endure in corporeal form over time") is appealing in this respect because it introduces *form* as a mediating term between kinship and corporeality. Rather than restricting genealogy to the inheritance of bodily substance, we might ask how somatic forms, borne in relations of care, can pass between bodies and through time. How are these forms and their modes of transmission reconfigured in response to the pressures of familial duty, profit-seeking, and same-sex desire set out by Iolaus in his prologue?

The children of Heracles are refugees, expelled from their homes in Argos and deprived of a civic community that could shelter them from their enemies. This outlaw condition intensifies the need for care within the *genos* and drives the Heraclids to improvise modes of kinship adequate to their plight. The most striking example is the episode in which Heracles' virgin daughter (Macaria; in *Children of Heracles* known only as "the Girl") offers herself as a human sacrifice in order to secure the aid of the Athenians against Eurystheus. The Athenian king, Demophon, has accepted the Heraclids as suppliants and vowed to protect them, but he reneges on his promises upon learning from oracles that he cannot win the battle unless he sacrifices a noble virgin girl to Persephone. Unwilling to sacrifice an Athenian, he implies that the Heraclids must seek refuge elsewhere. As Iolaus and the Chorus of Athenian citizens process the news, the Girl appears onstage for the first and last time. When Iolaus explains their predicament, she immediately offers herself as Persephone's victim.[10] She then seizes her moment in the limelight to explain how her actions realize a distinctive conception of kinship (578–83 and 589–92):

> We are your children, Iolaus; we have been reared by your hands. You see that I, too, offer up my youthful age of marriage, about to die in their place. And you, the company of brothers here with me, may you be happy, and may you enjoy all the things of which my heart will be deprived … For I did not fail to stand by your side, but I died for my kin (*genos*). In place of children and virginity, these will be my treasures.

The Girl represents her act as a genealogical exchange by which she trades the prospect of bearing her own children for the survival of her brothers. She thus follows the example of Iolaus ("I, too …") by preferring collateral over lineal descent and by transmitting care and protection to her kin rather than biological substance. This is why, presumably, she reminds Iolaus that "we are your children … we have been reared by your hands": by the same logic, the Girl's brothers become her children ("my treasures"), inheriting the life-sustaining legacy of her care.

This is not the only way in which the Girl advances a practice of non-procreative parenthood. Before exiting the stage for the sacrificial altar, she asks her family to remember her after her death and implies that her brothers will inherit the example of her character, a disposition toward self-sacrifice and duty (584–9). The genealogical force of her example also works backward in time: her act, Iolaus claims, proves that she is the daughter of Heracles (539–40), an inference that the Girl echoes soon after (563). Even though she claims that Iolaus is her genuine parent by virtue of the care that he provided, the Girl affirms Heracles' co-paternity. The latter is redefined according to an ethical conception of kinship in which a certain somatic disposition, an *êthos*, is what children inherit from their parents. The Girl, in effect, says that she has two fathers: Heracles and Iolaus, *erastês* and *erômenos*, one the source of her character, the other the source of her nourishment and care.[11]

This queer family structure complements the Girl's inversion of gender norms. When she appears onstage, she apologizes for intruding into the male space of politics and deliberation (476–7), adding a gloss of decorum over her deliberate refusal of the gender role assigned to her as a young woman. The Chorus and Demophon express (underhanded) admiration at her courage and outspokenness: "you are the bravest of all women I have seen with my eyes" (570–1). In other respects, the Girl's redefinition of kinship remains invested in a patriarchal vision of the family and traditional gender roles. The rationale for her sacrifice implies that daughters are more expendable as members of a family than sons, and although the Girl claims to have two fathers, the role of her biological mother (Deaneira) is passed over in silence. The queering of kinship represented by the Girl's act is deeply ambivalent: it expands the scope of parenthood to include sisters, non-biological fathers, and co-paternity, but it takes for granted the expendability of women's lives and invests the violence of the sacrificial knife with heroic virtue.

The Girl is forced to economize her body, to distinguish between its profitable and non-profitable capacities. Her capacity to die turns out to be more profitable to her kin than her capacity to survive, suggesting (as Iolaus hinted in the prologue) that the profit-seeking associated with Eurystheus bears a strong and volatile affinity with the logic of kinship. The Girl's queer parenthood is self-possessed and willful, much like Iolaus' devotion to Heracles; but it is also a survival strategy, a way of reinterpreting and outliving a grotesque situation in which her body is to be cut open in order to extract *kerdos* for her kin. This figure of queer resistance forms a constellation with modern queer experiences. Silvia Federici uses the figure of "vivisection" to frame the historical process by which the body's capacities have been rationalized and commodified under capitalist regimes of exploitation. Literally cut open with a sacrificial knife, the Girl is also vivisected in Federici's figurative sense: her body's capacity for procreation is excised and devalued in relation to its use as a commodity in a transaction with Persephone. At this point of unsurvivable violence, the Girl's speech envisions unlikely channels of survival through which somatic form can outlive the body and thus partially resist the forces of profit-seeking reason.

One could say that modern queer communities have formed under the shadow of a knife—the advancing edge of capitalist exploitation. John D'Emilio (1983) opened up a productive subfield of queer studies with his pathbreaking research into the emergence of gay and lesbian identities in the tumult of industrialization during the early twentieth century. The conditions of perpetual revolution under capitalism disrupted the traditional sex and gender norms of the conjugal-procreative family, creating spaces in which queer modes of desire and belonging could congeal into novel identities. But the historical task of queer communities has also been to find ways to *survive* capitalism as it extracts ever more value from the bodies of workers and places new burdens on relations of familial care.[12] Through an anachronic leap, the Girl prefigures this double-edged movement: queer kinship becomes a means of surviving the very profit-seeking forces that, by disrupting the nuclear family, opened up a broader space for queer existence.

Vivisection and Kitsch Bodies

In the preceding discussion, I have not done justice to the sardonic edge that corrodes the high seriousness of *Children of Heracles*'s moral dilemmas. The scene of the Girl's self-sacrifice in particular is riddled with lapses in tone. She asks Iolaus to comfort her as she is sacrificed, but he refuses her request with a limp excuse ("I could not stand by your death" 564). Demophon cannot bring himself to tell the Heraclids directly that he will expel them from Athens unless they find a suitable human sacrifice, so he resorts to embarrassed insinuations (420–4; cf. 494). Sometimes the humor comes to the surface of the script: in a later scene, on the verge of joining battle with the Argives, Iolaus finds that he is too decrepit to bear the weight of his armor and draws derisive asides from a servant (720–47). One could multiply examples of these kinds of disjointed and self-deflating heroic sentiments.

On a structural level, too, the play is full of holes. The Girl's role is not established in advance of her appearance and, after her departure, she is never mentioned again. But her character-form keeps cropping up: in the final act, Alcmene (almost silent during the first half) asserts herself as a vengeful matriarch, demanding Eurystheus' execution despite the appeals for mercy from her Athenian allies. Her sudden occupation of the stage echoes the Girl's defiant and dramatically incongruous entry into the male public sphere. Iolaus' miraculous rejuvenation is similarly abrupt: the other characters barely remark on it, and it serves no immediate narrative function. The vivisection inflicted on the Girl offstage takes on a life of its own—it becomes a virtual machine that rewires the vital capacities of the leading characters and turns against the drama itself, applying a knife to the plot.

The fractured quality of *Children of Heracles* is often explained as an effect of its concerted ideological work. Gunther Zuntz influentially labeled *Children of Heracles* as a "political play" that broadcasts Athenian civic optimism with its "brisk *allegro con brio*" (read: rushed, episodic) pacing (1955, 27). Indeed, Athens appears throughout the play as the moral protagonist, a community willing to go to war to protect refugees and promote freedom and justice. Recent critics, who are more likely to regard Euripides as a subversive or critical playwright, have interpreted *Children of Heracles* as a drama that questions or satirizes the values that it ostensibly promotes.[13] From either perspective, the play's unsatisfying structure is redeemed by its political and social resonances. The other possibility is that the play's form redeems itself—that it has its share of tragic pleasures but engenders them through oblique channels of disavowal and vicarious empathy.

"Kitsch" is the closest term in our contemporary lexicon for cultural products that induce these oscillating disputes about compromised form and complicity in the sociopolitical status quo. Kitsch is a polymorphous category exemplified by tchotchkes, souvenirs, and patriotic memorabilia, and extending, depending on taste, to virtually any work of art or entertainment that one could denigrate as "sentimental." Kitsch is a fellow traveler with queerness: it (too) was consolidated as a category in the early twentieth century as capitalistic modes of mechanical reproduction and mass culture challenged traditional canons of good taste. Queer appreciation of kitsch, which developed partly as a way of subverting the pretensions of high hetero culture, fostered the overlapping category of camp.[14] Eve Sedgwick (1990, 150–7) probably represents more current critical sensibilities in regarding the notion of kitsch with suspicion, as an instrument with which the highbrow and the avant-garde stage a paranoid defense against their lowbrow other. But as Walter Benjamin suggested,[15] kitsch persists as a valuable relict category: it identifies a family of cultural artifacts that delight, baffle, and irritate us partly because their market-oriented shoddiness resonates with the ways in which contemporary life as a whole has been both produced and damaged by the pursuit of profit.

Perhaps (let's fantasize) some Athenians experienced *Children of Heracles* as a piece of patriotic kitsch: its drive for cheap effects reflected back on them the conditions of life in imperial Athens, which some of their contemporaries regarded as a war machine in which any expediency could be justified in the name of civic profit.[16] This reflection might have prompted uncritical endorsement ("Athens is great because Athens is good") or critical recoil ("who could relate to this canned patriotism?")—Euripides' whole oeuvre tends to engage these kinds of dueling sentiments. But kitsch can also produce a spark of recognition, an "awe for the kindred," as Iolaus puts it: *Children of Heracles*'s capacity to give enjoyment through/despite its bad form reflects our own capacity to refashion relations of care and belonging under conditions of material degradation. This affinity becomes especially palpable for audiences (ancient and modern) who can recognize their own experiences in Iolaus' and the Girl's narratives of queer survival.

In *Aesthetic Theory*, Theodor Adorno identifies as one of the hallmarks of kitsch "the prevarication of feelings, fictional feelings in which no one is actually participating" (1997, 239). Adorno is probably repurposing Clement Greenberg's fundamental definition of kitsch as "vicarious experience and faked sensations" (1961, 10), but Adorno's definition deftly substitutes "fictional" for "faked." In his aporetic fashion, he concedes that it is impossible to distinguish rigorously between (fake) kitsch and (real) art, since all artistic feelings are in some sense fictive, rather than documentary. The distinction comes down to the possibility of disavowal: one identifies a work as kitsch when one imagines that "no one is actually participating" in its emotional fiction. As Sedgwick suggests, this structure of disavowal paradoxically opens up kitsch and camp to queer recognition.[17] We can imagine that although "no one is actually participating," no one is secretly someone, and someone is gay. Kitsch disavowal can thus register, by negation, queer subjects' eccentric affectivity, their resistance to aesthetic consensus. At the same time, queer appreciation of kitsch probably owes much to its affinity for overwrought depictions of family life, conservative religiosity, and nationhood. The most socially regressive sentiments can be cut out of context, ironized, and repurposed for queer enjoyment: "no one is participating" in the kitsch work as it was intended, but someone is enjoying it in some other, oblique manner.[18] This mode of attachment-through-disavowal concentrates the texture of queer survival in a heteronormative world, with the many acts of perseverance, accommodation, and reappropriation that it demands of us and of figures like the Girl and Iolaus.

The attribution of kitsch is volatile, dependent on circular and historically contingent criteria for evaluating expressive authenticity. Adorno's allusions to Aristotle's *Poetics* (e.g., "kitsch parodies catharsis" 239) point to one particular framework that has had an outsized influence on theories of fictional feelings. Aristotle claims that a tragedy's emotions are produced by the structure of the plot, especially by a reversal of fortune constructed through an intelligible sequence of events. This model construes tragedy's emotional efficacy as a consequence of its organic structure: in a celebrated passage, Aristotle compares the unity and size of dramatic plots to that of a living animal (*Poetics* 1450b–51a). Inorganic ("episodic") plots comprise a haphazard series of episodes that fails to produce tragic feelings. Kitsch fails, too, but it does not *simply* fail. If a kitsch drama happens to be episodic, as *Children of Heracles* certainly is,[19] its tragic emotions can be felt to survive the fragmentation of the plot, even though they survive in a spectral state that audiences tend to disavow.

In his biological treatises, Aristotle is fascinated with the ability of plants and certain animals to survive the division of their bodies, at least temporarily.[20] If *Poetics* contained a theory of kitsch, Aristotle might have illustrated it by vivisecting the drama-animal described in 1450b–51a: in a kitsch spectacle, the animal's disincorporated organs shiver with residual life, expressing at once the experience of grotesque damage and the weird endurance of corporeal form in new arrangements. This kind of vital disintegration appears in *Children of Heracles* as a sequence of disjointed emotional effects—fear for the Heraclids, pity for the Girl, joy for rejuvenated Iolaus; a host of canned feelings that might (or might not) survive the dismemberment of tragedy's narrative body. As kitsch, *Children of Heracles* waits for an adoptive audience, a "family of choice" to revalue it from an oblique perspective in which its vivisected form appears not only as a grotesque spectacle but as incandescent potentiality, suspended between survival and extinction.[21] The drama figures such audiences in its own queer characters, who find equivocal modes of recomposing and transmitting their corporeal form in the face of the deracinating exactions of profit.

The end of *Children of Heracles* turns toward a bleak future: Hyllus, Heracles' eldest son, defeats Eurystheus' army and thereby restores the male Heraclids to their patrimony in Argos. From there, we learn, they will become the founders of a Spartan bloodline that centuries in the future—in fact, during the play's first production—will wage war on Athens, opposed by the sanctified bones of Eurystheus. The Heraclids' sacrifices, queer or otherwise, end up endowing the patriarchal kin group and its civic projections with a stability that spans centuries and seems to foreclose the alternative forms of sociality that the drama presents in glimpses. Kitsch parodies catharsis: *Children of Heracles* relieves us of fears we never had ("will patriarchy manage to survive?") and instills hopes of queer futurity that it holds out of reach. Given the intractable negativity, the not-yet-ness, of its form, the drama resists reparative readings that would revalue its faults as campy exuberance. This sense of damage and incompleteness registers José Muñoz's claim in *Cruising Utopia* that "we are not yet queer . . . queerness is that thing that lets us feel that the world is not enough, that indeed something is missing" (2009, 1). Queerness remains incomplete, anticipating a future in which care and belonging are not subject to the rule of consanguinity and profit.

Notes

1. E.g., Mendelsohn 2002; Carter 2020; and Wohl 2015, 1–2.

2. Quoted respectively from Fitton 1961, 460; Rivier 1944, 169; Grube 1961, 176; and Jones 1971, 266. See Burian 1977, 2n3.

3. On "the hope of children" in Greek tragedy, see Bassi in this volume; see also Nooter.

4. On queering gender and genre, see Boyarin in this volume.

5. Plutarch, *Pelopidas* 18, which cites Aristotle, fragment 97 Ross; see Dover 1978, 199.

6. On the use of the prefix *sun-* to describe erotic and kin relations, see also Mueller and Olsen in this volume.

7. The duplicated *mu*'s in *lê(m)ma* also resemble the duplicated M's in Marx's formula for self-valorizing value in *Capital* (M-C-M'').

8. On the dating of *Children of Heracles*, see Mendelsohn 2002, 1–2n1.

9. Weston 1991. On queer disruptions of conjugal-procreative kinship, see Mueller, Andújar, Olsen, and Telò in this volume.

10. On virgin sacrifices in Greek tragedy, see Loraux 1987, esp. 39–41.

11. Heracles is called a "father" repeatedly (12, 24, 29, 53, etc.), but Iolaus' non-biological parenthood is not so overtly gendered. Iolaus is arguably coded as a maternal caregiver to his foster children, especially in the Girl's expression, "we have been reared by your hands" (578; thanks to Mark Griffith for this observation). When Iolaus refuses to accompany the Girl during her sacrifice, she asks to be allowed at least "to breathe out [her] life in the hands not of men but of women" (565–6), suggesting obliquely with this preference that Iolaus' parental hands are of the latter kind.

12. See Rosenberg 2014 and Chitty 2020.

13. See, e.g., Burian 1977; Mendelsohn 2002; and Roselli 2007.

14. On camp aesthetics, see also Olsen in this volume.

15. Benjamin 1999; see Menninghaus 2009.

16. E.g., Ps.-Xenophon, *Constitution of the Athenians,* 1.14–18; on Thucydides' critique of imperialism, see Foster 2010.

17. See Sedgwick 1990, 155–7; I have softened her distinction between "camp recognition" and "kitsch attribution."

18. On queer irony, see Freccero and Telò in this volume.

19. See Carter 2020, 98–104.

20. E.g., insects (*On the Soul* 413b) and tortoises (*On Youth and Old Age* 468b). See Bos 2007.

21. On suspension, *lifedeath*, and anti-cathartic aesthetics in Greek tragedy, see Telò 2020.

CHAPTER 7
SUPPLIANT WOMEN—ADRASTUS' CUTE LESBIANISM: LABOR IRONY ADHESION
Mario Telò

Although recent feminist and broadly political readings have destabilized the traditional view of Euripides' *Suppliant Women* as a work of straightforward Athenian propaganda,[1] this play—with its topicality and wearisome self-righteousness—may still appear resistant to a queer reading. While loose structure and multiple anachronisms lend themselves to some of the approaches represented in this volume,[2] my queering of the play will rely on irony as the carrier of an anti-reparative affect that disrupts the boundary between word and performance, doing and non-doing (or undoing). This is a play that, while apparently fetishizing Athenian devotion to political and military labor (*ponos*), aestheticizes the inertia, the inefficacy of Adrastus, which is underscored by the alpha privative in his name (*a-drastos*). Cutting through *ponos* and the connected dramaturgy of maternity, the disidentificatory force of irony extends to heteronormative reproduction, which seems to be supplemented by a laborious crafting, formal and physical, of queer intimacies. In particular, the affective negativity of irony translates into haptic adhesion or even a passing touch, which I link with the position of Adrastus within the play and with a trans mode of relational being that Roland Barthes called "male lesbianism."[3]

Encapsulating the central theme of the play, the restitution to their mothers of the young Argives fallen at Thebes, *ponos* is charged with irony, which arises from the collision, and convergence, of Adrastus' ineptitude and Theseus' vocation—"action" or "laboring" for the benefit of others. The first time that Adrastus presses Theseus to take on the "labor" of rescuing the Argive bodies at Thebes (185 and 189), *ponos*, appearing twice at the end of a line, draws attention to Adrastus' name, haunted by an alpha privative that casts him as constitutionally "ineffective, inert, lazy" (*a-drastêrios*)[4]—not simply suffering from the exhaustion of old age (166). Theseus hastens to echo Adrastus' praise of his characteristically Athenian energy—"I *labored* (*eponês'*) in arguing with others" (195)— signaling an anxiety to measure up to what the political Symbolic demands of him. The lack contained in Adrastus' name ironically comes out in the same scene, when, to flatter his would-be benefactor, he says that "many cities have been ruined for want (*en-deeis*) of a leader" (192). Adrastus' lack charges the play with a negative fixation that emerges every time an alpha privative is used, as when, in her own plea to Theseus to intervene on behalf of the Argives, Aethra, his mother, remarks that it is "useless" (*a-chreion* 299) for women to give good advice and criticizes "indecisiveness" (*a-boulos* 321) in governance. Through these adjectives, Adrastus is lexicalized in a rhetorical strategy that is ironized when Aethra tells Theseus, "Son ... don't do these things (*mê* ...

draseîs tade 320)." In this prohibition the deictic ("these things") signifies hesitation and delay that she codes as "cowardice," failed masculinity (*an-andria* 314), a word also conjuring A-drastus. But in urging her son *not* to do "these things," i.e., not to act like Adrastus, Aethra in effect tells him to *be* A-drastus (a "not-doer"). The irony of Theseus' fixation on doing things is intensified by repetition and chiasmus in the lines that formalize his commitment to the Argive cause (339–46):

> Having done (*drasas*) many noble things, I set this example for the Greeks ... Therefore it isn't possible to refuse labors (*ponous*). For what will my enemies say of me, when the woman who gave birth to me and is afraid on my behalf (*huperorrhôdous'*) is the first one to command me to take on this labor (*ponon*)? I'll do (*drasô*) this.

The freezing fear that Theseus projectively attributes to his mother—*huperorrhôdous'* (344)—is enacted in the formal immobility conveyed by the chiastic repetition (*drasas ... ponous* and *ponon/drasô*) but also in the cold irony of what follows. While the Athenian army is "sitting" (*thassei* 391), about to spring into action, Theseus declares, once again, that his city is eager to undertake this "labor" (*ponon* 394). However, seeing the Theban emissary approach, he holds back his herald, just in case this unexpected arrival might spare Athens the "labor" (*ponos* 397) of intervening. A timely bit of news may bathetically obviate the muscular doing touted in Theseus' lofty rhetoric.

Interpellated by the maternal Symbolic, Theseus draws attention to another irony surrounding *ponos* in the play: the overlap between productive and reproductive "labor" as well as between reproduction and non-reproduction. Waiting for the return of their dead children, the Chorus of Argive mothers lyrically laments the vanity of reproduction, a laborious doing undone by men's *ponoi* (918–24):

> Child, I raised you, wretched one. I carried you under the liver, bearing labors (*ponous*) in birth pangs (*en ôdisi*). And now Hades has my labor (*mochthon*), wretched that I am. Having given birth to a child, I don't have anyone who can take care of me when I am old, poor me.

Ponos aligns, or identifies, Theseus with the Argive mothers even as the lack of it aligns Adrastus with them, both as "passive" women and as old women subject to an infertility elaborated by a series of alpha privatives (*a-paidian* 170; *a-gamon* 786; *a-pais a-teknos* 966). This double alignment of the Argive women and, by extension, of reproduction as such, brings together *ponos* and non-*ponos*, Theseus' (re)productive "labor" and Adrastus' not-doing or un(re)productive "labor." Indeed, when Theseus announces, "I'll bury the corpses, taking them out of the land of Asopus ... I've endured many other labors (*ponous*) for others" (571–3), an alternative parturition is imagined in which (with obvious Oedipal undertones) dead children are placed in the earth. Speaking of them, Theseus challenges the Theban herald: "Are you afraid that after having been buried they would destroy your land? Or that they may beget children in the recesses of the earth?" (544–6). By the time we get to Adrastus' comment on Theseus' successful enterprise (951–5)—"Stop, and having ceased the labors (*ponôn*), guard your cities . . . The affair of life is brief; one should get through it as easily as possible and not with labors (*sun ponois*)"—we may wonder whether Adrastus is, in a sense, recapitulating the mothers' disillusionment with their own *ponoi* ("What was the use of children for me?" 789).

Irony, in *Suppliant Women*, amounts to queer affect in that it participates in the anti-reparative orientation of this play, which culminates in a blatant "ritual aporia" (Mirto 1984, 63), when Theseus prevents the mothers from seeing their sons' reclaimed bodies. Referring to Paul De Man's theorization of irony (1996), Lee Edelman explains its queer discursive force (2004, 24):

> Queer theory . . . would constitute the site where the radical threat posed by irony, which heteronormative culture displaces onto the figure of the queer, is uncannily returned by queers who no longer disown but assume their figural identity as embodiments of the figuralization, and hence disfiguration, of identity itself.

Stereotyped as figures, we might say, as parodic, "ironical" disfigurations of (wo)man (broadly speaking), queers embrace this disfiguring irony as a disidentificatory discursive device as well as a habitus enabling them not to be classified or identified. In Edelman's powerful theoretical framework, irony is the queer rejection of identity that opens the space of the Real within the Symbolic, revealing the disavowed death drive in reproduction's perpetual loop, its aspirational replication of the status quo—or "reprofuturity."[5] The nexus of irony, reproduction, and death drive integral to Edelman's Lacanian theory of queerness is dramatized by Evadne, Capaneus' wife, one of the Argive women, who, "desiring (*erôsa*) to die with her husband" (1040), commits suicide. As she announces lyrically, she seeks "the same pyre and tomb" as her husband, a dissolution into Hades of "the toilsome (*em-mochthon*) life . . . and life's labors (*ponous*)" (1003–5). The ironical duplicity of *ponos*, "(re)productive labor," turns Evadne's suicide—a regressive impetus toward the lack of "toil" of pre-organic (non)life—into a rejection of reprofuturity, the loop of which is formally suggested by *em-mochthon* and *ponous* at the beginning and at the end of the line, respectively. Evadne's declaration can thus be read as a restatement of the anti-reproductive position of the Chorus, a proto-feminist questioning of maternity as a subjection to the masculine state's demand for disposable bodies to use in war.[6] In her dialogue with her father, Iphis—whom Daniel Mendelsohn calls "the maternal father" (2002, 216)—Evadne seems even to mock the play's ongoing concern with decision and action by ironically exploiting his naivety and tardy understanding of her suicidal intentions: "You would get angry if you heard about my *decisions* (*bouleumatôn*)" (1050–1); "we have prepared ourself for some novel *action* (*pragma*)" (1057). The hyper-maternity of the play is predicated on an *ex-cess* ("self-exit"), which manifests in motherly mourning that can never stop ("I will always drench the fold of my robes with tears" 978–9) but also in a stepping away from motherhood, from the very idea of reproduction. This negativity—in the perennial unfinishedness of the mothers' mourning, or in the foreclosure of their participation in the funerals, or in their flirtation with the anti-reproductive, the anti-maternal—is the distinctive trait of irony. Kierkegaard says that irony is an "infinite and absolute negativity" (1989, 6), while for Damon Young, "as an infinite negativity, irony cannot be simply asserted," since "any such assertion is at risk of its own reversal" (2019a). Irony is a condition of discursive or affective suspension epitomized by Evadne on the cliff's edge: "Father, I am lifted in the air (*kouphizô*), in a wretched hanging (*aiôrêma*) over the pyre" (1046–7). Warning of complacency in the valorization of the reparative in queer theory, Young observes that "to the real power and terrifying opacity of the signifier in the era of finance capital"— "futures," "derivatives," etc.—"we [should] oppose the uncompromising negativity" of irony.[7] Hyper-maternity in *Suppliant Women* can be qualified as queer because it totters on the edge of an "infinite and absolute negativity."

In its constant hermeneutic swaying between touch and non-touch, supplication (*hikesia*)—a social, religious, political practice of physical connection—becomes an embodiment of irony. The scholarship on theatrical supplication in Greek tragedy is emblematic of the positivism of traditional performance criticism, caught in the conundrum of whether in each instance the haptic connection indicated by gestural language is dramaturgically enacted (in fifth-century theatrical practice or in the phantasmic *archê* of the playwright's own production) or whether it is purely "figurative" (Gould 1973).[8] For Maarit Kaimio (1988, 49–50):

> It is comparatively *easy* to discern certain cases where the complete supplication is *surely* acted out on stage in the form of physical contact, and other cases where supplication is plainly confined to mere words, but there remain quite a few passages where we can only guess the degree of realization of the ritual.[9]

This observation signals that supplication is subject to the same oscillation between doing and not-doing that is integral to the play's political thematics and to the irony around the name of Adrastus. When the Chorus of Argive women supplicate Theseus, first, with "I beseech you, falling at your knee (*pros gonu*)" (41), and, later, with "I beg you, by your beard, falling around (*amphi*) your knee and hand" (276–7), "it remains doubtful," Kaimio remarks, "how literally these references are to be taken" (1988, 61). Shall we imagine that the whole Chorus touches Theseus or simply moves toward him? Staging operates in the virtual space of a perennially creative flux and is differently actualized in plural historical contexts. What we can say is that, in the Chorus's supplications, the correspondence, or lack of correspondence, between word and action, between performative utterance and the expected embodied counterpart, is self-reflexively problematized or ironized. The Chorus's first supplication fails to persuade Theseus to act, as does that of Adrastus, whose words enact his onomastic inactivity, or non-agentic agency: "I am ashamed to fall to the ground to embrace your knee with my hands" (164–5). Even when the Chorus succeeds in its second attempt, supplication— physical? figurative? a hybrid?— amounts to a form of weak, hesitant, interrupted, or even ironical hapticity. This (non-)touch exemplifies the gesture as potentiality, as *anomia*, theorized by Agamben (2016). The gestural, for Agamben, captures "the dimension in which works—linguistic and bodily, material and immaterial, biological and social—are deactivated and contemplated as such in order to liberate the inoperativity that has been imprisoned in them" (278). Supplication, in the play, expresses an anomic "inoperativity," which queers the very idea of relationality, placing it in a liminal space between praxis and non-praxis.

Embodying this anomic inoperativity, Adrastus evokes the queer aesthetics of the cute, which is based on a disingenuous fetishization of powerlessness. When, as "gray-haired" Adrastus lies on the ground in tears, surrounded by the Argive mothers and a secondary chorus of children, Theseus asks him to uncover his veiled head and speak (110–12), he acts as the Law of the Father interpellating the child, removing him from his *in-fancy* (in an etymological sense), objectifying him while pretending to confer subjectivity upon him, turning him from a non-speaking object into a speaking one. However, when Adrastus apostrophizes the Theban herald with "You, most evil man!" (513), Theseus shuts him down ("Silence, Adrastus, shut up!" 513), denying him syntax, reducing his speaking role to a fragmented cry lost in Theseus' extended monologue, demoting him to the role of an extra. Adrastus' passivity may be thought of as part of what Sianne Ngai calls "an aestheticization of powerlessness" (2012, 98) typical of the commodity fetishism expressed in the notion of the "cute," whether it is applied to small and soft toys or animals, children, or old people—all seen as subject to "defenseless immobility" (Harris 2000, 6).[10] Produced by the apheresis of "acute," the word "cute" is, in a sense, the opposite of "acute"—as though the loss of the "a" corresponded to the loss of an alpha privative of the sort that de-activates the doing in *A-drastus*. The lack or rejection of the "point" (the *punctum*) of "acute" that is suggested by "cute" entails a refusal of the instantaneous "event," just as Adrastus' name opposes the instantaneity of decision and intervention. The amorphousness of no-action—of a time not divided up by events—aligns with the pliability and smoothness (the lack of "pointedness") of cute objects. The temporality of "cuteness" is, in fact, anti-eventral or "retro-futuristic," for it "reimagines the past as somehow occurring in the future (or the future as somehow occurring in the past), blending older technologies and styles with the yet-to-be" (Chambers 2017, 84). This retrofuturity—exemplified in the somewhat sentimental conflation of child and old man that Adrastus embodies—"mirrors the complex and ambivalent relationship between temporality and queerness" (Kao and Boyle 2017, 16).[11] The "cuteness" of Adrastus' powerlessness invites us to respond with an "Aww," rather than tragic "awe," supplicating us to match Theseus in his ostensibly active predisposition. On the other hand, as Kao and Boyle put it, the powerlessness of the cute "is a supplicant" that has power over us through the affective and rhetorical bond it establishes with us. Cuteness, as they observe, "engages and disciplines its viewer. Its disavowal of power is one of its powers" (2017, 56). This disavowal is another expression of the queer irony that shapes this Euripidean play, whose gloomy atmosphere does not exclude dissonant aesthetic effects.[12]

The proximity of Adrastus to the mothers, who are the emotional center of the play, allows us to draw out the queer implications of supplicatory (non-)touch. Adrastus is not so much a protector or an ally of the mothers, also including Aethra, as he is almost one of them, in that he displays a cathexis to them, an intimacy with their homosocial intimacy. In a game of parallel verbal-proxemic circularities, just as the Argive mothers surround (*en kuklôi* 103) Aethra, looking, like children, for care, the sons of the dead Argives are around (*amphi* 106) Adrastus, looking for a surrogate father or mother. As he is about to supplicate Theseus—to re-enact the Argive mothers' supplication— Adrastus first presents himself as a "gray-haired man" (*polios anêr* 166) and then ascribes to them a sterile, "gray-haired (*polion*) old age" (170).[13] In a sense, eliding the difference between himself and them, Adrastus might be associated with the figure of the "male lesbian," which Roland Barthes employs to read—theoretically, not biographically—the intellectual stance of Jules Michelet. In a section of his eponymous book (1987) entitled "Michelet's Lesbianism," Barthes observes that the French historian who dedicated multiple books to an understanding of female subjectivity instantiates the cis-male subject who "attaches himself amorously to Woman by a veritable lesbianism, and finally conceives of marriage only as a kind of sororal couple" (152–3). In Barthes's view, Michelet's historical mission turns him "into a woman, mother, nurse, the bride's companion" (153). Barthes continues, "To protect Woman, to cover her, to envelop her, to 'follow' her entire surface, is to do away with any discontinuity of substance. The ideal figure of the lover is ultimately the garment" (153). As he puts it, the sexual "preference" of the lesbian cis-male subject is "not ... penetration but juxtaposition (*élongement*)." Naomi Schor comments that the male lesbianism discussed by Barthes entails "an adhesive mode of sexual relations, where the ... male becomes, like Deianira's tunic, a textile membrane stretched over the female body" (2001, 392). As Caroline Dinshaw puts it, Barthes's Michelet "resolves surface/depth oppositions into sheer surfaces, following them, juxtaposing them, loving them" (1999, 48). This sororal lesbianism could be connected with Proust's narrator's infatuation with *les jeunes filles en fleurs* and with his cathexis to their choral intimacy (Ladenson 1999) and even with contemporary discussions in popular culture.[14] The disidentifications opened up by the idea of "male lesbianism" are reflected in the Euripidean play in the gradations of affective proximity to femininity enabled by multiple formal configurations of supplication and quasi-supplication as characters envelop each other. The queerness of supplication emerges from the multiplicity and opacity of the levels and forms of desired "towardness"—the spatial and affective projection distinctive of this play, which is animated by a proliferation of the preposition *pros*, the Greek equivalent of *ad* in "adhesion" (2, 27, 30, 33, 37, 42, 360, etc.). In a sense, the first two lines of the play—"De-*meter* (*Dê-mêter*) guardian of this land of Eleusis and those men who occupy the temples, the goddess's servants (*pros-poloi*) ..." (1–2)—epitomize Adrastus' proximity (*pros-*) to the mothers, what Schor would call his lesbian adhesion, even if it does not translate into physical clinging.[15] When Schor likens Michelet's lesbian adhesion to the robe used by Deianira in Sophocles' *Women of Trachis* to erotically bind Heracles to herself, she allows us to see Adrastus as a prosthetic object fastened onto the mothers' bodies. We can glimpse the possibility of a convergence between this affective attachment and supplication: "no one will put on (*amphi-dusetai*) the robe before [Heracles]" (605); "[the robe] clings (*pros-ptussetai*) to

[Heracles'] sides like glue" (767–8); "[the robe] was attached (*pros-machthen*) to his sides" (1053). In the interplay of closeness and distance, intimacy and detachment, touch and non-touch, supplication's haptic formalism tropes the opaque spectrum of Adrastus' sororal proximities—or approximations—to female intimacy.[16]

Alongside Adrastus' emotional adhesions, the Chorus's supplication of Aethra generates queer intimacies through which homoeroticism and parental/filial bonds defamilarize each other. After the initial ritual language—"Old woman (*geraia*), I beseech you from my old mouth (*geraiôn ek stomatôn*), falling to your knees" (42)—the Chorus continues (60–1 and 69–70):

> Please persuade your son, I supplicate you, to go to Ismenos and place into my hand (*eman t' es chera*) the bodies of our valiant dead ... I supplicate your son to place my dead son in my wretched hand (*talainai 'n cheiri*) so that I can embrace (*amphi-balein*) the baneful limbs (*melê*) of my son.

While looking ahead to the mothers' imagined reunion with their sons' bodies, the hands mentioned here index Aethra's arms, touched figuratively or otherwise, in the act of supplication evoked by the quasi-technical verb *amphi-balein*, a circular adhesion. The overdetermined performative language of the supplication is thus laden with the hyper-intimacy of the mother–child attachment that informs the later scene in which the Argive mothers lament over their children's ashes. Theseus has in fact forbidden them to see and touch the bodies before they reach the pyre because, as he claims, "the mothers would die if they saw them disfigured" (944): he has denied them the "pantomimic" (Butler 2003) sensuousness of mourning a corpse, the pleasure-in-pain of touching an inherently lacking presence. Mourning veers into "necrophilia" (Worman 2020, 770), but also into the *jouissance* of "animacy"—of human bodies striving to connect with, or adhere to, urns.[17] This aspirational bonding stretches into the indeterminacy of syntactical bonds in the maternal intervention (1134–7) that occurs when one of the surviving children laments that he will never be "in the hands (*en chersi*) of [his] father":

> Where is the labor (*ponos*) of my children? Where are the gift (*charis*) of childbirth and the nourishment (*trophai*) of the mother and the eyes' sleepless duties and the loving (*philiai*) pressures (*pros-bolai*) of the faces (*pros-ôpôn*)?

Subliminally associating the giftless "labor" of childbirth, which brought the young soldiers to life, with their battlefield labor, the ambiguous genitive (objective/subjective) exceeds its immediate referents, troping, as it were, the ambiguity of relationships that occupy the unseen, repressed areas where kinship and the erotic press against each other—as they do in an Argive mother's quasi-figura etymologica (*philan philêma*) imagining a phantasmic father placing a kiss on the "dear" cheek of the surviving son (1153). The queer excess of these liminal bonds, which emerge after and in response to Theseus' prohibition, expresses "the pressure both alien and internal to the logic of the

Symbolic ... the inarticulable surplus that dismantles the subject from within ... what the queer ... is called forth to figure: the negativity opposed to the every form of social viability" (Edelman 2004, 9).[18] The encounter of two instances of the same preposition *pros-* in line 1137 (*pros-bolai ... pros-ôpôn*) formally conveys this excess, which reflects back, as it were, on the Argive women's supplication of Aethra, a different yet similar haptic configuration of the towardness of *pros*. The paramorous mother–son intimacy, channeled through a father in ashes, alerts us to the spectral queerness of the pressing (metaphorical or not) of the Argive women's hands and mouths against Aethra's body (*geraia geraiôn ek stomatôn* 42).[19] The polyptotic convergence of *geraia geraiôn*, comparable to the formal rubbing against each other of *pros-bolai* and *pros-ôpôn*, suggests a homoerotic juxtaposition or lesbian adhesion, or a homo-kinship, a form of kinship generated without and against reproduction. *Ponos* seems to take on the additional meaning of the handmade labor—formal as well as physical—necessary for crafting queer relationalities.

Formal, physical, and social hapticity as dramatized in *Suppliant Women* bears on the relationship of the "queer" and the "refugee" to the state, figured by Theseus, which keeps itself at an immunitarian distance, limiting its intervention to a goal-centered, (re)productive *ponos*. Speaking of Derrida's reflections on hospitality (2000, 2005), which have greatly influenced the field of refugee studies (see, e.g., Pugliese 2004 and Chiovenda 2020), Daniel Hannah says that his "notion of an absolute, unconditional hospitality—of an openness that resists a stabilized, customary, and hostile fixing of language's demands on the stranger, the guest, the other—is ... queer in its antinormative ... structure, in its resistance to the monological" (2010, 184).[20] Such anti-normative queerness "enables" but also others (or "perverts") the host "even as the host expels queerness" (ibid.). In this perspective, "to play the host, then ... is to play queer." Similarly to the queer—a disturbance of "social organization as such" (Edelman 2004, 17)—the refugee "cannot be simply ... incorporated into the superordinate terms of the host/nation" (Pugliese 2004, 292). Derrida remarks that hospitality is "an exposure without limit to whoever arrives" (2005, 6). Consequently, notwithstanding the host's immunitarian efforts, "the ethical relation between two seemingly opposed orders—refugee/citizen, non-nation/nation ... is ... indissolubly fused" (Pugliese 2004, 284). Theseus commits to helping the Argive refugees in the course of a speech whose nervous texture, as we have seen, exhibits the *ponos* of decision-making, the pleasure-in-pain of oscillation, curtailed by the solemn performative futures "I will do [it]" (*drasô* 346) and "I will come" (*hêxô* 357), each at the beginning of the line, followed by end punctuation. This is a formal break that sets a boundary on the commitment, a barrier between host and guest. These futures appear to mark a climactic moment after the back-and-forth or in-and-out of his decision-making. The end of the transaction—political as well as crypto-sexual—is signaled by Theseus' command (359–61): "Old women, remove the holy wreaths from my mother, so that attaching her dear hand to mine (*philên pros-apsas cheira*) I may bring her to the house of Aegeus." Theseus is seeking to separate himself from the migrant, to keep apart "seemingly opposed orders—refugee/citizen, non-nation/nation." But that these orders are "indissolubly fused" is shown by the language of adhesion that he appropriates. It as though the refugee's diction adhered to the host's, and Athenian language, stripped of the illusion of self-possession and self-sufficiency, became suddenly inflected with the accent of the stranger. What formally adheres to this language is the gestural adhesion of the female suppliants and by extension Adrastus' queer proximity to the old women, the women's own homo-kinship, and their hyper-intimate attachment *around* and *toward* children, which saturates these lines: "Give the children's bodies to me so that I may place them in my arms, *attaching my hands in embracings (peri-ptuchaisi … cheras pros-armosasa)*" (815–17). In Theseus' speech, *pros-apsas* queers his enforcement of hospitality as a goal-centered and thus temporally contained transaction. An effort to restrict hospitality, then, expresses a non-reproductive queer hapticity—what Schor would call lesbian adhesion—which, in its lack of teleology, is homologous to unconditional hospitality.

At the end of the play, the assimilation of tragedy to a buried talismanic object, in a re-imagining of the finale of *Eumenides*, results in a pre-emptive queering of Platonic and Aristotelian theories of tragic aesthetics. In her final intervention *ex machina*, Athena supplies nearly parodically detailed instructions on the mechanics of the sacrifice that Theseus should perform before sending off the urns of the Argive bodies (1205–7):

> As to the sharp-edged knife (*oxu-stomon machairan*) with which you cut open the sacrificial victims and inflict a wound, hide it in the recesses (*muchous*) of the earth (*gaias*) by the seven pyres (*par'autas … purkaias*) of the dead bodies.

A Freudian—as well as "paranoiacally" queer—reading of these lines is suggested by the earlier moment in the play in which Theseus defiantly asks the Theban herald whether he is afraid that the bodies of the fallen "could beget children in the recesses of the earth" (545). Strikingly, in Athena's figurative suggestion of a reproductive apparatus, all the elements are feminine, either grammatically (the pyres, the earth, the knife) or symbolically (the recesses). This feminine knife (*machaira*) seems to qualify as what Judith Butler has called the "lesbian phallus," which through "discursive performatives, alternative fetishes" contests the phallus's "masculinist and heterosexist privilege" (1993b, 55 and 56).[21] Athena appears to condemn the play's queer orientations—male and maternal lesbianisms—to encryptment.[22] Yet when we hear from Athena that the *machaira*—the lesbian phallus—will instill fear (*phobon* 1208) in Athens's future enemies when shown (*deichtheisa* 1209) to them, we are brought back to the moment in Aeschylus' *Eumenides* when Athena archives the Erinyes underground as beneficial vehicles of fear that, however, are bound to generate (auto-)immunitarian fear.[23] The ironical uncertainties raised by the projection of future "revelations" of the knife—how will it be revealed? will it be wielded? by whom?—open up the crypt. What comes out of it is queer reproduction—as queer as Athena's own conception and birth—based on juxtaposition (*para*), an *a-ponos* (or *a-drastos*) *ponos* based on adhesion.[24] As Amber Musser has observed, "In their estrangement from a phallocentric economy, the mother, the lesbian, and the woman-loving woman *sit alongside each other*" (2018, 176 [my emphasis]).[25] This *sitting alongside* points to proximities, juxtapositions between various queer relationalities, and to the adhesive quality of queer relationality as such. Circulating *phobos* primarily through the visual, as Aristotle will suggest, tragedy is the counterpart of the *machaira*, an aesthetic object homologous to the lesbian phallus. Since Froma Zeitlin's influential theorization (1996), we have tended to see tragedy Platonically, as an aesthetic exercise in "playing the other," a provisional experience and embodiment of femininity from a male perspective. The formal and affective complexities of *Suppliant Women* may alert us to unexplored queer implications of this model. Playing "cute" Adrastuses, not simply (temporarily, unwittingly, unconsciously) feminized males like Pentheus in *Bacchae* but rather lesbians—male, female, or non-binary, cis or trans—we are woman-besotted sororal companions, keen devotees of the intimacy among women, approaching or adhering to "the eternal irony of the community."

Notes

1. See Mendelsohn 2002, ch. 3; Kavoulaki 2008; Wohl 2015 (ch. 4).

2. On anachronism in the play, see esp. Wohl 2015, 105. See esp. Andújar, Baldwin, Freccero, and Radcliffe in this volume, and Introduction.

3. By "trans" (or "trans*"), I mean, with Halberstam (2018, xiii, 4–5), "pressure on all modes of gendered embodiment . . . a name for expansive forms of difference . . . the disaggregation of identity politics predicated upon the separating out of many kinds of experience that actually blend together, intersect, and mix." For a different perspective, see Deihr and Ruffell in this volume; see also Introduction.

4. *Drastêrios* is a Euripidean adjective: see, e.g., *Ion* 1185 and *Orestes* 1554.

5. See esp. Bassi, Freccero, Orrells, and Youd in this volume. On irony, see also Freccero .

6. See Deutscher 2017; Lewis 2019; and Telò 2022 (ch. 3).

7. See also Telò 2020; see Stuelke (2021) for the connection between hermeneutic reparativity—what she calls "the ruse of repair"—and neoliberal politics. Dean (2020, 531) observes that "naming what you are doing as *reparative* functions, in queer criticism, as a kind of virtue signaling."

8. On queerness as the "impossibility" of performance, see Gurd in this volume.

9. The emphasis is mine. I, too, indulged in this exercise twenty years ago: see Telò 2002.

10. On the "cuteness" of old men such as King Lear, see Cochran 2017.

11. See also Baldwin in this volume.

12. On kitsch aesthetics in *Children of Heracles*, the "twin" play of *Suppliant Women*, see Radcliffe in this volume.

13. Mendelsohn (2002, 150–1) characterizes Adrastus as "feminized" or "womanish," conforming to an influential structuralist model of gender binarism that, as will become clear, my queer perspective pushes against.

14. See Daniel Lavery's characterization of Ryan Atwood from the show *O.C.* and the comic character Johnny Bravo as lesbians: https://the-toast.net/2016/02/25/reasons-ryan-atwood-from-the-o-c-was-a-lesbian/; https://the-toast.net/2016/05/03/reasons-johnny-bravo-was-a-lesbian/. Even though Adrastus' "lesbianism" could be connected with autogynephilia, "a love of women that entails the fantasy that one *is* a woman" (G. Lavery 2019, 122), or with the

female equivalent of the transgender or transsexual desire that Grace Lavery (2020, 388–92) locates, for example, in Eve Sedgwick's frequent self-characterization as a gay man or an aspirational one (1993, 256), as discussed by Goldberg in this volume, I resist this interpretive possibility in my reading of Euripides' play because of the psychologism that it entails: see the critique of Anne Carson's reading of *Bacchae* offered by Gabriel 2018. My position also differs from that of Chu (2019), who posits a universal desire to *be* female; see the critique by Halberstam (2020b).

15. Speaking of Audre Lorde's lesbianism, Chinn (2003, 190) observes that "the power of touching other women erotically allows her to connect with her mother, to empathize with her"; see also Musser 2016. On the Eleusinian subtext of the Euripidean play, see esp. Mendelsohn 2002 (ch. 3). On queerness and touch, see Nooter in this volume.

16. On the relation between hapticity and queerness/transness, see Vaccaro (2015, 283), who views "gender transformation as a process of assembly and disassembly in which bodies auto-engineer shape and form, building and remaking connections between the soft and pliable material forms of emotional and material life." See also Vaccaro 2011.

17. On "animacy" as a queer, affective interaction of human and non-human, see Chen 2012.

18. On formalism and queer excess, see Youd in this volume.

19. On queer spectrality, see Freccero 2013a; on incest as queer kinship, see esp. Butler 2000 (on Sophocles' *Antigone*).

20. See, however, the calcification of the notion of queer produced, as Eng and Puar (2020, 3) observe, by "LGBTQ alignments with nationalist and racist ideologies [which] are ... constitutive of a normative queer liberal rights project." See also Introduction.

21. On the lesbian phallus and lesbian maternal *jouissance*, see Musser 2018 (ch. 3).

22. On "containment crypts" in the lesbian literary imaginary, see Westengard 2019 (ch. 2).

23. See Telò 2020, 217–30.

24. On *para*-relationality and reproduction, see Mueller in this volume.

25. Musser (2018, 74–5) connects lesbianism with the desire for the mother; cf. de Lauretis 1994. See also note 15.

PART III
FAILURE

CHAPTER 8
MEDEA—FAILURE AND THE QUEER ESCAPE
Sarah Nooter

This chapter argues that Euripides' *Medea* represents a category of queer womanhood that arises in response to the social failure of a female life.[1] Medea is a character whom the audience understands to have submitted to a gender normative, and genre normative, life as wife and mother, having borne two sons and supported the ambitions of her Greek husband Jason. But when we meet her at the start of the play, this persona has already failed.[2] By the play's end, we see Medea shaping a new identity for herself, one which disturbs the other characters and Chorus onstage, even as it continues to confound the play's many critics, readers, and audiences, and yet one which also provides a "way out of the usual traps and impasses of binary formulations" (Halberstam 2011, 2). Moreover, Medea's transformation of self also impacts not just other characters, but also the entire structure of social life. For while the play is frequently read as a referendum on Medea's identity as mother—and thus as woman—much more attention is paid in the play itself to her relation to all things paternal: fatherhood, patrilineality, and the patriarchy itself. Medea's feat is to show men to be locked variously into states of dependence and failure, while she herself assumes an identity that is not captured by normative terms.

In shaping this identity, Medea is in fact returning to an intrinsic element of herself, as is made evident by references to her genealogy, other divine associations, and prior magical and violent deeds. The very first lines of the play remind the audience of this, when the nurse cursorily sketches out the history of Medea, dropping important clues about the Medea who will emerge again from the wifely shell onstage (6–11):

> For then my mistress
> Medea would not have sailed to the towers of Iolcus,
> struck in her breast with desire for Jason.
> Nor would she, having persuaded the daughters of Pelias
> to kill their father, live in this land of Corinth,
> having become bereft of her own family and fatherland.

Aside from simply supplying helpful details of the setting for the play, the nurse also reminds the audience that Medea's particular experience of love and marriage are non-normative, if only because she was the lover, struck by desire, not Jason (see his comments thereon at 526–31).[3] Moreover, the lines both name and make more allusive reference to the crimes she committed to attain the object of her desire: she not only murdered Pelias by proxy but also became "bereft of" (*amplakousa*) her own relatives by murdering one of them (her brother) in her bid to escape her father's wrath (see also 483–7). That these crimes both involve (slightly redirected) strikes against fathers is not insignificant. One by one Medea engages with the continuance or (more often) lack of a patrilineal line, including those of Jason, Creon, and Aegeus. She does not engage as a reproductive body, a womb, or (in the immortal words of Aeschylus, *Eumenides* 657–61) a host to the paternal seed, but rather as an external influence, one whose support or censure is dispositive.

The internal truth of Medea's queer character is signaled even before the references to her past deeds. It is implied first in the nurse's famous series of backward-moving contrafactual wishes, including both a wish that the Argo, Jason's ship, had never sailed and that the pine trees cut down to shape the ship had never been hewn (1–5). Some of the unmaking or deconstruction wished for by the nurse upon the Argo is ultimately visited not only by Medea upon the patriarchy but also by Medea upon herself.[4] As she loses her socially constructed shape and purpose, she also moves backward to her wild, rooted self—the fate the nurse wishes for the trees cut down to bring glory to male heroes. Jason ultimately dubs Medea a monster, but if there is an ancient category for the old/new Medea, it might be *witch*, perhaps ancient Greece's best approximation of an independent, non-family-oriented woman who occupies a remote and otherwise uninhabited space and consorts with men (if she does at all) as an equal or superior interlocutor, inhabiting a queer loophole to the normative expectations of gender.[5] The association of Medea with witchery is first signaled by her claiming of Hecate as "helper" (396), goddess of magic and witchcraft, but takes on ever more queer qualities as the play progresses. Even Hecate's own connection with the crossroads is significant, signaling not just uncanny encounters, but also the ability to change course. This identity is more significant, inasmuch as Medea asserts—against tradition—that Hecate "inhabits the innermost regions of my hearth" (397). As Donald Mastronarde (2002, 236) notes,

> In Greek cult Hecate was worshipped outdoors, in streets, and at crossroads, so Medea's statement that the goddess dwells within her house, virtually in displacement of Hestia, conveys both erotic transgression of the norm and a special personal intimacy.[6]

We might see here the idea of the crossroads imported into the household, or the queer displacing the normative. In this chapter, I trace the turning of Medea from failed female to queer witch, whose departure from family brings the whole structure crashing down.

Good Wife/Good Life

The play initially portrays Medea as held within, though already betrayed by, the generic structures of a heteronormative, Greek family. She is a wife and mother, seeking to serve the goals of her husband. As the opening monologue continues, the nurse opines upon the prior success of Medea in these terms (12–17):

And before, even here, she had a blameless life
with her husband and children, a refugee but pleasing
to the citizens to whose land she had come,
and a helper to him, Jason, in all things.
This is the greatest salvation,
when a wife is not at odds with her husband.

The framework of the Good Life for a woman is laid out here: she is irreproachable, invested in her husband and children, pleasing (thus) to her community but—most importantly—a partner who acts in line with her husband. Indeed, security for a woman consists in such staying in line, not standing apart (*dicha*) from her man, for, as Medea states, a husband is the one "in whom there is all that [she] has" (228) and is the "master of her body" (233). In his will alone can she find safety.

And not just safety, but reproductive futurity, too, perfectly enacting the theory of Lee Edelman, whereby children (or, really, "the Child") act as the telos in a "fantasy of meaning's eventual realization."[7] It is through the "figure of the Child" that identity gets fixe[d] "through identification with the future of the social order."[8] Accordingly, playing one's fixed role in the normative family structure promises continuity into the future, as best expressed by Medea when she mourns to her sons the loss of the future she had thought she was building (1024–7):

But I will go to a foreign land as exile
before I have the benefit of you and see you flourishing,
before I can exalt in your baths and wives and marriage
beds and hold up the wedding torches.

Moreover, Medea makes clear the exact economy of childbearing, that is, of assuming the normative role to which she had devoted herself (1029–31):

In vain did I raise you, O children,
in vain did I labor and was I torn apart by the pains of childbirth,
enduring harsh pains in labor.

Here the double valence of the word "labors" becomes significant: a woman's bodily pain is her work, her down-payment to futurity, "the return [on] the debt of [her] life," to quote Sara Ahmed (2006, 21),[9] a system of trade-offs that is meant to be guaranteed by marriage. Medea is a notoriously eloquent critic of the patriarchal institution that is marriage and the value and pain of childbirth as a form of female labor (230–51). But what could be better understood is how the play portrays her in a pivotal moment of critical engagement, in the process of turning from the experience of marriage to an acute understanding of it.[10] It is from this pivotal stance of critique that she can seek another outcome.

To be sure, when it comes to Medea and Jason, there is a certain haziness around their marriage bond, inasmuch as they did not perform the ceremony in the normative fashion—with father giving away daughter—but rather in a fashion that has left her both acting on her own behalf and isolated from her natal family and homeland (cf. 25–8 and 505–8), thus accentuating the potential for peril implicit in marriage. Here, instead of an agreement between (new) husband and father, Jason's oath is to Medea herself (495).[11] Yet it is paradoxically not his oath but his act of abandonment that presumes to impose gender normativity on Medea once and for all. His act threatens not only to reify Medea's helplessness within normative family structures—making her the more dependent on himself, his bride, and her father—but also to fossilize Medea's role as a precursor to the fully dependent daughter of Creon, "the one," says a messenger, "that we now hold in awe instead of you" (1144).[12] Thus she would be shown to be intrinsically replaceable by other reproductive females. The role of reproductive wife is generic in terms of Athenian family structure and also in terms of tragedy itself: the paradigms of wifehood and motherhood are familiar impositions of the particularly domestic staging of the genre, which frames life as lived inside and outside the house—most often the seat of a family.[13] Jason's act of re-marriage would merely reset the staging of his family at the palace of Corinth.

Failing Up

But when Medea flies away in the chariot of the sun drawn by dragons,[14] she jumps both genders and genres, simultaneously breaking free from the normative family structure and removing herself from the limitations of tragedy.[15] In so doing, she (re)asserts her line of descent from Helios, and thus Circe, the original witch of Greek literature (1321–2):

> For such a chariot did Helios the father of my father
> give me, a defense against a hostile hand.

Here the several references to Helios throughout the play are at last cashed out. Medea claims her defense and identity through her paternal grandfather, with the implication of direct relation to Circe (her aunt)[16] and to various tales of monsters and men—a connection that Jason soon makes explicit, as I will explore below. She had previously referred to Helios twice, once to rev herself up to do her filicidal deed and again as the god on whom she asked Aegeus to swear to protect her whenever she should arrive at Athens (401–6 and 746–7):

> But on, Medea! Spare nothing of what you know,
> having planned and contrived.
> Come to the terrible deed. Now is the contest of courage.
> You see what you suffer? It cannot be that you incur laughter
> because of this Sisyphean marriage to Jason,
> *you*, born from a noble father and Helios.

and

> Swear by the land of Gaia and by Helios father of my father
> and add all the race of the gods.

Medea's first citation of Helios comes as she calls upon herself to *become what she was born as,* namely no victim or laughingstock, but a fighter and the granddaughter of the sun. Her second citation reminds Aegeus—another male whose relationship to fatherhood is ultimately mediated by Medea—of her divine heritage. In each case, the sheer paternality of it all is stressed by Medea to the umpteenth degree: *patros Hêliou t'apo* (406), *patera th'Hêlion patros* (746), *patros Hêlios patêr* (1321).[17] Each case is an example of Medea's assuming of paternal powers for herself, if implicitly.

But the third reference to Helios in the play is the most revealing. This one, mentioned above, comes when she offers to Jason the gift of her shining raiment to his new wife (952–5):

> She will be blessed not only in one thing but in countless ways,
> having happened upon the best man as partner
> and come into possession of the adornment which once Helios,
> father of my father, gave to his descendants.

This reference is equally emphatic on the matter of paternity: Helios is enjambed as *patros patêr* and his relationship to his descendants is the significant point. (By contrast, who can name Medea's grandmother? Her mother?) It is notable that Medea has not offered gifts that she has woven by her own hand—a more typical symbol of the industrious female—but rather ones she has inherited from the father of her father. In this gesture, she both echoes and appropriates male strategies of patrilineal wealth maneuvering, whereby select goods are used as gifts to "guest-friends" (*xenoi*) to create bonds and stave off enmity. Medea gives the appearance of using her paternal legacy to strengthen the position of her sons, but in fact she is infiltrating and poisoning the patriarchal home and seat of power by use of *pharmaka,* her god-given magic and true paternal inheritance.[18]

Medea thus sets up gender binaries only to break them in several ways, and flirts with the power of paternal lineage only to turn it into the plaything of Medea, a woman who—to quote Jason—is no woman (1323–6 and 1339–43):

> O hated thing, O most greatly despised woman
> to the gods and to me and to every race of men,
> you who have endured to cast a sword against your own
> children whom you bore and destroyed me, childless.

and

> There is no Greek woman who would have
> endured to do this ever, but before I thought it worthy

to marry you over them, a hated and deadly bond to me,
you lioness and no woman, bearing a fiercer nature
than the Tyrrhenian one, Scylla.

Jason makes some good points here: Medea has accomplished precisely what she set out to do in making Jason "childless" by killing his sons and new wife with all her reproductive capability (cf. 803–6). Medea, he repeatedly asserts, is no "woman" and, moreover, no *Greek* woman, a point that is repeatedly made in the play and by its critics.[19] Indeed, she has become unrecognizable in the terms of Greek gendered conformity. Rather she is an "other"—a monster for whom he struggles to find a suitable comparandum. The comparisons he does manage—lioness, Scylla—point both backward into tragic precursors and beyond tragedy, into a different generic field.[20]

For precursors, we find Aeschylus' *Oresteia*, whose specter hangs over the play, providing paradigms to be replicated and then shattered: it is, after all, Clytemnestra who is the grandly monstrous woman of tragedy. Though her pain and rage originate from Agamemnon's slaughter of her daughter Iphigenia, her self-defense against the onslaught of her son Orestes in *Libation Bearers* and her urging the Furies against him in *Eumenides* paint her as fully murderous of her own offspring. Medea might seem to exist, then, in her shadow. Yet, unlike in the *Oresteia*, in *Medea* one husband is not replaced with another;[21] no line of descent sets the course of family aright.[22] Medea does not (re)enter her palace to join a new (however corrupt) marriage; she departs from the household altogether. This picture, this possibility, fits better with archaic epic than classical tragedy. Here we find, specifically, Circe, the witch who lives by herself on a wild island on which she tames wild animals (and men), who consorts with Odysseus variously as danger, consort, and adviser, and who occupies no recognizable gendered structure or institution.[23] This model lies in wait—legible in the terms of gender fluidity of the *Odyssey* but largely excluded from tragedy, which tends to keep its women in the house. Medea's magical escape is thus not just from the institution of normative gender, but from the genre of tragedy itself.[24]

But, as I have tried to demonstrate, there has been no sudden shift here. Not only has this identity been signaled as Medea's previous and true self, but the audience has watched her turn ever more witch-like, and queer, as the play proceeds, in terms of both the religious language she uses (i.e., the gods she invokes) and the poetic language used to describe her. Deborah Boedeker has explored some of the "poetic mechanisms" that grant Medea the "profound and disturbing power" often noticed by audiences of the play, particular comparisons to "beasts, legendary killers, and natural elements such as rock, sea, or storm," and also the way in which Medea is "gradually dissociated" from such "simple terms" as woman and mother (1997, 127–8).[25] Yet she does not push this sense of dissociation to its logical conclusion in tragic terms. Unlike Clytemnestra, Medea does not depart (dissociate) from womanhood into manhood,[26] but rather into a queer, or non-normative, womanhood where new designations become possible.

Not Touching/Not Feeling

In what way is this chapter performing a queer reading rather than a feminist one? Certainly it *is* a feminist reading, picking up from excellent work done in this regard on tragedy in general and this play in particular.[27] If it is also a queer reading, it is so in its attempt to follow the play in its explorations of spaces beyond the patriarchy and even beyond its downfall, beyond failed womanhood and its triumphant replacement with witch or its re-appropriation of the tropes of monstrosity. As per the readings of Jack Halberstam,[28] Euripides' *Medea* opens up a space occupied by an "unbecoming woman"—an imagined space, for it becomes possible only when she departs from the household on a chariot drawn by imaginary beasts that are, in any case, occluded from the text. In a fit of fantasy, Medea no longer touches the earth, and Jason can no longer touch her. What we do know about this chariot is that it holds the bodies of her dead children. As Mario Telò (2020, 91) has written,

> Driving a chariot burdened with corpses, Medea sets off on a literal *death drive*, embodying a materiality that, while disintegrating others, is also in danger of disintegrating itself . . . [S]he enacts the death drive's violent refusal of the future's reproductive logic and life itself.

For as Telò makes clear, the story of *Medea* is not only one about freedom from exploitative standards of womanhood and oppressive fantasies of futurity; it is also about the vertiginous detachment from life that is the price of this freedom—an ambiguous result or "uncomfortable suspension" (2020, 109)[29] between possibilities that leaves the audience uncomfortable, too, unresolved in their ethical and affective positioning.

Earlier in this chapter, I quote Medea on the bargain of parenthood, whereby the pain and labor of childbirth and childrearing are meant to pay the parent back through the joy of celebrating the child's ascension to adulthood and marriage, and thus the promise of still more reproductive futurity. Moreover, Medea continues, her sons should have cared for her in old age and lovingly buried her corpse when she died (1032–6):

> Truly I once, wretched, held many
> hopes in you, that you would tend to me in old age
> and that, when I had died, you would lay me out well
> with your own hands, an enviable fate for mortals.
> But now this sweet thought is lost.

All of these hopes, she sees now, were rather fantasies (or, as here, a "sweet thought"). So, too, does Edelman assert: the futurity of the Child is a fantasy around which we are made to build our lives and societies. He advises, rather, to live in the present, in presence that he configures as like to the death drive, a cry of resistance against the machine, a refusal to become a legible alternative or structure. "[Q]ueerness," he insists, "insist[s] on the Real of a jouissance that social reality and the futurism on which it relies have already foreclosed" (2004, 24–5).

Perhaps, but as Halberstam has shown, there is a thread of anti-womanhood, the idea that womanhood equates with the oppressive structures of life, that runs through this theory.[30] There is also a blindness to the presence of the now—indeed the *jouissance*—that is offered by the very thing that fundamentally ties one to the dictates of the machinery of reproductive futurity—that is, children. If, indeed, children were merely arms of social oppression, they would be an easy loss to bear. Even their offerings of continuance into the future, maintenance of familial wealth, and care in old age would be small—particularly from the perspective of a semi-immortal witch, who has other means to her ends. The confounding complexity of Euripides' *Medea* arises from its more nuanced demonstration of childbearing. The play itself does not accede (only) to Jason's understanding of children as the path to reproductive futurity, or even to Medea's spirited resistance to this path. It shows, too, another aspect of having children, which might be thought of as their affective hold, their own offering to their parents of *jouissance*. This it does in a very brief span through its exploration of touch, the ultimate sensory experience of presence, "the single sense that no animal can live without:" it dwells, then, at the "core of sentient life" and yet, or perhaps consequently, is "particularly resistant to language and description ... surprisingly ungraspable as a single sense or concept" (Purves 2018, 1–2).[31]

Though Jason willingly leaves his children, though Medea unwillingly kills them,[32] the play shows also how both receive a nearly erotic level of pleasure and pain from them, its own kind of escape from oppressive systems of success and failure, winning and losing, futures and pasts. We are shown this through how they both feel and long for the touch of these little ones. We see their shared obsession with this touch. Hence Medea (1074–7):

> O sweet embrace,
> O **soft skin** and most lovely breath of my children.
> Go away, go. No longer can I stand to look at you,
> for I am overcome by pain.

And Jason (1399–1400 and 1402–3):[33]

> Alas, I long for the loving faces
> of my children, wretchedly, to clasp them to me.
> > Give it to me by the gods
> to touch the **soft skin** of my children.

The grief of each parent devolves upon the haptic embrace of the soft skin—the texture itself— the very element of their children that no memory, portrait, ritual, or narrative can preserve or restore. As Eve Kosofsky Sedgwick (2003, 14) has written,

Even more immediately than other perceptual systems, it seems, the sense of touch makes nonsense out of any dualistic understanding of agency and passivity; to touch is always already to reach out, to fondle, to heft, to tap, or to enfold.

In the parents' pleasure and longing to touch the skin of their children, systems of agency fall away; something far more potent and less amenable to discursive engagement is at work. Thus, Medea must stop touching her children to let them go (*Go away, go*), to become other, to disconnect from her normative identity as mother and take on the mantel of monster, witch, goddess, and thus take on oppressively normative structures of the world. This is the true battle, and one which she nearly does not win. In winning, she transforms the touch of her children on her own skin into the weight of their corpses on her chariot. She thus redraws the lines of success (for herself) and failure (for the patriarchy). Jason notes, however, that she has made herself suffer as well as he (1361), and he is right.[34] Shall we forget her suffering, as she commands herself to forget the children—and implicitly the pleasure of their bodies—to tell a story of triumph? Shall we ignore queer suffering in general, seeking to fold it into a success story? Shall we submit to accepting existence as merely resistance? One cannot read or watch the *Medea* without wondering, for the umpteenth time, if there is really no other way.[35]

Notes

1. Much work in queer scholarship of the last decade or so confronts questions of failure, the feeling of being "backward" or otherwise falling short of normative expectations. See Ahmed 2006; Love 2007; and Halberstam 2011.

2. See Boedeker 1997, 148 on the eradication of Medea's early identities.

3. That Medea, rather than Jason, desires is traditional, from at least the version of Pindar, *Pythian Odes* 4.213–19.

4. See Telò 2020, 92, 93, and 95 on the deep links between Medea and the "destructive and self-destructive energy of the Argo." The connection is not just to be found in events but also in identity: "The Argo also amounts to an *archê* as a figure of primordial trauma, which is felt through the participle *tmêtheisa* ("cut down" 4), uncannily resonant with the name of Medea, three lines later, in the same position (*Mêdeia* 7)" (93). See also Konstan 2007 on how the sounds of Medea's name in the opening lines of the play may point to her ultimate ascension to divine status, and Rutherford 2014 on the potentially divine implications of Medea's flight by crane.

5. We might appropriately dub Medea's witchery a version of Halberstam's (2011, 4) "shadow feminisms [which] take the form not of becoming, being and doing but of shady, murky modes of undoing, unbecoming, and violating."

6. See Hall 2014, 129 on Medea's "offbeat divine associates in Hecate and Helios." To be sure, Euripides does not turn Medea into a full-fledged sorceress in the mode of Apollonius of Rhodes or Seneca (both later, of course), and Knox (1977) is right to point to how Medea's humanity is stressed in the play, at least until Medea all but becomes divine at the end. Witchery does not take over the plot here, so much as point the character toward non-normative constructions of womanhood.

7. Edelman 2004, 4.

8. Edelman 2004, 25. See Telò 2020, 97 and 103 on how Jason's (supposed) plans for his children are scripted in accordance with the logic of reproductive futurity.

9. As Ahmed puts it, "For a life to count as a good life, then it must return the debt of its life by taking on the direction promised as a social good, which means imagining one's futurity in terms of reaching certain points along a life course. A queer life might be one that fails to make such gestures of return" (2006, 21).

10. See Kasimis 2020, 14 and 19 on the view that "women have no political value outside of a kinship system" and on how Medea's "motherhood . . . undergoes a crisis in meaning."

11. See Sourvinou-Inwood 1997, 256 on Medea's "form of marriage" as "transgressive" in the eyes of the audience, and Kasimis 2020, 15–16 on how Medea has "brokered her own arrangement with Jason," something we see her do onstage as well, when she pretends to submit to his new marriage plans.

12. See Boedeker 1997, 143 on the manifold ways that Medea is "assimilated to" the princess, including the terms used to describe their physiques, their feelings toward Jason, and their (once and future) susceptibility to his methods of persuasion.

13. There are exceptions of course, such as Sophocles' *Philoctetes* (a play without women), but the family household remains a mainstay of tragic space.

14. The play falls short of being entirely explicit about the staging here, but both the visual tradition and the play's *hypothesis* present Medea as being carried off by a dragon-pulled chariot.

15. In *Poetics* 1454b Aristotle would seem to disapprovingly agree.

16. This connection is picked up by later authors, such as Apollonius of Rhodes and Madeline Miller.

17. Cf. Telò 2020, 103 on how the "almost self-identical repetition in the polyptoton *patros patêr* resumes the overlapping logic of reproductive futurism and of the patriarchal archive, their shared notion of the child as a faithful imprinting of the father." Medea adopts this phrasing for a mission of subterfuge and deceit, to use rather than serve the ideology imposed by this language.

18. See Mueller 2001 on the implications of Medea's use of these gifts and her (pretext of) adopting a (generally) male system of gift exchange, one of several examples of her enacting exchanges with men in the play.

19. See Sourvinou-Inwood, 1997, 289–92 on the possibility that Medea's costuming might have changed from Greek to Asiatic by the end of the play, emphasizing her "otherness," but also the instability of the Greek/"other" divide.

20. Medea accepts the designation (1358–69). See Boedeker (1997, 132), who links Jason's association of Medea with Scylla to his (epic) experiences on the Argo expedition, as well as to *Odyssey* 12.55–100, where Scylla and the Argo are briefly linked.

21. The tradition that Medea shacks up with Aegeus is not relevant here, since it is made clear that Aegeus is already married and that Medea plans to help him in his reproductive troubles through the use of *pharmaka* (673 and 716–18), not sexual union.

22. Here Love's (2011, 207) portrait of Lady Macbeth's "dangerous maternal ambivalence" is especially enlightening. According to this reading, Lady Macbeth's prayer to have her milk exchanged for poison is of a piece with her hunger for a future that does not accord with succession or genealogy.

23. This picture also accords with a general account of Greek witches as explicitly sexualized, as opposed to Roman witches. Roman witches are evil; Greek ones are just dangerous. See Spaeth 2014, 46–9.

24. *Contra* Hopman (2008), who argues that Medea's destruction of the male glory of the Argo expedition turns the play away from epic, but ignores (in my view) Medea's models in the *Odyssey* and her departure from (certain) tragic tropes of womanhood, particularly in the *Oresteia*. As she herself notes, "Medea . . . manages to undermine those expectations [of undergoing Clytemnestra's fate]" (178). How this happens and what this means are where these interpretations part ways.

25. Medea as a rock or the sea can be found at 28–9 and 1279–80.

26. Cf. *Agamemnon* 11, for starters.

27. See Foley 1989; Haley 1995; Mills 2014; Kasimis 2020; and Cairns 2014 (a feminist reading inasmuch as it argues that *Medea* is far from having been a feminist play in its time). See Hall 2014 and Van Zyl Smit 2014 (as well as Haley 1995 again) on how the play has been adopted as a feminist text in performance and adaptations.

28. As Halberstam (2011, 125) puts it, "The texts that I examine in this chapter refuse to think back through the mother; they actively and passively lose the mother, abuse the mother, love, hate, and destroy the mother, and in the process they produce a theoretical and imaginative space that is 'not woman' or that can be occupied only by unbecoming women."

29. See also McDermott 1989, 78. Cf. Lawrence 1997, 55 on how "Euripides invites questioning of rigid categorisations, stereotypes and antitheses." See also Pucci 1980, 158–9; Rabinowitz 1993, 125–54; Segal 1996; Mossman 2011, 353; and Roisman 2014 on the problem for the audience of grappling with violence and vengeance in the play.

30. Halberstam 2011, 118: "But Edelman always runs the risk of linking heteronormativity in some essential way to women and, perhaps unwittingly, woman becomes the site of the unqueer: she offers life, while queerness links up with the death drive." Cf. Deutscher 2017 (ch. 2).

31. Purves (2018, 1) cites Aristotle, *Parts of Animals* 4.5.681a27–8. For a different take on queer touch, see Telò in this volume.

32. See Foley 1989 on how the internal debate of Medea on whether to kill her children takes place between two genders, of which the masculine part wins, pointing to a critique of a "social structure."

33. Segal (1996, 39–40) suggests that Jason's "intensely corporeal relation to his children's bodies at the end suggests . . . perhaps an implicit feminization of Jason."

34. See Telò 2020, 99, and Pucci 1980, 158 on Medea as "mangled and suffering, just as Jason is."

35. I am deeply grateful to the editors of this volume for having created such an encouraging and communal space for thinking this through. I received the invitation to participate in the volume while in the hospital, having just given birth to my (third) son Ezekiel. In light of my immediate and enthusiastic request to write on *Medea*, I hope this essay will be understood ultimately as a reflection not on the violence but rather the *jouissance* of childrearing.

CHAPTER 9
ALCESTIS—IMPOSSIBLE PERFORMANCE
Sean Gurd

I am trying to imagine a way to perform Euripides' *Alcestis* so that it has a strong emotional arc or a characteristic tone. *Alcestis*, in my imagining, shares with a number of other Euripidean works an interest in the problematic nature of moral righteousness and in the extraordinary mechanisms needed to critique or overturn it. Think of the zealously abstemious Hippolytus, capsized by others' desire, or Electra, who discovers the horror of matricide only in the act, or the absolute rationalist Pentheus, who is seduced and destroyed by what he suppresses. In *Alcestis*'s Admetus I find the same righteousness, the same insidious plot to overturn. But here Euripides' focus is on what we could call, following Jack Halberstam, queer strategies of subversion: strategies that come from a position of weakness and look as though they are designed to fail. For Halberstam, "what looks like inaction, passivity, and lack of resistance" can be characterized "in terms of the practice of stalling the business of the dominant," while failure can be seen as "a way of refusing to acquiesce to dominant logics of power and discipline and as a form of critique" (2011, 88). The degree to which such strategies can indeed subvert righteousness and other systems of domination is a central question in these reflections, as is a nagging worry about how failure as a strategy of critique interfaces with performance: what happens if one's performance fails, and how is this related to the performance of failure?

I

At the beginning of *Alcestis*, Apollo is ending a period of enslavement to the Thracian landowner Admetus. This enslavement came about because of a dispute over sovereignty in the strongest sense: the right to set the limits of life and death, which Zeus claims as his alone.[1] Apollo's son Asclepius violated this prerogative by practicing the art of resurrection (Apollo pointedly leaves this well-known detail out of his account at the beginning of the play), for which Zeus blasted him with a thunderbolt. Apollo avenged his son by shooting one of the Cyclopes, who forge these thunderbolts; this is the crime that led to his servitude under Admetus (3–7).

Now at the end of his punishment, Apollo grants to Admetus a gift: if he can find someone else to die for him, Admetus will live a long life. But this gift looks like an act of defiance, a further refusal to grant that Zeus alone has the right to set the limits of life and death, since allowing someone else to die in Admetus' place smudges the limits of one life. Admetus' wife Alcestis agrees to die in Admetus' place, an act that secures his longevity and seems like a sacrifice; by the end of the play Heracles will have prevented

Alcestis' own death, and Apollo knows this at the beginning (64–71). In other words, Apollo succeeds in doing exactly what Asclepius was punished for: he has stopped a fated death from occurring. But this is no outright rebellion: it is an act of cunning. After all, his servitude has established that direct resistance will not work. Apollo would need to resort to trickery, to use what James C. Scott called "the weapons of the weak" (1985). His gift could well be taken as a Promethean trick: as Prometheus concealed bones by wrapping them in fat, so does Apollo conceal an attack on the cosmic hierarchy in what otherwise looks like a generous gift of gratitude to his former master.

The gift seems suspicious in another way as well: what reasons had Apollo to be grateful to a man who upset the normal social order by operating as the owner of a divinity? Surely an act of retribution, something to rebalance the scales, is more in order. Apollo claims that he gives Admetus this gift because the latter is "holy" (3–7). But Admetus' "holiness" has curious characteristics. True, he observes correct form, not merely as a matter of course or habit, but for reasons that he can articulate. For example, when Heracles appears at his door just after Alcestis has died and he has proclaimed a period of mourning, he welcomes Heracles into the house and throws a feast for him. When the Chorus expresses astonishment at this, Admetus gives a worked-out justification (553–60). He asks what people would say if he turned Heracles away, a question that shows a concern for his public "face." He wonders how he would be treated the next time he needs hospitality somewhere else, an admission that there is self-interest lurking at the base of relations of reciprocity. And while his self-justification provokes the immediate admiration of the Chorus, who expostulates in praise of his virtue (569–605), his act of hospitality is hardly uncontroversial. It causes real upset inside the house, as we learn from a servant who has been set to serve Heracles as he carouses (747–72). This servant shows agony in having to serve an increasingly rowdy visitor when he wants to be mourning. He also drops hints that, in the absence of Alcestis, Admetus may not turn out to be a positive force in the lives of his slaves: Alcestis is mourned not least because she "warded off many evils by softening the anger of her man" (770–1). A foreboding phrase, whose exact meaning we can only imagine. At least we can infer that Alcestis knew how to manage him, to mitigate and mollify what could otherwise be a dangerous temper. Admetus' position is that of a master: feared, perhaps even respected, but by no means beloved.

Such is also implied by the encounter between Admetus and his father Pheres, who has offended his son by refusing to die in his stead. Admetus will by no means forgive his parents; he calls them old, useless, past having any value to anyone other than in their ability to die for them (629–72). Pheres' reply is equally harsh. Admetus is way out of line (679); he is less courageous than his wife (696–7); Alcestis' choice to die was foolish, since she died for a husband of little worth (728); Admetus bears the guilt for her death, and will pay retribution to her father (730–3). Admetus' final words banish his father from the house (734–8).

How unreasonable would it be, I wonder, to take Alcestis' choice to die for Admetus as a kind of resistance from below, akin if not identical to Apollo's gift? Unlike some of Euripides' other sacrificial maidens, she seems to have a plan. Perhaps she theatricalizes her death and uses the drama of the situation to extract from Admetus the promise that he will never accept another woman into his house. In a short play her death scene is long and theatrical, even campy, or at least one could easily play it that way. Could we make an audience see that Alcestis, far from being the passive victim of horrible death throes, is in fact performing for her husband to extract this vow? That certainly would not be unusual for Greek tragedy, which loved the surreptitious-play-within-a-play format, and especially loved to cast women in such roles (Clytemnestra, Electra, Medea, for example).

In any case, the situation at the end of the play is at least uncomfortable for Admetus. Heracles has wrestled death to the ground and won Alcestis back from the shades: he presents her to Admetus, as a parting gift, though she is veiled at first and Admetus does not know who she is. He tries to refuse the gift, in observance of the promise he had made to Alcestis, but in the end he gives in to Heracles, and thus breaks his promise to his wife; at this point she takes off her veil and he realizes that he has broken his vow before her very eyes. What happens to him here but defeat? We might ask who leads whom offstage at the play's end: does Admetus take his wife within, or is it she who leads him, finally convinced that his furious piety is an impossible ideal to maintain?

Thus does Apollo's war with Zeus continue to work itself out, through the twists and turns of generosity and gift, via kindness deployed like a weapon. Really imaginative readers can even fantasize that Alcestis, who, after all, shared walls with the prophetic Apollo, knows as Apollo knows that Heracles is coming and that her death will be revoked, knows in advance that the oath she extracts from Admetus will be violated before her very eyes.

II

"Wonderful!" Someone says after reading my concept for the play. "But we are supposed to be talking about *Euripides'* play here, and your cunning—not to say perverted— scenario seems unlikely to reconcile itself perfectly with the *ink*, the actual words of Euripides' text." After all, Apollo calls Admetus a "holy man" and cites this as the reason for his gift. Hardly the words of a god who hates or wants to humiliate Admetus. And the Chorus praises him as a model of virtue and virtuous action (569–605). And what about Admetus' final lines, where he declares that he is happy? Surely here Euripides is saying that Admetus is happy with the outcome of this tale. How are we not contradicting the text when we describe this ending as a scene of humiliation and cruelty?

If such an objection were raised I would offer the following response. First, the ink alone will never be able to constrain a performance in one direction or another; and, second, *Alcestis* seems to have a built-in indeterminacy about it—there are multiple ways to play it.

As it happens there is a long tradition of imagining tragedy in performance. But this tradition does not get me off the hook vis-à-vis the authority of the text. For the defining law of performance studies as these have evolved around ancient theater is that nothing may happen on the stage that is not mentioned in the text. This principle was originally promulgated by Oliver Taplin to support his work on entrances and exits in Greek tragedy (1977, 2003). But its value as an interpretive principle is very limited, and I would contend that the relationship between what happens on the stage and what is said in the text is both a variable and a source of dramatic energy, not a predetermined constraint.[2] Consider the moment at the end of Admetus' argument with his father, when Admetus says to the Chorus "let *us* go and perform a mourning ritual" (740). The next scene is an exchange between Heracles and a slave, with no intervention from the Chorus. We naturally infer that, after this line, Admetus leaves and takes the Chorus with him, since the text has him use the first person plural to mark the exit. An unusual, not to say strikingly theatrical moment; in tragedy, Choruses are typically onstage permanently once they have entered. But imagine for a moment that a director decides to leave the Chorus onstage at this moment. "Let us go and mourn," says Admetus to the Chorus, then leaves—and they do not follow. This violates Taplin's principle, to be sure. But it is a very interesting thing to do dramaturgically. In such a play, Admetus' authority would be considerably weakened: perhaps the Chorus is so gobsmacked by the way he handles his own father that they choose, then and there, to insert some distance from him. What such a staging does not do is reduce the play to nonsense: it just changes its charge. I mean to suggest with this little experiment that the text does not constrain staging: rather whatever happens onstage will be given context by the text (and vice versa).

Ultimately, it is not a sustainable position that the tragic text alone is an adequate signifier of performance. Large parts of tragedy were sung, and while we can tell the rhythm of the singing from the text, the MSS do not preserve the melodies (if they ever had them). There is ancient debate about the degree to which the music should follow the words or vice versa, so we can presume there was some variability in practice (see Plato, *Republic* 3.400d). On this very important front we cannot reasonably posit immediate control of performance by the text of the play: in repertoire a producer or performer would have to decide what the words meant, then design music that fit those meanings. Here the text serves as only a limited constraint on performance.

The same may reasonably be said about the non-sung parts of the text. When Apollo says that Admetus was a holy man, a performer must make a decision about *how* to say this: he could choose to use his voice to indicate rage, or irony, or joy. Likewise Admetus' declaration that he is happy at the play's end. Say this with a tone of exhaustion and defeat and you will fundamentally change the feeling of the play. Prima facie it seems hard to imagine any living theater ignoring the dynamics of vocal tone. And in fact we are told by Aristotle that dramatic actors treated vocal performance in a self-conscious manner. We do not get much more information than that—Aristotle is interested not in dramatic performance but in the manipulation of the voice and body in rhetoric, which he says was derived from what actors were doing (*Rhetoric* 1404a). But something that we could call a psycho-thermo-dynamic theory of the voice seems to have connected states of soul or *êthê* with vocal quality, in particular vocal pitch. Peripatetic sources, for instance, connected fear with high-pitched vocal expressions.[3] The mechanism appears to have been well theorized: as heat affects the quality of the voice, so does emotion affect the temperature of the blood around the heart, where voice was produced and conditioned. We also run into the recommendation that the best way to represent *êthos* and emotion was to actually see the situation you were talking about, to actually feel the relevant feelings.[4] Although the passages that discuss this technique are concerned with the way it can inform diction and rhetorical argumentation, they could also be expected to affect tone, if one believed in the nexus of emotion and voice articulated by the Peripatetics. Connecting these threads, we might say that actors could develop their expressive ability by learning to feel what the characters felt; this would then affect their tone of voice.

This is all speculation. But it suggests that then, as now, a text's affective content, its emotional meaning and the dramatic arc of a play, depended on choices made by the performer about who his character was and what they were feeling: Who is Apollo here? How humiliated is Admetus at the end? The performer would seek to vividly feel these things, and the vocal expression would follow.[5]

III

What a producer or a performer needs to do, then, is develop a theory of the play that includes but is not completely dominated by the ink. From this theory, both thought and felt, will proceed choices about tone, tune, and staging. *Alcestis* offers multiple affordances to a dramatist wanting to do this. The choices start with the problem of the play's genre. Tragic productions were conceived and performed in tetralogies, sets of four plays performed on a single day. Plays 1–3 were tragedies in the strictest sense; large plays on grand mythical subjects with momentous themes. Play 4 was normally a "satyr play," using the same musical and dramatic structure as the tragedies but shorter, and featuring a Chorus of satyrs, mythical man-beasts with goat lower ends, large phalloi, and major impulse-control issues. From what we know (and we do not know much: only one complete satyr play survives, the *Cyclops*),[6] satyr plays reflected the character of their Chorus: they were transgressive, obscene, and hilarious, making comedy within the weighty form of tragedy. *Alcestis* was put on *instead* of a satyr play (*Alcestis Hypothesis* 18; cf. 24). In form it is a short tragedy (just over 1,000 lines), but its placement suggests that it should be light, even funny. Indeed, the play seems built to teeter on a thin edge between these two tones.

Another choice a producer must make is how to distribute characters to actors. Tragedy adhered to what is usually called the "three-actor rule," according to which producers had a total of three speaking actors.[7] In practical terms this meant that performers had to take on multiple roles during a single play. Euripides was entirely capable of playing with this constraint in a thematically significant way. In *Hippolytus*, for example, Aphrodite, Theseus, and Phaedra are played by the same performer, a pairing that sets husband and wife "against" their problematic son/in-law, and "with" the goddess who wants to destroy him. Now *Alcestis* has a small glitch (actually it is more like a loose screw) that allows for more freedom than one usually has in assigning roles. With some juggling, it can be played by two actors. If it is performed with three actors, one actor (let us call him Actor A) must play Admetus exclusively, but for the rest there are multiple possible distributions. Here are four:

1.

   Actor A. Admetus

   Actor B. Apollo, Alcestis, Therapaina, Pheres, Therapôn

   Actor C. Death, Child, Heracles

2.

   Actor A. Admetus

   Actor B. Death, Alcestis, Pheres, Therapaina, Therapôn

   Actor C. Apollo, Child, Heracles

3.

   Actor A. Admetus

   Actor B. Apollo, Alcestis, Therapaina, Therapôn

   Actor C. Death, Child, Pheres, Heracles

4.

   Actor A. Admetus

   Actor B. Death, Alcestis, Therapaina, Therapôn

   Actor C. Apollo, Child, Pheres, Heracles

Option 2 would align the two opponents of Death (and sons of Zeus)—Apollo and Heracles—in one performer, and add the irony of having these two ultra-masculine roles matched with that of a child (who perhaps symbolizes their status as children of Zeus); it would also put Death "in the house," as it were, having that character share a performer with Alcestis and her father. Here, I propose, we have a casting that suggests an interpretation of the play as a conflict over the limits of death.

Option 1 introduces the irony of having Heracles and Death, who wrestle offstage, played by the same actor; but also ranges Apollo, Alcestis, Pheres, and the household servants in a single role. That is, here Apollo operates with the household (to which, after all, he was enslaved) and against its head—a kind of subaltern revolutionary lineup.

Here is a fifth option, which takes advantage of the fact that Alcestis does not speak in the final scene and makes the conflict implied by option 1 even more extreme:

5.

   A. Admetus

   B. Apollo, Alcestis (speaking, in death scene), Pheres, Heracles

   C. Death, Child, Therapaina, Therapôn, Alcestis (silent, in final scene)

This distribution is in some ways perfectly conventional. It is not unusual for the third actor to have a series of subaltern roles, and both servants have messenger speeches, which we might conceive of as a specialist role. This casting also ranges Admetus against *all* of the socially recognizable characters, including Heracles, who would be an unwitting instrument of Apollo's revenge. It would be odd to have Alcestis played by two actors— even if the second one did not speak. But we might recall the stunning moment close to the beginning of the play when Admetus promises that, instead of a wife, he will take a statue to bed (348–54). At the end of the play, in a sense, Alcestis *is* this statue—a visage, nothing more—and Admetus finds himself (re-)betrothed to her.

It seems to me that the multiple possible role distributions, each encoding a different set of themes and dramatic tensions, is part of a pattern that we find repeated in the *Alcestis*'s generic ambiguity, as well as in the ambiguities surrounding Apollo's gift to Admetus and Alcestis' self-willed death, both of which could be taken as simple acts of generosity, or as something more complex and ambiguous, even cruel. It seems important, in other words, to acknowledge that undecidability is important to the construction of this play. The problem is that it is hard to imagine preserving such ambiguities in performance. A producer will have to choose one role distribution and use it. Apollo can either be rewarding Admetus or punishing him, but not both; Admetus can either be rewarded or humiliated at the end, but not both. Something of the text would be incurably lost.

IV

Could we approach this from another direction entirely? The three-actor rule requires performers who can play (and delve into the psychologies of) multiple characters. Even when we choose a casting and thus reduce the play's structural ambiguities, we nonetheless reproduce them at a different level, for now we have performers who exist in a kind of psychic plurality. Indeed, one might observe that the necessity of doubling roles often placed greater demands on "second" or "third" actors, and I can imagine audiences being drawn to such performers and their ability to move from one role to the next. Such considerations upset the hierarchy that is often assumed, favoring not the title performers but the ones who have to be physically and emotionally plural, endlessly performing their own difference on the stage. Perhaps it was these actors, too, to whom Plato's Socrates objected in the *Republic*, on the grounds that they were inherently unstable (10. 600a–607e). Say we pursue this line of thought, and aim not to reduce but to maximize *Alcestis*'s ambiguity on the stage: one could arrange for music or bodily movements that somehow clashed with the words, or with each other; one could build simultaneous conflicting messages into the performance. In doing this we might succeed in communicating the play's ambiguities to an audience.

But I suspect that this is a play that prefers failure. Let us return to the story and remind ourselves *why* there are so many ambiguities here: the power hierarchies of the Olympian court and the house of Admetus mean that resistance can only proceed obliquely, through indirect strategies. In Apollo's case, this was an act that looked like gratitude to his enslaver, and in Alcestis' case it looked like choosing to die. These could be described as what Halberstam called "the queer art of failure," "a radical form of masochistic passivity that not only offers up a critique of the organizing logic of agency and subjectivity itself, but that also opts out of certain systems built around a dialectic between colonizer and colonized" (2011, 131). Change "colonizer and colonized" to "master and slave" or "husband and wife" and you get close to the dynamics of *Alcestis*. Alcestis yields, displays a perfect passivity, and in doing so she fundamentally alters, though without supplanting or overturning, the patriarchal hegemony represented by Admetus and his Olympian emblem Zeus.

Halberstam's is an elegant articulation of what it would mean to step outside the dialectical structure of modern politics, as well as a convincing description of the phenomenology of such a step sideways, including the affective consequences of the invisibility that would inevitably result. Halberstam's work is also rousing in its call to sketch out alternatives to the correct or the righteous: "let's leave success and its achievement to the Republicans, to the corporate managers of the world, to the winners of reality TV shows, to married couples, to SUV drivers. The concept of practicing failure perhaps prompts us to discover our inner dweebs, to get distracted, to take a detour, to find a limit, to lose our way, to fight, to avoid mastery ..." (2011, 121). In pursuing a performance, perhaps what we should do is submit to the necessity of failing—own the fact that we will not succeed in mastering this play. That might subvert those social logics that insist on success, victory, mastery as the only meaningful articulations of value.

But I want to push the logic just a step further. How can one *own* failure? What does it mean to *want* to fail? Asking this question is, I think, inevitable and requisite: otherwise "failure" remains a disposable term, too quickly reconverted into a new language of domination. As the negative side of success (if winning matters, I will lose), failure would be little more than the dialectical obverse of mastery, and would be unsustainable as an alternative or a viable critique. Failure may be merely apparent; it may be what appears to the world when one commits oneself to a set of values that are not those of one's context. But this failure is no failure at all: it is just the public face of private success. One lives as one believes is right at the cost of seeming wrong. Here the logic of succeeding continues to prevail, but is taken underground, as it were. If failing as such is to become a means to achieve an alternative to forms of domination, it must somehow be an absolute failure, a failure in and for itself, with its own logic that supplants the logic of success. Consider the following passage from Tom Johnson's "Failing" (1976), a very difficult piece for solo string bass: this text is to be read by the performer as he plays the score:

> The piece called "Failing" is extremely difficult. There are a few relaxed moments now and then, but most of the time I am required to play a tricky chromatic melody at a fast speed, and by now I am probably beginning to fail in one way or another. Of course, I don't particularly enjoy failing. Sometimes I think it would be better if I cheated a little so that I would not fail too badly and so that people would

be more impressed by my playing ability. But on the other hand, if I do my best, and play most of the music well, it should be clear that I am doing the task as well as anyone could expect me to do it. Moreover, I will be interpreting the piece accurately, since it is obvious that "Failing" is about failing, and if I succeed in playing everything accurately without slowing down my speaking, or cheating, or anything, I will fail to fail, and thus will miss the point. In a way, I almost want to fail, because everybody fails at certain times and in certain ways anyway, and because that is what the piece is about, and because I want to interpret it appropriately. But of course I must not try to fail. I must try to succeed in doing the task well, without slowing down, and without missing notes, even though, by now, it is almost impossible to succeed for very long. If I tried to fail, and then failed, that would be a kind of success, and not a failure at all. So I must try to succeed. That way, when I fail to succeed, I will succeed in communicating the essence of the piece, even though I will fail to accomplish the task as it is set up. In other words, I will not be able to fail unless I am trying to succeed, and I won't succeed in interpreting the piece sensitively unless my performance turns out to be a failure. Or, putting it another way, I will probably succeed in failing to succeed, not only because the music is so difficult, but also because, if I fail to succeed in failing to succeed, I will fail to fail and will miss the point, since "Failing" is obviously about failing, and since any successful performance must be a qualified failure.

Say we commit to the logic of failure implied, perhaps, by the queer resistances of Apollo and Alcestis and choose an unambiguous line of approach for our performance of *Alcestis*. We will have *succeeded* in developing the logic of failure. And so we would have failed. Say, on the other hand, we preserve the play's ambiguities in a complex, difficult production. We will have failed to communicate the failure that seems to be one of its concerns. And so, we will have succeeded. Which means, of course, that we will have failed. The logic of failing, once it is fully owned, proves deeply corrosive. Few philosophers have time for lines of thought like this: they think of them as sophomoric high jinks or as signs that one's intellectual premises are flawed. But I am not trying to be cute. The circular, rebarbative logic of deliberate failure is commonplace. "Damaged life," as Adorno called it, is the lived logic of failing. Owning it may be the only thing you can do.

Perhaps what happens in *Alcestis*, knowingly performed as an impossibility, is the dramatization of lives that have been altered by the possession of failure. Alcestis voices the agony of her position by a seemingly generous suicide and is returned to life within a household where even her last act of agency has been obscured and obviated (even her death, a last act of resistance from below, is cancelled; she is, in the end, not allowed to die). Admetus submits to Alcestis and the law of hospitality, and is rewarded with a form of life that is both perduring and stripped of any pretense of mastery. "Let no one say that I am not happy," says Admetus at the end. Maybe that expresses neither celebration nor defeat, but a simple fact. He has come to know a happiness without uplift. Ordinary life.

Notes

1. See Agamben 1998 for the way this sense of sovereignty unfolded through twentieth-century politics and political theory.

2. On the staging of supplication, see Telò in this volume.

3. Aristotle, *Problems* 11.13, 900a20; 11.32, 900b36.

4. Aristotle, *Poetics* 1455a22–5. Developed further by Quintilian 6.2 and 10.7, with Gurd 2007, 46.

5. See Aristotle, *Rhetoric* 3.1413b21ff. on the importance of being able to vary one's tone to say the same lines in different ways.

6. See Boyarin in this volume.

7. See Pickard-Cambridge, Gould, and Lewis 1988, 135–8 for the standard overview.

CHAPTER 10
ION—INTO THE QUEER IONISPHERE
Kirk Ormand

Queer Texts

One of the many advantages of the notion of queer is that it functions as an inclusive term, allowing a wide range of non-normative behaviors, identities, and political stances to adopt it in a mode of resistance. Because queerness is rigorously non-identitarian, it seems that a range of non-hegemonic social stances—and particularly oppressed identities involving the body—can claim queerness.[1] Indeed, to police the boundaries of what might be considered "queer" becomes an oxymoron, both because the police have traditionally not been queer-friendly, and because queerness consists in part in confounding boundaries; as Madhavi Menon says, "One is not queer by acts and chronologies alone. One cannot be queer while insisting on barricading queerness" (2011, 10). And yet ... and yet. I want to resist reading the *Ion* as queer, to suggest instead that the *Ion* is anachronistically neoliberal: I argue that the *Ion* borrows all the trappings of queer identity in order to firmly establish, for the Athenians, the status quo and to enact its future as such. Exemplifying a perverse meta-level of the "queer art of failure" (Halberstam 2011), this chapter stages the impossibility of a queer reading, as it were.

In denying that *Ion* is queer, I do not insist on a strict chronologism. We see ancient texts as queer, in part, expressly because they leap over chronological boundaries, but queerness must be more specific than simply an anti-normative stance. Many texts buck the norms of the culture that produced them. For a text to be queer, it also has to strike *us* as queer, in some way—to challenge or violate our cis-hetero-normative standards, especially as they relate to bodies, in the moment of reception. Ancient texts, in other words, are queer not in a strictly historicist reading, nor in a strictly contemporary one, but in the interaction between the ancient modes of thought and our own.[2]

What, then, are our requirements for a text to be considered queer? Writing in 2011, Teresa de Lauretis began an exploration of this question (244):

> I may provisionally call queer a text of fiction—be it literary or audiovisual—that not only works against narrativity, the generic pressure of all narrative toward closure and the fulfillment of meaning, but also pointedly disrupts the referentiality of language and the referentiality of images ... a further and, to my mind, not sufficient but necessary specification: a queer text carries the inscription of sexuality as something more than sex.

We see, then, two critical components of queerness in a text: a resistance to the production of meaning according to the usual modes of argument and reference—what we might call a disruption of signification; and an interaction with the body (most often through non-normative sexuality) that creates disruptive meaning in other realms (the social, the political).[3] The first of these components has been most forcefully championed by Lee Edelman, who sees queerness as a kind of denial of signification especially in so far as narrative coherence allows one to posit a future: "[T]he queer comes to figure the bar to every realization of futurity, the resistance, internal to the social, to every social structure or form" (2004, 4).[4] Edelman's reading has, to be sure, met critics who find it too restricted and too negative, and who posit queerness precisely in a future that we have not yet attained. I think here especially of Muñoz and the idea of a queer utopia: "The not-quite-conscious is the realm of potentiality that must be called on, and insisted on, if we are ever to look beyond the pragmatic sphere of the here and now, the hollow nature of the present" (2009, 21). But even Muñoz, in opposing Edelman's more negative "antirelational" approach, posits queerness as an idea that cannot be fully represented. It is utopian precisely in so far as it is unrealizable using the tools of the present.[5]

To this heady mix, I would like to add one more concept, what I think of as the persistent double bind of queer embodiment. More than twenty years ago, David Halperin discussed an idea of power defined by Michel Foucault, in which power is "not a substance but a relation" (1995, 16). This understanding of power requires that we accept that acts of gay liberation (and analogous movements) take place within new structures of governmental, medical, and social control that also serve to oppress, "for the effect of sexual liberation"—as Halperin puts it— "has been not, or not only, to *free* us to express our sexuality but to *require* us to express—freely of course—our sexuality" (20). I will raise this double bind again later in this essay; I see variations on it in recent work on trans* and racial queerness, and in an interesting way I think the *Ion*'s deployment of categories of identity might be seen to invoke it for modern readers.

The Queer Foundation of Athenian Citizens

Ion is fundamentally a play about the production of Athenians as a closed and coherent race, established by blood ties. In the Athenian imaginary, the lines between citizens and non-citizens were clearly demarcated, even if not visible to the naked eye: Athenians were those descended from a race of originary founders, and there was no easy or regular process to become a naturalized citizen. Resident aliens, called "metics" (from a Greek word meaning "one who shares a house"), were regular members of the social system but, with rare exceptions, could not acquire full citizenship rights.

Underlying this strict definition of citizenship is the bizarre but absolutely accepted narrative of the first kings of Athens, who were said to be literally born from the Athenian soil—autochthonous, as we say. The story, which fulfills many of our requirements for a queer text, goes as follows: Hephaestus, a god known as a craftsman, conceived of an overwhelming sexual desire for Athena, the somewhat gender-bending, perpetually virgin, motherless daughter of Zeus. As Hephaestus pursued Athena—and she resisted—he prematurely ejaculated onto Athena's thigh. Athena wiped the offending seed off with a tuft of wool, which she threw onto the earth; thus Hephaestus impregnated *the earth itself* (Gaia), who gave birth in time to Erichthonius. Athena received the baby from Gaia, and entrusted him, hidden in a basket, to the three daughters of Cecrops—an earlier king of Athens, also autochthonous. The daughters were given strict instructions not to look in the basket, but of course they did—and seeing either the baby as a monster with snakes for legs, or seeing the baby protected by snakes, went mad and threw themselves from the Acropolis to their deaths. Through this narrative, as Nicole Loraux has shown, the birth of Erichthonius bridges the gap between autochthonous birth and sexual reproduction, and he becomes a son both of the Athenian earth, and of Athena herself (1993, 37–71). Crucially, Athenian imaginary made use of this story of sexual assault to order the fundamental structures of civic society, in the form of citizenship: Athenians were descended, metaphorically at least, from the semi-autochthonous Erichthonius. Resident aliens did not share this bloodline, and would always be strangers to the city of Athens to some extent (Kasimis 2012, 234). This story is referred to repeatedly in *Ion* (see especially 265–74). Ion, as things will turn out, is a direct descendent of Erichthonius through his mother Creusa, and his birth echoes that of Erichthonius. But he takes a winding path to reach this realization.

Ion is thus expressly concerned with the myth of the Erechthonid bloodline, and is perhaps one of the easiest of Euripides' plays to read as queer. In an early essay, written long before the first instance of the term "queer theory," Loraux laid out the play's kinky political trappings: the play is "a drama about citizenship in which not a single character is a citizen, and in which it is the women who embody legitimacy and slaves who speak for the city, while the eponymous hero has no name, as befits the child of a woman; in a word, a drama that tells of all the ways to be an Athenian outside Athenian orthodoxy" (1993, 201). The play, as Loraux, Froma Zeitlin, Victoria Wohl, and others have shown, is a carefully perverse investigation into the formation of Athenian political identity, and especially the identity of Athenians as *Ionian*, the descendants of Ion (cf. also Foucault 2010, 78). In order to establish this political-familial identity, the drama revolves around the identity of its title character, and formulates that identity as contradictory, contingent, and dependent on the characters (and audience) maintaining a series of open secrets.[6]

Ionic Identity

As often in Greek tragedy, the audience of the play knows what the characters onstage do not. We learn from a prologue spoken by the god Hermes that Ion was born when Creusa, the only surviving daughter of the king of Athens and direct descendant of Erichthonius, was raped by the god Apollo. She abandoned her child in a cave on the Acropolis, and though Hermes transported him to Delphi (on Apollo's orders) nobody onstage is aware of this fact. The truth comes out only through a tortuous 1,300 lines of chance meetings, near misses, and deliberate misdirections.

When we first meet Ion, he literally has no identity. He does not know who his parents are, and declares that he is "motherless and fatherless" (109). He is living and working as a temple attendant at Delphi, and ironically calls Apollo "father" (136), not realizing that this is literally true. Though he will turn out to be a direct descendant of the Athenian royal line, he has been displaced to Delphi and does not know his homeland. It will moreover turn out that a priestess of Apollo at the temple has kept secret a basket of tokens that were with Ion when he was brought to the temple—the tokens that will eventually prove his familial identity, and genealogical birthright as a king of Athens (1340–52). Everything about him has been socially displaced and made into a secret.

The first social identity that is granted to Ion, the one that will give him his name and his political standing, is provided indirectly by Apollo, through Xuthus. Xuthus is the king of Athens, but not a native of Athens; he married Creusa after providing military assistance to the city, but the two of them have been childless, which is why they came to Delphi in the first place. When Xuthus consults the oracle of Apollo about his childless state, the oracle tells him that the first person he meets on leaving the temple will be his son (527–37). He meets Ion, and after a confusing conversation, conveys the contents of the oracle to him. He simultaneously gives Ion his name, from the act of meeting him as he came out (the participle for "going" in Greek is *iôn*; 661–2). Ion, confused, has two critical questions: "Your own son, or a gift of others?" which Xuthus answers with supreme ambiguity: "A gift, but my own" (537). This opposition between being a "gift" (*dôron*) and being born from Xuthus will be repeated throughout the play, thus confounding the putatively clear distinction between blood right and adoption. As Xuthus' son, Ion is both born and made, the very tension that we ascribe to most social identities. But Ion's second question, and ironic deduction, is even more to the point (540–3):

> *Ion* From what mother was I born to you? *Xuthus* I cannot say. *Ion* Did Phoebus (Apollo) not say? *Xuthus* I was pleased with this, and did not ask that. *Ion* Then I was born from the earth as mother! *Xuthus* The ground does not bring forth children.

In line 543, Ion's conclusion that he is born from the earth is, to the Athenian imagination, ironically correct; he is the descendant of the autochthonous royal lines. At this moment, however, Ion understands this comment as a joke; if he does not know who his mother is, then he has, in a sense, no mother—which, if true, would make him not a citizen of Athens. His bitter statement thus contains both ends of the spectrum: he is literally the descendant of the Athenian soil, and he is an illegitimate interloper with no mother. We might indeed see this moment of belonging/not belonging as analogous to modern queer identities, particularly to the extent that Ion's real identity is literally latent, hidden from both Ion and Xuthus.[7] Over the next twenty lines or so of dialogue, however, Xuthus and Ion abandon this line of reasoning and establish that long ago, Xuthus raped an anonymous young woman from Delphi, and the two conclude—wrongly—that Ion was born of that union.

Ion's real birth identity is a confusing double of the identity that he receives from Xuthus. As we learn no less than six times in the course of the play, Ion was born after Apollo raped his mother Creusa, who exposed him in a cave on the Athenian acropolis.[8] Since the audience knows Ion's birth identity from the prologue, when Xuthus adopts him in Delphi we can easily read that social identity as a displacement, if not queer. It is a false identity, arbitrarily assigned to him through the political mechanism of adoption, and the apparent chance (*tuchê*) of his meeting with Xuthus. More to the point, Ion imagines how this identity will look to the Athenian people, and as he sees himself through their eyes, he adopts an alienated subject position. In a speech that begins, famously, "Matters that are seen from afar, and those seen up close, do not appear with the same form" (585–6), he goes on to describe himself as a stranger in the land of his birth: "I will intrude, having acquired a double sickness, being the son of a stranger, and myself of illegitimate birth . . . if I should desire to be someone in the first rank of the city, I will be hated by the powerless" (591–6). In social terms, Ion is acutely aware of how others will see him in this political reality where he does not belong. We are, perhaps, not far from the queer phenomenology that Sara Ahmed describes, of non-white and mixed-race bodies and their experience in a world that is "oriented around" whiteness (2006, ch. 3).

Ion's political self-distancing, however, has a more specific historical meaning in the context of the play. Because Ion believes himself to be the illegitimate son of a woman from Delphi, he realizes that he will not have full citizenship rights in Athens, even if adopted by Xuthus. He would be, in technical terms, a *metic*, and Ion calls attention to this fact by saying that he must learn who his mother is: "and may the woman who bore me be an Athenian so that right to free speech (*parrhêsia*) may exist for me from my mother. For if a person comes into a pure city as a stranger, he may be a citizen in name, but he has an enslaved mouth, and does not have free speech" (672–5). In other words, Ion recognizes how fully out of place he will be in Athens.[9] He will have political standing but be a social outcast, so much so that he initially concludes that he would rather stay in Delphi, occupying the identity of temple servant with no familial or political ties whatsoever (645–9).

What neither Ion nor Creusa knows at this intermediate point is that Creusa really is Ion's mother (and that Xuthus is not his father). This fundamental misapprehension leads to significant moments of peril in the plot: first, Creusa uses poison from her father to try to kill Ion, thinking that he is the son of another woman, and that he will displace her in her own household. Then Ion, who is rescued by a bit of divine providence, hatches his own plot to kill Creusa, calling her a "foreign woman" (1221), which must have been jarring to the Athenian audience. At this point, a priestess reveals the hidden tokens that were left with the baby Ion some twenty years previously, and by correctly identifying them from memory Creusa establishes that she really is Ion's mother.[10] Ion's previous concerns have been answered, but now the manipulations of identity reach their highest rate of convolution: Ion's mother is not only an Athenian, but in a sense, *the* Athenian, the daughter of the born-from-the-earth king of Athens. Ion should, therefore, have full citizenship rights—except, of course, that Xuthus is still not a native-born Athenian. Ion has two parentages to choose from: he can be the illegitimate son of the king of Athens, or the illegitimate son of the queen of Athens, and neither identity is without problems. As Demetra Kasimis (2012, 236) puts it:

> Yet on both occasions, shortly after each recognition scene, Ion's political standing fluctuates: he moves from a statusless temple servant to an Athenian metic to an autochthonous Athenian back to an Athenian metic. In each case, Ion's political membership is (re-)constituted by some act of concealing or disclosing of status—what is supposed to be mere uncontroversial facticity.

There can be only one solution to this knot of interwoven social and political identities, and this solution is brought about by (literal) divine intervention. Toward the end of the play, Ion asks Creusa why Apollo, if his true father, says that Xuthus is. Once more, Creusa answers his queries with language of gift and birth, here invoking the idea of adoption: "You were not born from him [Xuthus], but Apollo gave you as the son of himself. Just so a friend might give to his friend his own son, as ruler of the house" (1535–6). Ion declares that this answer is insufficient, and is on the verge of entering the temple to ask Apollo himself about his parentage, when Athena comes down, and sets everything straight. Athena echoes Creusa's language, but grafts onto it a larger political purpose: "This woman gave birth to you, and Apollo was the father but he gave you to this man, not because he begot you, but so that you should be thought part of a most well-born house" (1560–2). Ion's personal birthright has now become his political identity.

Perhaps the most important of Athena's injunctions, however, is that Ion must go to Athens as Xuthus' son, hiding his real parentage from his adoptive father: "But now say nothing about this child being born from you so that the idea should take hold of Xuthus pleasantly, and you may go having your own nobility, woman" (1601–3). Only in this way, it appears, can the true descendant of Erichthonius occupy the role of the future king of Athens: he is the right person, in the right place, at the right time, but his legitimacy depends on this act of secrecy and subterfuge. This is the queerest moment of Ion's adventures in identity. At this point in the play, he knows exactly who he is, but in order to occupy his legitimate political identity, he must pretend to be the illegitimate, adopted son of Xuthus, from whom his birth identity is hidden. This role, moreover, is larger than himself. As Athena explains in the same speech, the name Ion will become the name of the Athenian people, who were *Ionians* (1584–6). In this way, the Athenian audience of the drama must participate in Ion's legitimate-but-secret identity; as Wohl explains, this becomes a matter of the audience's desire for the plot to end as the myth required: "Athens's glorious history, which at the beginning of the play we confidently took for granted, by the end emerges as an object of our longing, a longing the play generates, frustrates, and finally satisfies" (2015, 36).

It is an old story, and a familiar story. A boy, on the verge of manhood, discovers that he is not exactly who he always thought he was. He finds his father, who is all too ready to give him a name, an identity, a birthright, and a seat in the family business. But he also finds his mother, who gives him another, secret, much-longed-for identity. As long as he keeps the latter identity a secret from exactly nobody except his father, everything will turn out just fine. He will be a success, his family will flourish, and the family business will become an empire. All that is required is that not one person openly acknowledge the secret: that he occupies his position as CEO legitimately, even though he was given it by nepotism. It is no wonder that Kasimis has seen in this play a structure analogous to the closeting of sexuality: for, as Kasimis argues (citing Sedgwick 1990), it is the act of closeting that "moves sexuality out of an economy of activity and into an economy of knowledge" (2012, 249). Or to cite Foucault, one of the fundamental moments in the medicalization of sexuality was the codification of confession in scientific terms, and that codification required the principle of "a latency intrinsic to sexuality." Under this principle, confession "tended no longer to be concerned solely with what the subject wished to hide, but with what was hidden from himself, being incapable of coming to light except gradually and through the labor of a confession in which the questioner and the questioned each had a part to play" (Foucault 1978, 66). Ion's discovery of his real identity takes place through an agonizing series of interrogations and confessions. But once realized, that identity must be closeted—a seeming political analogy to the process by which nineteenth-century sexologists gave rise to this new, powerful aspect of one's personal identity, to the invention of sexuality itself. Only by simultaneously acknowledging and closeting his identity can Ion fulfill his destined role (Kasimis 2012, 249).

But Is It Queer?

And yet. Ion may be in a closet, but it is a political closet, not one of sexuality or gender identity. Does that trouble us? Despite the fact that an act of rape—allegedly a secret, but spoken of repeatedly—is the initiator of this drama, there is nothing pertaining to sexual drives in the definition of Ion's identity. In other words, one of the fundamental aspects of queerness is its use of a political metaphor to define the sexual self (de Lauretis 244). The *Ion* is concerned not with how Ion will function sexually or in a gender-non-normative way, but how he will negotiate his public and secret familial identities. To be sure, phenomenological theorists like Ahmed have seen race in queer terms along such lines, but even there we are dealing with questions of embodiment, of sensing that one's own physical self does not belong in the ethnonormative environment. Ion, by contrast, *does* belong.

Perhaps even more important is the fact that in terms of structures of power, Ion seems not so much queer as an inversion of queer. That is, whether the queer is expressed in terms of sexuality, trans* identity, race, or some combination of these categories, the person who is queer (but not openly so) is generally thought to be queer because they are hiding the non-normative aspect of themselves in order to fit into the straight world. They pass while maintaining a latent queer self. Ion, by contrast, must end the drama pretending to be a *metic*, a resident alien of somewhat marginalized status, but is hiding the fact that he really is an Athenian by birth. The identity that he is hiding, then, is the one that guarantees his authority, not the one that risks making him an outcast; his "latent" identity quite literally authorizes his status in the city and in Xuthus and Creusa's family. Though Kasimis has productively compared the status of *metics* to the idea of closeted sexual identities, as she points out, ultimately the play "does not focus on a man with the wrong blood who nevertheless infiltrates Athenian society undetected by virtue of his active participation in the polis's institutions" (2012, 250). Ion is not an illegal alien who does not belong; that is only the role that he plays.

What, then, about the level of discourse? To be sure, *Ion* creates a fiction whereby the natural identity of all Athenians is the product of a kind of open secret. But in so doing, the play creates the present of the Athenian audience as the future of the dramatic action, and uses each to reinforce the other. It is not a coincidence that Creusa and Xuthus come to Delphi in search of children: they must have a child, and that child must be Ion for the Athenian state to come into being, for the drama that the audience watches to take place. If, as Edelman suggests, "*queerness* names the side of those *not* 'fighting for the children,' the side outside the consensus by which all politics confirms the absolute value of reproductive futurism" (2004, 3), then *Ion* places itself firmly on the side of reproductive futurism. Not only will Ion lead to the production of Ionian Athenian citizens, but once he returns to Athens with Xuthus and Creusa, they will have children of their own, who will become the progenitors of the Dorians and Achaians (1587–93). This is not just a matter of children, but is a question of children as producers of social significance: the story of Ion and his miraculous identity functions in this play to bolster the idea of Athens as natural by birth, as the offspring of autochthonous ancestors.

Queerness is also determined in part by its relation to power. And here, perhaps most critically, is the point at which *Ion* begins to look neoliberal. As Halperin explains, "Modern liberalism . . . has championed an ethic and an ideal of personal freedom while making the exercise of that freedom conditional upon personal submission to new and insidious forms of authority, to evermore deeply internalized mechanisms of constraint" (1995, 19). *Ion* would seem to trouble the idea of political identity as determined by birth, but ultimately it does not question the form of power that those structures hold. At the penultimate moment of the play, Ion still does not quite believe Creusa—he suspects that this story of having had sex with Apollo is a subterfuge, hiding an illegitimate affair with a mortal man (1523–8), and he threatens to question Apollo directly (1547–9). It is at that moment that Athena steps forward and stops that act of questioning. She tells Ion that Apollo is his father, and reveals the regenerative future that I have been discussing. Unsettling though this may be, Ion accepts Athena's pronouncement, and Creusa declares herself pleased with Apollo's past actions. Ion's words here are worth examining: "O Pallas, daughter of greatest Zeus, without distrust we have received your words, and I believe that I am the son of Loxias (Apollo) as father, and this woman. Indeed, this was not unbelievable before" (1606–8). In the popular translation of R. F. Willetts in the Chicago series, a stage direction just before these words indicates that they are to be delivered "ironically."[11] The direction for ironic delivery is Willetts's attempt to resolve a tension in these words, the tension that springs from the previous 1,500 lines of misdirection and subterfuge, juxtaposed in the end with Ion and Creusa's capitulation to Athena's declaration of the Way Things Are. In this play, Ion's overdetermined birthright ultimately serves to establish the status quo; Ion's final moment of doubt becomes only the stage cue for Athena to close down any suggestion of a remainder, any hint of queer identity that might cast the Athenian system of civic genealogy into doubt.

I spoke at the start of this essay of the queer double bind, and perhaps we can think of Ion as queer, or queer-analogous, in these terms. One of the strongest expressions of this sort of catch-22 has recently been expressed by Grace Lavery, discussing the ways in which trans* queer folk sometimes express positions "willingly," because doing so has been made a condition of their existence (2019, 125):

> The speech act *I identify as a woman* has been, it will be remembered, extracted from the trans woman as a condition of transition; it was not, so to speak, *spoken* freely, even though it was *chosen* freely. It was a speech act that we might characterize as felicitous but faithless: in context, it works perfectly and is understood by all, but it is, nonetheless, extorted from trans people as a condition of medicalization.[12]

We might see Ion's acceptance of Athena's pronouncement as analogous to these sorts of moments. Though just a few lines before he had rejected Creusa's virtually identical explanation of events, once Athena explains the situation, he declares that he believes this advantageous state of affairs, and indeed, suggests that it always was believable— rewriting the past in the service of his future. But if the structure is analogous, the relations of power are not: Ion accepts, and agrees to hide, a position of authority, not a position of oppression. Though the play toys with the idea that Ionian identity is contingent, merely the product of a vertiginous series of chance occurrences, ultimately the play denies those contingencies to the disenfranchised. Ion *is* the son of Creusa, he accepts the pronouncement of Athena, and, though we can find rifts and cracks in the text if we look hard enough, *Ion* guarantees the normative Athenian present, and expansion into empire.

Notes

1. See Edelman 2004, 4; de Lauretis 2011, 248–9; and Halperin 2019, 418. See Introduction.
2. See Halperin 2002, 23. On queer unhistoricism, see Introduction.
3. See Introduction.
4. See Halperin, 2019, 418 on the "categorical ... illegibility" of queer love. See Freccero in this volume.
5. See Edelman 2022.
6. See Kasimis 2012 and Wohl 2015, 23.
7. Kasimis 2012, 235; see Lavery 2019, 130.

8. Not coincidentally, he was left in a basket, a clear echo of the basket in which Erichthonius was placed. See Zeitlin 1996, 299.

9. See Foucault 2010, 104, and Kasimis 2012, 233 and 236.

10. The fact that Creusa does not look into the basket to identify the tokens makes this scene into a successful re-enactment, in imaginary terms, of the revelation of Erichthonius (discussed above); Ion has become the new Erichthonius, and Creusa replaces the earlier, unsuccessful daughters of Cecrops.

11. On irony, see Telò in this volume.

12. See also Deihr in this volume.

PART IV
RELATIONS

CHAPTER 11
HERACLES—HOMOSEXUAL PANIC AND IRRESPONSIBLE READING
Alastair J. L. Blanshard

Wife fatally strangled by husband who planned new life in Australia with gay lover

Mirror (July 22, 2020)

Russian immigrant pleads insanity in murder of lesbian lover's husband

New York Daily News (June 8, 2009)

Foreigner claims insanity for murdering wife and children, plans new life in Athens with so-called "friend"

Plot summary of *Heracles*

Putting Heracles on the Couch

Among the many terrors that the queer elicits is the threat that it poses to the domestic. The most dangerous form of queer is the one that passes, the one that lurks in the bosom of the family while plotting its destruction. Nothing brings out this fear more than stories about "seemingly straight" actors whose true nature is only revealed too late in scenes of horrific bloodshed. These fears haunt the normative, requiring endless rehearsal and recapitulation. As the tabloid headlines above attest, even the merest hint that homosexuality is at play in cases of domestic homicide instantly reorientates and reinvigorates the narrative. Discussions of gender give way to allegations of desire. History becomes rewritten as one of deceit and duplicity—every action rethought, every gesture revisited, every absence queried anew. The protagonist becomes alien, a person who stands apart, all too knowable in their unknowability.

In bringing out the potential tabloid qualities of the plot of *Heracles*, this essay shines a light on the queer potential that lurks within this play. This is a play that interrogates key concepts that lie at the heart of the entanglement of queer/straight identity.[1] Through its relentless ironies it queers subjectivity, through its disorders it queers bodies, through its invocation of the tragic it queers reproduction, and through its disavowals it queers relationships. In its increasingly desperate attempts to define friendship, it compresses the homosocial hard on the homosexual.

Among all this queerness, I want to examine what happens when we read or perform *Heracles* as a text of "homosexual panic." In evoking the phrase "homosexual panic,"

I want to keep two complementary definitions of the term in view. The first is the general sense of societal anxiety caused by the public presence of queer desires, and which finds its way into concepts such as the "gay panic" defense.[2] In thinking about this aspect, I want to think about ways in which the play operates to highlight issues of queer practice in order to alarm the desires of the audience. The second definition that I keep in play is the specific psychiatric condition of "homosexual panic" from which this first definition is ultimately derived. In diagnosing Heracles' madness as a case of "homosexual panic," I want to see what this brings into view and what it occludes, what horizons it opens up, and what claims it facilitates. I want to lean into the troubling and problematic neuroses that animate the idea of "homosexual panic." What follows is, in many ways, a thoroughly irresponsible—and thus quintessentially queer—reading.[3]

"Homosexual panic" is a curious condition. Although grounded in Freudian ideas and typologies, especially in relation to Freud's connection of paranoia with the homosexual component of libido, this condition received its most elaborate discussion in Edward Kempf's *Psychopathology* (1920). Kempf was an enthusiastic follower of Freud and one of the key promoters of Freudian theory in the United States. Kempf's vision of this condition would become so persuasive that "homosexual panic" would also become known as "Kempf's disease." In the chapter entitled "The Psychopathology of the Acute Homosexual Panic: Acute Pernicious Dissociation Neuroses," Kempf laid out what he regarded as the key features of the condition. These were summarized by Hinsie and Shatzky in their *Psychiatric Dictionary* (1953) in the following terms: "an acute schizophrenic episode, characterized by intense fear, marked excitement, and paranoid ideas; usually of short duration, occurring in individuals whose homosexuality is unconscious." The condition survived in psychiatric literature until the sweeping revisions on the topic of homosexuality that attended the publication of the seventh printing of the *Diagnostic and Statistical Manual of Mental Disorders* (*DSM*)-II in 1974, and the subsequent further refinement of the topic in *DSM*-III. It now survives only in an attenuated form in *DSM*-V under section 302.9 ("unspecified paraphilic disorder") which reworks the classification offered in *DSM*-IV (1994) of "a persistent and marked distress about sexual orientation."

As a psychiatric concept, "homosexual panic" has limited diagnostic use. However, as an animating myth that agglomerates "our medical, social, legal, and religious homophobic attitudes" (Chuang and Addington 1988, 616), it proves useful to think with. In particular, what I want to explore is the seemingly easy susceptibility of *Heracles* to a diagnosis of "homosexual panic" and what this might illustrate about the nature of Heracles' masculinity and homosociality. Let us start with an observation about the apparent absence of interpretive violence—*Heracles* is, after all, a play that asks us to consider the presence and absence of violence in all its forms—in the imposition of such a diagnostic frame onto this text. The presentation of his bout of madness following the strenuousness of his labors along with the attribution of his madness to an external agency in the form of the goddess Lyssa, the nature that the madness takes, and the final turn to suicidal despondency are all features associated with "homosexual panic." Indeed, the very first patient offered as a case study of "homosexual panic" by Kempf ("Case PD-13") shares a number of physical and emotional characteristics with the hero. PD-13 is described, among other things, as "rather well-built, but undersized." "He had never been able to adapt himself to society, and had attended school irregularly, had a poor education, [and] was fond of playing truant"; in addition, he "was unable to submit to the dictations of an employer, feeling that it referred to some inferiority." Other sufferers are a similar Heraclean type. Some other cases, we might note, include Case PD-20 "an illiterate, irresponsible soldier … a shiftless worker … [who] wasted all his earnings in carousals and alcoholics" and Case PD-21 "a soldier … [who] said he learned with great difficulty … [and] indulged in alcoholic debauches." Among such characters, Heracles does not look out of place.

Similarities also exist between the circumstances of Heracles' madness and the types of situations in which "homosexual panic" is said to occur. Triggers for bouts of "homosexual panic" include fatigue, misfortune, and homesickness. It is a cocktail of emotions and feelings that maps onto Heracles' state as he emerges from his long sojourn away from his family and the ardors of his trip to the underworld. Amphitryon awards him the title of *ho poluponos* ("the man of many toils" 1190) and the exhaustion of Heracles is a theme that runs throughout the play.

Focusing specifically on the form that the "panic" can take, we should note that its primary form includes "delusions about, and hallucinations of, situations, objects, and people" (Kempf 1920, 478). Significantly, especially for our reading of Lyssa, in almost all cases, such delusions are "disowned by the *ego* as a foreign influence, and the ideas and visions, or sensations … are treated as being due to foreign influence" (478). We might also note that although these paranoid delusions assume a variety of different appearances, within them, snakes ("the phallus symbolized") are a regular feature, an element worth bearing in mind given the description of Lyssa as "hundred-headed with serpents" (883–4). Case PD-15 describes visions of being tormented by snakes that "appeared all about him." Like Heracles, PD-15 reported to his doctor that he had been tormented as a child by snakes.

Finally, Kempf notes that "suicides in such conditions, usually by cutting the throat, hanging, or plunging on the head, are quite common. I know of two young men who killed themselves by several days of terrific pounding of their heads and bodies; another by plunging from an elevation onto his head" (1920, 491). Again, we might note the congruency with the Euripidean Heracles' desire to die by stabbing himself with a sword or leaping off a cliff (1148–9).

The only missing element in the syndrome is, of course, the patient's "unconscious homosexuality." And here it is perhaps worth dwelling on the fact that it is only a refusal to see Heracles as queer that prevents us from diagnosing *Heracles* as a paradigmatic case of "homosexual panic." There is a lot at stake in such a refusal. We need to hold fast on Heracles' straightness if we wish to avoid the queer diagnosis. However, seeing Heracles as unquestionably/authentically/irrevocably "straight" becomes an increasingly fraught activity as the play progresses. Indeed, if we code Heracles as "straight," he perversely ends up standing alone in a sea of queerness.

Piling Up the Queerness

The queerness of this play is signaled from its very first line where Amphitryon, in a remarkable and unprecedented moment of self-definition, introduces himself as the "bed-sharer" (*sullektros*) of Zeus. The term comes as an unexpected jolt in the play. Given that the scene opens with Amphitryon seeking succor at the altar of Zeus and that such suppliant openings are almost a cliché of Euripidean staging, we are expecting a word that invokes ideas of rescue or supplication, not sexual congress, to follow his invocation of Zeus.

From the beginning, Amphitryon wrong-foots us with imagery that he refuses to give up. Lycus ruthlessly mocks Amphitryon for his boast that "he was united by marriage to Zeus" (149). But that does not stop Amphitryon from using the same language later in the play when he again describes Zeus and himself as "joined in the same marriage" (339). Some commentators have chosen not to be alarmed by this turn of phrase. "The relationship is commonly most respectable: Amphitryon uses *sullektros* proudly," remarks G. W. Bond (1988 ad loc.). Proud is right, but respectable seems a stretch. The use of a similar construction (*homosporos*) to describe the incestuous relationship between Laius and Oedipus might give us pause in seeing this language as too unproblematic (*Oedipus the King* 260 and 460).

Euripides' only other use of a similar compound term outside of *Heracles* supports a reading of *syllektros* as a queer signifier. In *Orestes*, Tyndareus is also described as sharing the same bed as Zeus (476). The context is telling. As David Youd remarks in this volume, *Orestes* is a play that is driven by a "widespread failure of conjugality." It is a play that skewers the heteronormative at every turn. Just as *Orestes* makes an obscenity of marital relations, so, too, does *Heracles* expose the fundamental violence, strangeness, and horror that lurks in cycles of heterosexual reproduction.

Questions of family dominate the opening speeches of *Heracles*. Yet, if we are expecting uncomplicated genealogies and respectable lineages, we are sorely disappointed. Amphitryon's start is promising ("My father was Alcaeus, son of Perseus, and I am father of Heracles" 2–3), but matters quickly unravel. These confident patronymics hide an uncomfortable truth. Amphitryon may know his father, but nobody knows for sure his mother (see [Apollodorus], *Library* 2.4.5). Already, by the second line, mothers are proving disposable (awkward). This point is emphasized by the turn Amphitryon's speech suddenly takes toward Thebes. Once again, mortal mothers are proving unnecessary. Amphitryon determinedly reminds us that Thebes is a city of the "earth-born" (4), no fleshy wombs required.[4] And here he introduces a theme that will swell as the play develops—being part of a family is a murderous business. To reproduce is to commit yourself to a cycle of violence. The earthborn men are the perfect exemplars of this. Procreate and kill[5]—they exist only to do these things. In the tight compression of Amphitryon's speech, murder and reproduction are separated by only a few words. These men are born, slaughter one another, and "stock the city of Cadmus with children" (6–7).

Death dances with reproduction throughout the rest of speech.[6] Megara, daughter of Creon, "son of Menoeceus" (8) enters the story. A woman from the line of Menoeceus!

Now there is a name to conjure with. Nothing says happy families like reminding us that a cousin of Jocasta will soon be entering the stage. Amphitryon cannot stop pointing out to us just how queer this family is. But wait, the speech offers a respite. We are treated, following this mention of Megara, to "a pleasant little picture of Heracles' marriage . . . in the tradition of choral lyric" (Bond 1988, 65). Well, yes, pleasant, but not for long. Three lines later we are once again reminded that murder attends matrimony. This time it is the ill-starred Electryon, another figure who exists "only to beget and die," who comes along to fill out the body count and decorate this scene of domestic bliss with his corpse. Again, we might note myth's carelessness. Did Amphitryon murder Electryon? Was it an accident? No definitive answer exists. The only imperative is to put blood on Amphitryon's hands.

Amphitryon is keen to smear all families with this blood. His description of the family of Lycus shows it to be one similarly reproductive of/in death. Again, the names provide hooks onto which we can hang a tableau of internecine killing as the line of Menoeceus clashes with the line of Lycus. In the figures of Dirce and Amphion and Zethus, we are encouraged to contemplate one of myth's most macabre spectacles, namely nephews tying their aunt to a bull in order that she be trampled to death—a death of such queerness it came literally to embody the spectacular. The logical, cyclical nature of this violence is stressed in which "murder quenches murder" (40). There is no way out of this cycle except more killing (43–4).

"Joining in marriage . . . is a great evil" (35–6), Amphitryon concludes. Marriage leads to children and children lead to murder. In making his observations, Amphitryon has throughout his speech emphasized the queerness of his speaking position. He reminds us that he barely counts among men. He is "useless" as a man (41). His role as father has been supplanted by his feminine role as nurse (*trophos*) and housekeeper (*oikouros*). In his opening speech, then, Amphitryon attempts to triangulate queer positionality, heterosexual reproduction, and violent death. In doing so, he embarks on a project that is, in one sense, very familiar to queer critics from Arthur Rimbaud to Lee Edelman and beyond. Indeed, in exposing the ghastliness of tragedy's reproductive futurity, Amphitryon is aligned with the intellectual agenda set out most provocatively in Edelman's *No Future*. Everyone clearly wants children, but as Amphitryon points out, they just prove a catalyst for the enactment of violence and hate. What then stops Amphitryon in joining Edelman in saying "fuck the social order and the Child in whose name we are collectively terrorized"? What makes him, despite the logical consequences of his arguments, never fully repudiate this tragedy's reproductive futurism?[7] The answer lies in hope. As Megara constantly complains, he loves the light too much (90–1).

From its opening, then, *Heracles* proves susceptible to a queer agenda. Indeed, at times *Heracles* seems positively brazen in its queering. There is no more palpable example of the extraordinary transgressive ambitions of this play than in its queering of the bow of Heracles. Queer this and you queer the entire Trojan War. Sophocles had spelled out the stakes earlier in *Philoctetes*. Seize the bow and you seize the city, it is on this bow that the fate/fame of Troy rests. *Philoctetes* plays up the penetrative power of the bow. It is simultaneously nurturing and unstoppable. "Will you allow me to worship it as a god?" Neoptolemus asks (657). The line is duplicitous, but the reverence feels real. Rarely in Greek drama has a physical object elicited such desire.[8] Watching *Philoctetes* is an exercise in watching an unseemly scramble over a barely disguised phallus. It is for this reason that the unmanning of the bow in *Heracles* is so potent. Seminal even. As Lycus and Amphitryon make clear in their *agôn* in the transvaluing and the revaluing of the bow, masculinity is interrogated. Lycus says (157–64):

> Worthless though he is, Heracles has acquired a reputation for courage spearing beasts, but in other respects there is not an ounce of bravery in him. His left arm has never sported a shield, nor has he ever been face to face with the tip of a spear, no, instead with a bow, the worst of weapons, he has always been ready to flee. A bow provides no test of a man's courage—that is done by standing fast, not flinching from the rapid damage done by enemy spears, and instead keeping formation.

Lycus does not hold back here. His target is the bow. Heracles is collateral damage. He is even prepared to concede that there might be some value in Heracles when he puts beasts to death by the spear (158). It is his use of the bow that makes him unmanly. Such disparagement of archery is a common topos of aristocratic prose. Many people would be only too happy to endorse Lycus' rhetoric.

In extolling so firmly the hoplitic values of holding one's position in the line of the phalanx and not flinching from the spear, Lycus deploys exactly the same rhetorical strategies as Creon in his *agôn* with Haemon in Sophocles' *Antigone*. For Creon, as Lycus, it is the man who remains where he is placed against the storm of spears that shows his justice and his goodness (669–71). Such an invocation of Creon operates on a number of levels. First, in general terms, it invites us to contemplate how we are going to figure this play within the wider sweep of Theban history. It knits the play into the web of previous dramatic imaginings. In doing so, it reinforces previous points about the cyclical nature of violence. Lycus replaces Creon who replaced Oedipus who replaced Laius.

It also invites us to re-read *Heracles* again anew. In more specific terms, this allusion invites us to reflect again on an earlier passage in the play, namely the last time that Creon was mentioned. This is Megara's description of her father. In Megara's opinion, her father, Creon, was extremely fortunate (64). The sentiment is conventional; what makes this passage so extraordinary are the terms in which Megara expresses Creon's good fortune. Namely, what made Creon so fortunate was that he was a man for whom "the long spears leapt in lust for the bodies of the blessed" (65–6). It is a deeply erotic image. Long shafts lunging toward beautiful (how could the blessed not be beautiful?) bodies. If we saw something of the phallus in Sophocles' bow, Euripides' *Heracles* rejigs the Symbolic order and reclaims this role for the spear with gusto.

Nothing that Amphitryon subsequently says alters this shift. His defense of the bow fails to reinstate its status as masculine signifier. If anything, it confirms Lycus' judgment.

Amphitryon defends the bow on the basis of its cunning: it is the wiliest of inventions (*to pansophon ... heurêma* 170). Cleverness is hardly the most masculine attribute (*pace* Odysseus). His claim that "a hoplite is a slave" sounds promising until you get to the end of the line "... of his weapons" (190). The mastery of the spear remains undisturbed. Most tellingly, at the end of his speech, it is a spear, and not a bow, that Amphitryon wishes that he had in his hand to challenge Lycus and send him packing (233–5); reinscribing that running from the spear is a sign of cowardice, not cleverness. The Chorus echoes these sentiments, also wishing that they had a spear in their hand. "O right arm, how you long (*potheis*) for the spear" (268). Masculine desire and the spear remain firmly wedded.

Heracles is shot through with such queerness. We have not touched upon other aspects of the play that could, for example, be productively coded as queer, such as its cavalier treatment of myth, the radical, subversive theology of lines 1340–6, or its "flawed" dramatic structure.[9] Instead, let us conclude this discussion of the queerness of the play by noting that above all these specific examples, a general queer aura hangs over this play. We see it in the overarching ironic sensibility that permeates it. Ever since Susan Sontag's "Notes on Camp" (1964), irony has been regarded as a quintessential element in queer sensibility. While Sontag's essay has not gone without criticism, few would challenge its stance on the queerness of irony.[10] Irony is fundamentally queer because it plays with knowledge and knowing, it interrupts relationships of meaning, dislocates strategies of audience identification, and recodes every utterance. This matters for *Heracles* because few tragedies are so relentless in maintaining the audience in such a heightened, unremitting state of ironic awareness.

The audience always knows that murder is on the cards. From the moment she enters onto the stage, Megara is a dead woman walking. Watching *Heracles* is an exercise in waiting for the shoe to drop. Within this environment of delayed horror, language inevitably takes an ironic turn. When Megara declares in her opening speech "I am about to die" (70), we are torn by her simultaneous knowledge and ignorance. Time and again, characters speak lines of unwitting truth. The sentiments are often right, just the context is wrong. The misplaced hopes put on Heracles' return ratchet up and multiply the levels of ironic interchange. How exquisite are the multiple levels of irony when Megara orders her children to "cling to your father's peplos, go, hurry, do not let him go, since he is no less your savior than Zeus the Savior is!" (*epei Dios sôtêros humin ouden esth' hod' husteros* 521–2). How prophetically right these words are. Heracles will prove just as much a savior to these children as the god whose deafness to their plight will facilitate their slaughter. Between the ringing echo of *sôtêros* and *husteros*, irony seals the fate of Heracles' family.

"Cling to your father's peplos." Of course, the children should cling to the garment that is both simultaneously cloak and funeral shroud. Throughout the play costuming exacerbates irony, and there is no more ironic garment than the peplos. Its gender ambiguity, just one of the many ambiguities it carries. As both Nancy Worman (1999) and Rosie Wyles (2013) have observed, costuming plays a particularly significant role through the metatextual signals that it directs to the audience for thinking about the tragic and the theatrical. The "vigorous cloak of flesh" that Heracles wore as young man (1270–1) becomes a veil in which he seeks to hide himself. Within such a metatextual frame, Megara and the children's costuming heightens our sense of the dramatic ironies at play. Time and again, our attention is drawn through diction and register to the way that they are accidentally/appropriately dressed for their upcoming slaughter.

This ironic sensibility reaches its climax in the interchanges between Amphitryon and Lycus following the return of Heracles in which the already high level of irony, at least, doubles if not grows exponentially; the position exacerbated, not least, by the fact that the audience knows that the actor playing Lycus also played Heracles. From the audience to Amphitryon to Lycus there is a sliding scale of knowledge and ignorance with which to calibrate each utterance. When Lycus describes Megara begging uselessly for her life inside (716), he will prove to both spectacularly wrong and spectacularly right. As Lycus goes inside to meet his fate, we remember his opponent Heracles' words before he entered that fatal abode: "What fame shall I have if I fight with a hydra or do battle with a lion at Eurystheus' command, if I do not manage to prevent the death of my children?" (578–81). Pity an audience that knows so much. How can it ever think straight?

Playing Tugboat with Daddy: Some Queer Commitments

Let us now return to the question that we postponed earlier. Among all this queerness, how straight is Heracles? In particular, in what sense is his madness symptomatic of a much more fundamental queerness that flows through him, and which finds its resolution in his connection with Theseus? A starting point might be the observation that, when it comes to Heracles, *eros* and *nosos* often go together.

Discussion of the symptoms of Heracles' madness have traditionally focused on points of intersection with fifth-century BC medical writings (frothing at the mouth, deep breathing, rolling of the eyes, etc.). What symptoms might a reading of the mad scene that is attuned to ideas of "homosexual panic" reveal? First, it would move our critical eye away from the descriptions of the physical symptoms to an analysis of the form of the delusion and the language in which it is expressed. Secondly, it would ask us to consider any latent eroticism in this paranoid delusion. One of the recurrent features of paranoid delusions associated with "homosexual panic" is that they exhibit features that allow the analyst to see the repressed homoeroticism of the subject.

By paying attention, then, to the language of Heracles' delusions as well as the symbolic associations implicit in them, a reading of Heracles' repressed queer desires emerges. A psychoanalytic reading of the delusion would emphasize the metaphors of space at play; how the action moves directly from the "men's room" to the "bedroom." It would see through the athletic fictions that allowed Heracles to perform these acts of violence naked (959). Given previous case histories and their "pernicious oral erotic cravings," it would not miss the palatal pleasures of the undulating tongue in Heracles' triumphant cry of *alala* (981). It would enjoy the challenge of unpacking the polysemous richness of figuring Athena ("the *virgin* goddess") as the agent of deliverance. Above all, it would keep a firm reckoning of the plethora of phallic signifiers that jostle in the fantasy, all those weapons (bow, club), not to mention "the torch carried in the right hand" (928), the crowbar, the pitchfork, the chisel, and, of course—for how could one forget?—*that* column.

Masonry as metaphor. The column is both the scene of the bloody rejection of heteronormative domesticity and the object of salvation. It is the place where the child (or with Edelman "the Child") seeks sanctuary from the death-dealing queer. The text (977–9) relishes the way Heracles hunts the child in terrible circles, whirling round the column, making it the center of their relationship, before Heracles slays the boy with his arrow, wetting the column with the child's lifeblood. Binding himself to the column is of course the only way to end the madness. In his extreme bondage to the column, Heracles finds rest. Seeing Heracles as trapped in queer crisis makes us appreciate how *overdetermined* his heterosexuality has always been. What other hero feels the need to sport the epithet *philogunês*? How did we see the act of deflowering fifty virgins in one night as anything other than *pathological*?

In such an internalist reading, a reading that sees the madness emerging from Heracles' own queer nature rather than an external agency, we would find ourselves in good company. Not just Wilamowitz, but Wilde. For Wilde, Euripides was the poet of the interior self. As he observed in his review of a production of *Alcestis* performed in Oxford in 1887, what distinguishes Euripides as a poet is "his extraordinary psychological insight into the workings of the human mind."[11] The influence of Euripides on Wilde was profound. Wilde's copy of Tyrrell's edition of *Bacchae* is full of passionate underlining and annotation.[12] The famous "handbag" scene in *The Importance of Being Earnest* takes its cue from the recognition scene in *Ion*. However, as Kathleen Riley has shown, it is *Heracles* that Wilde responded to most out of all Greek drama (2018, 178–86). On leaving Oxford, Wilde had initially proposed to the publisher George Macmillan that he produce an edition of the play.[13] While this edition never eventuated, the play continued to resonate with Wilde for the rest of his life. Heracles became a prototype for his suffering queer existence. In particular, it was this play to which Wilde turned during his incarceration in Reading gaol for the crime of gross indecency. In the figure of Heracles, Wilde saw a model for his own explosive passion, tortured regret, and resigned endurance. Heracles became the pattern on which Wilde modeled his own queer modus vivendi.

Of course, in focusing so much on the internal desires exposed in Heracles' madness, we inevitably reduce the agency of Lyssa. The history of the reception of *Heracles* is a history of dissatisfaction with the role of Lyssa.[14] From Seneca onward, we scarcely see her. It is the mad, frenzied Heracles that occupies the spotlight to the exclusion of all others.

Yet, before we jump on this bandwagon, let us examine what demands such a position requires; that is to say, what are its politics? The play neatly dramatizes the commitments that we need to make to buttress a notion of an interiority. If we want to give Heracles a queer inner life, we need to sacrifice female agency. Of course, requiring commitments is nothing new in drama and let us not forget that this is not an undemanding play. Requiring that we both see and do not see Lyssa is just one of a series of commitments that this play has demanded. Its stagecraft has demanded that we suspend time. It has not only required a suspension of disbelief, it has required a suspension of the laws of physics—the scene with *ekkyklema* literally warping space so that the interior becomes the exterior. Requiring Lyssa to operate on a different order of causality seems a trifling matter in comparison.

Trifling, but also tragic. In diminishing Lyssa, we also devalue her queer potential. In our rush to establish Heracles/Theseus as the queer pairing at the center of this play, we blind ourselves to that other queer coupling of Iris/Lyssa.[15] In her capacity to undo the Symbolic order, Lyssa is iconic in her queerness. She cannot be domesticated. She is in the words of Iris, *anumenaios* "unable to be sung into a wedding" (834). She refuses to play by the rules. What god appears *mid-play*? As written, she is so flamboyant, so excessive as to be practically unstageable, requiring hundreds of serpents, invisibility, and a full team of flying horses with which to make her escape. Her very presence alters the register of language, causing the Chorus to exclaim in elevated, mannered diction. She excites the beating heart. Her trochaic tetrameters pick up the tempo in the play, making the drama dance to her beat. She knows how to (literally) bring the house down. All this fabulous potential is lost, if we reduce her from cause to symptom.

Yet, such a move would of course be in keeping with a general trend in *Heracles*, namely its explusion of the feminine. We observed in passing the disappearance of Amphitryon's mother. This is, of course, the least of the female disappearances in this play. We now need to face up to the fact that Heracles' happiness, his union with Theseus—the moment when he gets to play tugboat with daddy—is predicated on murder. This is the uncomfortable and transfixing truth of this play, namely that male homosociality is founded on the corpses of women and children.

In casting the relationship between Heracles and Theseus as "homosocial" rather than "homosexual" and/or "queer" (both categories to which I reserve right to name this relationship), I am, naturally, deliberately evoking Eve Sedgwick who foregrounded the "homosocial" as a sphere of relationships crucial to understanding the operation of queer identity, most notably in her groundbreaking *Between Men* (1985). Two points that emerge from this work are crucial for my understanding of this moment in the play. The first is Sedgwick's notion of "continuum" and it is not difficult to see the slippery continuum between homosociality and homosexuality hard at work here as we dramatize the relationship between Theseus and Heracles. Theseus and Heracles' relationship may be grounded in *philia*, but as Plato's *Lysis* so eloquently demonstrated, the jump between *eros* and *philia* is shorter than you think.[16]

For Sedgwick, it was the radical disruptions in the visibility of this continuum that helped to give texture to the mid-eighteenth- to mid-nineteenth-century novel and later modern discourse on male relationships. In this "the unbrokenness of this continuum is . . . a strategy for making generalizations about, and marking historical differences in, the structure of men's relations with other men" (1985, 2). In this respect, the project and the dynamics that Sedgwick analyzes in *Between Men* shares an affinity with one of the great sources of anxiety in *Heracles*, namely what constitutes *philia*. From its opening this play has worked over the concept of the "friend" in numerous ways. At the end of his first speech, Amphitryon remarks on the difficulty of knowing with clarity (55) what constitutes "a friend." And nothing throughout the rest of the play provides any resolution to this fundamental dilemma. The idea of the "friend" is left open. As a result, as we contemplate what life Heracles and Theseus will have as they go off together, the world seems full of possibilities.

A world of possibilities for everyone, of course, but Megara. And this is the second way that Sedgwick is important for my reading of this play. In the way that Sedgwick framed her discussion within a politics of the male "traffic in women" and the way that "men are able to exchange power and confirm each other's value" (1985, 160), we see most appositely the dynamics of this play at work. Sedgwick reminds us that, when we triangulate the relationship between Heracles, Theseus, and Megara, we should be attentive to the asymmetries of power, desire, and affection. She reminds us that we need to be wise to the gendered economies in which this genre participates. Tragedy does not lament the death of Megara, it lusts for it. Indeed, in the violent elimination of the mediating woman, *Heracles* achieves homosociality's greatest fantasy.

Notes

1. On the queer discomfort with the very idea of identity, see Introduction.
2. For a survey of the major early cases relating to the "gay panic" defense and its underlying jurisprudence, see Tilleman 2010, 1666–8, and Capers 2011, 1278–84.
3. On the theoretical implications of queer reading, see, in general, Introduction.
4. On this theme, see also Andújar in this volume.
5. See Kraus 1998 on the pun between *tiktô* ("to beget") and *kteinô* ("to kill").
6. See also Bassi in this volume.
7. For the commitments to reproductive futurism in this play, see Telò 2020, 114. See also Bassi, Freccero, and Telò in this volume.
8. See Telò 2018.
9. Compare the delightful irony of the queer appropriation (following the novel by Annie Proulx and the film of Ang Lee) of the term "Broke Back" (Urban Dictionary: "A secret relationship between two closeted gay men," "used to describe anything of questionable masculinity") with Murray's famous description of the structure of the play as "broken backed" (1946, 12).
10. For these criticisms of Sontag's essay, see Meyer 1994, esp. 7–11, and Pellegrini 2007, 169–71. See the observations of Castle on the coded nature of Sontag's evocation of homosexuality in the essay (2009, 29–30). On camp, see Olsen and Radcliffe in this volume; on irony, see Freccero and Telò.
11. "The 'Alcestis' at Oxford," *Court and Society Review* 4 (no. 151), 1887, 485–6 quoted in Ross 2013, 33.
12. For discussion of the edition, see Ross 2013, 185–7.

13. Letter to George Macmillan (22/3/1879) reproduced in Holland and Hart-Davis 2000, 78.

14. For the tendency to minimize the role of Lyssa, see Riley 2008, 53–4, 211–14, 288–9, 313, and 353–4.

15. See esp. Rabinowitz and Bullen in this volume.

16. Although shorter for some than others. Cf. Poole's description of the relationship between Heracles and Theseus as a "male friendship that lacked a homosexual dimension" (1990, 134).

CHAPTER 12
ANDROMACHE—CATFIGHT IN PHTHIA
Sarah Olsen

"It is no good," declares Hermione, in Euripides' *Andromache*, "for one man to hold the reins of two women" (177–8). Her use of equine imagery underscores the erotic nature of the relationship that she describes, for images of horses and horse-taming appear across ancient Greek poetry in highly sexualized descriptions of girls and women. The archaic poet Anacreon, for example, envisions his female addressee as an untamed "filly" who needs a "skillful rider" to "mount" her.[1] Hermione, whose own marriage to the hero Neoptolemus is complicated by his concurrent relationship with the enslaved Andromache, thus vividly expresses her discontent with her own marital state: a configuration wherein "one man" enjoys the sexual possession of "two women" (178).

Yet, whether "good" or not, the simultaneous possession of a wife and one or more enslaved concubines is hardly unusual for the heroes of Greek myth. And while Greek literature from the *Iliad* onward attends to the problems arising from such arrangements, Euripides' *Andromache* explores the relationship between women in a polygynous household in a particularly explicit way.[2] The play opens upon a scene of intense domestic drama: Andromache, once the royal wife of the Trojan hero Hector, is now living in Phthia (northern Greece) as the enslaved concubine of Neoptolemus, son of Achilles. Hermione, daughter of Helen and Menelaus, has recently married Neoptolemus and regards Andromache as a treacherous rival. When Neoptolemus departs on a trip to Delphi, the conflict comes to a head, and Andromache takes refuge in a shrine as Hermione seeks to kill her and her young son (fathered by Neoptolemus). After an opening scene and a choral ode, Hermione arrives at the shrine to confront and threaten Andromache, who responds by defending herself and lobbing insults at Hermione (147–273).

This encounter between Andromache and Hermione has been described as a "catfight," a term clearly intended to capture the dramatic, feminine quality of the conflict.[3] It is also a modern term that does ideological work comparable to that of the ancient equine imagery mentioned above: characterizing women as "fillies" or "cats" aligns them with a bestial sexuality, an alluring energy that requires "taming" or domestication. In this chapter, however, I would like to further explore how the concept of "catfight" as a queer theatrical and cinematic form can illuminate the dynamics of Euripides' *Andromache*. To that end, I will first trace the history of the term "catfight" and its relationship to queerness, demonstrating that the modern use of "catfight" to describe interactions between women in polygynous marriages resonates with Euripides' play. I will then turn to the relationship between the catfight and "camp" aesthetics, suggesting that while Hermione insists upon the perversity of Andromache's sexuality, her obsessive hostility to her rival ultimately exposes the queerness of her own impulses and orientations. For the purposes of this analysis, I define as "queer" those forms and relationships that challenge, undermine, or unsettle normative social and familial structures, whether explicitly sexual or not, and I will focus primarily on the first encounter between Andromache and Hermione in the play (141–273).[4]

Catfights and Sister Wives

One of the earliest uses of the term "catfight" in English occurs in a description of polygynous domestic arrangements among nineteenth-century American Mormons. Benjamin Ferris, contending that "polygamy poisons every thing; it seems to break down all the barriers of female virtue," explains that men kept their wives in separate apartments in order to "prevent those terrible cat-fights which sometimes occur" (1854, 306–8). Ferris provides a series of examples that highlight the explosive combination of anger and eroticism at the heart of these catfights: his stories repeatedly feature a jealous first wife witnessing the sexual relations between her husband and a new wife, then interrupting them in order to attack her rival. In Ferris's account, polygamy transforms potentially "virtuous" women into angry and vengeful sexual voyeurs. He elsewhere claims that the living arrangements of less wealthy Mormons result in a "manifest struggle between poverty and licentiousness," implying that the necessity of keeping two or more wives within a single-room dwelling creates the conditions for decidedly non-normative sexual arrangements (307). Ferris thus suggests that the relationships (and resulting "cat-fights") between women in polygynous marriages reflect a hostility animated by sexual jealousy and (often unwanted) physical proximity.

The TLC reality show *Sister Wives* (2010–present) offers a modern-day counterpart to Ferris' book—an intimate and sensationalized glimpse into the domestic lives of polygamous Mormons. *Sister Wives* is far more sympathetic to its subjects than Ferris, and it also more directly raises the possibility of erotic relations between the multiple wives ("sister wives") in a polygynous family. Courtney Bailey argues that the show "[flirts] not only with female homosociality but also with female homoeroticism," observing how its depiction of relations between its four wives "gestures towards something like Adrienne Rich's lesbian continuum, in that it acknowledges a range of female desire beyond the hetero/homo binary per se" (2015, 44). The women of *Sister Wives* also, of course, engage in their fair share of "catfights." As Bailey suggests, Rich's "lesbian continuum"—her influential project of discerning "lesbian existence" within female relationships and experiences that are not (explicitly) sexual—offers one framework for exploring the queerness of sister wives. I would especially highlight how, in tracing the "emotional importance" of female–female relations, Rich observes that "'emotionally important' can of course refer to anger as well as to love, or to that intense mixture of the two often found in women's relationships with women" (1980, 636).

Sara Ahmed's conceptualization of "sexual orientation" is also useful for describing the queer possibilities lurking within polygynous marital structures. As Ahmed shows, spatial, temporal, and motor metaphors play an important role in many accounts of sexuality, and such metaphors contribute powerfully to a sense that "bodies become straight" (or, conversely, queer) by "tending toward" certain objects and avoiding others (2006, 79–94). In Ahmed's analysis, "straightness" develops through repetition, the persistent and often compulsory orientation toward and alignment with an opposite-sex partner and the various trappings of normative heterosexuality. In both Ferris's treatise and the many seasons of *Sister Wives*, we see that polygynous marriages are notionally organized around a man, whose sexual relations with multiple women may be seen as a form of "hyper-heterosexuality" (Bailey 2015, 45). Yet these marriages also unsettle normative forms of heterosexuality by enabling women to form intense and complex attachments to one another. As the term "sister wives," with its doubling of familial roles, already indicates, women in polygynous households repeatedly orient themselves, not only toward their common male partner, but also toward each other—whether in affection, anger, or *eros*. The "terrible cat-fights which sometimes occur" between "sister wives" lay bare the intimate nature of female relationships within polygyny.

The Intimacy of Polygyny

We might say, therefore, that one important way in which polygyny becomes (potentially) queer is through its ability to create the conditions for various forms of female intimacy. In Ferris's view, such intimacy leads to "licentiousness" and "cat-fights" (307–8); for some viewers of *Sister Wives*, the sense of camaraderie and affection between wives generates a longing for a kind of female community precluded, they feel, by their own monogamous arrangements (Bailey 2014, 46–7). Queer theory has taken a particular interest in the delineation and construction of intimacy, and especially, in exploring the significance of intimate relationships beyond the monogamous, heterosexual couple. With James Bromley (2011, 5–6), I am interested here in drawing upon the superlative quality present in the Latin root of "intimacy"—*intimus* as "innermost" and "closest"— and considering how Euripides' *Andromache* explores the relationship between two women forced into a "most intimate" engagement with one another through the practice of polygyny.

   In the ode preceding Hermione's entrance, the Chorus sings of the "troubles" (121) that have "joined" Andromache with Hermione "in hateful strife" (122). The verb used here for "joined" or "locked" (*sun-kleiô*) stresses both the intimacy and the intensity of the women's connection, combining the prefix *sun* ("with") and the root verb *kleiô* ("close"). The Chorus further explains that the conflict is focused on the "double marriage bed" (*lektrôn didumôn* 123–4) that the women share with the singular Neoptolemus (125). This description anticipates Hermione's subsequent claim, quoted at the outset, that "one man" should not possess "two women" (178). And just as Hermione's assertion uses equine imagery to gesture to the erotic nature of Neoptolemus' relationship to his "two women," the choral ode refers specifically to the marriage bed (*lektron*)—the site of sexual relations. In Ferris's account, the marital bed is a frequent focal point for the catfight, a locus for contesting claims of sexual ownership as well as a reminder that polygynous sister wives themselves, however unhappily, share a bed (1854, 308–11). Bailey observes how the Browns (the family featured in *Sister Wives*) carefully deflect questions about their own sexual practices, making it "difficult, if not impossible, to know once and for all whether the Browns toe the heteronormative line," and she suggests that this "slipperiness" resonates with Eve Sedgwick's understanding of queerness as marked by possibilities, gaps, and a certain kind of unknowability (2015, 45).[5] In Euripides' *Andromache*, both the Chorus and Hermione figure the marriage bed as the source and site of conflict, thereby underscoring the uncomfortable intimacy that animates the relationship between wife and concubine.

When Hermione later contrives to have Orestes take her away from Phthia, she makes a speech disavowing her relationships with other women. She specifically claims that the "visits of bad women" (930) were the source of her downfall, insisting that these women, treacherous "Sirens" (936), encouraged her to persecute Andromache, asking why she tolerated the enslaved concubine who "shared [her] marriage bed" (933). The words that Hermione attributes to these "women" underscore the intimacy of the relationship between wife and concubine: they "share" (933) a marriage bed, and Andromache is even described as "reaping" that "bed" (935)— an allusion to her reproductive fertility. The description of these visitors as "Sirens" (936) is also provocative, in that the Siren is specifically a figure of treacherous feminine allure. Hermione, who argues here that intimate female friendships threaten the integrity of male/female marriage, also describes such relationships in terms of spatial orientation: she stresses the movement of these women "into" the home (*eis-odoi* 930 and 952; *es-phoitan* 945), "toward" (*pros* 945) the wife whom they seek to "corrupt" (*sum-phtheirei* 947); she also repeatedly uses the preposition/prefix *sun*, "with," to characterize the engagement between women (*sum-phtheirei* 947; *sun-nosein* 948). Drawing upon Ahmed, we might read Hermione's speech as articulating a queer order, a situation in which women are oriented toward (*eis, pros*) and entangled with (*sun*) one another to the detriment of marriage. A "sensible man," Hermione declares, "should not allow women to visit his wife in the home" (944–6).

Hermione voices anxieties about female relationships that course through Greek tragedy. Nancy Sorkin Rabinowitz, for example, demonstrates how normative marital order as represented by Euripides relies upon the containment and separation of women (1984 and 1993). In this case, of course, Hermione's repudiation of female intimacy is motivated by the collapse of her own plot against Andromache, and the audience receives this speech in light of Hermione's own complicated entanglements with her husband's concubine. Hermione's words, then, reinforce the relational ideology implied by the development of the plot: female intimacy, whether forced by polygyny or facilitated by female friendship, is a potentially destructive force, capable of rending apart the marital relationship between man and wife.

As I suggested above, "catfights" make the uncomfortable intimacy of polygyny visible—exposing how this marital structure, while ostensibly organized around a man, also creates the conditions for disruptive and explosive relationships between women. The term "catfight" is further bound up with a kind of queer history, entering into

American discourse in part through the discussion of the unusual marital arrangements practiced by a religious and sexual minority.[6] Whether or not this particular history has informed the past scholarly use of the term to describe the conflict between Andromache and Hermione in Euripides' play, it has hermeneutic value. Andromache and Hermione's "catfight" interrogates the nature and terms of Neoptolemus' sexual and domestic arrangements and exposes these women's entanglements with one another, revealing the queer relationship that has developed in the context of their polygynous household structure.

Close Combat

A volatile combination of intimacy and hostility courses through the debate between Hermione and Andromache. Hermione asserts that Andromache uses drugs (*pharmakois* 157) to make her infertile, and declares that "my womb is barren, destroyed by you" (158). In the Greek line translated here (*nêdus d'akumôn dia se moi diollutai* 158), the reference to Andromache (*dia se*) is nestled between Hermione's references to her womb (*nêdus*) and herself (*moi*); the word order thus displays the entanglement of the two women. In addition, the repetition of the preposition/prefix *dia* ("through") underscores how these women's lives are woven "through" one another.

Andromache, for her part, begins by offering advice to Hermione. Picking up on Hermione's argument, Andromache suggests that Neoptolemus "hates" (205) Hermione because she does not make herself "suitable" or "pleasant" to live with (206). She then encourages Hermione to become a more accommodating wife by making extravagant claims about her own support of Hector's infidelities (222–5). While there is undoubtedly hyperbole and even sarcasm in Andromache's speech, she also enacts a particular kind of female intimacy: the exchange of relationship advice between women. Such dialogue reflects a female homosociality that can thrive among polygynous sister wives. In their opening speeches, Hermione and Andromache thus gesture to two different models of polygynous female intimacy: Hermione constructs Andromache as an invader of her marriage bed and womb, while Andromache nods to the possibility of a relationship based in shared female experience.

In the rapid-fire dialogue that follows these initial speeches, open hostility between the two women drowns out the Chorus's plea for reconciliation (*sum-bênai* 233). Yet despite the women's failure to live harmoniously "with" (*sun* as in *sumbênai* 233) one another, the use of the preposition/prefix *sun* ("with") throughout their exchange reveals the attachments at stake. Both women use *sun* when speaking about marital and sexual relations. Hermione criticizes Andromache for "sleeping with" (*xun-eudein* 172; *xun* is a variation of *sun*) the son (Neoptolemus) of the man (Achilles) who killed her husband (Hector). Andromache, in turn, declares that Hermione is not pleasant "to live with" (*xun-einai* 206), explaining that "virtues delight bedmates (*xun-eunetas* 208)" and insisting that Neoptolemus has rejected Hermione as a result of her own interpersonal failings. Andromache subsequently describes herself having "helped" (*xun-êrôn* 223)

Hector in his extramarital affairs, even to the point of breastfeeding his offspring by other women (224–5).

Given the repeated use of *sun* to characterize marital and sexual relations, its remaining two uses in this dialogue are striking. At the outset, Hermione emphasizes her possession of wealth and luxury, the fact that she arrived in Phthia "with" (*sun*) "many bride-gifts" (153). As we will see, Hermione's attachment to her natal family and its material trappings represents its own form of queerness, a failure to fully orient herself toward her husband. Euripides' representation of Hermione as more closely linked "with" (*sun*) her wealth than her husband, her "bedmate," gestures toward this decidedly non-normative dimension of her character. And in the passage of rapid-fire dialogue (stichomythia) that follows the women's initial speeches, Hermione, suggesting that Andromache is not "chaste" (235), remarks: "May your mind (*noos*) not dwell together (*xun-oikoiê*) with me" (237). The combination of *sun* ("with") and *oikos* ("household") in the verb used here draws attention to the intimacy created by Neoptolemus' domestic arrangements: the two women dwelling unhappily within the same *oikos*. Hermione's wish thus reflects a deep desire to ensure that such unavoidable physical proximity not lead to any kind of psychic or intellectual intimacy—to make sure that Andromache's *noos* ("mind," "sense," "purpose") not become her own. Yet despite Hermione's desires, she is already thoroughly enmeshed "with" Andromache: she fears that her rival has invaded her womb with hostile drugs (158), and she resents the fact that she is figuratively yoked to her husband's concubine, as two women under the "reins of one man" (177–8).[7] The uses of *sun* within this particular "catfight" thus expose Hermione's entanglements with her natal family and her sexual rival—forces that prove "queer" in their ability to undermine her relationship to her husband.

In the course of their debate, Andromache and Hermione further attempt to cast each other as sexually perverse, with each woman in turn insisting that her rival is the real source of problematic and unorthodox erotic practices. Hermione, for example, insists that Andromache's "foreign" or "barbarian" (*barbaron* 173, 261) origins have made her sexually promiscuous, willing to "sleep with" (*xun-eudein* 172) the son of husband's murderer. Claiming that "the barbarian race" (173) readily practices both incest and murder (174–6), Hermione not only attempts to racialize Andromache's alleged sexual "deviance," but also associates her with the kind of deadly violence that Hermione herself is attempting to deploy against Andromache and her son.

Andromache is subtler in her accusations, but she, too, links Hermione with non-normative forms of female sexuality. In particular, she twice reminds us of Hermione's connection with her mother, Helen: first cautioning Hermione against "surpassing" (230) her mother in "love of men" (*philandria* 229), then answering a jab from Hermione with a harsh claim about Helen's responsibility for the Trojan War (248). Helen is herself a queer figure, and while her promiscuity is distinct from Hermione's possessive attachment to Neoptolemus, Andromache seeks to cast Hermione as an inheritor of her mother's wayward sexuality.[8]

Through their heated debate, Andromache and Hermione expose the tensions generated by Neoptolemus' polygynous domestic arrangements and their consequent entanglements with one another. The two women also articulate various models of normative sexual order, ranging from Hermione's denigration of Andromache's sexual ethics (170–8) to Andromache's advice to Hermione about proper wifely behavior (205–28). Yet on the level of plot, it is Hermione's obsessive pursuit of Andromache and her son that threatens to destroy her marriage with Neoptolemus. Hermione's later speech about the negative impact of intimate female relationships upon a marriage (929–53) thus underscores a message already implied by this "catfight": the orientation of one woman toward another, whether in anger or in affection, poses a threat to normative male/female relations.

Catfights, Camp, and Hermione's Queerness

It may seem counterintuitive to cast the "catfight" as a queer form, since it clearly draws upon normative, male stereotypes and fantasies about female desires and behaviors. This is already evident in Ferris's treatise, but, in the modern American cultural imagination, we might further observe that theatrical and cinematic catfights often reflect lurid fantasies of eroticized conflict located within women's schools, colleges, and prisons. As Dana Heller notes, "Feminist critics have not been entirely wrong in arguing that the catfight luxuriates in images of femininity as wanton eye candy, an erotic fantasy composed of soft-porn clichés and crude homoerotic sensationalism, or an enactment of damaging feminine competition" (2017, 88). The spectacular debate between Andromache and Hermione likewise activates specific misogynistic fantasies: it has been described as "salacious" (Chong-Gossard 2015, 143), potentially titillating to a male viewer, and it provides support, in the argument later articulated more clearly by Hermione, for the social segregation of women.

Yet Heller, focusing on twenty-first-century American television, also argues that the catfight "has always functioned as an acknowledgement of the shared stock of fantasies, anxieties, industrial techniques, and intertexts out of which queerness—or its media affect— becomes manifest" (2017, 88). For example, she notes "*The L Word* [Showtime, 2004–9] made particular use of the catfight as a convention of queer aesthetics or camp, by which I mean performances of excess aimed at exaggerating the artificiality of the gender and sexual divide" (2013); Heller similarly analyzes the "camp aesthetics" of the catfight in Netflix's series *Orange is the New Black* (show ran from 2013–19). Heller, to be clear, is using the term "camp" to refer to a specific twentieth- and twenty-first-century tradition of queer performance, an archive from which the producers and actors of shows like *The L Word* and *Orange is the New Black* may consciously draw. Yet I believe that specific aspects of "camp," especially as enacted by the "catfight," are also evident in Euripides' *Andromache*, and I would like to suggest that this framework enables us to better appreciate the queer energy that drives Hermione through this play.

While "camp" itself has been variously defined, I am drawing upon Heller's definition and its theoretical antecedents. In her framework, "camp" is characterized by parodic excess that exaggerates and thereby undermines normative models of gender and sexuality; the performance of "camp" is thus a process through which "queerness ... becomes manifest" (2017, 88)—a process that subverts as it enacts. In the words of Moe Meyer, "camp, as specifically queer parody, becomes ... the only process by which the queer is able to enter representation and produce social visibility" (1994, 11). In Euripides' *Andromache*, both the parodic and the revelatory dimensions of camp play an important role in the *agôn*, the catfight, between Hermione and Andromache.

Hermione's opening speech emphasizes the luxury of her bridal gifts and accoutrements. Her words exaggerate familiar marital tropes, especially when compared with Andromache's more restrained description of her own nuptials. Andromache begins the play by recalling how she once "arrived" at the house of Priam, with the "rich, golden luxury (*poluchrusôi chlidêi*) of bridal gifts," to marry Hector (1–4). Hermione, for her part, enters and declares that she wears the "adornment of golden luxury (*chruseas chlidês*) about [her] head," part of the "many bridal gifts" with which she "arrived" in Phthia to marry Neoptolemus (147–53). Andromache gestures briefly to her wedding gifts; Hermione calls attention to the rich adornment of her body itself, underscoring the links between her costume and her character. Indeed, scholars have observed that the markedly Dorian quality of Hermione's costume contributes to the play's alignment of her sexual "deviance" with her ethnic (Spartan) origins.[9] While Andromache's description of her marital past recalls her role in epic and lyric as an ideal wife, Hermione's emphasis on her nuptial trappings serves to underscore the ongoing failure of her marriage. Like Andromache, she was transferred from father to husband with the rich bridal gifts associated with aristocratic marriages, yet unlike Andromache, she has not produced a child, and her wrathful orientation toward her husband's concubine, rather than her husband himself, has caused the crisis at the heart of this play. Hermione's entrance is thus consistent with "camp" aesthetics in its ability to expose, through amplification, the fissures and failures of normative sexual order. Hermione's indulgent, "campy" description of her own bridal "adornment" becomes parodic in light of the current absence of her husband and her failure to fulfill her wifely role.

Hermione's entrance sets the tone for the remainder of the exchange. Both Hermione and Andromache offer sweeping and exaggerated claims about the proper construction of marital relations: Hermione declares that "the whole barbarian race" regularly practices incest and murder (173–6), while Andromache amplifies her own image as loyal wife to the point of absurdity by claiming that she "often" nursed Hector's bastards (221–5). Both women "over-perform" their roles: Hermione as the self-involved and vindictive villain, Andromache as the archetype of the faithful and circumspect wife. By intensifying elements of normative femininity (bridal luxury, loyalty to an unfaithful husband), their performances veer toward parody, inviting the audience to question the very values that they so dramatically voice.

Hermione also stresses that her gifts and ornaments do not come "from the halls of Achilles or Peleus" (149–50); rather, her "father Menelaus gave them to [her], from the Laconian land of Sparta" (151–2). This turn toward her natal family points to a potential source of Hermione's marital failures. Hermione insists that her independent (paternal rather than spousal) wealth empowers her to "speak freely" (153). But as Aspasia

Stavrinou demonstrates, the dissolution of Hermione's marriage to Neoptolemus is tightly bound up with her striking attachment to her natal family. Stavrinou observes that, in the absence of Neoptolemus, Menelaus' eventual presence onstage results in a "substitution of father for husband," underscoring Hermione's "deviant" loyalties; she further suggests that Hermione's eventual decision to abandon Neoptolemus and attach herself to her cousin Orestes reflects the culmination of her failure to make the expected female transition from natal to marital *oikos* (2014, 388, 394, and 402). In this respect, Andromache's impulse to link Hermione with her mother Helen (229–31) proves revealing: Hermione, like her mother Helen, rejects the marital role arranged by her father and husband, thereby enacting a form of female agency that undermines the finality and permanence of nuptial bonds.

Stavrinou's account of Hermione's failure to perform the role of normative "wife" does not use the term "queer," yet I believe queer theoretical perspectives enable us to appreciate how Hermione deviates from marital and reproductive norms not only through her attachment to her natal family, but also through her relationship with Andromache. Before Hermione runs off with Orestes (881–1008), she instigates a catfight that exposes her underlying queerness. Hermione embodies a kind of exuberant excess, manifested both in her lavish descriptions of her own wealth and her relentless persecution of Andromache. Her catfight, with its "campy" elements, underscores the fact that her entanglements with her natal family and her husband's concubine leave no room for meaningful attachments to her husband himself, whose physical absence serves to underscore the point. Through his "catfight in Phthia," Euripides thus explores the queer possibilities lurking within Neoptolemus' polygynous household—possibilities that emerge provocatively, though by no means exclusively, in the character of Hermione.[10]

* * *

Insofar as Euripides' *Andromache* has enjoyed a queer reception, it has been mediated through Jean Racine's *Andromaque* (1667). Leo Bersani, in *A Future for Astyanax* (1976), takes Racine's play as a point of departure for a wide-ranging discussion of literature, desire, and the construction of the self—a discussion that anticipates many of Bersani's later contributions to the development of queer theory. In Dorothy Bussy's novel *Olivia* (1949), the basis of Jacqueline Audry's film of the same name (1951), the titular schoolgirl Olivia's desire for her teacher, Mlle Julie, is awakened in part by a reading of *Andromaque*. Mlle Julie even takes apparent delight in introducing Olivia to the character of Hermione, adding "[T]onight you shall hear of her, and I hope never forget her" (28).

Yet the sense of queer potential that Bersani, Bussy, and Audry found in Racine can also be found in Euripides. While Greek tragedy as a genre is often concerned with familial and marital structures, *Andromache* is a play that is particularly interested in those topics; indeed, while its dramatic unity has long been maligned, many scholars have identified domestic relations as its defining theme.[11] And even as this play valorizes normative marital structures at various turns, it is also constantly deconstructing those models and gesturing toward alternatives:[12] Hermione's entanglement with Andromache and subsequent rejection of her arranged marriage; Andromache's embrace of Thetis' statue; Thetis' radical reorganization of her own marriage.[13] Euripides' *Andromache* is, at heart, a play about the queer and unsettling conditions that emerge, primarily among women, in the absence of Neoptolemus. *Andromache* is rarely performed, but perhaps, in the era of *Sister Wives* (TLC), *Orange is the New Black* (Netflix), and a re-booted *L Word: Generation Q* (Showtime), Euripides' dramatic exploration of queer femininity deserves greater creative and critical engagement.

Notes

1. Fragment 417 Page. Cf. Griffith 2006: 324–9.

2. I prefer the term "polygyny" throughout this chapter, in order to indicate my focus on a specific marital configuration: one man with two or more female sexual partners (whether these women are legal "wives" or not). Some of my primary and secondary sources, however, use the broader term "polygamy" to describe this arrangement, and so that term also appears at certain points.

3. See Allan 2000, 18n55, and Chong-Gossard 2015, 143.

4. See Introduction, and Radcliffe in this volume.

5. See Sedgwick 1993, 8.

6. On the queerness of early Mormons, see further Coviello 2019, 89–131.

7. On queer proximities, see Telò in this volume.

8. On Helen's queerness, see Lesser 2018.

9. See Battezzato 1999–2000 and Stavrinou 2016.

10. Andromache, too, displays certain queer impulses—in her case, directly primarily toward the goddess Thetis, who concludes the play by re-orienting Andromache toward normative patterns of marriage and procreation while forging her own queer (non-reproductive, female-centric) re-marriage to Peleus (Olsen 2022). On female queer bonds involving divine figures, see Haselswerdt and, especially, Rabinowitz and Bullen in this volume. We might, therefore, see Hermione's "catty" and "campy" form of queerness, specifically as enacted in the *agôn*, as one of several modes of queer femininity explored by this play.

11. See esp. Rabinowitz 1984; Storey 1989; Kyriakou 1997; Papadimitropoulos 2006; and Mirto 2012. On camp aesthetics and "bad" dramatic form, see Radcliffe in this volume.

12. On queer alternatives to the couple form, see Youd in this volume.

13. On those latter examples, see further Olsen 2022. Stavrinou (2014) offers an account of Hermione as a figure of non-normative sexual and social orientations, while Rabinowitz (1984, 122) suggests that, in Thetis, we might find "a new model of female behavior, a new model of gender relations."

CHAPTER 13

ORESTES—POLYMORPHOUSLY PER-VERSE: ON QUEER METROLOGY

David Youd

Greco-Roman antiquity has long served as a *locus classicus* of queer self-understandings: an archive well-suited to the denaturalization of sex and gender norms and categories, and a space for the collective envisioning of alternative ways of being. The comparatively recent institutionalization in classics of the study of established forms of "Greek love" is doubtless one of the triumphs of the modern field; yet while writing the history of ancient sexuality (as well as of the emergence of the very concept of "sexuality") has furnished an invaluable foundation for queer theory, there remains a particular sense in which the former is not entirely flush with the latter: the concept of "queerness," after all, has largely aimed at the *subversion* of such institutionalized forms and categories, at their proliferation and breakdown; has aimed, in short, at sexuality's ineluctable *excess*. An exclusive emphasis on ordering the past in keeping with ancient typologies, to the degree that it works to the exclusion of their interstices, would risk re-inflicting afresh the epistemic damage of a mutilating normativity. Epistemic damage: not of the modern homo/heterosexual definition that Eve Sedgwick so salutarily probed, but of the ancient consolidation of sexual identities and behaviors around the activity of the phallus. Re-inflicting: because, however serviceable the reconstruction of the ancient system of sexuality has been for the deconstruction of the modern, its newly buttressed framework may function as a monument that excludes as much as enshrines, precluding the very appearance of non-normative forms of intimacy,[1] which, already scarcely legible in antiquity, must be evicted anew as ahistorical, anachronistic, alien.[2]

In tandem, then, with the historicist preservation of the moth-eaten fabric of antique sexual discourse, a specifically queer theoretical approach might rather attend to its stray threads, snags, and tears as marking so many sites of categorial stress, and strain, and abrasion under the pull of the social body, and seek in those tears the evidence of creative refashioning. To borrow the formulation of Joshua Weiner and Damon Young (2011, 226),

> If sex is—or becomes queer when it is—a force of tearing and symbolic rupture, queer theory teaches us that it is, however, also a forging of sociabilities in this space of rupture. In other words, the antisocial force of (queer) sex is fundamental to [its] world-making inventiveness.

With this orienting premise, I offer one example of how a formalist mode of reading might provide an additional site for the elaboration of queerness, while simultaneously contributing to the formation and multiplication of queer discourses within the field of classical studies. A compelling and innovative model of such an approach can be found in the recent monograph *Archive Feelings*, in which Mario Telò tenders a wide-ranging re-evaluation of the aesthetics of Greek tragedy, strongly inflected by queer theory (2020). For aesthetic form, from an Adornian perspective, would constitute precisely the register in which the work of art attempts to go beyond the realm of the sayable and thinkable within a given historical moment; attempts, in the fragmentation of its facture, to express meanings, desires, and bonds that are discursively impossible. In its formal rifts, the aesthetic object can be said to index a toil, Penelope-like, to unweave and weave again a queer web of intimacies and relations, a ceaseless refashioning that would forestall forever the socially mandated domestication of desire.

To this end, I would like to dwell on but a few critical passages to suggest that the widespread failure of conjugality staged in *Orestes*—the explosive marital breaches that supply its content and catapult its plot forward—is tied to a fundamental triadicity of aesthetic form, wherein the foreclosed intimate third spectrally reappears as a persistent prosodic excess.[3] The play has been said to mark the apogee of Euripides' late style, and is characterized by a radical multiplication of metrical resolutions: an intrinsically queer rupture and transformation of the closed rhythmic couple into an open assemblage of three.[4] For the disyllabic pair that serves as the basis of the two predominant recitative meters in Greek tragedy is founded on a formal disequilibrium, both iambic (˘ ‾) and trochaic (‾ ˘) rhythms shaped by the uneven, unbalanced coupling of a dominant long syllable with a subordinate short, and these prosodic figures of an unevenly yoked pair comport with what David Halperin has called the Greeks' "generalized ethos of penetration and domination, a sociosexual discourse structured by the presence or absence of its central term: the phallus" (1989, 266). Moreover, this nexus between the erotic binary and hierarchic inequality is bound up with an exclusionary conception of intimacy itself, since in this discourse "sexual pleasures other than phallic pleasures do not *count* in categorizing sexual contacts" (266n29 [my emphasis])—the fallacy of such a phallocentric discourse, of course, consisting in its limitation of what "counts" as erotic to a penetrative binary, whereby the count of such arrangements always adds up to two.[5] It is this constitutive exclusion, the erasure of sex from every domain outside of the privileged couple formations, that results in a return of the repressed, the third that haunts both our play's content and its queer metrology. Thus, whereas Claude Lévi-Strauss argued in his foundational structuralist reading of Oedipus that the myth's underlying logic takes the form of the question "born from one or born from two? born from different or born from same?" (1955, 434), Euripides' *Orestes* can be thought to stage the somewhat queerer question "born from two or born from three?" and thus read as a programmatic deconstruction of the couple form.[6]

In returning to the issue of the couple, cast in an admittedly less than flattering light, I am taking aim not only at the "cultural chauvinism" that continues to reserve—often with political muscle and disproportionately with an eye to policing women—the aegis of respectability for monogamous and coupled over non-monogamous, promiscuous, or group sex, as circumscribed in Gayle Rubin's "charmed circle" of sexuality (2011, 152–4), but more particularly at the attempt to cordon off the subversive, suffusive reach of sexuality within the romantic halo of the (indicatively heterosexual) couple, as well as the ontological and epistemic enlistment of the erotic dyad to underwrite broader paradigms of oppression. The couple, as it were, remains in bed with power. As Monique Wittig brought out, ever since Aristotle's *Politics*, "male and female, the heterosexual relationship, has been the parameter of all hierarchical relations" (1992, 42),[7] and, with the due refinements of subsequent scholarship, this unholy alliance can be extended back to earlier, power-infused constructions of the penetrative–receptive dyad— Halperin's "ethos of penetration and domination" (1989, 266).[8] Against this brassbound and seemingly indestructible frame built upon binary difference, the radical parity of Euripides' resolved feet (ˇ ˇ ˇ) aesthetically incarnates a form of relationality giving body to sameness, a formal "*homo*-ness" which, to invoke Leo Bersani (1995, 76), "necessitates a massive redefining of relationality … a potentially revolutionary inaptitude … for sociality as it is known," a prosodic reflex of the queer bonds fronted in the play.[9]

That sexual and metrical conventions were felt in the classical period to bear certain contiguities is indicated most plainly by their overlapping conceptual vocabulary. For before their application to the measure of verse, *metron* ("measure") and *metrios* ("moderate") came to measure out a normative ideal of moderation, temperance, and respectability, evidenced for example in the aphorisms, variously ascribed to Cleobulus or another of the seven sages, *metron ariston* ("measure is best") and *metrôi khrô* ("use moderation"). It is only in the second half of the fifth century, precisely contemporaneous with Euripides' dramaturgical career, that *metron* first appears as a technical term for poetic meter, and play on the word's moral and metrical acceptations shows up in a sportive little poem attributed to Critias, our playwright's contemporary (*IE* [2] 4):

> And now I give a crown to the Athenian, son of Cleinias,
>> Alcibiades, in a song of novel character (or "meter:" *neoisin . . . tropois*):
> For it was not possible to fit his name into the elegiac,
>> but now he reposes in an iambic not without measure (*ouk ametrôs*).[10]

The verses turn on the fact that Alcibiades, in addition to his well-known immoderate character (*tropoi*), happens to possess a name that does not fit in the dactylic elegiac meter. The upstart "son of Cleinias" (*Kleiniou*, a patronym evoking the sympotic couch) is therefore made to "recline" in a new line accommodatingly written in a novel meter (*neoisin . . . tropois*). Although this flourish has been read as integrating Alcibiades' "new ways" in conformity with the old (where "not without measure" would signify a reimposition of moderation),[11] the form of the resulting poem, a hybrid iambo-elegiac fusion, gives poetic expression to the ideological rupture occasioned by Alcibiades' return to Athens by metrically encapsulating a collapse of the traditional structure of poetic genres, as well as the social hierarchies it has been thought to underwrite.[12] By the time of our play, then, the semantic nexus of the *metrios*, wherein characterological decadence came to require its commensurate cadence, had surfaced as the subject of poetic and aesthetic exploration, with direct political ramifications.[13]

As for its subject matter, *Orestes* has been characterized as "a kind of 'domestic' or 'social' drama, a step on the road to the New Comedy of the fourth century" where, compared to its predecessors, "the themes of (extended) family, inheritance, the house, gender roles, and marriage are brought much more emphatically (and literally) back to center stage" (Griffith 2009, 279 and 283–4). The play follows the disastrous fallout of two marital crises, triggered by the adulterous affairs of the sisters Helen and Clytemnestra, and has been read as a "sequel" that returns to the themes and narrative compass of not one but two dramatic predecessors, forming a sort of triad together with the *Helen* and the *Oresteia*.[14] In the first half of the play, Orestes and Electra seek in vain the political intervention of Menelaus (their reticent uncle) to secure an acquittal for the murder of their mother (some days before the events of the play); in the second half, Orestes, Electra, and Pylades, now sentenced to death, make a bold but divinely thwarted attempt on Helen's life—an attempt that largely transpires as a repetition of their murder of Clytemnestra—before Apollo, appearing as a *deus ex machina*, brings matters to a close by imposing a series of marriages. By thus tracking these dual murder plots, both excused by reference to their victims' adultery and the ensuing repercussions, the play becomes a dramatic orchestration of the cultural fantasy in which an otherwise consonant social harmony is felt to be marred by the discordant notes sounded by the adulterous wife— notes I am suggesting are replicated in the play's lavishly resolved meter.

For the formal homology, adumbrated above, between the micrological structure of metrical form and the social structuring of sexual arrangements, together with their constitutive instabilities and susceptibility to transformation, is foregrounded in *Orestes*, cemented, at several critical junctures, in neat dovetails of form and content. When, for example, Menelaus greets Tyndareus as the polyandrous "<u>bedmate of</u> Zeus" with a pronounced metrical resolution (*Zênos homolektron* 476), he formally "embeds" the threesome in the line's sonic texture. Given the context of the utterance—Menelaus freshly returned from Troy with his wayward Helen in tow—this show of metrical virtuosity might be read as a little good-natured ribbing, one cuckold to another. For in the next line Tyndareus replies in kind, with a matching resolution—in the very same metrical position—placing Menelaus in a parallel prosodic throuple, albeit with any reference to Paris tactfully omitted: *kai su, Meneleôs* ("you too, <u>Menelaus</u>" 477).[15] It is perhaps, on this reading, only by careful diplomacy that such banter remains anodyne, the sportive admission of their cuckoldry licensed by Zeus' divine status, on the one hand, and Paris' erasure, on the other. But by aesthetically couching the material crisis of conjugality in the scene's prosodic armature, the brief exchange both highlights the instability of the couple form, haunted by the specter of its supernumerary, and forwards through literary form the possibility of resolution—and radical equality—in refashioned intimate arrangements. Thus, bearing down further on these measures, the intimation of "sameness" intoned in *<u>homolektron</u>* resonates not only through the quantitative parity of the metrically resolved units ($\smile\ \smile\ \smile$), but qualitatively through the assonance of -*<u>os homo</u>*- and *<u>Menele</u>*-.

In fact, whenever Helen and Clytemnestra are mentioned in the play, a trail of resolutions follows in their wake, metrically encoding the "bad multiplicity" the adulterous wife is felt to introduce into the social order.[16] In the opening tableau, as the recumbent Orestes is apprised of Menelaus' return, "bringing Helen (*Helenên agomenos*) back from the walls of Troy ..." (246), he complains that "if he brings that spouse, he comes with a great evil (*alokhon agetai, kakon ekhôn*)" (248), while Electra agrees that "Tyndareus fathered a(n in)famous group of daughters (*episêmon eteke Tyndareôs ... thugaterôn*)" (249–50). Again, in the subsequent *agôn* between Tyndareus, Menelaus, and Orestes, the first denounces his own "impure" (*anosious* 518) daughters and berates Menelaus for going to Troy for one of them: "Helen, that spouse of yours" (*Helenên te, tên sên alokhon* 520).

In response, as if cottoning on to the purport of these prosodic undertones, Orestes musters an impressive column of resolved feet as he tries to shift the blame for his matricide onto Tyndareus himself for having fathered such a woman (585–90):

> By fathering (*phuteusas*) a wicked daughter (*thugater'*), it was you, grandfather,
> who caused my downfall; because of (*dia to*) her temerity
> I lost my father, and that made me (*egenomên*) a matricide.
> Do you see? Odysseus' wife (*alokhon*) has not been killed
> by Telemachus; that's because she did not remarry (*epegamei*) husband on husband,
> and her bedchamber remains untainted (*ugies*) in the house.[17]

In this update of the conventional comparison of Clytemnestra and Penelope, Orestes extends the traditional indictment of the former to encompass Tyndareus, perhaps tacitly implicating his procreative triad to the extent that *phuteusas* ("fathering") implies a paternal contribution to his daughters' polyandrous *phusis* ("inborn nature")—as if theirs were a congenital inaptitude for conjugality. But what arrests us in Orestes' harangue is its bravura sequence of resolutions, the steady division of two into three in the middle of the central *metron*, that clandestine extra beat pulsing like a rhythmic arrhythmia at the heart of each successive line. If in the first three lines the broken-up measures can be said to chart the breakdown of domestic harmony imputed to Clytemnestra's intrigues, in the latter three, as Orestes invokes the irreproachable devotion of Penelope as a foil to his mother's perfidy, the persisting resolutions serve instead to rhetorically underscore the contrast ("*his* companion," "*she* didn't take a paramour," and so on). The chiaroscuro of these contrastive portraits, however, not only inscribes in its metrical triads the shadow of the erotic third that overshadows and overdetermines Penelope's place in the cultural symbolic, but also adumbrates and aesthetically prefigures a more commodious world where her name might be uncoupled from the mere monogamous devotion of which she has been made (as here by Orestes) the *beau idéal*: the "wholesome" bedchamber (*hugies*) metrically made roomy enough for three.

A similar imbrication of the metrical and sexual materializes in the eroticized embrace of Orestes and Pylades (776–95). As Froma Zeitlin notes in her aptly (if unwittingly so) named article "The Closet of Masks,"[18] this scene bears a strong resemblance to a parallel scene in Euripides' *Heracles*, recalling the (homoerotic) bond there between Theseus and the eponymous hero (1980, 56).[19] But if our play is a closet, its epistemology remains fraught, coming out only obliquely when Pylades and Orestes embrace (792–3):

> Orestes. It is odious to touch (*duscheres psauein*) a sick man. Pylades. Not for me to touch you. Orestes. Take care (*eulabou*) you don't catch my madness. Pylades. Never mind about that!

This scene, construed by critics as a "genuinely touching" (Wright 2008, 57) display of fraternal intimacy, begins nevertheless to intimate something more when the "touching" comes to dominate its action, its metaphors, and its meter.[20] For Orestes' cautionary *duscheres psauein* ("it's odious to touch . . .") foregrounds the *che(i)r* ("hand"), and likewise the successive *eu-labou* ("take care") comprises the hand's "grasp" (*lab-*). But what grabs our attention is how the pair divvy up the metrical line, their shared syntax intimating a cohabitation of the same mental plane. This poetic device is known as "antilabe," where the shared poetic line is conceptualized as a "handing over" of the verse (*labê* being a handle or grip), and this metrical handling, already advertised by Orestes' "*eu-labou*," can be said to be subsequently literalized in Orestes' affectionate hypocorism (795):

> Orestes. Come now, tiller of my foot (*oiax podos moi*). Pylades. Yes, with loving care (*phila g' ekhôn kêdeumata*).

Not only does Orestes here clasp Pylades by the hand at the very moment of metrical handover, but, in dubbing Pylades the "tiller of my foot" (*oiax podos*), the latter is made to grasp the rudderly handle of a metrical "foot" as well. What is more, the "foot" (*pous*) is also a noted stand-in for the "penis" (*peos*),[21] of which the "tiller" here forms an obvious image: the antilabic handoff of the metrical line, figured as a shaft, is thereby rendered a tender rhythmic caress. This erotic frisson is slight but unmistakable, yet the erotics of this exchange, and more precisely the role of the phallus, are hard to firmly grasp: the tiller belongs to Pylades, the "foot" to Orestes, while the actors' hands are what make contact. Rather, with dexterous navigation, Euripides handily steers clear of committing the pair to a stable couple, while, at a stroke, granting their cheirophilic clasp a charge of erotic intimacy in excess of homosociality and irreducible to models of hierarchy and penetration.[22]

The fundamental ambiguity of their bond, the inadequacy of the conceptual tools ready to hand to apprehend the affinities that bind them, is indicated by the number of models and classifications brought to bear over the course of the play.[23] As if to pinpoint the singular nature of their kinship by triangulation, Pylades dubs Orestes "dearest of my age-mates (*hêlikôn*), / and friends, and relations: for you are all these things to me" (732–3). In 882–3, their relationship is compared to that between brothers, friends, and *pais/paidagôgos*; in 1072 to a *hetaireia*. But the Chorus also registers the nebulous erotism that surrounds these cousins when they sing, "Pylades, a man/husband equal to a brother, straightening out Orestes' sickly limb/member" (*isadelphos anêr, ithunôn <hoi> noseron* *kôlon* 1015–16): while the fraternal *isadelphos* seems to dispel any soupçon of desire, the spondaic *īthūnôn ... kôlon* conveys an obscene suggestion of erection ("rousing his member"), aesthetically rendered in its distended cadence. This intangible yet tactile *philia* thus manifests as a queer bond—"not reducible to sexuality" but "more insistently erotic than friendship" (Young 2016, 209)—supplementary to both Pylades and Electra's engagement and the incestuous notes sounded between Electra and Orestes.[24] Accordingly, *phila* is emplaced in the metrical triad of a resolved foot at the moment of contact, to wit, in Pylades' gentle *phila g' ekhôn kêdeumata* ("<u>with loving</u> care"). Precisely because of its excessive nature, conforming neither to meter nor prevailing discursive categories, it is at the level of aesthetic form that this immoderate friendship finds its measure.

Subsequently, these two become three when they are joined by Electra, whose tender embrace ("O my dearest, whose body is lovable [*potheinon*] and most delightful to your sister" 1045–6) is passionately returned by Orestes ("Now I want to respond with loving arms. Why go on feeling inhibited, damn it? O sister's breast, O beloved embrace of mine ... these endearments take the place of children and the marriage bed for both of us poor creatures ..." 1047–51).[25] Condemned to death, Electra pines for an eroticized demise with her brother—"if only the same sword (*xiphos*) could kill us both!" (1052)—while Orestes machinates to "lie together" (*koinônein*, encompassing sexual intercourse) in a shared grave (1055; cf. 1066–7).[26] Somewhat awkwardly, however, Pylades—who is, we have just learned, Electra's fiancé—has not gone anywhere, but demurely idles by, made to play the passive voyeur to their incestuous display. Yet in his turn, and of his own accord, he vows to join them in death (1091–3), giving birth thereby to an explicit "threesome"—thrice avowed: "salvation for you, and this man and myself makes three (*ek tritôn*)" (1178); "a remedy for us three friends (*trissois philois*)" (1190); "for us three friends (*trissois philois*), one contest, one act of justice" (1244). As Mark Griffith notes apropos of this decidedly queer bond, "the dynamics of three-way devotion are as intimate as could be imagined" (2009, 294–5).

The trio crystallizes around the plot they hatch to avenge themselves on Helen and thus mete out "a bitter pain for Menelaus" (1105). The erotic side of this pact has been brought to the fore in Mary Kay-Gamel's recent adaptation "Orestes Terrorist," appearing as the threesome of pornographic fantasy when, in the summary of Fiona Macintosh, "Elektra's incestuous attachment to her long-lost brother, and her betrothal to her brother's lover, are elaborated in a three-way erotic encounter fuelled by the excitement of revenge" (2011). As the title of the adaptation suggests, this threesome in a sense anticipates the orientalizing fantasies of contemporary discourses that invest the figure of the "terrorist" with a queer perversity unassimilable to the co-optive homonormativity of Western liberal democracies, namely what Jasbir Puar has called "the Orientalist wet dreams of lascivious excesses of pedophilia, sodomy, and perverse sexuality" (2007, 14), the polygamy and "pathological homosociality ... ascribed to terrorist bodies" (25). Like the "terrorist" or gay man who are constructed as "always already dying" and thus embracing and inflicting on others an erotically charged death, so the queer trio of *Orestes* invests not only their own death with desire (as above), but the death of their foes: "since I'm breathing out my life-breath regardless, I want to die having inflicted something on my enemies" (1163–4).[27]

Yet although they hook up for the express purpose of avenging themselves upon Helen, the play adverts to a subtending alliance between these ostensible antagonists by dint of their shared existence in overflow of proper intimate arrangements. For like Alcibiades in the Critias poem discussed above, Helen's anapaestic name—a name made to condense by *figura etymologica* the imputed "destruction" of the Trojan War—resolutely overflows the iambs and trochees of the play, just as her marital bounds are persistently troubled by her plethoric attachments to her daughter (her "only solace," 62–6) and her paramour (e.g., 1362–5). When Paris polyandrously "marries" (*egêm'* 1409) the already-wed Helen, he inadvertently engages not just Helen, but all the Hellenes in battle (*agag' Hellad'* 1365; *Hellênas eis hen . . . sunêgagon* 1640).[28] Significantly, however, this marital and martial *ménage à Troie* is ultimately not resolved through any restoration of conjugality; for although the *deus ex machina* who hastily brings the play to a close does so by arranging a series of marriages,[29] Helen is enshrined, extra-maritally and extra-metrically, in a divine troika with Castor and Polydeuces (*Kastori te Poludeukei . . . kath' Helenên* 1636 and 1643). As with Orestes' "brotherly" bond with Pylades and his incestuous relation with Electra, Helen is loosed from the confines of matrimonial subordination to Menelaus and katasterized: constellated in a triadic and lateral assemblage figured as fraternal. In Apollo's closing declaration, "now take the positions I've assigned you, and resolve your quarrel" (*neikos te dialuesthe* 1678–9), "resolve" both evokes the technical term for a metrical resolution (*luô*) and is in fact couched in a metrically resolved foot.[30] At the final moment, then, the reconciliation coinciding with the play's denouement (*lusis*) is conflated with metrical resolution and divorce (likewise *dialuô*), and for the remaining lines of the play, as he relates the luminous throne and divine renown that await her together "with the Dioscuri" (1682–90), Apollo switches to anapests, a triadic meter (˘ ˘ ‾) uniquely suited to accommodate Helen's trisyllabic name (*Helenên* 1684).[31]

Orestes can thus be said to transpose the problem of configuring intimacy in the wake of conjugal disaster into its stylistic register, the problematic dramatized in what we have called its queer metrology. As Adorno would have it, "the unsolved antagonisms of reality return in artworks as immanent problems of form" (1997, 6), and, in the teeth of the divine but suspect repair tacked on with the dramatic finale, the play evinces in its late style a refusal of marital and metrical closure: the impossibility of their suture.[32] But while the crisis of conjugality remains unresolved, as perennial as the couple that gave it birth, this breach in its bounds provides the space for counter-intimacies—perhaps a bit "offbeat"—structured laterally and no longer formed by disequilibrium and binary difference. And like the indeterminate bonds glimpsed in the play, Euripides' metrical praxis also performs a becoming-imperceptible within the prevailing regimes of erotic and prosodic legibility, through a multiplication of the forms and modes of relationality in his aesthetic architecture. A queer architecture: gesturing beyond the limits of cultural norms and conventions by its formal deviations and creative renovations. Could this not be excavated, reconstructed, creatively re-appropriated as an alternative abode alongside the marmoreal edifice of "Greek love?" In this way, by firmly planting at least one leg of our queer hermeneutics in aesthetic form, it might be possible not only to further expose the queering effects of ancient constructions of sexuality, but to detect the at times barely audible strains of an already immanent resistance to history's normative rhythms, and, in such moments of formal unruliness, to discover new allies in antiquity and forge new bonds within and between interpretative communities today.

Notes

1. See Berlant 1998 and 2012.

2. Compare Freccero (2006, 69–104) on historicism's melancholia, whereby the dead are "consumed and entombed within categories that are meant to lay to rest troubling uncertainties and that at the same time foreclose the possibility of a future open to what is not already known" (73), as well as the critique recently leveled by Gunderson (2021, 200) against the odd but compulsory limitation of hermeneutics to "the reproduction of the (would-be) ego-speech of the ancient world." See also the Introduction.

3. Compare especially Edelman and Litvak 2019.

4. More resolutions than any other play: see Willink 1986, liii, and West 1987, 27.

5. On the "ontological calculus" of the couple form, see also Brilmyer, Trentin, and Xiang 2019.

6. Olsen (2012) offers an analogous reading of the erotic third disrupting the "heterosexual romantic pair" in the *Aethiopica* of Heliodorus, where the heroine's conception (and complexion) is inflected by her mother's gaze at a painting of the naked Andromeda during intercourse with her husband, thereby producing "a child born, apparently, of three parents" (312). On queer models of reproduction, see also Andújar and Mueller in this volume.

7. This point is valorized in Bersani's otherwise acid reappraisal (1995, 37–47).

8. Compare Amin (2017) for a contrasting treatment in which pederasty is approached as a perverse "*eroticization of social power differentials themselves*" (42).

9. The queer triads presented in the *Orestes* are almost without exception male-male-female (thus "polyandrous"). For a complementary reading of polygyny and the attendant intimacies and tensions between "sister wives," see Olsen in this volume.

10. Trans. Ford 2002, 43.

11. So Ford 2002, 44.

12. See Wohl 2002, 124–5.

13. Compare Wohl 2015, 6: "For its critics the formal innovations of [the New Music]—its greater melodic flexibility, metrical heterogeneity, and syntactical freedom—were not only symptoms of the license and chaos of the radical democracy, but in fact their cause: Plato attributes Athens's degeneracy to the mixing of musical genres."

14. See esp. Wright 2006.

15. By calling Menelaus "my relation by marriage" (*kêdeum' emon* 477), he points up the fact that they are connected by marriage—and by their marital woes.

16. Tanner 1979, 3, cited in Zeitlin 1996, 240 ("the best kept secret of cultural ideology: the reality of the sexual, even adulterous wife").

17. Trans. modified from West 1987.

18. A reference to the dense allusive texture of the play, where "the repertory of tragedy and epic provides, as it were, a closet of masks for the actors to raid at will" (1980, 69).

19. See Blanshard in this volume.

20. On the dialectic of intimacy and intimation, see Berlant 1998.

21. See Telò 2018, 140–1 (on the queer atmosphere of Sophocles' *Philoctetes*).

22. On queer adhesion, see Telò in this volume. On Orestes and Pylades, see Rabinowitz and Bullen.

23. On their *philia* and its broader thematization in the play, see recently Griffith 2009 and Wohl 2011.

24. On incestuous queer kinship, see further Andújar in this volume.

25. Trans. West 1987.

26. His envy of Pylades' "happy marital bed" (*makarion . . . lekhos* 1208) manifests throughout. Compare Telò's (2020, 190) reading of Orestes' "patriarchal aspiration of impregnating his sister Electra through Pylades" in *Iphigenia in Tauris*. On the complexity and indeterminacy of these relationships, see also Griffith 2009, 318n69.

27. Orestes is "dead" throughout (*nekros* 84), plagued by the madness of pollution. The erotics of their scheme, "the sword in the bridal chamber (*xiphos . . . pastadôn*)" (1369–71) of Helen's "marriage to Hades" (*Aidên numphion* 1109), are brought out in the exoticized, extravagant monody of the enslaved Phrygian, styled by Anne Carson "a sort of hysterical Trojan version of Venus Xtravaganza" (2009, 177). On the Phrygian, see Introduction.

28. For this connubial sense of *agô*, cf. 246–8.

29. An ending whose "implausibility seems only to reemphasize the impossibility of resolution" (Wohl 2015, 129).

30. Similarly, the enjoined positioning (*protassomen*) suggests the positioning of words in verse.

31. Likewise, although earlier referred to as the "daughter of Tyndareus" (1154, 1423, 1512), the divine component of her parentage—and its triadic nature—is now re-emphasized: "Helen, Zeus' child" (*Zênos Helenê . . . pai* 1673).

32. On refusal, see esp. Radcliffe in this volume.

PART V
REPRODUCTION

CHAPTER 14
HECUBA—THE DEAD CHILD, OR QUEER FOR A DAY
Karen Bassi

Above all else, Hecuba is a mother. Queen to Troy's King Priam, she is reported to have had as few as nineteen and as many as fifty children. In Euripides' *Hecuba*, the focus of this chapter, Hecuba herself claims the latter figure (421). In the *Iliad*, she is the mother of Troy's most valued and most notorious fighters, respectively, Hector and Paris. Her defining characteristic in the epic is the grief she expresses at the death of the former. She is also a mother who seems to outlive most of her children.[1] In Euripides' play, she suffers the death of her youngest (*neôtatos* 1133) and only remaining son, Polydorus; the sacrifice of her daughter Polyxena; and the predicted death of her last living child, Cassandra. After these events, Hecuba takes revenge on Polymestor—her son's murderer—by murdering his sons. Throughout the play, the Dead Child is a structural element (in the plot), a temporal and ontological marker (in the divide between the living and the dead), and the source of a forestalled future (defined by Hecuba's transformation into a [dead] dog). In short, the play's formal, temporal, and ethical effects are driven by children who predecease their parents. As I have argued elsewhere (Bassi forthcoming), there is ample evidence in the Greek sources, beginning with the Homeric poems, that this sequence of events runs counter to the normative expectation that children past infancy should outlive their parents. It is true that tragedy offers radical counter-examples of this expectation in the form of children who kill their parents (Orestes) and parents who kill their children (Agamemnon, Medea, Agave). But these exceptions only prove the rule. In this chapter, I argue that the Dead Child in Euripides' *Hecuba* exposes the precarity of the normative temporal sequence (that parents should predecease their children) and queers the narrative arc of what Lee Edelman calls "reproductive futurism" (2004).

First performed during the Peloponnesian War, probably in the mid-420s BC, *Hecuba* superimposes legendary and historical accounts of the effects of war, including its (war's) role in subverting this expectation. In Thucydides' *History of the Peloponnesian War*, Pericles' famous funeral oration for the war dead, dated to 431, culminates in its extreme application. There the general encourages parents of child-bearing age who have lost sons to the war to provide more fighters for the state (2.44.3). Doing so, he says, will have two good outcomes: it will help those parents forget the children they have lost and it will help to save the city from future destruction. What Pericles refers to—by use of the objective genitive—as the "hope (*elpis*) of other children" has two related effects. First, it establishes hope as a constituent feature of Athenian political/imperial discourse.[2] And second, it establishes a logic of human reproducibility as the source of that hope.

Relatedly, the city's future is predicated on the maintenance of the traditional family unit or what we can call by anachronism the "nuclear" family.[3] In the Athenian context, legitimate male children secure that family's claims to property through inheritance. As a compensatory response to the limits of mortal existence, the rights of ownership, and the maintenance of imperial power, "the hope of children" is strictly gendered.

Fulfilled by replacing (male) children who have died, as in Pericles' speech, this hope also interrupts the linear progression of time that, at least in theory, structures narrative history. The injunction to replace children who have died, in other words, requires taking a step backward in the mandated trajectory of generational succession. This temporal interruption is also proof that compensation always comes with a cost, measured here in the dead children of living parents. The "hope of children" also necessarily brings some underlying political and social conditions to the surface. The constant threat of violent death in war during the fifth century necessarily tests the idea that death should happen according to a normative temporal sequence. The high infant and child mortality rates in Athens also reveal the fragility of this expectation. In a society in which women often died in childbirth, moreover, the principle that children should outlive their parents only makes these harsh realities more acutely felt. It explains why hope is blind.[4]

As the expression of a temporal and ontological sequence, the "hope of children" constitutes a future defined by the preservation of the human species. But, as suggested above, it simultaneously reveals the contingency of that future. I argue that this contingent future is an inherent feature of Greek tragedy, in both its form and content. As a dramatic form, tragedy literalizes the Greek metaphor of mortals as "creatures that live for a day" (*ephêmeroi*, as, e.g., at *Prometheus Bound* 255). Each plot, as Aristotle recommends, occupies a single day. All the characters, most of whom are out of myth and legend, walk and talk on the single day of the performance. Each play is generally performed only once, i.e., on a single day. And while the ancient plays continue to be performed, modern productions only magnify their essential ephemerality by anachronism: they are out of place and out of time. Finally, the fact that the corpus of extant Greek tragedy comprises only a small subset of all the plays produced in the fifth century confirms the genre's ephemerality in material terms. In short, Greek tragedy's purported universal and transhistorical (even immortal) value is an ironic effect of its essential ephemerality.

This ironic effect raises in turn the question of the *genre*'s reproducibility. Similar to the political future invoked by the reproduction and replacement of (dead) children in Pericles' funeral oration, the future of Attic tragedy names a relation to what is short-lived, in the ways enumerated above.[5] If reproduction always posits an original or a model whose features are necessarily observed in its offspring, moreover, that future arises out of the simultaneous creation and destruction of the model, here the canon of Greek (Western) literature. It refers to an art form that died too soon.[6] In this sense, the funeral oration is the ideal form for positing the convergence of sexual and ideological reproduction. But tragedy queers this convergence, as illustrated in *Hecuba*.[7] "Queer" is defined here in temporal and ontological terms, where each is complicated by the fact that tragedy is a fully embodied mimetic form. On the one hand, queer refers to a resistance to linear or teleological narration, i.e., it comprises what Carol Atack calls "asynchronous temporalities" (2020, 16–19).[8] In the current context, as stated above, this asynchronicity is epitomized in parents who outlive their children.[9] It also comprises the gap between the dramatic date of any given tragedy and its date of composition. On the other hand, queer refers to an uncertain or fluid distinction between the living and the dead. In *Hecuba* this uncertainty is manifested in the surprising appearance of Polydorus' ghost.[10] Both of these terms revolve, in turn, around the relationship of a living mother to dead children, both her own children and those of others. In murdering the children of Polymestor, Hecuba gives what she gets.

Consequently, the play abandons hope as the source of both a political and a reproductive future. Hopelessness signals instead the futility of replacing (a fantasized) past with a future that promises more of the same. What Edelman calls the "ascription of negativity to the queer" (2004, 4) is constituted in a refusal to "fight for the children" as the means of guaranteeing and perpetuating sedimented political and social orders. As Edelman explains, this negativity is advanced:

Not in the hope of forging thereby some more perfect social order—such a hope, after all, would only reproduce the constraining mandate of futurism, just as any such order would equally occasion the negativity of the queer—but rather to refuse the insistence of hope itself as affirmation, which is always affirmation of an order whose refusal will register as unthinkable, irresponsible, inhumane.

If, as Edelman concludes, "the image of the Child invariably shapes the logic within which the political itself must be thought" (2004, 2), the image of the Dead Child— defined as the child who dies before his time, i.e., before his parent/s—complicates that logic. As the subject, perhaps *the* subject, of a non-normative or out-of-sync temporal sequence, the Dead Child is a figure for both the power of and resistance to reproductive futurism.[11] Situated in contemporary American political discourse, reproductive futurism is activated in the desire to "fight for the children" in the hope of making a [better] future. As the title of Edelman's book indicates, the queer alternative to this better future is a radical insistence on "no future."[12]

This "no future" arrests the constitutive repetitiveness of the psychoanalytic death drive, defined by Edelman as a desire "to begin again ex nihilo" (2004, 9), i.e., to have no past. According to Edelman, the death drive "names what the queer, in the order of the social, is called forth to figure: the negativity opposed to every form of social viability" (2004, 9).[13] In the order of the temporal, "The Queer"—in opposition to "The Child"—is a figure for suspending the lockstep march toward a [better] future. As a consequence, Edelman's arguments offer a cautionary tale for the current crisis of sinking birth rates, met by calls in China and elsewhere to increase production, as it were.[14] Here reproductive futurism, with its "fetishistic fixation of heteronormativity" (2004, 12), constitutes a belated, predictable, and empty response to the co-present threats of economic and ecological catastrophe.[15] The irony of producing more children to replace those who grew up to endanger the planet is lost in the act of passing the buck onto unborn "innocents." I think this is what Edelman means by the "Ponzi scheme" of reproductive futurism.

If the Child does the hopeful work of reproductive futurism, the Dead Child begins the hopeless work of starting over again, of repeating the past and its failures. In *Hecuba*, this work is carried out in the political, ethical, and affective consequences of pedicide and the resulting condition of being *a-pais* ("childless"), where the alpha-privative is the sign of a child's violent death. The play thus reveals the "fantasy of survival" that drives reproductive futurism by subjecting the false promise of living forever to the brutal fact of dying too soon. This subjection also helps to explain the weird prophecy at the end of the play where we are told that Hecuba, having been transformed into a dog, will die after falling (*pesousan*) into the sea from the masthead of a ship. And that her tomb (*tumbôi*) will become a *sêma* and a *nautilois tekmar*, i.e., a protective sign for sailors (1271–3). Here aetiology as a rationalizing discourse offers weak compensation for the deferral of meaning that attends the Dead Child.

Scholars often divide *Hecuba* into two loosely joined halves. The first half begins with the appearance of Polydorus' ghost and includes the scene of Polyxena's murder; the second includes Hecuba's murder of Polymestor's sons and the aetiological prophecy. In what follows, I pursue an alternating path between these two halves. The question posed by this method is, "What do we miss in reading the play from beginning to end?" Or, conversely, "What do we gain in resisting a linear and teleological reading?" The play begins with a Dead Child, namely, the ghost of Hecuba's son Polydorus who, unburied (*a-taphos* 30), has come out of the sea (*pontou* 27) to get a tomb (49–52; cf. 701):

I asked the powers below that I get a tomb (*tombou*) and fall (*pesein*) into my mother's hands (*cheras*). And so the very thing I wanted will come to pass.

The verb "to fall" (*piptô*) thus brings the end of the play back to its beginning; the prophecy of the mother who will die by falling into the sea recapitulates—in the form of a reversed trajectory —the Dead Child who returns from the sea in order to fall into her hands.[16] There are a lot of falls in *Hecuba*, beginning with Troy's "fall" to the Greek spear (*dori pesein Hellênikôi* 5; cf. 1112). The verb's semantic range is wide in the play, but is principally predicated of humans in a precarious state, close to death, or dead. This is vividly illustrated in the Chorus's simile regarding the fate that awaits Polymestor (1025–32):

As one who falls (*pesôn*) into the hold of a ship with no harbor so you shall fall away (*ekpesêi*) from your heart's desire, deprived of your life. For when what is owed does not fall together (*sumpitnei*) with justice and the gods there is deadly evil. The hope of this road will prove false and has led you towards Hades, o miserable man. And you shall leave life by an unwarlike hand (*cheiri*).

Anticipating Polymestor's prophecy about Hecuba's fall into the sea, his own "fall" to a watery death is correlated with the working out of justice (*sumpitnei*), enacted in the reciprocal killing of children. This imagery also extends to Agamemnon's watery death in the "bloody bath" (*phonia loutra* 1281) that awaits him in Argos. Also prophesied by Polymestor, this watery death is Clytemnestra's revenge for her husband's murder of their daughter, Iphigenia. At the center of these images of falling into water, the Dead Child functions like a whirlpool, a figure that repeatedly draws the play's characters and plot into itself.[17] As a recurring leitmotif in the play, "falling" (into water, into hands) is thus a metaphorized symptom of the death drive, a succumbing to gravity that has both physical and ethical weight. The "fall" of Troy, denoting the destruction of the city and the death or enslavement of its inhabitants is, of course, the ur-event in Greek literature. Endlessly referenced in all genres, its repetition literalizes the desire to "begin again ex nihilo" while simultaneously asserting the impossibility of doing so.[18]

In *Hecuba*, the Dead Child—in the form of a ghost who comes out of "the hiding places of corpses and the gates of darkness" (*hêkô vekrôn keuthmôna kai skotou pulas* 1–2)—is the drive's mediating figure. This is made clear when the now-blinded Polymestor falsely explains that he murdered Polydorus in order to prevent the boy from re-founding and re-populating Troy (1132–44). Held off until near the end of the play, his explanation both reveals and attempts to mitigate the equivalent of a repressed childhood trauma. As the putative source of hope for a future defined by the restoration of a lost past (the fallen city of Troy), Polydorus corrects Polymestor's lie in retrospect: he explains in the prologue that, after Troy fell, Polymestor killed him "for the sake of gold" (*chrusou* 25). In short, the Dead Child—the child who dies before his parent—inhabits a past and a future that oscillate between repetition (including replacement) and revision.[19] Comprising both the form of the tragedy and its plot, this spectral (dis)ordering of time gives the lie to what Edelman calls the "order of survival through reproductive futurism" (2011, 154):

> Survival depends on preserving, as an archive anticipating a future whose very anticipation effectively prevents it, an *or*der kept in motion by its persistent repetition and, in consequence, by the death drive.[20]

If, as Edelman says, the figural Child of reproductive futurism "signifies survival" (2011, 156), the Dead Child signifies survival's impasse. This impasse is expressed in the first word of the play, spoken by Polydorus' ghost, i.e., *hêkô*, "I have come" (1). The word is a provocation in the form of an assertion. On the one hand, the first person foregrounds the ontological and temporal fundamentals of the play qua play, i.e., the mimetic and ephemeral nature of the genre. But more to the point, it summons a future posed in the question, "Why has he come?" In the *Iliad*, Polydorus is killed in Troy by the raging Achilles (20.407–27). In *Hecuba*, Euripides brings the boy back to life only to die again in another plot. In this sense, his ghost has come to revise the past only to repeat it. This includes the "fall" of Troy, repeated in Polymestor's false justification for killing the boy.

More immediately, however, the Dead Child has come, as quoted above, to "get a tomb and fall into [his] mother's hands" (50), to be memorialized in a future punctuated by a sequence of "falls" and culminating in his mother's fall into the sea. But here, too, his words mark a disruption in the normative sequence of events. Greek funerary rites require the corpse to be washed by the women of the family before being taken to the site of the tomb. The ghost's words invert this sequence by placing the "tomb" syntactically prior to his "mother's hands." This may seem unworthy of comment. But I suggest that it epitomizes the temporal distortions of the play, structured first of all by the child who dies before his parent.[21] As noted above, "to fall" is to be in the throes of death in the play. What the ghost wants—the reason for his return—is, in effect, to die again, expressed both paradoxically and poignantly as falling into his mother's hands. The Dead Child, in opposition to the Child who "assures and embodies collective survival" (Edelman 2011, 148), exists in a "no future" of perpetual restoration, replacement, and repetition. Falling outside the normative sequence of procreative events and giving the lie to the "hope of children," the Dead Child denies the means through which its parents "live on" and leaves behind instead a future without posterity.[22] On seeing Polydorus' corpse Hecuba laments, "I am dead . . . I no longer exist" (*apôlomên . . . ouket' eimi dê* 683). If the ghost of the Dead Child makes a mockery of survival, its corpse breaks the normative promise of maternity, i.e., that a(nother) child may be born again.

The death of the Trojan ("barbarian") queen-mother, preceded by her transformation into another species (known for both its slavishness and its fecundity), and monumentalized as a defense against human precarity, threatens the consoling fiction of the survival (into eternity) of the human species.[23] Consumed by the events of a day, as outlined above, tragedy as a form actualizes this threat as summed up by the Chorus in the tag with which the play ends, i.e., "necessity is unbending/barren" (1293–5):

Go toward the harbor and the tents (*skênas*), friends, to experience the sufferings of the enslaved. Necessity is unbending/barren (*sterra gar anankê*).

The final words in Euripidean tragedy are often understood as throwaway lines having little to do with the plot. Or as predictable aphorisms. In this sense, they stand in opposition to the explanatory prologues for which the tragedian is also known, like that spoken by Polydorus in *Hecuba*. These aphorisms suggest that—at the end of the day—the plays in which they appear have fallen into the moribund and repetitive domain of received wisdom. Here, of course, the aphoristic final line follows the Chorus's admonition to go toward the tents and the boats that will take them into slavery in Greece. This admonition repeats, with a difference, the words of Agamemnon that immediately precede (1287–92):

Go, miserable Hecuba, and bury the twofold corpses (*diptuchous nekrous*); and you, Trojan women, draw near your masters' tents (*skênais*), for I see a breeze just rising to escort us home. May we have fine sailing (*eu d'es patran pleusaimen*) to our native land and may we see (*idoimen*) all well in the house (*en domois*), released from these troubles (*tônd' apheimenoi ponôn*).

These lines, too, constitute something of a commonplace in tragedy. The hope that things will turn out well generally means that the opposite will happen. Expressed here in the optatives *pleusaimen* and *idoimen*, this hope for a better future "released from troubles" only signals the coming catastrophe of Agamemnon's "bloody bath." More to the point, however, these two formal devices (prologue and final tag) work against a linear reading and instead oscillate between the past and the future and between necessity and prophecy.

The two corpses are, of course, those of Hecuba's two children, Polydorus and Polyxena. But Agamemnon's reference to a favorable breeze summons another corpse, that of his daughter Iphigenia, sacrificed in order to activate the winds that will send the Greek fleet to Troy. In *Hecuba*, ships, winds, water, and corpses comprise a congeries of images in which the aftermath of the Trojan War seems to inevitably bring us back to its beginning, and always back to the figure of the Dead Child. The phrase "twofold corpses" (*diptuchous nekrous* 1287) appears to be the only example of *diptuchos* ("twofold") predicated of *nekros* ("corpse") in extant Greek literature. In *Medea* (1136), *diptuchos* refers to the two children of Medea, about to be killed by their mother. In *Phoenician Women* (1354), it refers the two sons of Oedipus—here called the sons of Jocasta—who have recently killed each other. In its other occurrence in *Hecuba*, Polymestor describes how the Trojan women stripped him of his pair of spears, which he refers to as his "twofold equipment" (*diptuchou stolismatos* 1156). Coming just before he describes the murder of his children, *diptuchos* functions here as a transferred epithet whose effect is to stress Polymestor's inability to save his two sons. But these references are not simply numerical. Supported by the fact that the verbal root of *diptuchos* is *ptussô*, "to fold or wrap around," they present an image of the past and the future folding in on each other in the repetitive return of dead (or soon-to-die) children.

This brings me back to the play's final line, "Necessity is unbending/barren" (*sterra gar anankê*). The adjective *sterros* in the play's final line has two possible meanings: "hard, stiff, unbendable" and "barren." Most editors and translators opt for the former. But given the decisive role of the Dead Child in the play, both meanings are present.[24] Barrenness, we might say, is the flip side of the Dead Child, the absolute unproductive source of No Child.[25] But what does it mean to say that necessity is "barren"? "Necessity" (*anankê*) can be predicated both of what has happened and of what will happen, as in Polymestor's reference to Cassandra's death, "It is necessary (*anankê*) that your child Cassandra die" (1275).[26] In *Hecuba*, this prophecy, together with that of Agamemnon's death as noted above, are in effect *ex eventu*; they refer to events that have already happened, most memorably in Aeschylus' *Agamemnon*. *Hecuba* includes numerous allusions to the *Oresteia* (see Thalmann 1993). Lines 1291–2 above, for example, recall the first line of the *Agamemnon* where the Watchman asks for a "release from troubles" (*tônd' apallagên ponôn* 1). In *Hecuba*, the words—if not the exact words —of the Watchman are put into the mouth of the king whose troubles are only beginning. Here the play's temporal landscape—its returns and repetitions—is entwined with performance history to deny the hope of a better future, i.e., that "all will be well in the house."[27] This of course includes the life of enslavement that Hecuba and the other women of Troy will suffer in Greek houses.

As Edelman has argued, "no future" or, we might say, a barren future, opens up the possibility for a different future, one not founded on the hope of children which, through a "logic of repetition," perpetuates the existing social order (2004, 25). In *Hecuba*, the failure to which this hope responds is literalized in the fact that Polydorus, the last remaining son of Hecuba, is also her youngest child (*neôtatos* 1133). Here narrative sequence and birth order coalesce to provide further assurance that there will be no more sons to "restore and repopulate" Troy (1139). So, too, the force of the root *polu-* ("many") in the names of Hecuba's two dead children, Polydorus and Polyxena, extends beyond etymology. It lays stress on the large number of children whom she has outlived. This observation also pertains to *polu-* in the name of her enemy Polymestor, whose (unnamed) children Hecuba murders in revenge for Polydorus' murder. *Polu-* thus signifies "many" in a negative but reciprocal register, measured in the corpses of dead children and in the ideological work of the Dead Child. Insofar as the Dead Child summons its impossible replacement, moreover, these reiterated instances of *polu-*, beginning with the name of the ghost child, expose the "haunting excess" of queer temporality, an excess that "pierces the fantasy screen of futurity" (Edelman 2004, 31).[28]

This screen is also pierced by the ephemerality spoken about at the beginning of this chapter. At the very beginning of the play, the ghost of Polydorus prophecies what is to come (43–6; cf. 285):

> Fate (*hê peprômenê*) is leading my sister to death on this day (*tôid' hêmati*).
> And so my mother will see two corpses (*duo nekrô*) of her two children,
> mine and that of my ill-fated sister.

The use of the dual to refer to the two corpses (*duo nekrô*) specifies both an ontological and a temporal homology comprising what the titular protagonist and the audience will see in the single day that comprises both the plot and the play in performance.[29] Serving as a counterweight to the forces of necessity and prophecy, ephemerality is the temporal marker of the Dead Child, the child who dies before his time and, in doing so, gives time over to no future.

Notes

1. It is unclear from Polymestor's prophecies (1259–75) when Hecuba dies in relation to Cassandra. The fact that Hecuba's death is prophesied before Cassandra's may indicate its priority in time. The various sources are less than clear about the fates of Hecuba's numerous children. As Sarah Olsen reminds me, the end of *Andromache* implies that Helenus survives to marry Andromache. Conversely, in *Trojan Women*, Hecuba's singular longevity extends to the next generation when she must bury her grandchild, Astyanax.

2. On hope as a historical variable in Thucydides' *History*, see Schlosser 2012.

3. The relatively recent concept of the "nuclear family" is anticipated in the legal relations that comprise the ancient Greek household or *oikos*. See Maffi 2005, 255.

4. In *Prometheus Bound* 250–2, Prometheus says that he stopped humans from seeing the day of their death and compensated them with "blind hopes" (*tuphlas elpidas*).

5. See Atack 2020 on the ethical effects of "foreshortened lives" in times of crisis, in an argument about the "queer" temporality of the Platonic dialogues.

6. My comments here are indebted to Mercier (2021).

7. This conclusion complements Mario Telò's dismantling of the reparative value of tragic catharsis (2020).

8. See Introduction.

9. McCallum and Tuhkanen (2011) discuss the stereotype of the queer who never grows up.

10. I discuss Polydorus' ghost in more detail in Bassi 2017.

11. See Telò in this volume; cf. Nooter.

12. See Freccero in this volume.

13. For a critique of Edelman's queer anti-social thesis, see, for example, Freeman 2019 (ch. 2).

14. See Tavernise 2021.

15. Sheldon (2016, 2) analyzes nineteenth- and twentieth-century catastrophe narratives in which the child is a "resource."

16. Telò (2020, 163) discusses the connection between tomb and mother in the prologue.

17. See Telò 2020, 30–1 on falling into water as a singular instance of the death drive.

18. See Telò 2020, 173 and n117 on the "archontic" effect of re-founding Troy, with reference to Derrida 1996, 95.

19. On queer temporalities, see Baldwin and Freccero in this volume.

20. Edelman (2011) discusses the "or" of categorical thinking as epitomized in Hamlet's "To be, or not to be."

21. See Gregory 1999 ad loc.: "By reversing the actual chronology of events (hysteron proteron), Polydorus gives pride of place to the more important of his two requests."

22. See Freccero in this volume.

23. On queerness and the animal or non-human, see also the Introduction and Baldwin in this volume.

24. Other uses of *sterros* in Euripides confirm this conclusion. At *Iphigenia in Tauris* 206, Iphigenia speaks of her *sterran paideian*, i.e., her "hard" or "barren" childhood. At *Medea* 1031, Medea speaks of her *sterras en tokois algêdonas*, her "hard or barren pains in childbirth." In *Trojan Women*, Hecuba complains of her *sterrois lektroisi*, her "hard or barren bed" (114).

25. In the other occurrence in *Hecuba*, the Chorus comments that "human nature (*phusis*) is not so *sterros* that it would not shed a tear hearing your extended complaints and laments" (296–8).

26. Cf. *Agamemnon* 218 where the Chorus states that Agamemnon "put on the yoke (or strap) of necessity (*anankas edu lepadnon*)." The reference is to his decision to kill Iphigenia.

27. On the future, see Radcliffe in this volume; cf. Nooter.

28. On queer excess, see esp. Telò and Youd in this volume.

29. Haselwerdt in this volume offers further reflections on queer doublings.

CHAPTER 15
PHOENICIAN WOMEN—"DEVIANT" THEBANS OUT OF TIME
Rosa Andújar

In "Paranoid Reading, Reparative Reading," Eve Kosofsky Sedgwick (2003, 147) discusses a "paranoid" temporality, "in which yesterday can't be allowed to have differed from today and tomorrow must be even more so." Because of its regular and repetitive nature, this is a "generational narrative" that she labels "Oedipal." Particularly telling is the fact that Sedgwick here uses a label that has been central to psychoanalysis in understanding heteronormative sexual and familial relations to designate a *temporal* relation. This is a microcosm of the way in which the focus in queer theory has, to an extent, shifted over the past few decades, from complicated entanglements with psychoanalysis—involving the adoption (and repudiation) of theoretical models like the Oedipus complex that are themselves bound up in heteronormative and teleological assumptions of sexuality—to explorations of queer ways of being in time that enable more affective and multitemporal readings. Following Sedgwick's lead, I propose a shift away from the usual (repetitive) tragic narrative of Oedipus and his family, who embody unacceptable familial entanglements and social norms, to a broader consideration of the Oedipal family in all of its temporal forms.[1] Specifically, this is an invitation to travel beyond Sophocles' plays, and toward what is arguably the most sexualized and "deviant" (and least-known) account of the myth: Euripides' *Phoenician Women*.[2] This is a play that provides a broader perspective on the Theban family: Euripides not only features Oedipus, Jocasta, and their grown children together onstage for the first time, but he also reframes the myth through Laius' initial failure to check his desire, ignoring Apollo's explicit order not to procreate.[3] Wayward sexuality is a pronounced and unifying theme in the play, which furthermore features two virgins—male and female—who eschew their reproductive and familial responsibilities.

This chapter explores prominent queer aspects of a play that is typically seen as a variation on fraternal strife.[4] I first discuss the ways in which Euripides provocatively alters the myth by challenging the already fraught expectations surrounding this abnormal family. My discussion reframes the play's episodic and ensemble-cast nature to reveal an asynchronous reality that resonates with recent conceptualizations of queer time. I also examine how the new emphasis on Laius' failed desire transforms his descendants into products of a dissident sexual act. Queer time is an alternative temporality that exposes both the cyclical rhythms ruling over Thebes as well as the family's "deviant" nature. Secondly, given *Phoenician Women*'s inordinate emphasis on the Theban (epic) past, I note the manner in which the Chorus activates the past as an erotic and embodied encounter through monstrous figures who transcend human reproductive processes: the serpent of Ares and the Sphinx. Finally, I consider Euripides' subversion of heteronormative roles through a focus on Antigone, who is transformed from a dutiful maiden at the outset to one who actively refuses marriage with Haemon at the close of the play, as well as on Menoeceus, the only male virgin sacrifice/suicide in extant tragedy. I interrogate to what extent their actions—as well as the play as a whole—might be said to embody Lee Edelman's (2004) notion of an anti-social queerness that is invested in "no future," for both the Labdacids and Creon, who is the last of the pure autochthons. Throughout, I draw from the rich work addressing the "temporal turn" in queer theory, in particular the work of Edelman, Elizabeth Freeman, and Jack Halberstam as they discuss the organization of bodies in time and reproductive futurity. Their work enables us to see the ways in which *Phoenician Women* is fundamentally concerned with the intersections between power and time, particularly as these relate to gender and sexuality.

Queer Time and Myth

Phoenician Women is a play of excess: it is the only known tragic version of the myth that features in the same dramatic space all the surviving descendants both of Laius and of the *Spartoi*, the autochthonous people who emerged from the serpent teeth sown by Cadmus. It in fact brings together multiple generations and family branches that are kept separate elsewhere in the tragic corpus: this involves not only the entire immediate nuclear family (i.e., Jocasta, Oedipus, Antigone, Eteocles, and Polyneices) together onstage, but also Creon and his youngest son. Teiresias likewise appears accompanied by his daughter instead of a nameless attendant. Even Laius is "present" in the play: from the outset his desire is identified as the cause for the family's unique troubles. The presence of numerous characters (eleven in total) and compound generations leads to extreme and unique situations: for example, Jocasta now watches her sons die for the first time, which leads the messenger to label her "excessive-suffering" (*huperpathêsasa* 1456), a rare and superlative adjective in a genre that is well known for accentuating women's pain.[5] The ancient hypotheses likewise single out the play's excessive nature, which stems from this unusually large cast of characters (*poluprosôpon*), with one calling the drama "overstuffed" (*paraplêrômatikon*) and another remarking on its overly emotional nature (*peripatheis agan*).[6]

These excesses spill over into the play's notions of time. Though scholars recognize the play's "open" structure, or its "variegated" nature,[7] which stem from its ensemble cast, they rarely acknowledge the transtemporal spaces that are created by the inclusion of multiple characters and realities. I contend that *Phoenician Women* is a productive play with which to think about queer time and narrative orientations, as Euripides constructs new temporal and mythical trajectories for this notorious Theban family. Elizabeth Freeman's work on "time binds" is especially useful to understanding the play's excesses, both temporal and sexual. As she explains (2010, xvi), "binding" is intimately related to excess, not only as a term used by Freud precisely for the management of excess, but also as "a kind of rebound effect, in which whatever it takes to organize energy also triggers a release of energy that surpasses the original stimulus." These "binds" are established in the play's extended (i.e., excessive) prologue featuring Jocasta and Antigone: in two separate opening scenes, Euripides introduces minor but impactful changes that challenge the normative arrangement of sequences surrounding this already abnormal family.

The prominence of Jocasta, a character who elsewhere in surviving tragedy has a minimal role or is simply dead, gives the first clue on the queerness of time in *Phoenician Women*. Her appearance in the first part of the prologue (1–87) offers a sweep of Theban history, from Cadmus' arrival to the quarrel between Eteocles and Polyneices, but one that is crucially structured around particular repetitive patterns that illustrate the cyclical nature of the family's suffering. These include life milestones, such as marriage and sons' coming of age, and other critical events, such as oracles and fateful realizations. These repetitions, which forge visible links between each generation, collapse notions of linear time and its irreversible and cumulative nature, since each of the family's generations is now organized in a series of lateral and parallel sequences of looping time. The past in Thebes is unfinished and never-ending, as the same seminal events hover over each generation, from Laius to Eteocles and Polyneices. Jocasta's prologue thus exposes the cyclical rhythms of the Labdacids, illustrating in particular the synchronicity of the bodies of the noble house's "male heirs" (16).

In defining chrononormativity as "the use of time to organize individual human bodies toward maximum productivity," Freeman (2010, 3) explains that she is concerned with the multiple ways in which "people are bound to one another, engrouped, made to feel coherently collective, through particular orchestrations of time." Freeman's notion of chrononormativity enables us to see not only the ways in which the women of the family are subjugated to these cyclical (male) rhythms but also how *Phoenician Women* offers new queer possibilities for Jocasta, who did not commit suicide at the appropriate or expected time. Besides revealing the temporal loops that underpin Theban past and present, this older Jocasta reveals herself to be a mediator between her sons who attempts singlehandedly to end their strife (81–3). Indeed the play's second episode features Jocasta as arbitrator (443–637). Her continued presence in Thebes—as well as that of Oedipus, who was hidden away by his sons instead of exiled and is indeed unseen for most of the play—upends the "straight" time line of Theban mythology, which typically rests on a linear sequence of events: first the oracle to Laius leads to Oedipus' exposure and Corinthian adoption, then Oedipus' return results in the murder of Laius and marriage with Jocasta, and finally, once the truth is revealed, Jocasta commits suicide and Oedipus is exiled. In this new alternate reality, Jocasta has access to an old age and experience that is typically denied to her.[8]

Even in this new queer and discontinuous time line, perhaps most surprising of all is its cause, also revealed in Jocasta's opening monologue: Laius' unchecked desire. She divulges that Laius had received an oracle from Apollo that explicitly forbade him from having children, which was "against the gods' will" (18–19). Laius, however, "yielded to pleasure in a drunken moment" (21), and upon "realizing his error and remembering the god's command," the Theban king then exposed Oedipus (23). The entire family is subsequently the product of what is presented as Laius' uncontrolled desire. In re-routing the family's myth through Laius' unruly body, Jocasta's speech thus gives a new spin to the entire Theban myth of the Labdacids, re-casting the entire family as the product of a dissident sexual act. By contrast, the account found in Sophocles' *Oedipus the King* relates that the curse was caused by Oedipus himself in cursing the murderer of Laius. The result of that curse is infertility: Thebes is plagued with sterility both on the crops and its people (25–30).[9] *Phoenician Women* instead showcases the uncontrolled and fecund sexual acts that shaped and continue to plague the Theban royal line.[10] Other textual evidence furthermore suggests that other acts of sexual "deviance" hover in the background. A scholion explains that Apollo's pronouncement is motivated by Laius' abduction and rape of Chrysippus, which led to the boy's suicide and a curse by his father Pelops.[11] According to Aelian, Euripides depicted Laius as the first to practice pederasty (*On the Nature of Animals* 6.15), which has led many to believe that this account featured in his lost play *Chrysippus*.[12] Gilles Deleuze and Felix Guattari (1983, 186) pick up on this when they highlight the "perversions" of Laius: "everything begins in the mind of Laius, that old group homosexual, that pervert who sets a trap for desire." If we consider this external evidence, which likewise highlights Laius' inability to control his desire, the "deviant" excesses responsible for birthing the family further expand and multiply.

Like Jocasta's opening speech, Antigone's first scene not only extends the prologue, as it also occurs before the Chorus's entry, but it likewise expands the play's queer sense of time. Here, Antigone, whose defiance against Creon has been especially noted by modern political, philosophical, and feminist scholars, appears as a secluded and dutiful maiden. Throughout the scene (88–201), which begins when an elderly servant leads Antigone to the roof of the house, her youth is emphasized, as is her dependent status: for example, the servant mentions at the outset that Jocasta has allowed Antigone to leave her "maiden chambers" (*parthenônas* 89). The entire scene, in which she excitedly asks the servant to identify the leaders in the battle, serves partly to emphasize Antigone's naive and sheltered nature in advance of her later transformation, as I discuss below. At the same time, the scene opens up new tragic vistas, both spatial and temporal, enabling the audience to experience the arrival of the Seven precisely as it occurs. Typically, violent action (e.g., murders, fights, suicide) is experienced retrospectively in tragedy, through a messenger's report. In the specific case of the Labdacids, the onslaught of the Seven is likewise mediated and never staged. Antigone's vista from the roof enables an innovative form of mediation and staging in the present, "[as] in a picture" (<*hôsper*> *en graphaisin* 129). The army comes to life through Antigone's excited questions to the servant, which are aptly conveyed through lyric dialogue: the account of Polyneices in his golden armor, for example, includes Antigone's wish to hug him (163–9). What was abstractly an "Argive army" for Jocasta in 77–8, one furthermore subjugated to Labdacid rhythms, becomes discrete individuals and actions in the now, experienced through the sympathetic eyes and emotions of Antigone.[13] In Aeschylus' *Seven against Thebes*, the scout provides descriptions of each of the Seven leaders. Despite his closer proximity, they remain hazy, as the messenger eyewitness reduces them to weapons and positions, focusing on the crest on their shields and at which gate they stand. There is a hint of this haziness in Antigone's initial reaction upon first reaching the roof as she claims that "the whole plain flashes with bronze" (110–11), but this is quickly supplanted by her more subjective responses. Later in *Phoenician Women* a messenger produces a more standard "catalogue" of the Seven resembling the account found in Aeschylus' play (1104–40). Because it repeats material from Antigone's earlier scene, some scholars have rejected this messenger's report as spurious.[14] Treating the scene as authentic involves recognizing the play's ability to create a sensation of asynchrony and dislocation through repetition, and the ways in which Euripides can manipulate the experience of time.

The scene additionally resonates beyond the tragic space. It recalls the "viewing from the wall" (*teichoskopia*) scene in the *Iliad* when Helen and Priam view heroes from the walls of Troy (3.161–244), an episode that is equally problematic and innovative: not only does it introduce a skewed and asynchronous time line into the epic (why would Priam suddenly query the identity of heroes in the ninth year of the war?) but it also enables the audience to experience the fight between Greek and Trojan (especially the duel between Paris and Menelaus) as if from the start. The Euripidean *teichoskopia*, however, does not pose such problems: given her seclusion, Antigone does not know the Argive champions, and from this perspective the entire scene is more plausible than its Iliadic counterpart, which hinges upon the audience baldly accepting Priam's ignorance. At the same time, if taken seriously, this affinity with Homer's epic produces some dissonance, as genders and ages are reversed: in providing answers, the servant, who is described as old, takes on the role of Helen, whereas the youthful Antigone impersonates the elderly (and allegedly ignorant) Priam. In drawing the audience's attention away from the immediate Theban past and beyond the tragic stage, the scene forges novel connections with other geographic and temporal spaces across the Greek mythical spectrum, while re-enforcing the disjointed nature of the play's sense of time.[15]

As Jocasta's prologue makes clear, the house of Laius is governed by repetition. However, through a focus on (young) Antigone and (old) Jocasta, Euripides rewrites the famous family's past, present, and future in surprising ways. The extended two-scene prologue of *Phoenician Women* establishes that Theban time is malleable and even "out of joint."[16] In going beyond the normative order of tragic sequences that typically keep the Labdacid generations apart, Euripides shows the queer possibilities and contingencies of mythical order and time, and the new uncertain models that can be built precisely by collapsing the temporal and generic divisions between the generations.

The Chorus's Monstrous Soundtrack

Crowded around the middle of the play is a curious soundtrack, three odes by the Chorus that delve deeper into Theban mythical history, from the foundation of the city by Cadmus to the more recent arrival of Oedipus (638–89, 784–832, 1019–66).[17] Lurking throughout these songs are the monstrous figures of the Theban past: the serpent of Ares and the Sphinx. In the last few decades, scholars have emphasized the manner in which these odes provide contextual and continuous links between Theban past and present, in particular through the conquest of these monsters. Marylin Arthur (1977) argues that the slaying of these figures by Cadmus and Oedipus denotes civilization's conquest of nature. This is a symbolic association that is furthermore connected to sex and marriage, as Laura Swift (2009) has recently shown; she furthermore sees these odes as "allegories for the taming of human sexuality into a regulated and socially beneficial form" (73). In marginalizing and subsuming Thebes's monsters into wider Theban narratives of civilization, scholarly accounts gloss over the queerness of these monstrous figures, who cannot be confined to human reproductive processes or biological clocks.[18] They likewise fail to recognize the manner in which their invocation across these odes transform Theban history into a series of embodied and erotic encounters.

Ares' serpent has the peculiar ability to birth men through its teeth, to which fact the Chorus draws attention throughout the odes. In the first stasimon, for example, the Chorus relates how Cadmus learns that this feat is possible from the word of Athena, who is described as "motherless" (*amatoros Pallados* 666–7), an epithet that further highlights the serpent's queer mode of reproduction. At 1060–6, the Chorus again appeals to Athena, this time paradoxically wishing that they "be mothers of fair children like these" (1060–1), referring to the sown progeny. Whereas critics have focused on the absurdity that such a wish is expressed by a group of women who are the temple servants of Apollo,[19] they fail to recognize it as a desire for a non-normative mode of external birthing that produces instantaneous grown children. Even when the Chorus declares that Earth "bore" (818) the *Spartoi*, perhaps an attempt to obscure their motherless nature, they nonetheless describe the sown people as a "race sprung from teeth" (*gennan odontophua* 821), adding in oxymoronic terms that they are "the most glorious shame" (*kalliston oneidos* 821). Since antiquity, scholars have noted the ambiguities around "most glorious shame,"[20] but rarely do they comment on the adjective *odontophua* ("sprung from teeth") occurring in the exact same line, other than to say that it is a hapax legomenon. In fact, the previous ode also included another hapax adjective, *gapeteis*, which like *odontophua* attempts singlehandedly to explain this unique mode of reproduction: in relating how Cadmus threw the teeth "onto the luxuriant plains" prior to the "birth" of the *Spartoi*, the Chorus describes the teeth as "fallen from earth" (*gapeteis* 668). The use of hapax legomena aptly captures a reproductive mode that is beyond the comprehension of the human world; their double use by the Chorus insists on its queerness.

Unlike the serpent, who is confined to these odes, the Sphinx haunts the entire play, also appearing at its beginning and end (45–9 and 1760). Her monstrosity is continuously emphasized: she is a "monster" (806 and 1023), possessing claws (809 and 1025), a creature from the underworld (810 and 1019–20), who plagued Thebes (46, 807, and 1030). As the Chorus specifies, however, she poses a particular threat to men, whom she would "disappear" (1041); in the same passage, the Chorus describes at length the mourning and grief of the women whose lives she affected by seizing these men.[21] As Timothy Gantz (1993, 495–6) reports, various sixth- and fifth-century vases show her in the process of killing—or raping?— young men. Her description in these odes (808–10 and 1021) and elsewhere in tragedy as a "man-snatching plague" (*harpaxandran kêr'* Aeschylus, *Seven against Thebes* 776–7) seems to confirm her status as a sexual predator, one who furthermore disrupts normative regimes of reproduction precisely by taking young men away from their intended brides. However, in the second and third stasima, the Chorus draws attention to her "virginal" status: "winged virgin" (806 and 1042) and even "half-virgin" (1023), perhaps as an allusion to her birth,[22] or perhaps to downplay her sexual voraciousness. Despite snatching these men, the Sphinx continues to be a virgin, thus representing an alternative and non-reproductive sexual practice, which destroys her partner while leaving her unblemished.

Patricia MacCormack (2012, 257) identifies the monster as a key element informing theories of alterity:

> The monster is alterity as both wonder and horror, as the limit of humanity and proof that the human always exceeds the parameters of what we think it is capable of. The monster crosses species and boundaries; it is hybrid, metamorphic, but it is not properly something that is so much as something that fails to be something else—the traditional dominant human subject.

Despite claiming that they are unmusical (785, 791, 807, 1028), the Chorus continually appeals to the unique combination of fascination, horror, and intrigue that these monsters inspire. Instead of reading these songs as evidence of how threats of monstrosity (and alterity) were overcome—in other words, as triumphs of the "normal"—a queer reading helps recover these as figures themselves worthy of celebration in the play's central soundtrack.

Antigone and Menoeceus: No Future in Thebes?

In a play of cyclical succession and violence, the future is always fraught. *Phoenician Women's* unique visions of Thebes's future are valuable to revisit in relation to the queer turn toward temporality. At distinct moments Euripides places a spotlight on the youngest Thebans, Antigone and Menoeceus, who are identified as both virgins and the last of their respective families, the Labdacids and the *Spartoi*. Since their bodies are intimately connected with the survival of these family lines, they enable an examination of the future orientations of the city. A consideration of these two figures extends my exploration of queer theories of time more directly into the reproductive sphere. Halberstam and others have examined the normative pull of the biological clock that not only assumes sex to be procreative but also structures lives around "institutions of family, heterosexuality, and reproduction" (2005, 1). Despite the unseen and offstage presence of Ismene and Haemon, the reproductive futurity of Thebes is arguably bound in Antigone and Menoeceus, as the play emphasizes that their bodily choices are not autonomous but instead reverberate across the city.

Antigone, who appears as a modest maiden as discussed above, undergoes an extreme transformation in the final scenes of *Phoenician Women*. In seemingly rediscovering her defiant politics by insisting on accompanying her father in exile, she embodies Edelman's concept of an anti-social queerness that is invested in "no future." In her second appearance (1264–83), she continues to be the same dutiful maiden from the rooftop in the play's extended prologue, in a manner that is "not only unusual but extremely ostentatious" (Swift 2009, 63). She is directly summoned by her mother, with an emphasis again on Antigone leaving her "maiden chambers" (*parthenônas* 1275), as Jocasta now wishes that Antigone accompany her to the battlefield to end the quarrel between Eteocles and Polyneices. The young girl initially objects, on account of "feeling shame before the crowd" (1276), and they depart the stage. However, in her third and final appearance, Antigone has abandoned her maidenly modesty, no longer concerned with shame or covering herself (1485–8). Faced with the death of her two brothers and mother, she broadcasts through song that she has become "a bacchant of the dead" (1489). Her aria (1485–1529) is filled with sounds of mourning and grief so powerful that they coax from inside the blind and aged Oedipus, who describes himself as "a grey and obscure phantom" (*polion aitherôdes eidôlon* 1543) in a nod to the way in which he has haunted the play.[23] His appearance—his first—is so surprising that scholars have dismissed the scene as inauthentic.[24] When Creon announces Oedipus' exile, she resolves to look after her father, though he himself tells her that it is "disgraceful for a daughter to be exiled with her blind father" (1691).

For Creon, Antigone's value lies in her reproductive ability, and the promise of the (grand)Child that she enables.[25] He tells her to go inside and to "live as befits a virgin" (*partheneuou* 1637), until her marriage with Haemon (1636–8). When Antigone threatens to kill Haemon (1675), Creon immediately stands down, declaring, "You shall not kill my son" (1682), and in fact exits, which leaves father and daughter alone onstage. The dramatic space, previously crowded with bodies, now contains only the old and blind Oedipus with his daughter, in fact dramatizing Edelman's adage (2004, 31) "the future stops here." This is literally the end of the Labdacid line, an end so final and irreversible that Antigone, elsewhere known for the extremes that she takes to bury her brother's body, now leaves several unburied bodies behind, including that of Polyneices, as she marches off to an unscripted life.

Antigone is often paired with Menoeceus, as another virginal figure who embraces a different life than that already scripted for him. Though he appears briefly, he does so in the center of the play (834–1018), in a poignant episode in which Teiresias reveals to Creon that the gods require the sacrifice of his son to guarantee the safety of the city (911–14). Faced with the prospect of no Child, Creon's immediate reaction is to disclaim his own ties to the city (919); later he offers himself to die in his stead (968–9) and urges Menoeceus to flee. However, Menoeceus deceives his father and kills himself.

In *Children of Heracles, Erechtheus, Hecuba*, and *Iphigenia in Aulis*, Euripides features the death of a young girl that likewise operates on the notion of heroic self-sacrifice. Elise Garrison (1995, 130), however, distinguishes Menoeceus (along with Ajax) as a "clear case of suicide" from the "suicidally motivated self-sacrifices of Macaria and Iphigenia," the latter of which she identifies as "noble suicides." In the case of Menoeceus, she argues that Euripides deliberately blurs the lines between self-sacrifice and suicide as Menoeceus claims to sacrifice himself for a greater good while actually plunging the knife into his neck. Nancy Sorkin Rabinowitz (1993, 65) emphasizes how he differs from other sacrificial victims in both having a "real choice" and in killing himself: "[H]e is the actor, the one who delivers as well as receives the blow." In the end, however, his suicide has no real impact on the battle, neither preventing it nor lessening its severity. In fact, Jocasta dismisses his death, stating that, while it is a loss to Creon, it is "good fortune" (*eutuchôs* 1206) for Thebes. To what end, then, was his death? Helene Foley (1985, 133) contends that his suicide is a poetic salvation achieved by the playwright "to save a Thebes that would otherwise have fallen." She further claims that despite its position in the middle of the play, Menoeceus' action is in fact a substitute for the traditional *deus ex machina,* in that it offers an alternative course for Thebes. This reading emphasizes Teiresias' promise that Menoeceus' death would effectively stop the curse by Ares that has haunted the *Spartoi* since the slaying of their serpent parent, thus saving Creon and his family. Seen in this light, Menoeceus' actions oppose those of Antigone, who leaves a trail of bodies that in the future will increase to include her own unmarried corpse. In particular, his suicide might be said to cohere with José Esteban Muñoz's critical corrective to the anti-social turn in queer studies; in seeing the value of queerness as being "visible only in the horizon" (2009, 11), Muñoz counters Edelman's "no future" claims. In this reading, the Theban horizon is imbued with potentiality through Creon and his family, despite the play's stark ending, which dramatizes Antigone's choice to spend her life—death—in exile with her father.

Greek tragedy is arguably the perfect venue in which to think about queer time, given the recurring nature of the violence of the past, and how it continues to reverberate in the present and specifically over the course of a single day.[26] The Theban saga, with its incestuously entangled royal family, itself presents a fascinating case study on non-normative erotics and cyclical time. As a play of excessive characters, desires, and histories, *Phoenician Women* illustrates the queer potential of the "overstuffed" house of Oedipus.

Notes

1. For an anti-Oedipal approach to sexuality in the Theban saga, see Wohl 2005 on *Bacchae.*

2. Critics typically engage with the version of the myth that is presented in Sophocles' plays. The neglect of *Phoenician Women* is curious given its enormous popularity in antiquity and in Byzantium, as Mastronarde and Bremer (1982) attest. See Introduction.

3. As told in Jocasta's prologue (13–27, esp. 21).

4. E.g., Alfonzo 2021. Cf. López Saiz (2017), who reads the fratricidal discord in the play as a critique of the political situation in Athens in 411–409 BC.

5. As Mastronarde (1994, 550) notes, this word is in fact a hapax in the tragic corpus and indeed across classical Greek literature. See Telò 2020, 80–1.

6. Ancient hypotheses as cited in Craik 1988, 58–9.

7. On its "open" structure see Mastronarde 1994, 3; for its "variegated" nature, Michelini 2009. Cf. Telò (2020, 46) who argues that the play is afflicted by "archive fatigue."

8. The play emphasizes Jocasta's old age: see 302–3, 528–9, 1318. "That an older, wiser Jocasta should stand before us," as Falkner (1995, 194) writes, "seems another of the fantastical what-if situations with which Euripides often opens his plays".

9. In Aeschylus' *Seven against Thebes*, the Chorus hints that Laius' foolishness in disregarding Apollo caused the curse (745–51, 801–2, 840–2).

10. In her dialogue with Polyneices, Jocasta later includes herself in the sexual "deviance" (379–81).

11. See Mastronarde 1994, 31–8; West 1999, 42–4; and Swift 2009, 57–8.

12. This testimony tends to guide scholarly reconstructions of Euripides' *Chrysippus*, though only meager fragments survive.

13. See Scodel (1997), who argues for women's value as focalizers.

14. See Mastronarde 1994, 456–9. For queer approaches to questions of textual authenticity, see also Baldwin and Haselswerdt in this volume.

15. See Baldwin in this volume for further reflections on tragedy, epic, and queer temporality.

16. See, e.g., Freeman 2007b, 159 (quoting Shakespeare's *Hamlet*). See Introduction.

17. Foley 1985, 107: "No other Greek tragedy crowds three stasima into four hundred lines at the center of the play."

18. On queerness and monstrosity, see Nooter in this volume.

19. Mastronarde 1994, 444.

20. See Craik 1988, 215, and Mastronarde 1994, 388.

21. Swift (2009, 75) sees the Sphinx as a symbol of "corrupted marriage."

22. This is the term that Herodotus (4.9) uses of the Echidna, whom the Chorus at 1020 identifies as one of the Sphinx's parents.

23. Telò (2020, 68–88) speaks of the "archivization" of Oedipus, who nonetheless "possesses a viral force" (70).

24. See Mastronarde 1994, 554–5.

25. See Bassi in this volume.

26. On the ephemerality of Greek tragedy, see further Bassi in this volume.

CHAPTER 16
ELECTRA—PARAPOETICS AND PARAONTOLOGY
Melissa Mueller

"Queer orientations might be those that don't line up." These orientations cut "slantwise," writes Sara Ahmed (2006, 107), across the horizontal and vertical lines of natal and conjugal genealogies, allowing "other objects to come into view." One of the objects that comes into view with a queer reading of *Electra* is the "besideness," the athwart quality of Electra's own orientation toward other objects (human and non-human) in her world. From the Indo-European word for "twist," queer is, in essence, a spatial term, and perhaps for this reason the spatial preposition/prefix *para* ("beside," "next to," "alongside") is peculiarly well attuned to the play's "twisted" kinship dynamics and queer poetics.[1] Taking as my point of departure Ahmed's insights into the slantwise nature of queer orientations, I pursue here a reading that centers itself around Electra's *para*-being (her "paraontology").

Situating Electra athwart the known categories—living vs. dead, married vs. virgin, straight vs. queer—opens up new perspectives on this most maligned of tragic heroines and her very queer experience of motherhood. For, as Jill Scott has observed, "Electra never has a child to whom she can transfer her desire, never has sexual relations with a man, and from this perspective does not fulfill the requirements for psychosexual maturity" (2005, 170). Electra's non-normative development prompts Scott to ask: "Is she then a half-being?"[2] Her being a "half-being"—alive only in her repudiation of future life—is, in fact, key to understanding Electra's character and her queerness.

The Dead Don't Dance

Nancy Sorkin Rabinowitz (2015) denotes Electra a "queer figure" because "she is at odds with traditional femininity and heterosexuality," because, that is, "she pathologically hates the females of the family (her mother and sister)." And "at the same time," as Rabinowitz argues, "she . . . is overly attached to the masculine, almost to the point of expressing incestuous desire for the father and brother" (2015, 215). This desire orients Electra toward death and the underworld, where her dead father dwells.[3] "You have always loved your father" (1102), her mother tells her. It is a love that very nearly destroys her, as Electra disappears into her intense mourning, her life a living paradox: a married virgin, a mother only in name, a woman who resists the companionship of other women.[4] Electra holds herself apart from the Chorus of dancing girls who circle around her, begging her to join them in their procession to Hera's temple.[5] Electra in this way resists *choreia*.[6] No communality for her, and no future either. Her stepfather Aegisthus, fearing her future children, had married her off to a "weak" man with whom she would bear only weak offspring. But her husband, a poor yet well-born man ("Farmer" is this character's name), proudly proclaims in the prologue that he has never touched Electra. She is still a virgin, a *parthenos*. Theirs is a sexless marriage (44), one designed to preserve Electra's virginity and her nobility, and, we might add, to sustain her in her state of "half-being."

Heterosexuality has a distinctly sordid history in the house of Atreus. Electra's asexual marriage therefore functions in part as a generational response to the sexual crimes of the family's past. The children of Agamemnon sidestep, in their different ways, biological kinship and reproductive futurism—Electra by remaining a virgin, and Orestes by escaping to the land of the Phocians where he is taken in by his adoptive family.[7] He has been raised by a surrogate father (Strophius) and develops new familial ties, including his close friendship and future sibling relationship with Pylades. In the meantime, as we hear from Electra, Clytemnestra remains *beside* Aegisthus. She has even borne him children—children who are now pushing Electra and Orestes *to the side*, making them *parerga domôn*: "Having given birth to other children *by the side of* (*para*) Aegisthus, she makes them *side-appendages* (*par-erga*) of the house" (62–3).[8] In this description of Clytemnestra, the preposition *para* redoubles as a prefix: in the Greek, these two words, *para* and *parerga*, are placed sequentially, the first capping line 62 while the second begins line 63. *Para-parerga* could, in fact, serve as a verbal refrain for the twisted sexual politics of the Atreid clan. And for Electra's sidelining of the living as she chooses *not* to dance.

The Parapoetics of Recognizing Orestes

Although celebrated for its "realism," *Electra*'s extended opening scene paints the mundanities of everyday life in the elevated tones of tragic diction and meter. This is no Athenian farmer's reality but rather "tragedy's gesture toward something outside its own mythic world: 'reality' in tragic quotation marks" (Wohl 2015, 68).[9] The tragedy seems to invite us from the get-go into a world where true virtue will be recognized and rewarded, regardless of birth, class, and wealth. But the Farmer is praised for a kind of virtue that only reinforces the play's class biases: he is declared noble for knowing his place, for *not* feeling entitled to his well-born wife. Victoria Wohl argues that the play's promise of a utopian world is a false promise: "Whatever 'utopian tendency' may have lain in the rocky soil of Argos will not be allowed to grow: we will not even be given a chance to decide how utopian it actually was" (2015, 76). Likewise, the recognition scene, with its adherence to empty tragic form, destroys whatever potential the realism of the first episode seemed to provide. All we are left with is "a collection of hollow conventions and quotations." Scholars have characterized the scene as a form of metatheater: Euripides' deliberate misquotation of the Aeschylean recognition tokens is a self-conscious admission that he has come late to this genre.[10] But Wohl's description of the plot's adherence to hollowed-out, "empty" form, more aptly, in my view, captures the dynamics of the *para*-poetics at play here.

When we look at the recognition of Orestes from the perspective of form, a couple things stand out. The Old Man initiates the episode when he returns to the cottage bearing provisions. He addresses Electra as "daughter" (493) and announces that he has come with a suckling lamb, cheeses, and wine. But when Electra notices the tears in his eyes, the Old Man explains that he has also been to the tomb of Agamemnon. His digression (literally, a turning aside from his planned route) is what brings him into contact with a lock of a hair. And this object presents itself as a potential material link between our recognition scene in *Electra* and the one from Aeschylus' *Libation Bearers* on which it is modeled.[11] As the Old Man elaborates, "I went to his tomb, a sidestepping from my path (*parerg' hodou* 509), and fell down and wept when I found myself alone."[12] As he is pouring a libation, he notices the golden locks of hair lying on the tomb. Immediately, he wonders whether they might belong to Orestes. And so the recognition scene is formally launched, thanks to the Old Man's *parerga*, his side-trip: a narrative digression (i.e., *parekbasis*) stemming from feet having stepped off the main pathway.[13] *Parerga* is, moreover, the word Electra had used of herself and Orestes, as the shunted-to-the-side step-siblings of her mother's children with Aegisthus.

The Old Man next tries to have Electra hold up the shorn locks to her own head: he is convinced that they belong to Orestes and that blood relatives have similarly colored hair and bodily features (521–3). Electra is surprised that the Old Man would assume that the hair of a man and woman resemble one another. Or that brother and sister would have similarly shaped footprints (527–37). These are the moments most conducive to the "metapoetic" interpretation, as Electra becomes the mouthpiece for the poet, who is supposedly critiquing his rival Aeschylus' artistry. But things take a different turn when Orestes comes out of the house, wanting to know to whom this ancient "remnant" of a man belongs (*leipsanon* 554). The Old Man, like Electra, is a "thing left behind," the literal meaning of *leipsanon*. And, like Electra, he sits athwart the play's fixed categories. For one thing, he is temporally out of place, having been "left behind" or passed over by death.[14] But though he is old, he is still very much alive; and although he himself is nameless, he is the only one with the authority to recognize and name Orestes. That the act of recognition is entrusted to this anonymous *para*-being and his side-swerving gait is yet another symptom of the play's queer poetics.

We sense the scene building to some sort of climax, as the Old Man eyes Orestes. Walking around him and looking at him intently, he spots the scar that will verify the young man's identity.[15] The Old Man excitedly tells Electra to pray to the gods, and Electra, still doubtful, asks what it is she should pray for—about which "of the things that are absent or present?" (564). But after accepting as proof of Orestes' identity the scar *alongside* his eyebrow (*oulēn par' ophrun* 573)—a scar that he got when he fell as a child, chasing a fawn near his father's house—Electra asks him in disbelief if he is *that one* (581). As he draws closer to making his discovery, the Old Man "circles around" Orestes (561), a movement that mimes the arc of the scene itself as it circles from the Old Man's stepping-to-the-side to the scar's arch-framing of Orestes' eyebrow. From a formalist stance, the description of the scar brings the episode to a close, with the *para* of *alongside* his eyebrow (*oulên par' ophrun* 573) here picking up on and re-tracing the *parerga* from earlier (509 and cf. 63), and reminding us, also, that it all began with the Old Man stepping off the straight path (*parerg' hodou* 509).

After they have finished embracing, Electra turns to the Old Man for advice on how to take revenge on Aegisthus and their mother, "participant in an unholy matrimony" (600, cf. 926). Biological kin-relations are represented here as corrupted by the institution of marriage—not for nothing did the Old Man address Electra as "daughter" (493, cf. 563). Their kinship is based on a relationship of care and mutual sympathy; before he sees her, he describes her as "the child of Agamemnon whom once I raised" (488). And he, of course, is the one who provided the same care for their father, when he was a child (555), while also rescuing Orestes, after Agamemnon was killed (556). It is hardly coincidental, then, that the Old Man plays such a pivotal role in recognizing Orestes.

Later, Electra will taunt the corpse of Aegisthus for having made her an orphan (914–15). And she will use the same language with her mother, claiming that she is as destitute as her mother's slaves; like them, she has been orphaned of her father (1010). Natal and conjugal kin are not only incapable, in this play, of mutual acts of recognition, they are also at the center of plots to murder one another. Only a surrogate father/grandfather has the capacity here to reunite a long-separated brother and sister. The hollowness of traditional kinship bonds, moreover, is what enables Electra to dupe her mother into visiting her. Electra arranges to have the Old Man summon her mother to her cottage on the pretext that Electra has just given birth to a male child—and is at the end of her ten-day quarantine (652). Clytemnestra will be told that Electra is sick from childbirth, and she will come, lamenting the child's low birth. And then she will be killed. Or, as Electra herself puts it, at 662: "Won't the turn toward Hades then be a slight one?" There is no explicit *para-* language here. But as we have seen of the play's queer plot "twists," even subtle veerings to the side and seemingly innocuous turns of phrase can be dramatically consequential.

Electra's Extreme Pregnancy

In Andrea Long Chu's memorable formulation, "pregnancy is a form of body modification so extreme that its result is another person" (2018, 68).[16] Electra's "pregnancy" is a fiction, and thus leaves her own body unmodified, but it results, nevertheless, in the subtraction of another person. A daughter, Electra lures her own mother to her death with the fake news that she herself has become a mother. "Motherhood" is, in this sense, an act Electra tries on for only a few minutes—just so she can murder her own mother. Capitalizing on Clytemnestra's ignorance of her daughter's body, Electra alleges that she has recently given birth. She then asks Clytemnestra to make the appropriate tenth-day sacrifice. Electra claims not to know what to do, as this is her first, and she is inexperienced. Clytemnestra says she will make the sacrifice, and that she will then join Aegisthus in sacrificing to the Nymphs. Each of their performances of maternity—Electra's and Clytemnestra's—reinforces how hollowed out and empty traditional familial bonds have become for these women.

Ironically, though not unexpectedly, it is when Electra acts out the part of dutiful daughter that we should be most frightened of her. Electra's performance of filial dependency (her soliciting her mother's help precisely at the moment when she becomes a new mother) has been contrived to mimic normalcy, to lull Clytemnestra into believing that this daughter who has always loved her father more is at long last being tamed by her own body's rite of passage. Being man or woman, male or female, are, in the words of Judith Butler (1993a, 26), "for the most part compulsory performances, ones which none of us chooses, but which each of us is forced to negotiate." One might almost believe that in her experience of "pregnancy," Electra has yielded to just such a "compulsory performance." And yet, as spectators and readers, we know that Electra plays at being a mother as if it were a drag performance. In the same piece, Butler suggests that "as an allegory that works through the hyperbolic, drag brings into relief what is, after all, determined only in relation to the hyperbolic: the understated, taken-for-granted quality of heterosexual performativity" (27). The everyday forms of heterosexual performativity are the ones that go most bizarrely off the rails in *Electra*, turning this tragedy into a queerly camp comedy, a knowingly tongue-in-cheek version of the marriage plot—though one that contains its fair share of noir.[17] A mother visits her adult daughter, thinking that she will meet her new grandson (and perform the rites associated with his birth), only to become the victim of sacrifice. Her sword-wielding daughter kills her, just like a man, and then laments:[18] "Who will marry me?" "Who will be my husband?" "In whose bed will I sleep?"[19] (1199–1200) as if the great tragedy of matricide is that it ruins one's marriage prospects. Luckily, like any self-respecting comedy, *Electra* does, in the end, find a suitable husband for its heroine.

Castor announces at the end of the play that Pylades, whom we met earlier as a silent character and as Orestes' companion, will take Electra as his wife (1284–5). She is described as *korê* (virgin), to reflect the fact that, although she is married to the Farmer, their relationship was never consummated. As a marriage plot, the arrangement works out perfectly, perhaps even a little too well. Electra gets her proper, aristocratic husband and home (1311), while Pylades and Orestes are nearly guaranteed a future reunion; in any case, the homosocial bond between them is now sanctioned through Pylades' marriage to Orestes' sister.[20] The future looks bright indeed. But at what cost? In this play, there are only two dead bodies: those of Aegisthus and Clytemnestra, whose "unholy" marriage spawned the blood-soaked action. But looking back, as Clytemnestra does in her "defense" speech (1011–50), we recall how the promise of marriage to Achilles was weaponized to lure Iphigenia to Aulis. As Clytemnestra herself argues, her father Tyndareus did not give her away in marriage to Agamemnon so that either she or her offspring should die (1019). And yet, a death-filled marriage is precisely what she got. Agamemnon brought Iphigenia to Aulis where she was meant to marry Achilles. There, instead, he slaughtered her over an altar. And from this act sprang the seemingly endless sequence of "sacrificial" murders performed under cover of marriage. Little wonder then that Electra herself, at the start of the play, is so skeptical of the institution, associating marriage, as she does, with death.

When Orestes, still unrecognized, asks Electra why she is living so far away from town, she replies that she has entered a "deadly marriage" (*thanasimon gamon* 247). Her marriage to the Farmer, while not literally life-threatening, binds her in a sort of living death. Additionally, Electra's language evokes the ghosts of other "deadly marriages"—Iphigenia's, Agamemnon's, Aegisthus's, and Helen's, to name just a few. Thus, the shell of *Electra*'s marriage plot lightly conceals the much darker "twisted" stuff of counterfeit kinship bonds in which the Atreid clan so expertly traffics. I have underlined in my discussion thus far the parodic twists the plot takes in its parapoetic journey toward a "happy" ending. But it is time now to return to Electra herself as a queer character.

In her performance with Clytemnestra, Electra makes visible some of those barely recognizable norms and gestures that undergird heterosexual femininity in a classical Greek context. Because we know that she is pretending, we are that much more sensitized to the way that mother–daughter relations are supposed to play out. Just as with a drag performance, the "understated, taken-for-granted quality of heterosexual performativity" rises to the surface. Electra, as we have seen, enacts matrescence—in this way fulfilling societal expectations placed on daughters who are married women—only in her plot to murder her own mother. And this may make us wonder who the "real" Electra is. What sort of woman, or man, or being is she? That question turns out to be much harder to answer. There is no single scene or speech to which we can point for a clear answer. Nor is this the sort of question that avails itself of a straightforward response. What we can say is that, when Electra is called upon to participate in a group whose membership is configured according to strict delineations of age, life stage, and gender, she finds herself unable to comply.

Paraontology

Alluding to the work of Sara Ahmed, trans* and queer theorist Marquis Bey (2020,18) affirms: "[W]e learn about worlds when they do not accommodate us, and that refusal to accommodate is the marker of paraontology." Bey refers here to the unique status of trans(*) and Black individuals: "the Negro and trans do not accommodate the worlds of race and gender." Defying standard categorizations, whereby male and female are mutually exclusive terms,[21] and Black undergirds the ontology of whiteness,[22] Negro and trans* lie "in the interstices or beyond the scope of what can be understood" (19). I want to propose a similar interstitial, or "paraontological," understanding of Electra's nebulous status. For Bey, the Greek etymology of paraontology offers a way of capturing its "fissured besidedness."[23] "I wish to explore," Bey writes, "the implications of thinking the *para-* of *paraontology* in both eytmological senses, denoting the paraontologicality of blackness and transness as a fissuring besidedness to ontic and ontological meaning and making *and* a protection from the regime of ontology" (18). In order to "be" in the eyes of others, one must fit within the tyrannizing lineaments of ontology, as these are defined through race and gender. But what of those who do not fit, those whose very being is illegible because they are *beside*-being?

"In a simplistic sense, paraontology refers to something that cannot really be 'referred' to" (Bey 2020, 18). Is Electra then a "woman"? If she were, she would have to be a mother, given her age and marital status. She plays at mothering, as we have seen, but only to entrap and kill her own mother. In Bey's words, "[R]eferences hold sway by virtue of their allusions to something concrete, something rooted and grounded. A kind of sediment, if you will" (19). What is missing, in Electra's case, is the assemblage of features that would constitute, or sediment, her as either "woman" or "girl." As a virgin, she is still a *parthenos*, at the stage of being that precedes and is superseded by womanhood; and yet she is married, a social status that precludes being a girl. You cannot point at what is not there. The *para*-being, the "half-being," will always be slightly to the side of what is there, waiting to be referenced. So it is that when the Chorus tries to interpellate her into their group, they fail. As Naomi Weiss (2018, 69) observes, "[W]hile the Chorus see her as a potential member of a maiden Chorus, Electra through her refusal to join the dancing excludes herself from either category, and simultaneously underscores her lack of choral participation within the drama itself."[24] Her refusal to dance, I would add, is a consequence of her paraontological dilemma.

Electra dwells in the interstices, between unrecognizable and recognized states of being: "What arises nebulously, unintelligibly, in the interstices or beyond the scope of what can be understood has the residue of the paraontological" (Bey 2020, 19). There is no Chorus, no collectivity, that could welcome her into its fold because Electra desediments the very categories through which such groups constitute themselves.[25] In her intense mourning, moreover, she reaches beyond the human world, searching for a way of expressing her grief. At one point, she compares herself to a swan who cries out loud for its father as it is carried *alongside* the river's streams (*potamiois para cheumasin* 152). This is a swan whose father has perished in a hunting net. Electra empathizes with it in a manner in which her fellow humans no longer feel empathy for her. Electra has no desire to join the procession or the chorus of dancing maidens, nor to set her "whirling step" alongside the brides of Argos (180). She rounds out her lament by recalling again how she lives in a state of half-being, an impoverished exile within her own homeland (207–12):

> But I live in the house of those laboring with their hands, melting away my soul, a fugitive from my father's house, up among the mountain crags, while my mother lives, yoked in murderous wedlock, with another (*allôi sungamos oikei*).

Notice here the difference between the prefixes *sun-* and *para-*. *Sun-* marks relationships of merging conjuncture, where two become, or are already, one, whether in marriage (e.g., *sungamos* means "spouse"), genealogy (*sungonos* meaning "sibling"), or action.[26] *Para-* marks a turning athwart or bending to the side of such a merger. Because one who is *para-* skews to the side, a space opens up that can be filled by mourning—by, for example, the orphaned swan, or orphaned Electra.

But *para-* can also mark a turning to the other side, a swiveling from intense mourning to euphoria, as happens when, in the wake of Aegisthus' death, Electra joins the Chorus in a victorious song of celebration. Sharing an ode with her, in which they dance and sing in praise of Orestes' revenge, the Chorus compare Orestes to an Olympic victor, rejoicing that he has achieved a "crown-contest greater than those **by** the streams of Alpheios" (*kreissô tôn* **par'** *Alpheiou / rheethrois telesas* 862–3). These streams recall those of the swan's mournful song, as lamented by Electra earlier. But now being *alongside* flowing water is a joyful image. *Para*'s sense is never sedimented. It expresses relationality, not monumentality. In this respect, *para* captures a body's spatial position relative to other bodies, and other objects, in time. As these shift, so, too, does the meaning of *para*, and the meaning of "being" to which it attaches.

As one of only a handful of tragedy's *para*-heroines (Antigone is another), Electra brilliantly reveals the rigidity and hypocrisy of gendered and sexual identities, as well as of the social institutions such as marriage and motherhood that sustain and (re)produce them. Her very existence is, for all intents and purposes, a logical impossibility. And yet, by centering its action around those who dwell in between the normative categories, *Electra*, a play that is also precariously positioned in terms of its literary genre, desediments those ontologies, encouraging us to cast our gaze beyond—and to the side of—what is visibly there.

Notes

1. Ahmed (2006, 67) describes queer as "a spatial term, which then gets translated into a sexual term," becoming a "term for twisted sexuality that does not follow a 'straight line,' a sexuality that is bent and crooked" (here Ahmed cites Cleto 2002, 13). Telò (2020, 282) describes tragedy's archive feelings as "*queer* feelings of twistedness and fractured temporality." On Ahmed's concept of queer orientation, see also Nooter and Olsen in this volume.

2. Scott quotes Butler (2000, 40) on Electra's role within Freud's writings: "The daughter's incestuous passion is less fully explored in the Freudian corpus, but her renunciation of her desire for her father culminates in an identification with her mother and a turn to the child as a fetish or penis substitute."

3. Worman (2021, 69) suggests that Electra is "strangely situated at the intersection of sex and violence" and that she engages in an "angry flirtation with the dead."

4. See Rabinowitz (2015, 221), who remarks that Electra's "status is contradictory, married but a maiden still"; Rabinowitz settles on "melancholy heterosexual" as a way of capturing how her "gender construction is related to her mourning" (222).

5. On the Argive Heraion and the festival of Hera as backdrop to the action, see Zeitlin 1970 and Ormand 2009, 268–9.

6. See esp. Weiss 2018, 66–72. Ormand (2009, 251) observes that, for Electra, "exile is to be understood in terms of marriage and dances."

7. On "reproductive futurism," see also Andújar, Bassi, Nooter, and Telò in this volume.

8. See Ormand 2009, 252 on *parerga . . . domôn*: the phrase is "not a common one and, taken literally, means something like 'deeds standing beside the house.'"

9. On realism, see Introduction.

10. See Torrance 2013,14–31, with reference to earlier scholarship. Baldwin, in this volume, further explores the queer dimensions of belatedness.

11. See Telò 2020, 199–206 on the lock in *Libation Bearers* and hair as an archival object.

12. There is a parallel with the location of Aegisthus' murder insofar as the Old Man explains to Orestes that Aegisthus' fields have a road right beside (*para-*) them (636): *hodon par' autên, hôs eoik', agrous echei.*

13. Thanks go to Mario Telò for the observation about *parekbasis*.

14. Compare Jocasta's old age in *Phoenician Women*, as discussed by Andújar in this volume; I am grateful to Sarah Olsen for encouraging me to think more about *leipsanon*.

15. On the significance of this scar, see Mueller 2016, 99–100.

16. See also Andújar in this volume for a discussion of queer and monstrous modes of reproduction.

17. See also Olsen in this volume on camp aesthetics in *Andromache*.

18. See Worman 2021, 70 on Electra's "warrior affect."

19. Electra prefaces these questions with two others—"Where will I go, *and into which chorus?*" (1198). The latter question underlines the importance of chorality (choral life in ancient Greece) in producing and sustaining personal and group identities in relation to age, marital status, and gender. On Choruses in Greek literature, see now Steiner 2021.

20. See Rabinowitz 2015, 224–5 on the incestuous language and imagery of *Orestes*, where Pylades' presence "adds a note of homoeroticism" and Electra's presence seems to further the intimacy between the two men (along the lines of Sedgwick 1985). See also Youd in this volume on *Orestes* and its representation of relationships among these characters. See also Rabinowitz and Bullen on *Iphigenia in Tauris*.

21. For Bey (2020, 25), trans* is the "working-on and undoing-of the organizing frame of the gender binary."

22. See, e.g., Bey 2020, 24: "The white subject is the ground allowing all notions of 'subject' to come forth, no matter how 'black' it might be. This ground must be displaced, and the name Chandler gives for that displacement is the Negro, that figurative instantiation of desedimentation."

23. Bey 2020, 17: "Interestingly, the prefixal para- comes from the Greek word παρα-, meaning 'by the side of,' 'beside,' and hence 'alongside, by, past or beyond.' But it is also linked to French, Italian, and Latin, where it bears a strong affinity with *trans* (to the side of, across, beyond)." See Introduction.

24. On maiden Choruses in tragedy, see also Olsen 2020, 55–8.

25. Cf. Ormand 2009, 254 on how Electra's "ambiguity of status" bars her from "regular social activity that should be available to her in the form of dances and festivals."

26. On *sun-* to characterize sexual relations and marriage, see Olsen in this volume.

PART VI
ENCOUNTERS

CHAPTER 17

IPHIGENIA IN TAURIS—IPHIGENIA AND ARTEMIS? READING QUEER/ PERFORMING QUEER

Nancy Sorkin Rabinowitz and David Bullen

Nancy. When Mario Telò and Sarah Olsen first invited me to contribute an essay to a *Queer Euripides* volume, I enthusiastically said yes and easily chose *Iphigenia in Tauris* as "my" text, since I had already developed a gay positive reading of the relationship between Orestes and Pylades (Rabinowitz 2020).[1] I had shared my subsequent research with By Jove Theatre Company, and we were working on a performance piece that became the digital installation called *The Gentlest Work*. Thus, it also made sense to have By Jove's co-artistic director and theater scholar, David Bullen, join me in ruminating on what was queer in the play. In our conversations, I tended to emphasize the text and what a queer perspective made visible.

David. And I always added: "and performance!" When By Jove first crossed paths with Nancy in 2018, her interest in (re)asserting Orestes and Pylades' sexual and romantic connections intrigued us. Our work had been feminist, but we had not considered the possible queerness. Nancy posed a question that we explored through the devising process: how and why would it matter for these characters to be represented as in some way queer?[2] How and why would it matter to the queer members of the company to see ourselves represented in these particular ancient characters?

In this essay we reflect on the queer possibilities of *Iphigenia in Tauris*—a text that became important to By Jove's process, thanks to Nancy's work—and explore how the "feedback loop" between two different ways of knowing of this play, through text and through performance, facilitated new queer readings that go beyond Orestes and Pylades' desire for one another.

Into the Rehearsal Room

Nancy. To my surprise, By Jove paid much more attention to Iphigenia than to Orestes and Pylades. In the early stages of working together, almost none of the artists focused their attention on the pair; indeed some of them really hated Orestes. The character they were drawn to—Iphigenia—led to a revelatory reading. They imagined a queer bond between Iphigenia and Artemis.

David. We work by having the members generate ideas and text, before exploring it together in the rehearsal room. This process de-centers one vision, whether that is from a director or a single writer (new or old) and helps us make work collaboratively. As Nancy notes, almost everyone responded to Iphigenia. One early piece by Wendy Haines imagined how Iphigenia might have felt about Artemis:

> You took me, in that moment. I felt your pressure under my arms, my spine, lifting me out. Not taking flight but just being, in another way, I can't describe, like you were the stardust I'm made of. Your fingers scraping the molecules that make me. And I felt for the first time that I was nothing, in the grand scheme, because you were the whole universe in one grip, one wing. How could I compete with any relevance? My helpless body that you could dissipate into carbon on a whim. But you didn't, you moved me here, and left me unchanged in all but my perception of reality. It was cruel of you, cruel to show me the fabric of my own existence and then leave me to ponder it powerless. You wonder why I can't sleep, Artemis, because I'm scared if I close my eyes I might break apart, become liquid, ether, nothing. Without you I can't feel whole, I can't be, you're my glue, holding the bits and the dust together. Without you I feel my skin pulling away, my edges blurring, my voice cracking, my heart failing. Please take me back, take me into you, I'm only ever going to be an addendum of you, indebted, connected, a motherless child.[3]

Nancy. That text and the dance it inspired led me to rethink my initial focus on the men, and my earlier view of Iphigenia. Her rescue, as narrated in *Iphigenia in Aulis*, was not convincing to me, and I ignored it in my chapter on the play (Rabinowitz 1993). I saw trauma but no healing,[4] and I brought that cynicism to my work on *Iphigenia in Tauris*. I was not convinced that her life as a priestess at Brauron was anything but a living death. Certainly not what I, following Judith Butler in her work on *Antigone*, would call a livable life (Butler 2000, 23–4).

David. The interplay of trauma and the possibility of healing, of rescue, underpinned the company's explorations. It resonated with many of the company members' experience of negotiating a "livable life" as queer: we recognized the trauma and the search for return from exile. We were drawn to the scenes in *Iphigenia in Tauris* and in *Orestes* where Pylades cares for the ailing Orestes.[5] In July 2019 we thought about relocating the scenes of tender care from Pylades and Orestes to Iphigenia and the statue of Artemis. This led, on the spur of the moment in the rehearsal room, to the idea of a danced exchange between Iphigenia and the statue.

The implausibility and incongruity of such an exchange was directly inspired by Joint Stock Theatre Company's 1986 proto-queer devised response to *Bacchae*, *A Mouthful of Birds*, in which a character dances "tenderly, dangerously, joyfully" with a pig they loved that they had inadvertently sent to slaughter (Churchill and Lan 1986). Evoking a *pas de deux*, queering this kind of duet, the sequence enabled us to express, corporeally, the layers of trauma, violence, abuse, and regret that we felt between Iphigenia and Artemis—not only at Aulis, but in Iphigenia's new situation, transformed from victim to perpetrator of human sacrifice.

But the sequence also turned on the impossibility of a reciprocal desire between a deity and a mortal. In this instance, the scene recalled the violence that has marked Iphigenia's life so indelibly—and, indeed, the violence that has corroded the family from the start. Here, then, we had located a potential queerness in the Atreid myths that emerged from thinking beyond the confines of extant texts and myths as attested in antiquity.

It is queer in the sense of same-sex desire, but also in that it interrupts and reconfigures one of the central themes of the Atreid myths—the repetitive intergenerational trauma born of cyclical violence—away from Orestes' guilt and his expiation via Apollo to Iphigenia's extraordinary death, exile, and return as facilitated by Artemis and Athena. Unlike Orestes' relationship with Pylades, which we struggled to make relevant to a narrative retelling of the myths, Iphigenia and Artemis offered a queer reading that emerged from both character and plot—and potentially a feminist reading, too. It was, by far, the sequence most commented on by the audience at the work-in-progress performance in 2019.

Returning to the Text

Nancy. When I saw the piece in the rehearsal room, I was incredibly moved. David here talks about its "impossibility," but, inspired by what I had experienced, I turned to my traditional research methods to see what might be "there."

I started first by looking at the goddess Artemis. She has lots of potential for queerness given her associations with the wild and her confirmed virginity. She, along with Hestia and Athena in the *Homeric Hymn to Aphrodite* (10–13), is given the right to stay a virgin forever.[6] In Greek, the virgin has a kind of power—she is untamed (*adamastos,* from *damazein* meaning "to tame"). Modern lesbian authors like Adrienne Rich and Marilyn Frye emphasized the virgin's resistance, enacted or potential, to male domination. Rich calls her "she who belongs to herself" (1986, 107); Frye sees her as resisting the service to men required by patriarchy (1992, 124–37).[7]

Furthermore, Artemis is always surrounded by girls and young women. Artemis' cult at Brauron centers on girls and their transition to marriage. If a girl imitates the goddess fully and holds onto her virginity, she is a threat to the heterosexual marriage system.[8] But we must also consider what the girls were doing there. Pots found at the site show girls together, nude and dancing, which raises the possibility of female desire; certainly the *Partheneion* of Alcman indicates the presence of female homoeroticism in the worship of Artemis Orthia.[9] Moreover, Zeus, in Ovid's *Metamorphoses* (2.420–5), transforms himself into Artemis to seduce her female acolyte Kallisto. Thus, Artemis looks like a plausible object of queer desire.

What about Iphigenia? Going back to the play, I found signs of an attachment. Her first description of Artemis is powerful and evokes a sense not only of awe but of light, like that of a beloved: "But Artemis stole me away, and gave the Achaeans a deer in my place. She brought me through the radiant sky and settled me here in the Taurians' country" (28–30).[10] Since then, she has lived in the temple with the statue (*agalma*), and when the three of them depart, she is holding it in her arms (1158).[11] Furthermore, in the deceptive show they put on, she claims she must purify both the "strangers" and the goddess at sea (1225); thus she cares for the statue, bathing it (1230). Is the goddess then her beloved, represented in this "doll"?[12] She looks forward to a future with her: "Oh maiden mistress of Zeus and Leto, if I can wash the blood from these men and sacrifice where we should, your dwelling will be pure, and we shall enjoy good fortune (*eutucheis*)" (1230–3). She thus envisions a life together with the goddess. Can we imagine her lavishing on it the nurturing she received perhaps from her mother and from Artemis? Though this is a performance, the pretense may allow her to express what she really feels. At the least, the bond with Artemis enables Iphigenia to escape her deadly past in her family—the play opens with Pelops—as it saved her from the sacrifice.

Queer theory on the emotions and affect was productive for my thinking about other definitions of "queer" than the sexual one.[13] And it synced with what I was learning about performance. Actors, especially those working as By Jove does, must attend imaginatively to the emotions, as embodied.

David. This way of knowing the characters—imaginatively, through the body— uncovers what might exist between, before, and after the lines of the text. As theater-makers we cannot stop at the text: an actor, for example, needs to know what the characters are *not* saying as much as what they are—what they are holding back as much as what they are making known.[14] And while readers might do something similar, actors need not only to imagine the subtextual but enact it convincingly. The job of the writers in the group is to give voice to what the actors uncover beyond, or despite, the text.

And what is intriguing here—although not entirely unexpected—is that when it came to Iphigenia all of us kept returning to the sacrifice at Aulis as a point of trauma that informed our understanding of the way queerness manifests "in Tauris."

Nancy. Certainly I felt the trauma that brought Iphigenia to this place. The first half of the text amplifies her continued suffering; she mourns for herself, betrayed by her father, who held her aloft for sacrifice (23; cf. Aeschylus, *Agamemnon* 232). This passage is from her initial lament (203–13):

> From the start my star has been ill-starred ... And from that night when I was born ... The divine Fates who attended my birth have forced upon me a harsh upbringing. I was the firstborn child that Leda's ill-used daughter in her chamber †gave birth to, nurtured†, victim for a father's atrocity, a joyless offering promised by his vow.

She later returns to the memory of that day (361) and bewails her situation and her love for her father. She recounts her efforts to touch him as she simultaneously accuses him of giving her a shameful—or "ugly" (*aischra*)—wedding (364–5).

Furthermore, she feels isolated. She emphasizes the way in which her "upcoming" marriage led to separation from the rest of the family: she did not even say goodbye to those she assumed she would see later (376–7). Like Electra in her plays, she emphasizes her unmarried state (*agamos ateknos apolis aphilos* 220). The repeated alpha privatives here stress her loss. Moreover, though rescued from death, she is still in exile, a "stranger" in this "inhospitable" place (*axeinou pontou . . . xeina* 218). There is also evidence of her melancholy or self-mourning—she wants to know if anyone in Argos remembers her, the sacrificed daughter (*sphageisês* 563);[15] she cries for the "poor wretch and the father who killed her" (565).

But change of location and the passage of time have also given her new awareness. She notes her objectification—she was paid to the goddess to fulfill her father's promise to offer the year's "fairest thing" (21–3) like a calf (*moschon* 359). Her phase of father-love seems to be over. Now she understands that Agamemnon betrayed her, deceiving her with a promised marriage to Achilles just to get her to Aulis. Then she was excited, but now she recognizes the marriage as "bloody" and a deceit (370–1). She names Agamemnon a murderer (1083) and tells Thoas she hates Greece for destroying her (1187). This version of the story lends itself to a critique of marriage and heteronormativity, connecting marriage and death; it gives the lie to the idealization of heterosexual marriage.

This suffering has strong effects on her—the rescue has turned Iphigenia into a ritual murderer. At first, she disclaims the violence: she does not actually strike the blow herself (40–1; 622), which would be shameful for a woman, as Orestes says ("a woman slaying a man" 621—cf. Clytemnestra). She says she used to be careful, taking pity on the Greeks because one of them might be her brother (344–7). Now that she thinks her brother is dead, she is frankly angry at what happened to her—Cropp translates *cheiroumenoi* as "manhandled," the word also used to describe the Taurians' treatment of Orestes and Pylades (359–60; cf. 330 *cheiroumetha*). And she wants revenge; she regrets that she did not have the chance to sacrifice Menelaus and Helen (354–8; cf. 439–46) in payment for her sacrifice. Indeed, the sacrifices she performs or prepares for are seen as making up for her own "death" at Aulis, though they of course are not true sacrifices (1418).

Thus, Euripides reveals the torture she suffered and continues to experience. Though I do not want to seem to be arguing that this violence from her father turned her "queer," the other consolation in this bleak picture might come from living in a community of women. She and her servants are represented as sharing the fellow feeling of exiles, based in part on nostalgia for Greece. Working with By Jove and watching the installation also led me to see the hidden dimensions of a sisterhood.

David. And what affect theory leads to on the page was mirrored by what was occurring in practice. The Covid-19 pandemic interrupted our plans for a public performance, and transformed the final product: instead of pursuing a conventional theater performance we developed our multitude of ideas into a digital installation, explored much like an art gallery, with around sixty short films, audio clips, images, and fragments of text. One "room" of the installation was devoted to Iphigenia, her trauma, and her queerness. This included a further development of the Iphigenia–Artemis dance, now delivered solo by movement director Susanna Dye (the conditions of the pandemic meant we had to work independently), and *R.E.M.*, a film that reads Iphigenia's layers of trauma through the lens of EMDR (eye movement desensitization and reprocessing) therapy. This enabled us to articulate and make visible Iphigenia's traumatic relationship to her past outside of the restrictions of Euripides' play (for example, the adventure narrative or the focus on Orestes). It would be difficult to do this in the same way through scholarly analysis or, indeed, through a conventional stage production of *Iphigenia in Tauris*.

As Sarah Olsen pointed out to us, *The Gentlest Work* stands in a non- or even anti-teleological relationship to Euripides' play. In refusing both form and structure that "ends" in a narrative sense, the installation was able to repeatedly reflect on facets of Iphigenia, Artemis, and the other characters that may easily be missed in a dramaturgy oriented so keenly toward an end point, i.e., the return of the Greeks to Greece. Suspended in the installation's fragments, Iphigenia and the others both remain and do not remain among the Taurians, allowing the queernesses that became visible there to be explored via the stasis of that space, the recounting of their journeys into it, and the potentialities of their exit from it.[16]

Between Text and Performance: Among the Taurians

Nancy. With my eyes on the male homoeroticism, I had not paid sufficient attention to the setting of the play; it is often the case that having a goal (or a position or perspective) enables you to see some things but to overlook others. As I was working with By Jove, I became intensely aware of that oversight. There have been many challenges to feminism and queer theory for ignoring race and class; I was committed to taking an intersectional approach. So I pushed us to think about what the setting has to do with the sexuality theme per se.

The play disrupts the canonical treatment of the *Oresteia*; it is in a queer time and place (see Halberstam 2005).[17] Euripides finds the conclusion to the *Eumenides* inconclusive; Orestes' return to rule (and adulthood) has been deferred once again. He is still being pursued by a few Furies, and his new initiatory task is to rescue (steal?) the statue of Artemis. In this way the play displaces the centrality of Athens and its democracy in the *Oresteia*.

Coincidentally, women's homoeroticism, to whatever extent it was represented, was often located outside of Athens—in Sparta, Lesbos, or with the Amazons in Scythia. This play is set near those regions; the setting of the play is as wild as its patron goddess.[18] As we have seen earlier, the characters are in an inhospitable place, as the text reiterates through the many references to hostile sea and crashing rocks, the Symplegades: "the twin converging rocks of the Inhospitable Sea!" (*pontou* ... *axeinou* 124–5; cf. 241 and 260–3). Over and over again we hear how hostile the land is, how inaccessible. What we call the Black Sea in Greek is literally *axeinos*, "inhospitable," and the Greeks prided themselves on their code of hospitality. Thus, the land of the Taurians is quite clearly made the realm of the other—the hostility is not merely geographical. The Chorus makes the connection between place and behavior (392–406):

Dark, dark confluences of sea, where the gadfly that flew from Argos crossed over the unfriendly sea-swell < >, passing to Asian land from Europe … and come, come to this unwelcoming land, where for Zeus' maiden daughter altars and columned temples are soaked with human blood.

The characters are clearly in a deathly realm—the temple to Artemis is ghoulishly festooned with the remains of the bodies sacrificed. When Orestes and Pylades arrive, Orestes describes the "altar where Hellene blood drips down." Pylades replies: "Indeed— top-pickings from foreigners who have died here" (72–6). Human sacrifice and the use of those heads as decoration here typify the barbarian realm. The Chorus claims that the sacrifice would not be holy in their land, but is here (464–6). Thus, by a sleight of hand the Taurians are marked as those who commit human sacrifice, not the Greeks, though we know that Iphigenia is here because she was rescued from being rescued by that very civilized Greek man, her father.

We can see that the plot thread of peril and exile is closely related to the barbarian vs. Greek binary. Martin Cropp (2000, 40) argues that space and time show progress: "The play's allusions to the orderly ritual world of contemporary Athens, set against the perversions of the Taurians' ritual world and of Pelopid history, reinforce its mythical message of transformation, of a better order emerging from the disorder of the distant past … uncivilized practices of the mythical past [are] being refashioned as, or replaced by, civilized symbolic acts." The cowherd, who acts as messenger, and the Chorus are very impressed by the exploits of Orestes and Pylades (336–9 and 393–438), although they are to my mind more like pirates—gathering wealth (416–17)—than heroes. Finally, Thoas and his people are easy for the clever Greeks to fool, confirming another stereotype about the barbarian.

The plot itself is fully implicated in colonialism and the ideology of Greek supremacy over the barbarian.[19] The word "barbarian" comes up repeatedly in the text, sometimes suggesting "lesser," sometimes only suggesting difficulty (cf., e.g., 418). For instance, the three Greeks claim to be rescuing Artemis from a land where she is established, calling it barbarian; going to Athens is a step up for the divinity (1086–7). Iphigenia similarly asks for rescue for herself from the barbarian land (1400). The speech of Thoas reveals the Greek point of view of the whole play, since he uses the term *barbaros* of himself (1174, 1170, and 1422). Thus, as Edith Hall and others have established, here the barbarian is used to set off or establish the glories of Greece.[20]

David. Nancy's reflections on the location of *Iphigenia in Tauris* and the modern racist ideologies around the term "barbarian" affected By Jove's project. In devising processes that work fast and loose with mythic source material, it is common for narrative quirks to develop that quickly feel "canonical" to those making the project. One such quirk grew and established itself in the company's imaginary in the first two years of development: hesitant to describe the location Iphigenia is transported to as "Tauris," the company members began to refer to it as "the island."

Nancy. I objected to the word when it came up in part because I liked the specific reference to Crimea as a liminal space, attached to the mainland, not an island. But also because it reminded me of ideas of gay ghettoes, which tend to be very white (Nero 2005), as "Circle Jerk," an award-winning new play by Michael Breslin and Patrick Foley, points out with deadly irony (https://circlejerk.live/).

David. It was only with Nancy's further thinking on Euripides' play that we began to interrogate this misnomer. It underscored the company's understanding of Iphigenia as experiencing a kind of exoticized, improbable exile, which dovetailed with the strangeness of her relationship to Artemis' statue. But it also had implications for who the Taurians were. Our focus on Iphigenia's experience on "the island" rendered the Taurians themselves invisible, a function perhaps of Euripides' problematic identification of these people as "barbarians." We avoided them because we were wary of racializing the Taurians in a manner akin to the racializations of Caliban and Ariel in the performance history of Shakespeare's *The Tempest.*

As we moved to a digital project with *The Gentlest Work,* we were able to reconnect with artists outside of the UK. One such artist was Lilian Tsang. Possessing both British and Chinese nationalities, Tsang had worked in London for many years but at the time of the pandemic was in Hong Kong, where she grew up. After looking through the material the company had generated, and after conversations with Nancy and me, Tsang was drawn to Iphigenia and the colonial, racialized contexts of her exile to, and return from, living among the Taurians. For Tsang, this resonated with her experience of possessing dual nationalities and of growing up in a city shaped so significantly, within her lifetime, by colonialism.

Here both the company's existing threads of engagement—Iphigenia's complex relationship to Artemis and the somewhat more accidental relocation of the Taurians to an island—took on new meaning and informed the work Tsang produced for *The Gentlest Work.* Artemis—which might be imagined as the name for an indigenous deity that Greek colonizers imposed their existing goddess onto—took on the complex "love and hate" nature of the postcolonial condition in Hong Kong as Tsang experienced it, a phenomenon epitomized by the outright adoration for Britain and Britishness that many of her friends expressed. Tsang's major contribution to the installation, a short film titled "Colony," located the dysphoria of Iphigenia's experience of not belonging in either Greece or on "the island" of the Taurians within her own experience of growing up and starting a career while caught (geographically and culturally) between British and Chinese cultures.

In this way, the queerness of Iphigenia being among the Taurians and with Artemis— where queerness has more connotations of strangeness and discomfort than in the word's current associations with LGBTQ+ lives—is thus received in a context that gestures to the colonial ideologies in which Euripides' play is historically imbricated. A relatively straightforward performance of the play, set (for example) in Hong Kong, might struggle to achieve this complex temporal, cultural, and geographical mediation. The form eventually taken by *The Gentlest Work,* however, allows Tsang's film to stand alone and to be understood in the overlapping contexts of Iphigenia's mythic narratives, the complexities of queer identity, and the reception history of Euripides' play.

Nancy. In the end I found myself asking just how queer is this wild place, given its ethnocentrism. The barbarian place is hostile and wild—that is, not progressive

politically. But perhaps we can reclaim "wild." The perfor
participated in what Jack Halberstam offers, a "queer definiti
genres and breaks loose from history, reaching for new arrang
and temporality" (2020a, 53). In terms of sexuality this *is* a qu
been the site of the intensified love of Orestes and Pylades, and
with Artemis (and her statue).

It is, then, a complicated text, a potential site for identifi
progressive audiences—its strong woman, the women's community, the queer love—and
for dis-identification—the colonialism (Muñoz 1999, 4 and 9). We must see that
complexity: yes, the barbarian is comfortably used to shore up and praise Hellenic identity,
but the imagined space also allows Orestes and Iphigenia to escape heterosexual marriage.

Contemporary work on queer temporality and affect asks us to think about *our*
desire.[21] Heather Love assumes that there is a lonely lesbian in the present looking for
someone in the past (2007, 36). As a feminist classicist, the question for me is not so
much why go back as *how* to go back. I have always wanted something from tragedy—
trying to bring my research into sync with my political drive to make a better world. In
this return to tragedy, I have been looking for a ghostly lesbian (Freccero 2006, 18–20), a
figure that was made *invisible* by a certain philological variety of classics, and made
visible by the practice of theater—what I see as an empathetic and imaginative form of
research. The wildness of women leads to terrible ends (for instance, in *Bacchae*), or it is
shut down as the genre reasserts itself (see Telò 2020, 6–7). But performance practice and
adaptation can open readers and audiences to new possibilities, new ways of thinking
and feeling. I should add that, for me, it has offered a new kind of pleasure in the work, a
liberation from the weight of classical *Wissenschaft*.

David. The title of By Jove's piece came about when one of our artists, Alexander
Woodward, commented that the project was our "gentlest piece of work so far." Within
the installation the idea of gentle work takes on multiple meanings. It is the work of
carefully, slowly, and lovingly unpicking the web of myths and texts that constitute the
source material. It is an evocation of the quality of relationships-in-progress over the
course of a lifetime. And it is also the act of storytelling in which the unpicking of myth
and that evocation of lives marked by desire become entangled: it is the act of recounting
these violent stories in a way that makes room for desire and joy, both for the storytellers
and the characters, amid the traumatic and the tragic. Queerness, at least as connected
to sexuality, is ultimately one vector within this paradigm; race and gender also emerge
from it. Iphigenia and her relationship with Artemis on "the island," and Tsang's
contextualizing of this idea in her own lived experience of (post)coloniality, are
emblematic of this kind of gentle work offered in By Jove's production.

Notes

1. We want to thank Mario Telò and Sarah Olsen for welcoming all our efforts to change things
up, starting with allowing us to produce a dialogue.

refers to a generative theater-making process whereby a group of artists—in By [.....]se, a mix of actors, musicians, dancers, and writers (both playwrights and poets), with [...]y members of the ensemble acting in multiple capacities—create a performance through [...]n extended period of collaboration. With its roots in the 1960s, in many parts of the world it now constitutes perhaps the most popular alternative to a more traditional theater-making process that might be summed up as "putting on a play." For further information on the history and practice of devising theater, see Heddon and Milling 2005, as well as Oddey 1994. For an account of some major classics-oriented devised work, see Cole 2019.

3. Haines's unpublished draft text is here printed with her permission.

4. Cf. Haselswerdt in this volume.

5. See Youd in this volume.

6. See Budin 2016, 38–44.

7. On queer wildness, see also Baldwin in this volume.

8. See Tyrrell 1984, 64–7; and Rabinowitz 2015, 216.

9. See Calame 1997, 208–9, 244–58; Budin 2016, 25–8; and Rabinowitz 2002, 130.

10. References will be to the edition of Cropp (2000); the translations are his as well.

11. See Telò 2020, 191–3.

12. I owe this idea to a conversation with Mario Telò.

13. See Introduction.

14. On queerness and the impossibility of performance, see Gurd in this volume.

15. Love (2007, 34–7) discusses Sappho and Anne Carson and the desire to be remembered.

16. Our reflection here was prompted by Karen Bassi's fascinating remarks on *Hecuba* in this volume. On queerness and fragmentariness, see also Orrells.

17. Freccero uses the term "unsettling" to get at this sense (2007, 485); for a discussion and critique of the openness and attendant demand for "newness," see Amin 2017, esp. 178–82. Matzner (2016) discusses reception studies themselves as "queer." The "elision of race and class" in queer studies has been pointed out by many queers of color (Johnson 2005, 128). Cohen (2005, 25) addresses "the limits of current conceptions of queer identities and queer politics" and is "interested in examining the concept of 'queer' in order to think about how we might construct a new political identity that is truly liberating, transformative, and inclusive of all those who stand on the outside of the dominant constructed norm of state-sanctioned white middle- and upper-class heterosexuality." She calls for an intersectional analysis. Later, Cohen distances herself from the word queer as it has been deployed (2005, 36); cf. Johnson (2005, 124–8) on multiple identifications with queer. See Introduction.

18. On wildness and queerness, see Halberstam 2020a, 51–3.

19. See Hall 2013, 1–2. To one recent director of the play, Michi Barall, it seemed "very American." "It's the story of a guy and a gal with some magical object fleeing barbarians. You've seen that movie. It's *Raiders of the Lost Ark*" (Mark Blankenship 2010 https://tdf.org/articles/377/Get-the-Goddess-a-Coke). The possibly queer reading of buddy movies like *Star Wars* also comes to mind.

20. See Rankine in this volume on queerness and the construction of the "barbarian."

21. See, e.g., Love 2007, esp. 33–4, citing Sappho; and Amin 2017, esp. 177.

CHAPTER 18
CYCLOPS—A PHILOSOPHER WALKS INTO A SATYR-PLAY
Daniel Boyarin

Euripides' only preserved satyr-play, *Cyclops* (408 BC)—actually the only complete satyr-play preserved from antiquity—was composed only a couple of decades before Plato's *Symposium* (*c.* 385–370). They have one character in common, Silenus, patriarch of the satyrs. Moreover, the ante-climactic (not anti-climactic) scene of the Euripidean play is, itself, a *Symposium*, and similarly the climactic scene of the Plato is—explicitly—a satyr-play. I will read these two texts together, seeking to understand better via a queer juxtaposition the place of the satyr-play as significant—even corrosively so, perhaps—within Athenian culture and why Plato portrays an old gray-beard and very serious philosopher, Socrates, as Silenus father of the satyrs. Plato, at the end of the *Symposium*, comments on the structures of Athenian drama, including dubbing the final scene in his self-declared "tragic tetralogy" as a satyr-play. He certainly knew the rules and practices of which he was writing (which is not, of course, to guarantee that he is undistorting in his characterization of them), so the question this paper asks is what can be learned from the *Symposium* in reading *Cyclops*. R. G. Usher was probably the first to see *Cyclops* as a source for the *Symposium*, writing that "an awareness of the extent of Plato's use and adaptation of satyr lore in the *Symposium* is essential for a full appreciation of his philosophy of love, his technique as an author, and the purpose of the dialogue" (2002, 206). I wish to build quite high on Usher, reading *Cyclops* and the satyr-play altogether as a deliberate queering of the opposition between tragedy and comedy, precisely the one called for explicitly by Plato—an affirmation, if you will, of non-binary genre.

The *Symposium* thematizes and promotes genre-queering. The key moment in the last part of the *Symposium* is Socrates' "forcing" of both Agathon and Aristophanes to assert—entirely against Athenian tradition and rules—that the same person ought to be able to write tragedy and comedy. In order to get a sense of what might have been at stake for Plato, I will bring onstage the scenes of the *Symposium* that connect that text with Euripides', namely the "satyr-play" with which the *Symposium* ends, Alcibiades' inburst and outburst. These scenes have great implications for understanding Plato's take on Athenian drama. It is a matter of no small importance that Plato refers to Alcibiades' speech as a satyr-play, a silene drama (*saturikon . . . drama . . . kai silênikon* 222d) for, as we know well, the satyr-play followed the tragedies on the Attic stage. If Alcibiades produces a satyr-play, then that which came before (appropriately enough since Agathon orchestrated it) must be a tragedy. But since we know already that tragedy such as Agathon's is not true tragedy, not at all *spoudaios* nor even dedicated to holding on to truth—we know this in the *Symposium* from his speech, as confirmed, *ex post facto*, in the *Laws*—then the first tragedy, the conversations of Agathon and his friends is a false tragedy, because Agathon himself—true to the characterization of tragedians in the *Laws*—does not know or hold to the truth. Truth, it seems, begins to emerge in the second tragedy, the one spoken by Socrates himself. Satyr-play was penned by the same author who wrote the tragedies, in this case, then, Plato. This is Plato's satyr-play; it must, therefore, somehow be powerfully related to the search for the True word that animates Socrates' animadversions against the false tragedian Agathon and against rhetoric entirely. And indeed, Alcibiades has promised to tell the truth and not to be amusing (215a)—precisely echoing the moment in the *Apology*, when Socrates says: "And perhaps I shall seem to some of you to be joking; be assured, however, I shall speak perfect truth to you" (20d4–6). The truth Alcibiades has to tell is his satyr-play (215a). Diotima's speech, I suggest, is the true tragedy that follows on the false one of Agathon, the best, perhaps, that tragedy can pull off, while Alcibiades' true satyr-play supersedes even this trueish tragedy. The same person—Euripides/Plato—writes the tragedy and the comedy.

Let me begin, then, with a synopsis of the silenic drama. I will mention moments left out in others' synopses and leave out sometimes what others make much of. Socrates has just completed his speech to uproarious applause and Aristophanes is about to make some remark when a disturbance is heard near the door; drunken revellers and a flute girl (precisely the two things that had been excluded from *this Symposium* earlier on) appear. It turns out to be Alcibiades on a *kômos*, floridly staggeringly drunk with garlands for Agathon (the most beautiful) and looking, as *komasts* do, for sex. Between his drunkenness and the garlands, he does not notice the presence of Socrates until he has flopped on the couch between Agathon and Socrates. When he does, he remonstrates with Socrates for having chosen to sit next to the beautiful Agathon rather than the laughable Aristophanes. Socrates feigns jealousy and complains about Alcibiades' jealousy, whereupon the latter takes some of the garlands from the head of Agathon and places them on Socrates' head, declaring that "he [Socrates] is victorious in words over all people, not just the day before yesterday like you, but every day" (213e). After some byplay about drinking, Alcibiades is instructed in the agreement for the evening's entertainment and asked by Eryximachus to give his encomium to Eros. Alcibiades wittily proposes that he will praise Socrates himself, insisting that he "will tell the truth" (214e). He even invites Socrates to interrupt him and object if Alcibiades reports something untruthful in his praise. He then makes the following remarkable declaration:

> I'll try to praise Socrates, my friends, but I'll have to use an image. And though he may think I'm trying to make fun of him, I assure you my image is no joke: it aims at the truth. Look at him! Isn't he just like a statue of Silenus? You know the kind of statue I mean; you'll find them in any shop in town. It's a Silenus sitting, his flute or his pipes in his hands, and it's hollow. It's split right down the middle, and inside it's full of tiny statues of the gods. Now look at him again! Isn't he also just like the satyr Marsyas? Nobody, not even you, Socrates, can deny that you *look* like them. But the resemblance goes beyond appearance, as you're about to hear.

There are multiple levels of irony in this passage. Alcibiades has pointed to the familiar (almost standard) Socratic irony in his own critique/praise of Socrates. He describes him as ugly in mien and ridiculous in speech with all the beauty and divinity not in the outer form but in the inner (dare I say?) content, the golden *agalmata*—phallic images of the gods.

To this point, the irony is familiar to us as readers of Plato, all too familiar. There is, however, a different level of irony of which, it seems, Alcibiades is unaware and which comes out in the sequel. If his blame turned to praise is familiar, his praise turned to blame is not so. The terms within which Alcibiades praises Socrates are, as we will see, a mobilization of the charges against both rhapsodes and rhetors throughout the Platonic corpus. Socrates here is made to appear here as Ion, Agathon, and Gorgias all rolled up into one (215a–e):

> You are impudent, contemptuous, and vile. No? If you won't admit it, I'll bring witnesses. And you're much more marvelous than Marsyas, who needed instruments to cast his spells on people ... The only difference between you and Marsyas is that you need no instruments; you do exactly what he does, but with words alone. You know, people hardly ever take a speaker seriously, even if he's the greatest orator; but let anyone—man, woman, or child—listen to you or even to a poor account of what you say—and we are all transported, completely possessed.

Earlier in the *Symposium*, it was Socrates who mockingly feared that Agathon's speech would, like the Gorgon's head, turn him into stone. Now, all of a sudden, it is Socrates who spellbinds and makes his hearers drunk with his words. It is he who is the magician of rhetoric, the purveyor of drugs. And it is, most assuredly, "the truth," truth being here the truth of Alcibiades' experience and his report of it as the experience of others as well.

Alcibiades is not lying. Corrigan and Glazov-Corrigan have, moreover, pointed to the seriousness of the charge of *hubristês* that Alcibiades lays at Socrates' door. This is no laughing matter: "Anyone who struck, pushed, pulled, or restrained another person (and this could include a sexual element) could be liable for a prosecution on a charge of *hubris*" (2004, 13). Socrates' hubris displaces ordinary perceptions; like an irruption of the unexpected, it unsettles the comfortable course of normal life.

The speech continues with some further meditation by Alcibiades on the Academy versus the polis. Alcibiades declares that he has shut his ears in order not to hear Socrates, because, were he to allow himself to hear Socrates, he would not be able to leave his side and go about the Athenians' business (216a). Aside from the irony once again emphasized of Socrates as compelling, forcing Alcibiades to agree with him in something, there is other irony here. The Athenians' business at this particular moment was, of course, the Peloponnesian War and the calamity to which Alcibiades was about to lead them. The dramatic date of the *Symposium* is the summer of 416 BC, the summer between the Melian Massacre and the disastrous expedition to Sicily. This is the summer in which Agathon won first prize at the Lenaean festival and in which *Trojan Women* came in second. Given that Alcibiades was the architect of Athens's downfall and destruction, at least the last part of the dialogue seems to allow for a contextualizing reading of Alcibiades, one that enables us to see it as putting into question the single-mindedness and single-voicedness of that very "tragedy," the sustained attack on encomia and rhetoric of the text until now.

Alcibiades continues with his satyrical praise of Socrates, interpreting him as one who is deceptively unattractive on the outside, both in his person and in his behavior, his appearance of overweening desire for boys. Inside this clay statue of a Silenus, however, when "he comes to be serious" (216e), then one can see the beautiful statues inside, the golden *agalmata*. For Alcibiades, this inside is made of moderation; Socrates pretends to be profligate, but, when he is serious, he reveals the golden statues of his self-restraint, his resistance to the enactment of physical love. Alcibiades goes on to recount how, stricken with philosophy, he sought Socrates' body (precisely the reverse of Diotima's ladder) but Socrates "rebuffed" him, sleeping beside him, wrapped up in his arms, chastely, the whole night.

With this, I come to the denouement of Alcibiades' peroration, in which we find, once again, a justification, now well supported, of Alcibiades' comparison of Socrates to Silenus and satyrs (221d–222a):

> There is a parallel for everyone—everyone else, that is. But this man here is so bizarre, his ways and his ideas are so unusual, that, search as you might, you'll never find anyone else, alive or dead, who's even remotely like him. The best you can do is not to compare him to anything human, but to liken him, as I do, to Silenus and the satyrs, and the same goes for his ideas and arguments. Come to think of it, I should have mentioned this much earlier: even his ideas and arguments are just like those hollow statues of Silenus. If you were to listen to his argument, at first they'd strike you as totally ridiculous; they're clothed in words as coarse as the hides worn by the most vulgar satyrs. He's always going on about pack asses, or blacksmiths, or cobblers, or tanners; he's always making the same tired old points in the same tired old words. If you are foolish, or simply unfamiliar with him, you'd find it impossible not to laugh at his arguments. But if you see them when they open up like the statues, if you go behind their surface, you'll realize that no other arguments make any sense. They're truly worthy of a god, bursting with figures of virtue inside. They're of great—no, of the greatest—importance for anyone who wants to become a truly good man.

Plato's satyr-play about Silenus also produces an ugly and gross, grotesque exterior that has within it golden gods. In other words, the attack on Athenian aesthetics is also embodied in Socrates' silenic speech, his discourse that sounds more like a satyr-play than anything else—note Alcibiades' declaration that he can only be compared to a Silenus in his person and in his discourse.

The tragedies in this Platonic tetralogy are in tension with the satyr-play and the satyr-play in tension with them. Socrates is revealed to himself have a body which, while surely not lacking limbs, does not quite have a middle composed to suit the extremities. Neither, one can add, does his *logos*. Socrates and his discourse are both disproportionate and grotesque, with various features that are incongruous with each other: "internal division of the trait, impurity, corruption, contamination, decomposition, perversion, deformation, even cancerization, generous proliferation, or degenerescence ... disruptive 'anomalies'" (Derrida 1980, 57). This strengthens, I think, my suggestion that in reading Alcibiades' satyr-play—so-called by Plato—we are meant to read it as somehow a part of the Truth to which Plato's true tragedy aspires as well. Both the tragic and the comic (in the form of the satyr-play) are written, indeed, by the same author, and both, somehow, must contribute to the serious (and comic) enterprise of that most epistemic of authors, Plato. At one level, then, the explicit genre of the *Symposium*, which is a kind of hermeneutical key and synecdoche of the whole corpus, is the tragedy and the comedy, in one, the satyr-play.

Euripides' *Cyclops* is the best comparandum for Socrates' satyr-play. The issue is not atomistic—some diction here, some phalloi there—but holistic: what is Plato talking about when he talks about satyr-play? *Cyclops* is the only candidate for helping toward an answer, an answer, I suggest, that will illuminate *Cyclops* as well. I take seriously, much too seriously, Plato's explicit non-binary genre identification, indeed his overt attack on the very binary of tragedy and comedy. Plato is vaunting the *spoudaiogeloion* ("serious laughter") as the only way to Wisdom (maybe even truth). How, then, does Plato read *Cyclops* or, more, how can we imagine Plato reading Euripides' satyr-play via the construction of Plato's own?

Usher has already compared the action upon Alcibiades' arrival with a "similar episode of comic flirtation in the *Cyclops* beginning at line 503" (2002, 219–23). I wish to employ this comparison for purposes of better apprehension of Plato's interpretation of the anti-generic satyr-play, his (Socrates') so trenchant and truculent insistence that the same author must write tragedy and comedy—or rather, as I suggest, that tragedy and comedy must be one—and his (Plato's) apparent conviction that this purpose is best realized in the satyr-play. Why?

Cyclopes are strange creatures; satyrs more ordinary. In Euripides' play, Odysseus has developed a plan to rid them of the cannibalistic Cyclops, Polyphemus who holds them in thrall. The plot thickens. In a kind of "mock symposium," Silenus and the Cyclops are reclining, drinking in the latter's cave. The Cyclops decides to go on a *kômos*, a drunken peripatetic revel intended to culminate in sexual intercourse with somebody. The Chorus of young satyrs breaks out in a sort of wedding song with very alluring images of dewy, nude, young, and willing women alluringly arrayed on couches waiting for their lover. "They seem to know that it is not merely cannibalism that the Cyclops has in mind, but a sexual conquest" (Usher 2002, 220). The Chorus, on the other hand, hints rather darkly that the Cyclops will be murdered himself (517–19). In a conversation full of sexy innuendos to that ocular rape and murder, including at least one delivered unwittingly by the Cyclops himself, Odysseus and Silenus (the old fat father of the satyrs) persuade Polyphemus to abandon his *kômos* and recline there in place drinking the good Bacchic liquid.

Following quite a bit more drinking and mock symposiast conversation, the Cyclops turns once more his attention to love. He reports that he perceives the sexual union of heaven and earth and, moreover, that the Graces are tempting him to lie with them but (580–4, trans. Usher)

> I have a Ganymede here, and will enjoy myself with him in finer fashion than I would the Graces. Yes, for some reason I take more pleasure in boys than in women.

The scene is undoubtedly hilarious with two monstrous old male creatures playing the roles of Zeus and Ganymede, the beautiful couple on the stage. The superiority of the love of a man for an ephebe to male–female love is enacted parodically in the rejection by the Cyclops of the love of the lovely Graces in favor of sexual intercourse with an old, fat, decrepit Silenus. The satyr-play burlesques the ideals of beauty of the Athenian pederasty devastatingly, just as it burlesques the ideals of beauty enshrined in Athenian literary decorum. And Euripides dissolves, therewith, the social genre of pederasty.[1]

No wonder the satyr-play—I think maybe even *Cyclops* itself—appealed to Plato for his queering of genre as part of his destruction (attempted) of the Athenian ideals of beauty enacted in the institution of pederasty as well as in the drama for his own purposes (not entirely unrelated to those of Euripides). The satyr-play was a kind of ready-made for Plato's purposes, for his attack on beauty, at the end of his *Symposium*.

How do we queer or talk about queering in a sexual culture as different from ours as was that of ancient Athens? In what sense can Plato be said to be queering anything, other than as a gesture for me to fit what I have to say into the discourse? Closely related question: What is the difference between queering a binary and a deconstruction of that binary?

Let us begin, as one ought to, with a primary text. I refer to Derrida's "The Law of Genre" (1980). "Thou shalt not mix genres." As Derrida remarks, this can be heard as "a sharp order," as in ancient Athens, it was indeed. There was even a rule that the same person was forbidden from writing both comedies or tragedies, the limit case, one might say, of a law of genre (56):

> As soon as the word "genre" is sounded, as soon as it is heard, as soon as one attempts to conceive it, a limit is drawn. And when a limit is established, norms and interdictions are not far behind. "Do," "Do not," says "genre," the word "genre," the figure, the voice, or the law of genre.

This is where the satyr-play comes into its own, as antithesis to genre, to genre itself, not as a genre but as corruptive of genre. The theme of a satyr-play comprises exactly the same themes that we find in tragedies as well. The Chorus of old men or wise or lamenting women of tragedy is replaced by a Chorus of shepherds or satyrs, making the satyr-play a kind of grotesque double of the tragedy. As Richard Seaford has reminded us, "The actors of satyric drama . . . seem to have been tragic in appearance and to some extent also in utterance" (1988, 4). David Konstan, too, analyzing the meter of *Cyclops*, shows how the language, for all its grotesque effects, is not an opposite of tragedy but rather a fractured version thereof (McHugh and Konstan 2001, 18). Finally, Mark Griffith has shown that "in most formal respects satyr plays belong quite squarely with tragedy, and share very few of the characteristics of comedy" (2015, 10–11). Instead of the semantic opposition between tragedy and comedy—the binary that Socrates rejects—we have an intensification of tragedy, a kind of hyper-version of the "goat song" that is tragedy. Generically or genealogically speaking, the satyr-play might even be the origin of tragedy; the word, itself, after all, as is notorious, means "goat song." Derrida has sensed this himself, I reckon, even without quite naming it: "the mixing of genre that is 'more than a genre,' through the excess of genre in relation to itself, as to its abounding movement and its general assemblage which coincides, too, with its dissolution" (1980, 61). This is surely not "deconstruction" but may very well be what "queering" means or ought to.

As Konstan has written, "It would appear that the plots of satyr-plays, more than those of either tragedy or comedy, best corresponded to the ritual occasion" (in McHugh and Konstan 2001, 4), to wit, the Great Dionysia. In any case, I suggest, those approaches to the satyr-plays that treat them as a form of comic relief—the "orthodox view," according to Seaford (1988, 26)—are seriously missing the point. Seaford himself captures this when he writes of the satyr-play: "In its obscenity, hilarity, and joyful endings satyric drama resembles comedy; in form it appears to resemble tragedy; its content, like tragedy's, is mythological, *and it was written by tragedians as part of the tetralogy*" (5, emphasis added). I suggest, therefore, that the true tragedy of which Plato speaks is the satyr-play (the true goat song), and that true tragedy is the true meaning of philosophy, of Socrates. Just as Plato breaks, reverses, upsets the laws of gender/sex, in his brilliant riff on *Cyclops*, Plato breaks the law of genre, which is, I am claiming, the very charge of the satyr-play as well. Once again, as so often in the past decades, we see how close—and not only paranomastically or etymologically—genre is to gender.

"Queering," I suggest—with fear and love—is a different mode of critique than deconstruction. Deconstruction shows that the distinction between binary opposites is always constructed and exposing the construction is deconstruction. Typically the terms of the binary are both shown to be "contaminated" with what should be exclusively on the other side of the line. Queering undoes the very terms of genre itself in that Derridean sense we have just touched upon. (This, by the way, is why LGBTI is undone, not completed, by queer.) If a deconstruction sets a binary in oscillation and destabilizes it, queering makes its very terms impossible to imagine.[2] Konstan makes the point that Euripides' introduction of a third character, that is, from Homer's drama of Odysseus vs. the Cyclops to Odysseus, the Cyclops, and Silenus (with his satyrs) shifts Homer's "polar opposition" to a structure of "two extremes mediated by a middle term" (McHugh and Konstan 2001, 13).[3] The Cyclops himself, Polyphemus, as well as Silenus and the satyrs— both figures, as we have seen, of Socrates—are of hybrid *genos*, monstrous in that they neither fit into the category of humans nor of beasts. The satyr-play is also a monster, neither tragedy nor comedy. Are you a boy or a girl?, one asks the satyr-play, and they answer—of non-binary genre. This is, again, precisely the reason that his philosopher enters into the satyr-play, as it were, at the very apex of the *Symposium*, the chaos of which, I reckon, is the very point of the dialogue. The satyr-play breaks the opposition between the tragedy and the comedy, as Socrates has been fighting to do, and produces what for Plato is, I think, a truer understanding of the world in that it is neither tragic nor comic but tragic right in its comedy, comic right in its tragedy. And a new Plato emerges out of the intertextual relation between his silenic drama and that of Euripides' genre-bending satyr-play.

Queering has nothing essentialist to do with gay/straight—although it does, of course, historically in our *Lebensform*; it is the operation of breaking, scoffing the law of genre, of gender.[4] The attacks on the law of genre (in Athens, comedy and tragedy shall not be mixed) and of gender (Silenus/Socrates the beautiful *erômenos*; Polyphemus/Alcibiades the wise *erastês*) enacted in both of our satyr-plays threaten the apple cart of normal Athenian life. This is how a bourgeois institution such as pederasty is queered.

Socrates' coercion of his interlocutors in the very last scene of the *Symposium* is a perfect text for me to end on. Richard Patterson bases his interpretation of this moment on the passage from the *Laws* in which Plato indicates that the tragedians are not *spoudaioi*, or even tragic, but rather it is the philosophers who are both: "Let us return first to the *Laws'* combination, in the philosopher, of (true) tragedy and (popular) comedy. We may recall that the philosopher alone knows the nature of the noblest and best life, so that he alone can knowingly imitate it in *logos*. Since such a life will inevitably appear comic to the multitude, his tragic figure will just as inevitably be popularly comic. Thus he creates at once true tragedy and popular comedy, and is the only one capable of doing so by knowledge or *technê*" (1982, 84). As Patterson shows, at least one of Plato's charges against tragedy is that it cannot be genuinely *spoudaios*, because the tragedians are not philosophers, and cannot hold on to the "truth." They cannot show an audience what it is to be the best sort of human being, owing to the fact that they are devoted to beauty, and truth is *not* beauty, nor beauty truth. Tragedy is thus not "true," and only philosophy is truly tragic, *spoudaios*. "Any dialogue featuring Socrates as protagonist will qualify as *spoudaios*—hence 'tragic' in the sense appropriated by Plato in the *Laws*."

According to this view, when Plato has Socrates insist at the end of the *Symposium*, as his tragic and comic poets Agathon and Aristophanes are falling asleep, that the same person must be able to write both comedy and tragedy, his insistence grows out of this double meaning—on the literal level the authors of comic and tragic dramas; on the metaphorical, the authors of the truly "serious," that is, philosophers, must also be able to "write" comedy, to be *spoudogeloion*. For the ordinary dramatists, whether tragedians—including, of course, Euripides—or comedians, drama is not serious. *By rule*—a literal law of genre—drama is practiced by men skilled in either the writing of tragedies or comedies, not both. But Platonic drama (always in this sense tragic, whether externally comic or tragic in form), based on *epistêmê*, will always represent the same Truth, since Truth is always one, and the same philosopher can truly write in either mode. On this reading of Plato, there is a reversal of terms; for the *doxa* (standard Athenian opinion), Agathon appears *spoudaios* and Aristophanes, *geloios*, but from the aspect of *epistêmê*, neither Agathon or Aristophanes are *spoudaios*, and the genuine dramatis persona, the philosopher, can write tragedy or comedy equally *spoudaios* and *geloios*. I find here all the more the multiple ironies that I have noted above in the double-reverse of Alcibiades' praise of Socrates as ugly and ridiculous on the outside but beautiful and wise on the inside. This carnival of reversals is acted out in the narrative when Alcibiades asks of Agathon that he take some strands of the victory garland that he has won in the tragic contests and place them on the head of Socrates (213d), thus alluding to the idea in the *Laws* that the philosopher is the true tragedian, the true *spoudaios*, the one who holds to the truth. Diskin Clay argues that the importance of the hiccups of Aristophanes is that "unexpectedly a comic and a tragic poet are brought together" (1975, 242), suggesting by this that the final enigma of the *Symposium* is something that was deep in the plan of the work; indeed, that it is essential to the piece. Socrates ends up sitting between the one that Alcibiades calls *kallistos* (Agathon) and the one that Alcibiades names *geloios* (Aristophanes, of course). Socrates, the one who sits between the tragic and the comic poet and insists that, were they true, they would be one, imputes to himself the character of the *spoudogeloios*. This seems to me right; the question is to what end. Why the insistence in the satyr-play on Socrates as *spoudogeloios*, on the comic as tragic? If the only true *spoudaios* is the tragic philosopher, why the *geloios*? Why is he also a clown? Menippus may help us think.

Joel Relihan has located the primary impulse for Menippean satire in the tenth book of the *Republic*, just before the Myth of Er, which he takes as "in most of its elements a Menippean satire, with a statement doubting the ability of words to express anything other than the lowest level of phenomenal reality. Menippean satire accepts this caveat and takes the Myth of Er, and Platonic mythologizing in general, as perfect demonstrations of how *not* to go about proclaiming truth and defining reality" (1993, 11). Relihan has written of the Menippean satire: "Here [in Lucian's *Icaromenippus*] Menippus is identified as comic because he is lost in thought, mumbling about interplanetary distances; he knows that his friend will think that he is speaking nonsense" (105). I want to suggest that this Menippean moment in Lucian is virtually an open allusion to Socrates both in the battlefield and on his way to the *Symposium*, lost to the world while deep in thought, knowing that his associates will think he is speaking nonsense. Plato's satyr-play can be read, therefore, as a prefiguration of Menippean satire itself, the very upending of the solemn binaries on which official (bourgeois, as it were) Athenian culture rests, this being Plato's very own and evergreen project. Plato's own description of the satyr-play as "a-political" (*Laws* 815c), which means having nothing to do with the polis, underlines again his hostility to the polis, and consistent attempts to overcome it and its mores and rules including its law of genre. Whatever its "real" etymology, *satura* as in Menippus is constituted by a miscegnation of genres that is enacted in the satyr-play.

Coming back, then, to *Cyclops*, I will suggest—gingerly—that Plato was on to something: the role of the satyr-play, indeed the only one we have entire, Euripides' *Cyclops* may indeed be read as upending genre, queering genre, providing a kind of Menippean second accent within the solemnity of Athenian culture precisely and paradoxically by being so close to tragedy in its themes and forms. And more: the tragedy is characterized by beauty; the satyr-play by an overturning of beauty, the same beauty advanced by the tragedian, Agathon the beautiful. Beauty is *not* truth, truth *not* beauty. (Plato was clearly looking at a different Grecian urn than Keats.) This is the function of the satyr-play in the tetralogy as well, deepening the insight by stripping its own language of external beauty. As such, the satyr-plays are the "comedy" written by tragedians called for by Plato and vaunted as belonging uniquely to Socrates, greatest, in Plato's eyes, of the philosophers. The tragedy is not tragic owing to its commitment to the *kalon*, the beautiful, while only the satyr-play is serious, as manifested by its frontal attack on beauty, and this is not a Platonic fantasm but amply demonstrated by *Cyclops*. This reading is supported as well by a passage from Ion of Chios's lost *Visitations*, often cited as a precursor to the Socratic dialogue, in which the author of that text is reported to have said: "Like a tragic tetralogy, *aretê* should have its share of the satyric (*saturikon*)" (Plutarch, *Pericles* 5.4). The significance of this utterance is surely for the precise and close nexus it manifests between the form of drama and what we choose to call "real life." Plato has here, then, a model and a colleague, as it were. I am merely opening the possibility of thought that the satyr-play is about—and always was—genre-bending, and Plato is here a very wise and accurate interpreter. I must confess that the older I get the wiser Plato gets—but it's a different Plato. Philosophy, according to this new Plato, is the uncovery of the tragi-comic sense of life.

Notes

1. See also Youd in this volume.
2. On performative failure, see Gurd in this volume.
3. On queerness and throuples, see Youd in this volume.
4. See Introduction.

PART VII
TRANSITIONS

CHAPTER 19
HIPPOLYTUS—QUEER CROSSINGS (FOLLOWING ANNE CARSON)
Jonathan Goldberg

This investigation of *Hippolytus* takes off from and follows work by Anne Carson. An initial impulse comes from the final item in *Grief Lessons*, her volume of translations of four plays by Euripides (2006). Up until its final piece, the book is organized in a quite conventional way, opening with a general preface followed by each play with its own preface. After *Alcestis*, "Why I Wrote Two Plays About Phaidra" appears, its authorship identified in italics—"*by Euripides*" (309). Placing this piece as an afterword to *Alcestis* is a non sequitur—unless perhaps Carson means to suggest a relationship between the two Phaedras and the double Alcestis—if the final figure in the play even is her, something that, in her preface to the play, Carson questions in the name of Euripides the rule-breaker (249).[1] This final piece in the volume is another instance of rule-breaking in claiming to have been written "*by Euripides*" when it certainly was not: Carson authorizes her writing by disclaiming her authorship. These procedures, troubling sequence and ownership, are furthered by the fact that the author of that final piece writes about a first play "about Phaidra" that exists in a handful of fragments.[2] Only Euripides could know more. *Euripides* ends by quoting from it: "Instead of fire—another fire / *not just a drop of cunt sweat!* is what we women are—you cannot fight it!" (312).[3] What *are* women?

Carson's *Euripides* devotes half of his/her piece to why the earlier play "about Phaidra" was a failure, a presumed motive for the anomaly of Euripides writing another play on the same subject. Carson asks what an audience wanted from Greek tragedy in propria persona in her preface to the volume, devoted to tragedy as a "curious" art form. Its curiosity lies precisely in retailing violence and rage of a kind we find insupportable when it happens to us, but somehow can watch when actors act for us the rage and grief that we cannot handle on our own. Carson's *Euripides* supposes that his earlier play did not produce that catharsis; instead of relief through identification with the actor, Phaedra incited rage and refusal. Seemingly following "the Byzantine scholar Aristophanes" (167),[4] just about the only early source for knowledge about the reception of Euripides' lost play, Carson assumes that the later play, by not including a scene in which Phaedra declared her passion to Hippolytus, removed what was unseemly about the first. The veil that may have titled the first play, presumably donned by Hippolytus in response to his stepmother, becomes instead a veiling Euripides generalizes: "I would call 'feminine' this talent for veiling a truth in a truth" (309). In her preface to *Hippolytos*, Carson likens the relationship of its central couple to "two shapes ... disjunct and dissimilar" that "yet construct one form" (168). She finds evidence of this doubleness as well in the etymology of the name "Hippolytus," his loosening at once his being undone and yet set free by the horses he formerly controlled (an image of his mode of desiring not to desire).

"In general, I like women," writes Carson's *Euripides* (311). His first Phaedra, however, threatened to master him. Her desire is about something so central that even when its avowal to Hippolytus disappears in the second play, the question it raises does not. That desire may no longer be the disturbing essence of Phaedra; however, when its core is removed, it "spread . . . on all the surfaces of the play" that followed. "Shame" is the word for what spreads; the original core "reverberates everywhere in this so-called second version" (312). Reverberations like these also can be found when Carson crosses her authorship with Euripides, crossing her gender as well; her feminist (sapphic?) analysis of Phaedra's passion becomes *his*. This final piece of writing in *Grief Lessons* can be called *queer* in its movement across gender in a gesture of identification that, at the same time, confounds the parameters of identity; Euripides becomes his oeuvre; his translator becomes his author; a fragmentary text becomes the basis of identification. Euripides nonetheless prompts these crossings, spreading them across the extant *Hippolytus*. One fire ignites another.

These overlaps and indistinctions are not so far from what Froma Zeitlin claimed in *Playing the Other* about the hidden affinities between Phaedra and Hippolytus (1996, 219–84). Key words attached to self-making, words for shame and moderation like *aidôs* or *sôphrosunê*, are distributed across the text. (Hippolytus and Phaedra never exchange a word in the play, but the words exchange them.) Carson makes that point at the very opening of her preface to the play, describing it as "a system of reflections, distorted reflections, reflections that go awry." *Aidôs* ("shame") is her initial example of this, her scare quotes around her translation indicating that a word that functions doubly is not capable of a singular translation (163). Zeitlin's essay locates this doubleness in a feminine duplicity that threatens and destroys the carapace of the masculine self. However, as she acknowledges (and as Carson emphasizes), authority in the play is marked by the two female deities who frame it, Aphrodite and Artemis; their attributes are not as singular and oppositional as might be supposed. This may not be a play in which masculinity simply triumphs even if it ends with two men embracing.

Aphrodite opens the play, virtually hymning herself and her power, aimed both at Hippolytus who scorns her and Phaedra who succumbs to it. Aphrodite may be the force of erotic connection (Zeitlin takes the goddess to be the embodiment of a normative reproductive marital imperative that she describes as "the drama of life" [233]), but the deity's power is destructive. Eros is the child of a non-marital liaison. When Hippolytus appears, literally hymning Artemis, worshipping her as the exemplar of his self-containment and purity, his cross-gender identification with her is described as an act of adoration. Robert Bagg notes the "sexual implication" of the word Aphrodite uses to describe his self-relationship to Artemis at line 27: "It is Artemis . . . whom he adores" (1973, 9). Artemis is finally as indifferent to the man who worships her as Aphrodite is to the one who despises her. The "absolute cruelty" that Carson finds shocking in the goddess of love is not hers alone (312).

Carson ponders this relationality in *Eros the Bittersweet*, a book that claims the feminine—Sapphic—origin for the adjective that defines the decisive knot of an erotic contradiction that pulls together and apart (1986). Eros, the proverbial loosener, may find its way into Hippolytus' name, and the double end he wishes for himself as the devotee of Artemis. At the end of the play, she tells him that female virgins will dedicate a lock of hair to him upon their marriage. (Artemis also presides over childbirth.) Hippolytus' chaste career might well be one more usually gendered female, although his final embrace by his father also might conjure up the pederastic plot in which the boy, supposed to be unresponsive to seduction, will yet grow up to be a man who initiates it.[5]

This doubleness Foucault brilliantly characterized as "the antinomy of the boy" at the center of the problematization of pederasty in classical Greek thought (1990, 203). The boy, as an object of desire, is in the position of a slave or a woman; yet he must grow up to be a free man who can no longer be identified with the subordinate position he once held. While male–male sexual relations were certainly not outlawed in ancient Greece, as Foucault repeatedly insists, they were regulated in a direction that led to their final displacement (Plato's *Phaedrus* is one text that follows this paradoxical trajectory). Foucault describes the route as an "elliptical configuration" perhaps akin to Carson's two distinct and different figures that nonetheless form a whole. It involves the meeting of asymmetrical moderations; the boy who is the object of desire resists, while the man who desires him restrains his passion almost to the point where the boy is in control of the situation.[6] "A relationship between their two moderations" arises, Foucault writes. *Mutatis mutandis*, we might see this pederastic plot crossing Phaedra and Hippolytus, each resisting and joined thereby through that double negation. Foucault's male couple are in the grips of requirements of shame and moderation, key terms that Euripides transposes and doubles to describe his central couple.

In her end piece to *Grief Lessons*, Carson's Euripides sums up the path of desire in *Hippolytus* by insisting that it cannot be located in "human forms": "Human forms are puny. Desire is vast. Vast, absolute and oddly *general*" (2006, 311). Phaedra's desire for her stepson that she told him in the original play is not what made her unacceptable. "What do we desire when we desire other people? Not them. Something else" (310). The shame that Phaedra initially felt that spreads over the later play arises from being unable to meet the demand of Eros for "something else." In deploying this phrase, Carson may have had in mind a sentence from Proust's *In Search of Lost Time* (2003): "The most exclusive love for a person is always a love for something else" (2.563). Her preface to *Grief Lessons* likens Euripides to Proust by way of Walter Benjamin's essay "The Image of Proust" (1969a, 211), citing the phrase "a perfect chemical curiosity" to epitomize the qualities Benjamin admired in Proust that Carson finds in Euripides (2006, 8).[7] Benjamin applauds Proust's "constant attempt to charge an entire lifetime with the utmost awareness"—a "flash," like a chemical reaction or an electric shock—"that none of us has time to live the true dramas of the life we are destined for" (1969a, 211). Proust articulates this idea when his narrator finally realizes that his task as a novelist is to capture this "reality which it is very easy for us to die without ever having known and which is, quite simply, our life" (6.298).

Carson's interest in Proust has extended to *The Albertine Workout*, the labor involved in deciphering the uncapturable figure of Albertine. Through her, Proust refigured his own relationship to Alfred Agostinelli according to what Carson calls "the transposition theory" (2014, 6), the interpretive gambit of collapsing one figure into another (as when Carson writes as *Euripides*). As a rather literal-minded biographical ploy, this can be reductive, but its cross-relations between male and female same-sex desires suggests a more fruitful path to pursue (both can be tracked in Proust). A connection between Proust and Euripides is available obliquely when Proust's narrator, after learning of Albertine's death, thinks about their relationship, indeed the nature of his erotic attachments more generally, by way of Racine's *Phèdre*, a play, it hardly need be said, derived from Euripides. He examines the scene of Phèdre's declaration of love to Hippolyte.

In Racine, Phèdre tells him her desire by retelling the story of Thésée and the Minotaur, recasting herself as Ariadne and Hippolyte as his father. As in Carson's supposition about the original play about Phaedra, Racine's heroine does not offer Hippolyte his father's place and throne; rather, she invites him to imagine himself in a more general story that exceeds his and her own. Hippolyte accuses Phèdre of forgetting who she is, but she insists that she has forgotten nothing, not least her honor. Proust's narrator comments: "[I]f he had evinced no indignation, Phèdre, her happiness achieved, might have had the same feeling that it did not amount to much" (5.619). Racine's heroine, like the one Carson imagines Euripides first created, is not intent upon the boy but "something else" in the erotic relation that would not simply be satisfied by his capitulation to the older woman's desire. Although Proust's narrator, when he first thinks of his relationship to Albertine, does not fasten on the moment of temporal and personal transposition in replotting the story of the labyrinth, he does later in *The Fugitive* after seeing someone who might be for him a "new Albertine" (5.873; likewise, he recognizes Albertine as a reincarnation of his earlier love object Gilberte). Proust's narrator wonders whether he must again renounce his desire for this second Albertine "whom I loved 'not as Hades had beheld her … but faithful, but proud, and even rather shy'" (5.873). As Peter Collier notes, in this citation from Racine, "Marcel has transposed the gender of the speaker and the reincarnated loved one" (2002, 613n15); in Racine, Phèdre's lines imagine Hippolyte as his reincarnated father, the object of her and Ariadne's desire. Transposing the "new Albertine" into "what Albertine had been in the past" transposes gender; Proust's "her" is "him" in Racine.

The real of the narrator's life replays a previous literary embodiment in figures that Euripides staged and restaged. Gender crossing is only a step in the direction toward "something else": "We think that we are in love with a girl, whereas we love in her, alas! only that dawn the glow of which is momentarily reflected in her face": so Proust's narrator summarizes his realization (5.873). The reflection he sees is what Benjamin understood to be the function of the image: it condenses the possibility of something else; here it is a glow that grants visibility and the chance that affords of seeing what makes visibility possible. The etymology of Phaedra's name connects her to that condition of brightness.

The phrase "something else" recurs in *Eros the Bittersweet*. It follows from the answer that Carson gives (akin to the one her *Euripides* offers) to the question of what the lover wants from the beloved. It is not acceptance: "union would be annihilating" (1986, 62). Sappho's coinage of love as bittersweet points in two directions at once; in opening a space between, it posits the necessity of a third term. (Similarly, when Proust's narrator first contemplates the scene between Phèdre and Hippolyte, his focus is on the way love and hate stimulate each other.) Sappho's words depend for Carson on having been written, acts of alphabetization carrying a symbolizing function that conveys "an act of imagination ... in which the mind reaches out from what is present and actual to something else" (61). Elsewhere this is the erotics of metaphor "reaching out from what is known and present to something else, something different, something desired" (86). Hence, in a Greek romance, Heliodorus' *Aethiopica*, a character who becomes pregnant while contemplating an image, "Thinking of something else" delivers a child who resembles it, relocating biological reproduction (93). Sappho initiated this understanding of eros; Carson recurs frequently to fragment 31 to trace how coupling requires triangulation to accommodate the antithetical, double nature of desire.[8] Between the poet, almost annihilated by her desire, and the woman at whom she gazes, there is also a man looking at her impassively.

In the second half of her book Carson links sapphic desire to Socratic philosophy, joining "the testimony of lovers like Sokrates or Sappho" as exemplary (172). She looks first to Plato's *Symposium* for this transposition, citing the moment when Aristophanes declares that, in their sexual union, the male–male couple has not reached the goal of desire. "No, obviously the soul of each is longing for something else," Carson translates 192c–d (67); asking "what is this 'something else,'" she rejects the oneness Aristophanes provides as his answer in favor of "an edge between two images that cannot merge in a single focus" (69). Her reply matches her claim about the coupling/disjunction of Phaedra and Hippolytus, joined in life in death, but also in a vocabulary of cross-identification. In *Eros the Bittersweet*, Plato's *Phaedrus* is Carson's focus for the final fifty pages of the book. His name is the male form of Phaedra. Carson's coupling echoes Racine; in his preface to *Phèdre*, he writes: "Socrate, le plus sage des philosophes, ne dédaignait pas de mettre la main aux tragédies d'Euripide" (1962, 267).[9]

Carson concentrates her reading of Plato's dialogue on Socrates' rejection of Lysias' speech on love that Phaedrus champions. His claim for a lover who is not in love assures a relationship without the drawbacks of out-of-control desire, thereby answering the problematic of the asymmetrical relation. Carson takes Socrates to object to the shortcutting of the problem as forestalling the possibility that the boy ever will be anything but a boy. After giving his own speech on the perils of the love relationship, Socrates, modeling himself on the ancient poet Stesichorus, delivers a palinode.[10] The question for Carson and Foucault, following Socrates, shifts from how to be in love to its origin as the locus of its meaning. This moves the problem of the antinomy of the boy, without dispelling the question of exactly what sexual activity is condoned, as a question about the relationship between the body and soul. As Plato's Aristophanes also had affirmed, the desire that love incites is not one that only involves questions of bodily satisfaction.

Carson emphasizes that returning to the origin of desire is to grasp a now that never ceases to exist, to enter a time that only gods inhabit; it is to be seized by something outside oneself (like the gods) that yet is within. Indeed, in the myth of origins in Plato's *Phaedrus*, love returns us to our beginnings as souls that existed elsewhere. Love enables us to return; the soul grows wings to fly back. "It is the beginning of what you mean to be," Carson summarizes what Socrates declares (157). It initiates a "reaching out toward a meaning not yet known," she goes on to say (169), recalling once again the erotic triangle in Sappho's fragment 31 that narrativizes the paradox of bittersweet love in its configuration. The drive to know, like the drive to have, remains the motive of life. We never "get" Eros, she concludes, and "that is the most erotic thing about Eros" (167). The drive to overcome the difference between the known and the unknown keeps insisting on the difference it keeps driving us to overcome.

That difference can be restated as divine/human, soul/body, now/then; the slash between, like the space opened in erotic relations, is not simply an opposition. How do we become who we are in relation to someone else? By becoming aware that we ourselves are also someone else. That drive to realize an originary yearning for "something else" underlies Leo Bersani's exploration of homo-desire, a desire for the same. In *Intimacies*, a book co-authored with Adam Phillips (2008), Bersani looks to the *Phaedrus*, taking off from the point at which Carson arrives, as well as from Foucault when he suggests that Plato's dialogue finally argues that what the beloved recognizes and responds to is not the lover but his love. Desiring it, not him, the boy begins to grow the wings that will return him to his origin, to the being he is and is meant to be. "And here the answer to the challenge of Aristophanes transforms the answer the latter gave," Foucault writes: "[I]t is not the other half of himself that the individual seeks in the other person; it is the truth to which his soul is related" (1990, 243). The truth of their being is their shared object of desire and their shared *subjectivity*. The antimony of the boy is overcome in the antimony of a couple who become one in both becoming other than themselves, the "something else" that they are.[11]

In *Intimacies*, Bersani's discussion of queer desire in Plato's *Phaedrus* recasts Freud's relegation of same-sex desire to narcissism as "impersonal narcissism"; "what both beloved and the lover love are 'secrets' about themselves *and* the truth about the other" (Bersani and Phillips 2008, 77 and 84). Bersani locates this overcoming of difference in virtuality, the imaginative capacity to think beyond difference. He returns to this topic in *Thoughts and Things*, restating this possibility in two directions. One, the virtuality that is the reality of the image: "this activity of positing uncertain alikeness is to expand the field of being" (2015, 81). The other relocates Plato's origin in the one that modern scientists suppose for our universe, an explosion of stars: "we are, literally, starchildren, and our bodies made of stardust" (77). What is stored forgotten in our memory, and becomes available to us (involuntarily, Proust supposes, when we are drawn to a past still present), is the origin in the heavens that Euripides uses to frame *Hippolytus* in the contention and agreement of Aphrodite and Artemis. These deities, who might be taken to symbolize a reproductive imperative that may destroy the individual and an imperative to preserve the individual even when s/he succumbs to erotic demand, also are found in the detail in *Phaedrus* on which Bersani fastens: that the outside of themselves that joins the lover and the beloved is their original attachment to some particular god; it is that same god in each of them which they look for in each other. In Euripides, the sameness of Aphrodite and Artemis is the ultimate draw.

Bersani turns from Plato to Proust for this point, not, as it happens, to the erotic experience with Albertine in volume 5 of *In Search of Lost Time* (its title now seems like an echo of the question of love in Plato's *Phaedrus*), but to the aesthetic experience of hearing a septet by Vinteuil only discovered and performed posthumously. This experience cannot be separated from that love: "It was deep in my heart, and very difficult to extricate, that Albertine's double was lodged" (5.336); Albertine as an embodiment of the principle of a double reality remains lodged in Proust's narrator as he ponders the nature of works of art. What enables them, even as they bear the unmistakable stamp of the individuality of their creators, to draw us to recognize ourselves in them? The work of art shows "the irreducibly individual existence of the soul" (5.341), yet calls forth something "eternal and at once recognizable" (5.342). Proust's "at once" is the "now" that Carson insists upon in Socrates' palinode. "Each artist thus seems to be the native of an unknown country, which he himself has forgotten" (5.342), Proust continues; the artwork remembers what he has forgotten. Proust seems to me to recall Plato's *Phaedrus*, even uncannily anticipates the suppositions of physicists of our times about the origins of the universe that our bodies remember. "The ineffable something" (the "something else") recalled by the individual work of art, Proust continues, is "the residuum of reality which we are obliged to keep to ourselves" (5.343). It is not ordinarily communicable, but in the work of art we each recognize in its sameness to itself ourselves. We do not need "a pair of wings" or "a different respiratory system" to visit the other planets from which these work arise; hearing, seeing, reading them, "we do really fly from star to star."

In Proust that secret is often the secret of the closet; Hippolytus keeps the secret of Phaedra's desire, hiding it in his secret oath not to tell, leading his father to assume he affirms what he hides. Ontologized, this is the secret that another world exists alongside the one most people call reality, the queer secret of another life and a love that is and is not one's own. In Carson's *Hippolytos*, that origin is intimated in the two figures who flank the play; they embody the wish of its titular character: "So may my finish-line match my start" (177). Opening with Aphrodite and ending with Artemis, the play gets no further than the first letter of the alphabet. Carson's *Euripides*'s feminine veiled secret is its queer core. In *Time Regained*, Proust puts it this way, "The writer must not be indignant if the invert who reads his book gives to his heroines a masculine countenance" (6.321), almost lifting the veil on the fiction he has written and the significance of his jealous concern that Albertine might be a lesbian. Not that he articulates that possibility; rather, he transposes it: "Racine himself was obliged, as a first step towards giving her a universal validity, for a moment to turn the antique figure of Phèdre into a Jansenist" (6.321). This "masculinization" and generalization also queers her—and Racine. As for the antique Phaedra, we might recall a note in Foucault, "the long cited example of Euripides who still loved Agathon when the latter was already a man in his prime" (1990, 194), another example of Euripides the rule-breaker.

* * *

"Everything, indeed, is at least double," Carson ends *The Albertine Workout*, quoting "*La Prisonnière*, p. 362" (2014, 23). In the appendices that follow the numbered paragraphs of the prose poem, she ponders questions of doubleness by way of the difference between metaphor and metonymy and the relation of adjectives and nouns. The latter discussion bears on the question of translation/transposition in "Why I Wrote Two Plays About Phaidra," on how the specific object of love is a ruse and veil for something more general. "Nouns name the world; adjectives let you get hold of the name and keep it from flying all over your mind like a pre-Socratic explanation of the cosmos" (2006, 23). In this formulation, adjectives are the way we attach ourselves to specificity. Carson seems to let that notion stand, until we turn the page for another take on adjectives, this time by way of Roland Barthes in *The Neutral* (2002), dreaming of a language without adjectives and therefore without graspable meaning. This loosening of language is a utopic gesture past "binary situations" on the way to "a third language" that Carson commends to our attention (26). Her own volte face already invites this. She reiterates here questions she asked in *Autobiography of Red* where, contemplating the question as to "what difference did Stesichoros make," she answers, "making adjectives" (1998, 4). Adjectives attach "everything in the world to its place in particularity. They are the latches of being," she continues, only to complicate the question immediately by noting how generic adjectives are in Homer, and how Stesichorus' adjectives are unexpected like his palinode, refusing the conventional story about Helen in Troy. There she became unlatched; that let out "a light as may have blinded him for a moment" (5). In her own rewriting of the fragments of his *Geryoneis*, their fragmentary state, like that of Sappho, withholds in telling and tells by withholding. Between truth and its veiling, another truth can be glimpsed. Her novel in verse avoids adjectives.

* * *

In her 2004 interview with Will Aitken, two biographical facts about Anne Carson stand out: her attraction to Greek and her attachment to Oscar Wilde (Carson 2004). Their connection is not noted but figures in Sam Anderson's essay/interview with her, "The Inscrutable Brilliance of Anne Carson" in the context of a performance of *Antigonick*, Carson's version of Sophocles, in which she took the role of the Chorus (Judith Butler played Creon), and donned her Oscar Wilde suit (a photo of her in it heads the essay).[12] Asked about her Greek attachment, Carson tells Anderson "that part of her desire to learn Greek came from her childhood desire to be Oscar Wilde—classically educated, elegantly dressed, publicly witty." He follows up, asking "when she stopped wanting this." Her reply: "I didn't . . . Who could stop? It's unachieved, as yet."

What Anderson does not ask is Aitken's question, inspired most immediately by *Autobiography of Red*; he invites Carson to talk about her "young life as a gay man." In answer to this she refers to her identification with Wilde; it provided her with "an ongoing carapace of irony" that she supposes "a lot of gay men develop" (2004, 207) as a response to the social pressures on our lives. It also means, she adds, that most anything she says-writes-thinks is bound to be a lie.

Carson's provocative claim about her identity as a gay man resonates in many ways.[13] It relates to what she characterizes as her own "unbearable" nature (196), how she pushes others uncomfortably to think. This drew her to the Greeks, not some humanistic belief that "we" all go back to them, but how the texts we have insist on their otherness, and, indeed, on otherness as a condition of existence, "the principle of being up against something" (199). Stories about fate and the gods lead one ultimately back to one's own alterity. In her writing, Carson affirms, she wants the reader to recognize and face the unbearable we bear, generalizing the gay man's situation. It is not left as an identitarian position when she goes on to speak of her own discomfort identifying either as female or male, her search for something that we, trapped so often in binarisms, cannot see our way past, "the 'floating' gender in which we would all like to rest" (210). Astonishing sentence: to rest so unmoored.

This conclusion relates to the subject that occupies the final part of the interview with Aitken, Carson's recent revisitation of Sappho's fragment 31 in which the fragmentary final line of the poem, "But all is to be dared," not discussed in *Eros the Bittersweet*, claims her attention. Daring is the other side to the recognition that comes from being unbearable—from an unbearable existence, from being strange and bound to be estranged from oneself (the condition of Phaedra and Hippolytus, to go no further). In the space of that recognition, of seeking to grasp the ungraspable, of knowing the unknowable, lies the possibility of thinking, of being a thinking being. It is what Carson's *Euripides* was drawn to and drawn to again (to recall Sappho's favorite reiterative modifier) in Phaedra's expansive invitation to self-annihilation.

* * *

In the foreword to *Tendencies*, Eve Kosofsky Sedgwick embraced the term "queer" for the project she had been intent upon for a decade, a word for now that resonated beyond and before the moment: "something about *queer* is inextinguishable" (1993, 188), she memorably wrote, attaching the word to etymological origins that suggest athwartness, movements across. While the "definitional center" of *queer* must be "same-sex sexual object-choice," Sedgwick went on to say (8), it ramifies beyond this core to the "fractal intricacies of language, skin, migration, state" (9), to all the specific ways in which people are different from each other to the generality of that difference.[14] Proust was the last object of Sedgwick's queer literary attention. In "The Weather in Proust" (2011), she contemplates the air we breathe the way he does, as something in us, something in which we must be to live, something that survives us as the life that persists, ours and not ours. At one point she makes a list of all the adjectives Proust summons up to describe the air (9); Carson makes a similar list in *The Albertine Workout*, suggesting that while it is "fun" (2014, 25) to do this it is rather beside the point of Proust, which is, after all, more general than particular. In "The Weather in Proust," Sedgwick finds in Proust what

Winnicott "hauntingly points out" through his "holding environment," the possibility "to think about *something else*" (2011, 12). "Something else," ventured by Carson and Sedgwick, I venture, is the "something" hauntingly inextinguishable in *queer* crossings.

Notes

1. See Gurd in this volume.
2. On these fragments, see Orrells in this volume.
3. This is a rendition of one of the surviving fragments of *Hippolytus Veiled* (Euripides' first version of the play): "In place of fire we women were born, a different fire, greater and much harder to fight" (fragment 429 Kannicht, translation by Collard and Cropp 2008).
4. Carson refers to the Hellenistic scholar Aristophanes of Byzantium.
5. On Theseus, see Blanshard and Telò in this volume.
6. On challenges to the pederastic model of male homoeroticism, see Boyarin and Youd in this volume. See also Introduction.
7. The cited phrase does not actually appear in Benjamin's essay, although the notion of "curiosity" that Carson applies to tragedy as a form does.
8. See Youd in this volume.
9. Racine probably has in mind the claim made in Diogenes Laertius 3.6 that Socrates collaborated with Euripides.
10. Stesichorus is Carson's avatar in her novel about the male–male love relationship between the winged Geryon and Heracles in *Autobiography of Red* (1998); it in fact includes a translation of the lines from the palinode cited in *Phaedrus* 243b.
11. As Brian says to Justin at the end of *Queer as Folk*: "Whether we see each other next week, next month, never again, it doesn't matter. It's only time."
12. All citations from https://www.nytimes.com/2013/03/17/magazine/the-inscrutable-brilliance-of-anne-carson.cmp.html.
13. Conversely, on Adrastus' lesbianism, see Telò in this volume.
14. See Introduction.

CHAPTER 20

ARISTOPHANES, *WOMEN AT THE THESMOPHORIA*—REALITY AND THE EGG: AN OVIPARODY OF EURIPIDES

L. Deihr

First, some ground rules: (1) by *egg* I mean a person in a stage, pre-transition, in the trans life cycle during which one may feel compelled to disprove one's own transness and/or to prove the impossibility of transition; (2) by *trans* I mean not trans- or trans*, but trans; specifically transsexual, or transgender.[1] Until Isabel Ruffell's recent article, scholarship on *Women at the Thesmophoria* had not, to my knowledge, engaged seriously with its potential for a trans-centric discourse. In the play's most well-known scholarly treatment, Froma Zeitlin (1981) approaches its preoccupation with crossdressing as representative of its "unstable and reversible" relations which "cross boundaries and invade each other's territories . . . to reflect ironically upon each other and themselves" (303). For Zeitlin, the comedy's cross-gender activity speaks to structure and genre, with crossdressing working together with parody to "expose the interrelationship of the crossing of genres and the crossing of genders; together they exemplify the equivalence of intertextuality and intersexuality" (304). In 2017's *TransAntiquity*, Filippo Carlà-Uhink, given crossdressing's institutionalization within the theater, considers the play's transvestism to be "perceived by the mind-set of the ancient world as functional" (12). Enrico Medda in the same volume recognizes the text as a "cornerstone" of "transvestism documented in Greek culture," treating this phenomenon as it regards disguise, impostorship, and metatheater (137). I do not, at least in this chapter, read the characters' crossdressing as referential to much more than crossdressing: what is important is that the cross-sex activity here occasions a reading of an accompanying discourse concerning transsexual desire. Here I care most not about transvestism or cross-sex behavior as strictly literary or theatrical devices but about transness as a discourse and as a reality.[2]

However, I must define against certain other notions of transness, although not because they do not in large part enable valuable readings. I do not, for example, mean transness as a "methodological stepping-stone for thinking about boundary-crossings of all sorts" (Chu and Drager 2019, 105), nor as a resource for relationality broadly. I do not mean to discount this methodology—it is true, as Stryker et al. write in their introduction to the "Trans-" issue of *Women's Studies Quarterly*, that "some vital and more generally relevant critical/political questions are compacted within the theoretical articulations and lived social realities of 'transgender' embodiments, subjectivities, and communities" (2008, 12). Where such an approach links "the questions of space and movement that [*trans*] implies to other critical crossings" (2008, 12), this chapter inversely considers those spatio-temporal crossings in order to ascertain a particularly trans self-knowledge.[3]

And so, in this chapter, while I do some abstracting of the metaphor of the transgender egg, I approach *transness* not as a reference to genre or literary structure, nor as a theoretical model for transitivity or resistance to categorization broadly, but rather as, simply put, transsexual desire, in whatever form that may take. However, let me be clear that (3) for the purposes of this reading, the characters of the In-Law and Euripides are not necessarily trans. This is not out of any anxiety about anachronism or the imposition of so-called modern identities onto ancient figures, nor do I suppose that such an argument could not be made; rather, I am simply not all that interested in assessing or ascribing to these characters anything resembling much of a gender at all. What I am after here is not identity so much as its packaging—that is, the ways in which *Women at the Thesmophoria* models a certain self-knowledge that at times precedes and constrains a trans identity.

This packaging takes the form of an egg, and it is a most paradoxical container. In her 2020 article "Egg Theory's Early Style," Grace Lavery considers how, much like a hatchling, "one only becomes an egg in retrospect ... An egg is displaced in time, 'retconned' back into one's own being" (384). She goes on to identify the logics and stylistics of what she calls egg theory—that is, "chiefly, [a person's belief] that they (he, she, ze, etc.) [sc. the egg] cannot transition. Not, generally, *must* not ... Egg theory is not generally ethical, but technical. One simply cannot" (384–5). The most important of Lavery's criteria for egg theory is the requirement that it "assure us that transition is both impossible and inevitable, without exposing the dialectical negative of that contradictory image to too much light" (385).

Lavery's theory, as well as the metaphor of the egg itself, has certainly to do with ideas of hatching and emergence, as well as the temporalities contained within such a model— such as, you might have guessed, whether primacy belongs to the chicken or to the egg (Lavery 2020, 396). I am interested in hatching and the egg's paradoxical temporalities, but I am interested also in the unbroken egg and its shell; here I take up not only the rhetoric Lavery brings to light, but also the form of the egg's vehicle.

And so this chapter has two major goals: the first is to map out, in a perhaps somewhat vulgar application, the technicalities of this theory of the egg at work in *Women at the Thesmophoria*; the second, to take the egg not just as a rhetorical model but as an image or object. In this parody of Euripides—where Euripides is himself a force that acts on reality with gender production as his tool—it is through the paradoxical potentialities of the egg image that the impossibility and inevitability of gender transition in Euripidean reality not only appear as a motif but also come to be inscribed on the body itself.

Eggs and their Logics

Women at the Thesmophoria begins with the hatching of a scheme for the infiltration of the Thesmophoria (a festival in honor of the goddesses Demeter and Persephone which only adult women may attend); the main role of spy is handed off until it reaches Euripides' witless In-Law, whose assumption of the role is preceded, as we will see, by exercises in the logic of the egg. It is the character of Euripides himself and the poet Agathon who engage first in these exercises, and for whom any sort of transsexual enactment becomes impossible, and inevitable indeed.

Euripides, introducing the seed of the comedy's plot, hopes that Agathon will accept the task of infiltration. As for why he cannot manage it himself, he declares: "First of all, I'm well known. Second of all, I'm grey and I've got a beard. But you—you've got a pretty face, pale and shaven, and a lady-voice; you're soft and nice to look at" (189–92). While Euripides' anxiety about what we might gruesomely call *passability* is expected in this context, the essential logic of his refusal is exactly the circular reasoning of the unhatched egg: Euripides cannot make efforts to become a woman, or even womanlike, because he is not already a woman. This comes with various implications and details: he could never be a woman because he is wizened and old, as though old women do not exist; he cannot be a woman because he has a beard, as though we will not witness in just a few lines a scene of brutal, comic depilation.

And so Euripides' potential for (even temporary) transition is indeed impossible, but it is also inevitable: he cannot conceive of the idea of the elderly woman, let alone of himself as such a figure, but by the end of the show he will have convincingly become one; similarly he escapes recognition until he reveals himself, retroactively invalidating his fear that he is too recognizable as is. Consider the Scythian archer, for example, observing Euripides-as-Echo: "What a chatterbox of a wretched woman (*"gunaiko"*) (1097); "Keep an eye on this old man, granny (*graidio*)" (1199). The audience has proof of concept that his femaleness is perfectly feasible, but his character is encased in the logic of the egg, who cannot transition, she reasons, because she has not already transitioned—and yet must, and will, transition. In this case, there is no becoming, only stasis; for the egg, change is an impossibility.

For this reason, Euripides approaches Agathon, since Agathon is already sufficiently feminine, disbelieving wholesale in the work it must take for him or anyone else to achieve a socially sanctioned femininity. But Agathon refuses, citing reasons that are different from Euripides' own but which are no less typical of the egg's logic: Agathon is beautiful, even for a woman, but he does not want "to seem to be stealing the women's nighttime deeds, / making off with sex that belongs to them (*thêleian Kuprin*)" (204–5).

While Agathon in his daily life is content "to dress in accordance with his feelings" (148)—thus exhibiting probably the only instance in the drama we can effectively consider something like a sense of gender presentation, or even gender euphoria—his confidence in the assimilability of his appearance is not the issue. Rather, he is concerned about the optics; in fact, he seems, like many trans women, apprehensive of being classified as a sexual trespasser. Inasmuch as Euripides' own misogynistic intentions of disguise and infiltration might remind one of the anti-trans narrative which "project[s] onto trans women the image of the untamable lesbian rapist . . . in public toilets, or any other female-centered environment" (Lavery 2019, 122), Agathon's own reasoning seems to map in response onto a contemporary trans wariness of moral panic. This, too, carries a particularly egg-like, impossible logic. Inversely of Euripides, Agathon's taking up of trans femininity is already foreclosed upon by its very success: his concern is not that he will appear some dog-whistle image of a man in a dress but rather that he, being so womanly already, will with his presence seem to skew the women's limited supply and plentiful demand for sex, clinging to *seeming* rather than to *being*. He is, somehow, too much of a woman already to attend the festival of women—too much of a woman to be a woman.

Egg Theory at Large

The presence in the text of this gender foreclosure based upon a fixed present state is not limited to the specific conditions for the infiltration of the Thesmophoria, nor is it a solely interior phenomenon drawn out from within the characters. While Euripides and Agathon express entirely egg-like sentiments regarding their own prospects as women, we also see the theory of the egg implemented (here by proxy) as a means to an end; in other words, Euripides exhibits the logic of the egg himself, but he also imposes it on the world around him.

Once among the women, in his attempt to clear Euripides' name, the In-Law himself engages in a tricky bit of egg theory as it applies not to the circumstances of his own gender experience but those of the world—of the women, at least—more broadly. The women lament the fact that Euripides "did them much harm, deceitfully finding stories where there was a wicked woman, writing Melanippes and Phaedras; but he never wrote a Penelope, since she seemed a temperate woman" (545–8). The In-Law's excuse for this shortcoming is simple: Euripides has not written any good women because no such women exist, or, more pithily, because "you couldn't say that there's a single Penelope among today's women, only Phaedras" (549–50).

This is a backwardly circular assessment of the situation: it is not reality that constrains Euripides' writing but rather his writing that constrains reality, if his literary misogyny causes the husbands of Athens "to come straight home from the theater with suspicious looks and to straightaway search in case there's some lover hidden inside" (395–7), and if his writing "has convinced the men that the gods don't exist, and so [the garland-maker] no longer sells half of what she used to" (451–2).

It is evident from these accounts—from the very assembly apparently necessitating Euripides' defense—that Euripides, through his literary practices, drastically and materially affects these women's realities. For the In-Law to claim that Euripides can write no Penelopes, no so-called good women, because they do not exist at present, again takes up the more broadly eggy philosophy that no gender-reality that does not exist already, let alone women of any sort, can become real—that transition is impossible and that there exist only polar loci divorced from change over time—even though it has been shown (both by mention of a Penelope and by Euripides' eventual inevitable womanhood) that this is not the case.[4] The possibility of the creation of a certain kind of woman is denied by the man whose denial recreates, constantly, an opposing kind of woman. From these exchanges it becomes clear (1) that Euripides is here a kind of arbiter both of a paradoxical reality and of gender, and (2) that in his reality, as in egg theory, gender production is inevitable, but only ever with disastrous consequences. Where the character of Euripides appears to have internalized the egg's primary theory, the man the character reflects exerts that same theory over the reality in which the women of Athens find themselves.

Egg as Image

Next I turn to the egg as an image, an object, a form. While the functions of hatching and emergence concern a certain trans self-knowledge, I want also to consider not just the egg's logics within *Women at the Thesmophoria* but also the implications of the form of the egg itself: its surfaces, insides, and outsides. To some degree I take after Jeanne Vaccaro, who writes on a certain capacity for a trans methodology in the biologies and hyperbolic geometries of corals real and handmade, asking "after the lush shapes and textures of many things" (2015, 276). Vaccaro finds that "mathematical concepts of excess of surface [and] dimensionality animate the transgender body," and that we might understand hyperbolic space as "a reorganization of form and matter" (292). Here I read through the appearance of certain egg-like images a similar sort of organization of form through rhetoric and rhetoric through form. To that end, the following reading of the form of the egg in *Women at the Thesmophoria* seeks out the sensory alongside the physiological as markers of (and as marked by) the egg's model of self-knowledge. I identify four major egg images, which I qualify as prominent in the text, heavy with the problem of gender, into which I read, again, a sort of egg theory.

What I specifically want to pull out of the egg image is the order of its constituent parts—that is, the egg as a whole versus the innards it contains versus the shell doing the containing. The object of the unbroken shell, membrane, and contents we call an egg; so, too, we call "egg" the contents alone: the white and the yolk, raw or cooked. The outer layer itself is not an egg, but just the shell. I cannot comment on the particularities of this order of assembly in other languages, but it is this figurative shell going forward that makes the egg images we will witness. It is, of course, only by virtue of a shell that there can be an inside and an outside across which interior and exterior realities can be troubled.

The Baby in the Pot

I begin with the egg image manifestly closest to a (hard-shelled) egg: that of the baby in the pot. Among the In-Law's examples of female misdeeds that Euripides graciously does not report comes this narrative (502–6) in which a woman claimed to be having labor pains for ten days until she bought a baby; her husband was running in circles looking to buy birth-inducing medicines. An old woman brought the baby in a pot (*chutra*) with its mouth stuffed with honeycomb so it wouldn't cry.

You see where this is going: we witness (allegedly) unborn offspring contained within a hard, rounded shell. The resemblance to the prototypical bird's egg is perhaps apparent, but I want to bring out the egg's logic in the image as well as in the circumstances surrounding its gendering. Immediately after the "birth," the old woman aggressively sexes the baby (514–16); the primary function of this is to assure the father of the child's likeness to him, but this invitation to a sexwise comparison as a means of avoiding scrutiny seems to me an instantiation of egg theory at birth, a postpartum concealment and revision of one gender-productive reality by means of gender examination.

The contents of this egg undergo a displacement both spatial and temporal: the baby has been born in one reality but remains, right up to its presentation to its unknowingly adoptive father, unborn from its new mother's uninvolved womb and unhatched from the eggshell formed by the clay of the pot. It kicks not the wall of the mother's belly but that of the pot (508–9), a "new" enveloping surface concealing and protecting not only that which lies within it (the baby) but also that which stands outside of it (the wife). This arrangement combines the problem of fertility and the shell encasement of the embryonic egg with the temporal displacement of the transgender egg, "cast back in time from a hatched present" (Lavery 2020, 385).

Let us note also that, in medical contexts as well as in comedy, pots can generally carry a vaginal or uterine sense.[5] Above I suggest *chutra* as eggshell: not as reproductive organ but as thing reproduced. If the *chutra* suggests the uterus and the uterus is here removed from the body and also cast back into time, it is less a wandering womb than an unimplanted ovum signifying a retrograde concentricity of space and time together on the grounds, per the old woman's insistent sexuation, of gender production as a relation-stabilizing force.

The Lover Beneath the Cloak

We see in *Women at the Thesmophoria* plenty of prominent circles, what with the *kuklos* and its relationship with the metatheater of the Chorus, who are always running around self-directing their own circular formations ("but first we've got to run in a circle as quickly as possible" 662; "nimbly set your foot to the round—the chorus' circling formation must cast its gaze all over," 954–8; and so forth).[6] Also important here is Agathon's proximity to the *ekkuklêma*: he is wheeled in on one, and Euripides indicates him as *ekkukloumenos*, "the one being wheeled in" (96). These self-referential circles abound in the text, and work in part to show the poet's hand. Here I want to focus on another *kuklos* which shows and conceals in the same turn.

It is the *enkuklon* of Agathon that Euripides instructs the In-Law to wear to the festival (261). Used generically to indicate a woman's upper-body garment, its literal meaning is simply "the round thing." This garment surfaces again in the In-Law's litany of female misdeeds excluded from Euripides' tragedies; he claims (498–501) that Euripides

> has never spoken of how a woman, showing to her husband the quality of a garment (*enkuklon*) against the light, sends away her well-covered (*eu kekalummenon*) lover.

I suggest that it is this image of the *enkuklon* concealing the lover that is so fraught with the egg's logic—in particular, its relationship to the man behind it and the light around it, for which some manuscripts give *hupaugas[ai]*, "to shine beneath," while others attest *hup' augas*, "against the light" (500). Regardless of this textual indeterminacy, the image of the woman's lover hidden behind some span of fabric is unquestionably well-lit.

The paradox here is this: the adulterous lover is "well-covered" or "well-hidden" because the husband's attention is diverted toward the quality of the cloth, but, generally speaking, to hold most woven fabrics up to the light is to ensure that we are more able to see any shadows behind them. The lover, then, is well-hidden both in spite of and because of this abundance of light, and therefore both in spite of and because of the husband's scrutiny (which, we might imagine, may well have arisen after some accusation made by Euripidean writing). It is for this reason that I find in this image the qualities of the egg: a feminized surface, one with circularity built into its signifier, conceals a secret man, enveloping him as though a shell. Read into this whatever "direction" of transness you like; what matters is that a gender-specific, rounded surface conceals yet more gender-specific contents in a manner quite paradoxical. To think about it spatially, this configuration presents a circle, spread flat, more dimensional by means of what it conceals. This hyper-dimensional, light-bending form both attracts and diverts attention, making gender examination (here, the search for the adulterer) impossible and inevitable, much as the egg might deny herself transition both by ignoring and by closely scrutinizing her interior and exterior realities as incommensurable but fixed.

The Wheel and the Funnel

At the top of the play, Euripides, having informed his father-in-law that he need not hear what he is about to see (5–8), reasons that this is true because the faculties of sight and hearing

> were once so divided: the Aether, when it was producing the first things and was begetting the living things that move around within it, devised first that thing which is necessary for sight: the eye, which is like the wheel (*trochôi*) of the sun; and it drilled the ear as a funnel (*choanên*) for hearing (13–18).

In the interest of being a little too neat about it, I propose that the images of the eye-wheel and the ear-funnel foreshadow and correlate to the egg objects laid out above, and that through them the concentric, impossible rhetoric of the egg is inscribed on the body itself.

Like the eye-wheel, the concealing *enkuklon* is a flat circle that engages with the light to do its work of sensory processing; like the ear-funnel, the pot containing the baby is a hollow shape fashioned for transportation—both pot (*chutra*) and funnel (*choanê*) maintain some formal trace of their function: *cheô* ("to pour").

As before, though this time directly instead of through the In-Law as his mouthpiece, Euripides commits a logic of incommensurability and atemporality to the human body itself, generating in essence, before producing the In-Law's womanhood and sending him off to the festival, an eggshell of rhetoric within matter itself. For the eye and ear to be shells, to be internal barriers, is to build into their respective forms and sensory faculties the egg's discursive impossibilities, creating a concentricity involving the body and a logic constraining its ability to change. Sight and hearing ought not be mixed, says Euripides—but the eye-and-ear-as-shell imply a latency embedded in the physiological forms that enable them, signifying the prohibition of new reality both in the material of the body where these mechanisms are physically located as well as in the consciousnesses to which they direct their data. Euripides, who is established as wielding against the women the power of the egg's paradox, inscribes that paradoxical rhetoric onto the body and its senses, enforcing the embodiment of a "protocol for a new, and newly incommensurable, sensemaking procedure" (Lavery 2020, 384).

Conclusion: Making Reality

I have so far avoided using the term "queer," despite the title of this volume and the queer nature of the temporal and spatial crossings of which my reading consists, especially as they have to do with the body and gender. I have maintained this avoidance in response to an institutional difference more than a theoretical one. At the outset I defined *against* certain sorts of trans readings, simply because my reading is different. Still, it should be said, as Cáel Keegan writes, that "trans studies is against queer theory" in that "queer theory is the disciplinary surface against which trans studies must constantly narrate itself, the field against which trans studies finds itself pressed in a stipulated intimacy" (2020b, 349). Keegan cites the various institutional weaknesses which fail trans studies, its scholars, and its subjects, and makes the important distinction that "transgender studies departs from queer theory's deconstructive mode to place high value on constative self-knowledge," explaining that "this value developed as a political response to the specific medical narratology of transgender (i.e. transsexual) life" (350).[7] Similarly, Susan Stryker, who famously once characterized trans studies as queer theory's evil twin (2004), describes "Egg Theory's Early Style" as illustrative of "a cis-centric queer theory's inability to imagine transition" (2020, 300). Egg theory in this sense is emblematic of queer theory's "insistence on universality and virtuality as key aspects of queer politics"

(Lavery 2020, abstract), as well as of the tension therein "between the life of the 'tr*nny' and that of the queer other whose transness has been sublimated into a more nuanced, sophisticated orientation toward gender" (386). It is by virtue of a similarly eggy contradiction that queer theory may cite "incommensurability, division, discrimination, and distinction as its characterizing techniques" while maintaining the uselessly universalist position (this from Lavery's reading of Sedgwick's first axiom [1990]) that "people may be different from each other, but everyone is differenced in the same way" (387).

I cannot say whether I have been "doing" trans studies or queer theory in this chapter, to the degree that we might want to distinguish between them at all. I think it is true that queer theory often discounts the material importance of the body, including insofar as such a body-forward approach is "so often wrongly counted as an essentialist (and therefore putatively antitrans) account of embodiment" (Lavery 2019, 139). It is also sometimes true that "in privileging discursivity and performativity over interiority and materiality, queer studies overwrites the felt reality of transgender identification as a form of false consciousness" (Keegan 2020a, 70). In that regard, the presence of egg theory, not only in the dominant discourse of *Women at the Thesmophoria* but also in its bodies, is perhaps another illustration of the need for a trans-centric queer theory, a queer theory which can and is eager to imagine transition.

A trans-centric queer theory might, for example, use a model of trans self-knowledge not simply to deconstruct but to reveal mechanisms of hegemonic stabilization. For all that *Women at the Thesmophoria*'s crossdressing may draw out a cross-wiring of genres and a reversal of gender inequities, a reading featuring a trans self-knowledge exposes an ideology to match the Thesmophoria's thematic "renewal of fertility" for which purpose, per Zeitlin's investigation of gender and genre, "comedy, tragedy, and festival have all converged" (1981, 318). *Women at the Thesmophoria* essentially reproduces its own conditions: the situations of gender scrutiny and gender foreclosure I consider to be egg-like maintain a regime of stereotype, a pattern of behavior. Because the egg is unhatchable, the egg images within the In-Law's litanies of female misdeeds only renew their own circumstances. The rhetorics and images attending the baby in the pot or the lover behind the cloak end up stabilizing a family unit from which opportunities for transgression derive; even the explanation of the incommensurability of the eye-wheel and ear-funnel appears within a narrative of the Aether's concentric production of life within itself (15).

Let us not forget also that Euripides, the arbiter of reality through gender production, gets away with it all in the end, making a pact with the women that they will hear "nothing else bad from [him], never," a promise technically kept for the remainder of the comedy but certainly broken outside of its immediate narrative scope. The women's alleged mischief is laid bare to the audience but is concealed at the diegetic level in order to maintain the narrative conditions that produce it.

Transition at the Thesmophoria, then, is impossible/inevitable in part because sex and gender must be just transgressible enough to be exposed on the level of parody, so long as those categories are stable enough for their further reproduction. Transition is inevitable because gender itself poses problems, but impossible because the conditions problematizing it must be renewed. The image of the egg, a seemingly closed circuit, paradoxically allows us a glimpse through to the mechanisms incubating it.

As much as any Aristophanic comedy, *Women at the Thesmophoria* "engage[s] with a range of social and political issues ... through the construction, discussion and manipulation of ideal worlds" (Ruffell 2014, 220); Zeitlin acknowledges Aristophanes' typical usage of the "comic device of role reversal to imagine worlds in which women are 'on top'" (302), and Ruffell remarks that women's presumption of power (as also in *Lysistrata* and *Assemblywomen*) is one of many markers of Old Comic utopianism (2011, 9.2.3 and 2014, 206, respectively). Both despite and because of its thickly applied egg theory, and because of its project as a parody of Euripides as a simultaneous interrogator and enforcer of the stabilizing force of gender, I myself would like to imagine another utopia in *Women at the Thesmophoria*, a utopia that defies its utopianism and comes to be real: a Thesmophoria at which women are the "primary movers" (Ruffell 2011, 9.2.3), to be sure, but also one on the verge of believing that gender transition can be reality.

Notes

1. For the merits of *transsexual* see, among others, Gabriel 2016. On trans/trans*, see also Introduction.

2. On gender and genre crossings, see Boyarin and Goldberg in this volume.

3. Cf. Mueller in this volume, especially on Marquis Bey's conceptualization of both para- and trans-ontologies.

4. Zeitlin remarks that, by parodying *Helen*, the play stages within itself a contradiction of the lack of Penelopes whereby Helen is herself "another Penelope" (315).

5. For the uterus and vulva as pots in medical iconography, see Dasen and Ducaté-Paarmann 2006, esp. 240–1. In his 2012 dissertation, *Slaves, Sex, and Transgression in Greek Old Comedy* (UC Berkeley), Daniel Walin outlines the popular availability of this imagery, and of *chutra* as comic vulva/uterus specifically, especially as it facilitates genital comedy (193–5).

6. For ritual metatheater in the Chorus of *Women at the Thesmophoria* particularly, see Bierl 2009.

7. See Introduction.

CHAPTER 21
BACCHAE—"AN EXCESSIVELY HIGH PRICE TO PAY FOR BEING RELUCTANT TO EMERGE FROM THE CLOSET"?
Isabel Ruffell

In his review of the National Theatre of Scotland's 2007 production of the *Bacchae*, *Guardian* critic Michael Billington objected at length to its gleeful engagement with sexuality and gender, its elements of camp and its use of humor. True tragic sensibility, he argued, only arrived with Agave's recognition of her dismembered son. Unable to reconcile the spectacle of trauma with the earlier style and content, Billington's comments betray a fundamental misunderstanding of the play, and, furthermore, suggest that a queer interpretation of the play is necessarily to trivialize it. Yet the play's story about Dionysus' punishment of Thebes for failing to accept him and the demonstrations of his nature and power are pursued overwhelmingly in terms of transgressions of gender norms. Such transgressions are, through Dionysus' homecoming, to be integrated into Greek culture. A reading in terms of modern queer and specifically *trans* identities is thus, despite some profound silences in classical scholarship, both relevant and pressing.

A decade and a half on, the need is even more pressing, where gains that have been made in trans rights and healthcare[1] are facing a sustained backlash through a perverse alliance between far-right extremism and a strand of essentialist feminism.[2] One element in the strategy has been a denial of any trans history before Hirschfeld (1910) and Benjamin (1966) started applying labels. This is demonstrably false.[3] So one important aspect of this chapter is to contribute to this pre-history of trans. It is axiomatic here that (just as with sexuality) expressions of gender are culturally contingent, and that also means that expressions of transgender are culturally contingent and specific. Nonetheless, I am also writing from the perspective of a twenty-first-century trans woman, and I will draw attention to both historicist and contemporary political perspectives.[4]

The play is perhaps best known (as Billington grudgingly notes) for the final appearance (alive and whole) of Pentheus, where he comes out dressed as a maenad, is styled and coached by Dionysus, and is led off to the mountain to meet his death at the hands of his mother, Agave. While it is the culmination of a trans-relevant thematic, it is not in itself the most decisive scene for a trans reading (and as such will not be discussed at length here). By this stage, the play is deep into a compulsion narrative, a staple both of fictional narratives on trans themes from a cishet perspective (e.g., films such as *Some Like it Hot*, *Tootsie*, or *Mrs Doubtfire*) and of the political backlash (children allegedly forced to transition by, variously, parents or GICs). Dionysus compels Pentheus by using persuasion, that it is necessary if he is to spy successfully on the maenads, and by affecting his mental state directly. The public spectacle of Pentheus is presented in terms of mockery and humiliation—rightly emphasized by Kay Gabriel (2018)—the first stage in learning the truth about the god. At the same time, both in the scene itself and, in particular, from the performance to this point, it is clear that Dionysus is giving Pentheus exactly what he wants but cannot acknowledge. Herein lies the tragedy of Pentheus. By virtue of his self-denial, obsession, and confusion, he models an aggressive patriarchal authority and an obsessive but fantastical heteronormativity including the espousing of transphobic tropes and outright violence—all of which are made to rebound upon him.

There are trans-positive elements in the play, but Pentheus is not one of them. They also need to be unpicked from the uncomfortable story of vengeance. Punishment in *Bacchae* entails a demonstration not only of divine power but of the nature of the god and those who reject that. It is very similar to Aphrodite's in *Hippolytus* where she forcibly inflicts it on a mortal (Phaedra), exemplifying Hippolytus' disrespect through the play. In *Bacchae*, however, there are explicitly social as well as personal targets: Pentheus, the new king of Thebes, is particularly singled out, but Dionysus is also targeting other members of the royal family—his mother's father, Cadmus, and her sisters, who have denied that Semele gave birth to Dionysus, although Cadmus did provide a tomb (10–11). But Dionysus is also targeting the city of Thebes more generally. His first demonstration is driving the women out of the city onto the hillside, mad as if afflicted by a gadfly (*oistreô* 32), like Io in *Prometheus Bound*. There is thus a very significant difference between the women of Thebes who are being punished, controlled, and afflicted by Dionysian elements, and the Chorus of women who have followed Dionysus from Asia, apparently willingly. There are also already suggestions of what Dionysian power entails. The overturning of social norms and hierarchy is particularly signaled: women, particularly elite women, are not only out of their homes (violating an ideological norm rather than social reality), but out of the city, too; even more shocking, and particularly flagged, ordinary Thebans mix with the royal family (25–42, esp. 37). As will become clearer, the women, including nursing mothers, have also left their children behind. At the same time, this location of the Theban women in the wild, while also possibly evoking actual Dionysiac worship in some areas of the Greek world, also draws on cultural stereotypes that associated women with wildness and monstrosity.[5] In that sense, there is a gendered ambivalence here: under the influence of Dionysus the Theban women are acting both like and unlike (Greek notions of) women. Again, the physical as well as social dimensions become thematized in the play.

One element distinct from other plays of divine vengeance is that Dionysus himself is a near constant presence onstage, albeit mostly in the guise of a foreigner from Lydia, leader of a band of maenads (the Chorus). His assumption of mortal form is explicitly to "teach" Pentheus specifically, and the Thebans in general, that he is a god. The personal interactions between the god and the king are indeed central to the demonstration of his divinity and its nature. A crucial element—less obvious textually, but obvious to an audience—is Dionysus' androgyny. This appearance is consonant with the development of Dionysus away from a mature bearded male, albeit dressed in a flowing himation and wielding a parasol (both at least exotic, with suggestions of the Greek East, but also ambivalently gendered), to a younger beardless male by the last quarter of the fifth century BC (see *Lexicon Iconographicum Mythologiae Classicae*, s.v. Dionysus). The play will amplify this gender fluidity. Unsurprisingly, cross-gender casting of Dionysus in modern performance has long been a staple (including such contexts as the 1989 Cambridge Greek Play). There is, then, a physical reminder of gendered ambivalence throughout. There are other ambivalences, too, not least ethnicity: Dionysus presents himself as a Lydian mortal, but seeks to establish himself as a Greek god. This insider/outsider duality is central to his cult (e.g., he is always arriving in Athens for the Dionysia each year). These cultic ambivalences are also heavily gendered through the relentless syncretism of the play. Dionysus is associated with the local fertility cult of Iakkhos (725), one of the minor Eleusinian deities, and through him with Demeter and Persephone (see 275–85). The Chorus in their entry-song (*parodos*) associate him with the exemplar of Eastern ecstatic worship: Cybele cult (79), although regrettably the associated cult and myth of Attis is not securely attested in Athens for another half a century.[6]

It is in Dionysus' absence, however, that the play orients toward human cross-dressing, and locates it squarely at the intersection of two discourses: rationalism and absurdity. The blind old prophet, Teiresias, arrives to pick up Cadmus, so that they can join the maenads on the hillside (170–5). Both are dressed and equipped as maenads in fawnskins, and equipped with thyrsus and ivy wreath (176–7), "the god's outfit" (180). They are the only men to do so (195–6), and the visual parallel with the similarly attired Chorus reinforces their cross-gender appearance. One frame here is incongruity—in other words, a kind of drag performance—which is amplified, verbally and visually, through great play with their decrepitude (175, 186, 190, 203–7), not least as they emphasize, and no doubt demonstrate, the dance moves of their aged bodies. Cadmus, indeed, acknowledges that they might be thought lacking in self-respect (*aidôs*). They feel rejuvenated (188–91), the gift of the god, although this is somewhat belied by Cadmus' proposal that they travel to the hillside in wagons (192), as Teiresias perhaps suggests (193). Another frame is rational choice. They are not (or perhaps not only) swept away by a Dionysiac contagion, but repeatedly emphasize their wisdom (*sophia* 179) and prudence (*sôphrosunê*) in taking up the costume and equipment and dancing for the god (196): "We alone have good, if unwelcome, sense (*eu phronein*), the rest of the men are foolish (*kakôs*)." It is not unusual for Teiresias to articulate good, if unwelcome, sense about the gods, especially in Sophocles (*Antigone* and *Oedipus Tyrannus*); here, though, it is consciously absurd.

Both absurdity and rationalism are problematized further on the arrival of an agitated (214) Pentheus, the new ruler of Thebes, who has been out of town (215) and rushed back to restore some kind of social and specifically gendered (217) order. He flatly refuses to accept that Dionysus is a god, and roots this in the conviction—stated here for the first, but far from the last, time—that the new rites are a pretext for drink and, above all, sex out in the wilds. Then he turns to the old men, and the spectacle they present (*thauma* 249). He points both to the look of their maenadic costume, which explicitly makes them ridiculous (*polun gelôn* 250), and to their age. They are demonstrating that they lack intelligence. The mockery is picked up and repudiated by Teiresias, who repeatedly accuses Pentheus of mocking the god (*diagelais* 274, 287, 322). The question of where mockery lies, and on what basis, is initiated in this scene—and not just in religious terms (fighting against a god, *theomakhein*, is rarely a good idea in mythology), but also politically, whereby glibness rather than good sense is, for Teiresias, the mark of the bad *citizen*.

The mockery theme is one of the many ways that *Bacchae* draws on tragedy's sister genre, comedy.[7] There, cross-dressing can both be used for humiliating laughter as a punishment in *Lysistrata* or through pretentious rationalism or compulsion in *Women at the Thesmophoria*.[8] Pentheus is here wallowing in the shallower end of the comic pool, both in his equation of laughter with abuse and in his reuse of gendered assumptions, that women are obsessed with drink and sex, a very old Greek stereotype. He thus believes women-only spaces need to be surveilled and policed, and that gender non-conforming individuals are themselves driven by sexual motives (353–5; cf. 234–9), which is still a widespread cultural trope[9] and is a staple of the current transphobic backlash (prominent among whom in the UK is a onetime sitcom author whose output traded in just such tropes). Dionysus' comedy *can* involve abuse and humiliation, and, as Teiresias hints, if Dionysus is the ultimate target of Pentheus, then he is liable to have it returned with interest. Thus Pentheus—but there is more to Dionysiac comedy than this, and there is more to this scene than a reversal of humiliation strategies. Rather, the Dionysiac laughter (*gelôs*) *embraces* the incongruous, the absurd, and the joyful: pleasure as well as anger.

A binary opposition between sense and madness is also problematic. Teiresias accuses Pentheus of madness (*mania*) in rejecting Dionysus; but his embrace of maenadism itself constitutes madness (a maenad is literally a "madwoman"), and he and Cadmus are proposing to rave with the other maenads. Conversely, both old men display odd or disquieting rationalizations of their own. Teiresias' explanation of the divinity of Dionysus covers more than conventional associations with the grape and thereby other fertility gods. It culminates in a tortuous explanation of the story of Dionysus' birth, and that after the death of Semele he was sewn up in Zeus' thigh. This he explains by means of a bizarre piece of wordplay: Dionysus was the pledge (*homêros*) of Zeus to Hera, but over time this became "the thigh" (*ho mêros*). This looks more like the rationalisms of contemporary speculative thinkers than it does the insight of a prophet with a hotline to the divine. Cadmus has already suggested to Teiresias that, if Dionysus is a god, then it will be a mark of distinction for his family. His final speech to Pentheus elaborates upon this theme. So although the old men are, like the Chorus, willing followers of Dionysus, they are, unlike them, adding an element of calculation or rationalization to the embrace of Dionysus' power and his ecstatic worship.

Pentheus, clearly, both views the cult of Dionysus as a cultural threat and denies his reality (it is a fraud). The position that emerges from the old men is more complex. The strong association of Dionysus with the natural world and the old men's embodied responses suggests very strongly that the ecstatic worship of Dionysus—including cross-gender practice—is embodying nature and not in conflict with it, even if it violates cultural norms. That they still feel obliged to rationalize it, either in terms of foundational *mythos* (Teiresias) or in terms of its personal benefits (Cadmus) speaks to (some) debates about the status and etiology of trans: as a part of culture, as some kind of irreducible supplement to, and production of, the gender system, or as having at least some physical basis (pointing to a greater biological diversity, down to the chromosomal level, than some are willing to admit), or (as seems more likely) a mixture of nature and culture. The need for the old men to *explain* the phenomenon is all too familiar.

Pentheus, however, is in no mood for nuance or reflection. The following scenes (episodes two and three) present the central confrontation between him and Dionysus, the latter masquerading as the Lydian stranger. Here is the core of the lesson that Dionysus will teach, rooted in Pentheus' own contradictions, which are slowly drawn out (434–861). This sequence begins with Pentheus, wielder of civic authority, waiting for men he has sent to arrest the stranger. He has already sought to arrest all the women he can find. It ends with the new king at the mercy of Dionysus, which is entirely not forthcoming. One dynamic of these scenes is the repeated presentation of evidence that Pentheus' preconceptions about Dionysus, his worshippers and himself are false. First, a servant who has arrested Dionysus reports that the women who had been imprisoned had escaped, with their fetters unaccountably falling off by themselves; following the first exchange with Dionysus, a choral song leads into Dionysus' staging an earthquake that shatters Pentheus' palace; and third, a messenger reports about the women on the hillside, and how he and his mates spied on them, how they were discovered, and the women's reaction. The latter report, in particular, foreshadows Pentheus' own fate, but all three also inform the main narrative arc, Pentheus' growing fascination with Dionysus himself.

Dionysus' mortal presentation is central to the lesson he will teach. Already, based on others' reports, Pentheus has discussed his long, blonde, perfumed hair (235) and described him as androgynous (*thêlumorphos* 354), or, literally, "female-shaped." While Dionysus has claimed earlier to have taken the form (*morphên*) to embody "a man's nature" (*andros phusin* 54), the text is suggesting a high degree of gender fluidity, and Pentheus himself obsesses over it, and from his very first words to the stranger (453–9):

> You have a great-looking body, at least for women—that's why you've come here to Thebes—your hair is long—you're no wrestler—and it flows down just to your jawline—so sexy—you've worked at your creamy complexion by keeping out of the sun in the shade, hunting down Aphrodite with your beauty.

The sequencing and qualifications in this passage are very revealing, as Pentheus passes judgment on Dionysus' feminine appearance. Dionysus is presented as both an object of desire and an agent of desire (literally "full of desire" 456), and both stem from this feminine appearance. Pentheus' attempt to focalize his evaluation through female viewers (453–4) is clumsy at best. His first qualification resists easy interpretation. Literally meaning something like "at least in relation to women" (*hôs es gunaikas* 454), it could suggest women's response, or Dionysus' sexual purpose, or even Pentheus' view that Dionysus has a great feminine body. The ambiguity leads quickly to a further qualification specifying that he has (hetero) sexual motives in mind (although even that is not quite clear-cut). Pentheus' elaboration of Dionysus' appearance—long hair and skin tone—play on culturally specific gender markers. Dionysus has clearly not been engaging in manly work or leisure activities in the open air. Pentheus again specifies that Dionysus is seeking sex (Aphrodite) but there is no disguising Pentheus' interest in the feminine Dionysus, even without projecting himself into the position of a female spectator.

Billington's attack on the excessively queer NTS *Bacchae* oddly picked out David Greig's "amusing" rendering of 453–4, which was an utterly faithful version of the Greek. It *is* amusing, and if anything Greig's version slightly underplayed the ambiguities, which are very hard to catch in English. The ambiguities and humor continue as Pentheus develops his sexual obsession and probes the stranger about the origin and nature of Dionysiac rites, with Dionysus archly playing up their nocturnal and secret nature, only to provoke Pentheus further. Pentheus' attribution of clever speech uses a curious adjective, "not unexercised (*ouk agumnastos*), suggestive of sexual activity, before qualifying it with speech as the frame of reference. Dionysus meanwhile, hinting vigorously about what the god thinks and feels, asks Pentheus coyly, "Tell me what I have to suffer: what terrible [or amazing] thing are you going to do to me?" (492). Pentheus' response is to threaten the god with a haircut, stripping him of his equipment, and "keeping his body inside in seclusion." Pentheus' punishments are about 1) removing signs of gender ambiguity, 2) removing signs of Dionysiac cult, and 3) imposing physical constraint and domination. The *heirktai* (497 and 549) in which he proposes confining Dionysus could be any enclosure, including a prison, but the plural, perhaps significantly, also indicates the women's quarters (see Xenophon, *Memorabilia* 2.1.5). Dionysus is supremely unbothered—except for the hair (494). The god will save him. Pentheus challenges Dionysus as to where this so-called god is, which is as ironic as other aspects of Pentheus' self-awareness. Dionysus sums up Pentheus' lack of self-awareness, which is further reinforced by Pentheus' ironically clueless response (506–7):

> *Dionysus* You don't know what life you are leading, nor who you are.
> *Pentheus* Pentheus son of Agave and Echion.

The humor is a key driver of these scenes. Dionysus' mockery may be more arch and less direct than Pentheus' mockery of Cadmus and Teiresias, but the irony is all too clear to an audience.

Pentheus' ignorance of the god is the immediate focus as Dionysus is imprisoned and engineers his own release, and Pentheus chases an imaginary bull amid the chaos. Pentheus is baffled by the Lydian stranger's reappearance outside the palace. But, as a messenger arrives, attention shifts back to issues of gender, sex, and sexuality. The messenger comes from Cithaeron to report strange and terrible actions by the women that to him prove the god's divinity and power. His account foreshadows later events, in that a peaceful, if strange, scene is followed by a violent reaction to the discovery of a male spy. The oxherds and shepherds, like Pentheus, exemplify patriarchal desire for surveillance and control of women, suspecting sexual license and immorality, and their incursion prompts a violent response. But it is someone from town, coded as a politician who proposes to them a physical intervention (717–21):

> And then some wanderer from about town, a fluent speaker, said to us all: "You men who dwell on the holy mountain-pastures—shall we chase Agave, the mother of Pentheus, out of her bacchic dances and curry favor with the king?"

The account of a male demagogue using gender nonconformism as a self-serving pretext for seeking to police women's spaces is sadly far from unknown in the current era of transphobic backlash. Nor indeed is the sight of an essentially metropolitan politician exploiting fears and anxieties of an extra-urban audience unknown in recent and ongoing political movements.

The rural men agree with him, despite seeing nothing that bears out their, or the king's, obsessions (685–9). The women are actually far stranger than that: certainly not conforming to gendered norms of dress or behavior (everything is *very* relaxed), but, even more disturbing for essentialist (sex-based) notions, those of the women still breastfeeding have left their children behind and are now nursing wolf cubs (699–702); the environment itself also provides spontaneous fertility (702–11). The consequence of the cis male attack is a different mode of gender transgression, violent not peaceful. The women dismember their tormentors' animals, tearing them in half or littering the landscape with body parts, and then they attack the villages throughout the area. For the messenger, the women are displaying super*human* strength, but also invert gender norms, putting the men to flight, despite being armed only with the thyrsus (731–5 and 759–65). Transcending such norms, he says, comes from Dionysus.

Pentheus' response is to call for a military assault. The gender transgressions are clearly the trigger: "Does this not cap everything if we suffer what we suffer at the hands of women?" (785–6). Against the women's hubris he proposes wholesale slaughter (966–8), a grotesque parody of sacrifice. Dionysus offers ever more elaborate hints that he is their god, suggests Pentheus consider calming down, and finally offers to mediate and bring the women down. Pentheus is not interested in a genuine or informed discussion: he calls for his weapons and tells Dionysus to shut up (810). The demand prompts Dionysus' enigmatic but pivotal monosyllable. At this point, Dionysus utters the single most important utterance in the play ("Ah" 810), followed by the apparently innocuous question "Do you want to see the women sitting on the mountainside?" (811). Dionysus' exclamation marks this as a turning point. While Dionysus is, of course, able to manipulate victims directly, as evidenced by the women on the hillside and Pentheus' perception of the bull, this question and this scene are about verbal manipulation, and it is a question that only makes sense in the light of Pentheus' persistent obsessions with the presumed sexual activity of the women.

Dionysus now starts unpicking Pentheus' self-perception and self-understanding. He steers discussion about mounting an expedition to a proposal that Pentheus go alone and adopt maenadic costume. Instead of rejecting Dionysus outright, as his earlier mockery might suggest, his protestation is distinctly muted: "What is this? Am I to be classed a woman after being a man?" (822). Pentheus uses the language of political classification (*telô*), and as a matter of gender, not sex. Pentheus goes further than he did with Cadmus and Teiresias: his perception of himself is that donning a frock entails a change in classification. To go further, the primary sense of *telô* is about finding fulfillment; the expression *es gunaikas* echoes Pentheus' earlier fascination with Dionysus' gender-fluid appearance "in relation to women." The parallels, and Pentheus' leap to social re-classification, suggest that what has been going on is not (or not only) barely concealed desire for Dionysus' body sexually but desire for it in terms of Pentheus' own gender expression.

Pentheus' earlier behavior is further explained as the scene explores the conflict between his fears and anxieties and his growing self-perception. As Dionysus coaxes him on, Pentheus alternates between denial and demanding to know more about his outfit. The language looks back to his mockery of Cadmus, Teiresias, and Dionysus. Pentheus worries about his *aidôs* ("shame" or "self-respect") (830); he wishes to hide from the male citizens, here labeled Cadmeioi ("men of Cadmus" 840); and he is terrified of mockery, and absolutely female mockery ("everything is better than the Bacchae mocking me" 842). The outfit itself quotes that of Cadmus and Teiresias. Although Dionysus adds more unambiguously feminine floor-length gown (*peplos*) and snood (*mitra*), the maenadic accoutrements are the ones that prompt Pentheus to demur about feminine dress. But before that Dionysus pays attention to his hair, saying that he "will extend it so that it is flowing," using the same adjective, *tanaos* ("long"), that Pentheus had used when singling out the god's hair. Dionysus' boast to the Chorus that he will send him off "in a woman's form" (*gunaikomorphos* 857) similarly evokes Pentheus' earlier characterization of him as *thêlumorphos* ("female-shaped" 353). Pentheus' (transphobic) verbal and physical repression of others is thus presented as a symptom of his own self-denial. Even as he departs into the palace he is still claiming, however unconvincingly, that it could still go either way (845–6).

This is not, however, a supportive environment for coming out, but still, a narrative of compulsion and humiliation. Dionysus keeps pushing Dionysus, but he is transparently working with the king's own conflicted desire, using that dim self-perception to create what Pentheus has dealt out and fears most: humiliation and mockery. Thus the scene when Pentheus re-emerges from the palace and embraces his new gender role adds less to Pentheus' characterization than to understanding of Dionysus' control. Yet, although Dionysus has overcome Pentheus' *aidôs*, he still needs to persuade him out of violence, and field Pentheus' continuing conviction about sexual outrages on the hillside (849–55): Pentheus has not yet unthought his adherence to gender norms or his own privilege. The scene abounds in double meanings as Pentheus fantasizes about exerting gender and sexual control, and Dionysus hints extravagantly at his imminent death at the hands of his mother and the other maenads: Pentheus here both is and will be a stark visual sign of the power of Dionysus and what he represents. The themes continue into the messenger speech: Pentheus' voyeuristic desire (1059–62), the visual symbol (1076), and vengeance for his mocking laughter (1080–1), his outfit re-emphasized at the moment of crisis (1115–16) and in the Chorus's song of triumph (1157–9). His increasingly unconvincing masculinity and patriarchal authority are brutally juxtaposed through Agave and the other women's understanding of him as a virile lion, and the physicality of their dismemberment of him.

This is a bleak picture and no less grim for the re-entry of Cadmus: as Agave celebrates the success of her hunt, Cadmus relates how he and Teiresias were coming back from their excursion when they heard about events on the hillside. He has returned to Cithaeron to collect what is left of his grandson and now talks Agave down from her exultation and leads her to see again with human sight. The traumatic scene of recognition and lamentation, some of which has been lost, sees father and daughter acknowledging Dionysus' nature, power, and vengeance—"just but excessive" (1228–9)—but it is not the end of the story. Dionysus returns, now undisguised. Unlike other concluding appearances by gods, he is not resolving conflicts or offering consolation. Rather, he is dealing further punishments. Dionysus explains that Cadmus will marry Harmonia, both will become snakes, and he will lead a foreign army through Asia and into Greece, where he will die (1330–9 and 1354–62). Agave will also go into exile (1362–70 and 1388), which is less picaresque and much less secure. Cadmus' further punishment is somewhat more puzzling, given his apparent commitment to the god. From his own explanation of his movements, he must still be dressed in maenadic costume himself, yet Dionysus emphasizes that Cadmus did not accept him as a god. This must refer back to the partially opportunistic dimension of Cadmus' worship: he is celebrating Dionysus just in case, and with an eye on familial advancement. It is consonant with his lengthy account of what the loss of Pentheus means for his own and Agave's security which is rather self-obsessed at this moment of loss (1313–24).

Amid this serial punishment, there is only one named character enacted who escapes and whose embrace of Dionysus is not apparently deemed to be flawed: Teiresias. Certainly, Dionysus' focus is on the family, and Teiresias needs to stay in Thebes to be a voice of obscure clarity about the divine for the mythological future, but, more significantly, Teiresias is the *only* Theban who voluntarily embraces Dionysus without any side agenda. Teiresias may, however, have better insight and experience, not only as a prophet but also as one of the more celebrated trans figures of antiquity.[10] The story is related perhaps most famously in Ovid's *Metamorphoses* (3.316–40) of how Teiresias saw two snakes having sex, struck them with his staff, and changed sex. After spending seven years as a woman he changed back when he encountered the snakes a second time. As a result Zeus (Jupiter) and Hera (Juno) called on him to adjudicate a dispute as to whether men or women gain greater pleasure from sex; his answer that women did caused Hera to blind him, and Zeus to give him the gift of prophecy. Ovid is drawing here on Greek sources, and both Apollodorus (*Library* 3.6.7) and Phlegon of Tralles trace this version as far back as Hesiod, which means it would probably have been in the original audience's cultural encyclopedia. It is also specifically congruent with Dionysus' own time line in Ovid, which may be significant. It would be entirely consistent with the ideological and moral framework of the *Bacchae* if the one Theban who embraces the gender fluidity of Dionysus is also one who has had this transgendered (and, indeed, specifically transsexual) perspective and experience.

The Greek gods represented different aspects of human experience and to deny the god is to amputate one part of that experience. The focus of the *Bacchae* on trans expression puts that aspect of Dionysus to the fore when considering the need for his inclusion within the social and political order. It also demonstrates to chilling effect the consequences of repression and violence both to the city and to the individual, and suggests that one etiology for acts of transphobic speech and action is, as well as unthinking parroting of patriarchal tropes, denial of self and society. The answer, it seems, is to embrace the trans and the queer, just as it is also to embrace diversity in gender and ethnicity, as embodied in the Chorus.[11] Pentheus' failure is also a social failure, and in that sense perhaps Dionysus' intersectional Justice is not so excessive after all.

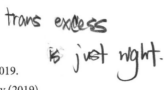

trans excess is just right.

Notes

1. For the UK, see Burns 2019.

2. Discussed by, e.g., Lavery (2019).

3. See, e.g., Herdt 1996.

4. See also Ruffell 2020 for further discussion and bibliography. See also Introduction.

5. Gould 1980. On queer wildness, see Baldwin and Rabinowitz and Bullen in this volume.

6. See Bremmer 2004.

7. See Jendza 2020. On the queering of genre, see Boyarin in this volume.

8. See Ruffell 2013 and 2020. On this Aristophanic play, see also Deihr in this volume.

9. See Garber 1993.

10. See esp. Salah 2017 and Corfman 2020.

11. See Introduction and Deihr in this volume.

CONTRIBUTORS

Rosa Andújar is Senior Lecturer in Liberal Arts at King's College London. She edited *The Greek Trilogy of Luis Alfaro* (2020), which was awarded the 2020 London Hellenic Prize. She is also co-editor of *Paths of Song* (2018) and of *Greeks and Romans on the Latin American Stage* (2020).

Oliver Baldwin is British Academy Postdoctoral Fellow at the University of Reading. He is currently working on the project *Queer Tragedy*, an international performance and cultural history of queer stagings of Greco-Roman tragedy between 1969 and 2019.

Karen Bassi is Professor Emerita of Classics and Literature at UC Santa Cruz. She is the author of *Acting Like Men* (1998) and *Traces of the Past: Classics between History and Archaeology* (2016). In 2010 she co-edited *When Worlds Elide* with Peter Euben. She is now working on a book titled *Imitating the Dead: Facing Death in Ancient Greek Tragedy*.

Alastair J. L. Blanshard is the Paul Eliadis Professor of Classics and Ancient History at the University of Queensland. He is the author of *Hercules* (2007) and *The Classical World: All that Matters* (2015). He also co-wrote *Classics on Screen* (2011). His most recent work includes co-edited collections on Oscar Wilde and his relationship with classical antiquity and the image of Hercules in the twentieth and twenty-first centuries.

Daniel Boyarin is the Taubman Professor of Talmudic Culture at UC Berkeley. He has published widely on matters of sex, gender, sexuality, and queer theory based on research on the Talmud and somewhat less widely in such topics relating to classical Greek literature and culture.

David Bullen is a theater practitioner and scholar. He is co-artistic director of By Jove Theatre Company and has taught in the Department of Drama, Theatre and Dance at Royal Holloway, University of London since 2013. He has published in a range of edited collections and journals, including a recent prize-winning article in *Theatre Notebook*, and he is currently writing *Greek Tragedy in Twenty-First Century British Theatre*. David's adaptations of works by all four extant Athenian dramatists have been performed in the UK and the US.

L. Deihr is a graduate student in Classics at UC Berkeley, interested in queer and trans theory and ecocriticism.

Carla Freccero is Distinguished Professor of Literature and History of Consciousness at UC, Santa Cruz. She has published several books, including *Queer/Early/Modern* (2006) and the co-edited *Premodern Sexualities* (1996). Her most recent work is in animal studies, and she has co-edited a special issue of *American Quarterly* on *Race/Species/Sex* and of *Yale French Studies* on *Animots*. Her book-in-progress is tentatively titled *Animal Inscription*.

Jonathan Goldberg is Arts and Sciences Distinguished Professor Emeritus at Emory University. His fifteen books of literary criticism often focus a queer deconstructive lens on early modernity, as in *Sodometries* (1992), *Desiring Women Writing* (1997), *Tempest in the Caribbean* (2004), *The Seeds of Things* (2009), and *Saint Marks* (2019). He has written on melodrama, Willa Cather, and Hitchcock's *Strangers on a Train* for the Queer Film Classic series (2012). As her literary executor, he edited Eve Kosofsky Sedgwick's *The Weather in Proust*. Two recent books especially relevant to his contribution to this volume are *Sappho] fragments* (2018) and *Come As You Are After Eve Kosofsky Sedgwick* (2021).

Sean Gurd is the author of four monographs: *Iphigenias at Aulis: Textual Multiplicity, Radical Philology* (2006), *Work in Progress: Literary Revision as Social Performance in Ancient Rome* (2012), *Dissonance* (2016), and *The Origins of Music Theory in the Age of Plato* (2019). He has also edited *Philology and Its Histories* (2010), and co-edited *'Pataphilology: An Irreader* (2018). His work focuses on aesthetics and media studies. He also has a secondary but related interest in twentieth-century avant-gardes, particularly in the Americas.

Ella Haselswerdt is Assistant Professor of Classics at UCLA. She is currently writing a monograph entitled *Epistemologies of Suffering* and co-editing the *Routledge Handbook of Classics and Queer Theory*. In 2016, she published a public-facing essay called "Re-Queering Sappho," and has gone on to develop a series of projects under the rubric of "Deep Lez Philology," exploring the sometimes intersecting lenses of queer theory and queer identity, with a particular interest in Sappho, lesbian separatism, and contemporary art.

Melissa Mueller is Professor of Classics at the University of Massachusetts Amherst. She is the author of *Objects as Actors: Props and the Poetics of Performance in Greek Tragedy* (2016), co-editor of *The Materialities of Greek Tragedy: Objects and Affect in Aeschylus, Sophocles, and Euripides* (2018), and series co-editor of *Ancient Cultures, New Materialisms* for Edinburgh University Press. Her current project is *Sappho and Homer: A Reparative Reading*.

Sarah Nooter is Professor of Classics and Theater and Performance Studies at the University of Chicago. She is the author of *When Heroes Sing* (2012) and *The Mortal Voice in the Tragedies of Aeschylus* (2017). She also co-edited *Sound and the Ancient Senses* (2019) with Shane Butler, and is editor-in-chief of the journal *Classical Philology*. She is now finishing a book that explores modes of embodiment and temporality in ancient Greek poetry and song.

Sarah Olsen is Assistant Professor of Classics at Williams College. She is the author of *Solo Dance in Archaic and Classical Greek Literature and Culture: Representing the Unruly Body* (2020), as well as articles on various topics in Greek art and literature.

Kirk Ormand is Nathan A. Greenberg Professor of Classics at Oberlin College, where he has taught since 2001. He is the author of *Exchange and the Maiden* (1999), *The Hesiodic Catalogue of Women and Archaic Greece* (2014), and *Controlling Desires: Sexuality in Ancient Greece and Rome* (2nd edition, 2018).

Daniel Orrells is Professor of Classics at King's College London. He has written two monographs, *Classical Culture and Modern Masculinity* (2011) and *Sex: Antiquity and Its Legacy* (2015). His third monograph, *Antiquity in Print in the Eighteenth Century* and his critical edition of Walter Pater's *Plato and Platonism* are forthcoming. He has also co-edited *African Athena: New Agendas* (2011), *The Mudimbe Reader* (2016), and *Richard Marsh, Popular Fiction and Literary Culture, 1890–1915* (2018).

Ben Radcliffe is Lecturer at Loyola Marymount University. He has published on domestic spaces in Hesiod's *Works and Days*, Odysseus' comrades in the *Odyssey*, and has forthcoming work on the politics of form in Aeschylus' *Persae*. His interests include critical theory, aesthetics, and the utopian imagination.

Nancy Sorkin Rabinowitz is Professor Emerita of Comparative Literature at Hamilton College. She is the author of *Anxiety Veiled* (1993) and *Greek Tragedy* (2008), and co-editor of *Teaching Classics in US Prisons* (2021), *Sex in Antiquity* (2015), *From Abortion to Pederasty* (2014), *Among Women: From the Homosocial to the Homoerotic in the Ancient World* (2002), *Women on the Edge* (1999), and *Feminist Theory and the Classics* (1993). Currently she is at work on a handbook on theater for incarcerated women with Rhodessa Jones and an interactive e-book called "Queering the Past(s)."

Patrice Rankine is Professor of Classics at the University of Chicago. He is the author of two monographs on the classics among African-American writers, one on literary reception, *Ulysses in Black* (2006), and another a study of performative aspects of classical reception, *Aristotle and Black Drama* (2013). He is also co-editor of *The Oxford Handbook of Greek Drama in the Americas* (2015). More recently, he has been exploring the entanglements between classical reception, racial identity, and queer theory for his work with Critical Ancient World Studies and for his book, *Theater and Crisis: Myth, Memory, and Racial Reckoning in America, 1964–2020*.

Isabel Ruffell is Professor of Greek Drama and Culture at the University of Glasgow, and her major publications are *Politics and Anti-Realism in Athenian Old Comedy* (2011) and *Aeschylus: Prometheus Bound* (2012).

Mario Telò is Professor of Classics and Comparative Literature at UC Berkeley. He is the author of *Aristophanes and the Cloak of Comedy* (2016), *Archive Feelings* (2020), and *Resistant Formalisms* (2022).

David Youd is a PhD candidate in Classics with a Designated Emphasis in Critical Theory at UC Berkeley. He has published on Plautus and is writing a dissertation on queer style in Latin literature.

BIBLIOGRAPHY

Abi-Karam, A., and K. Gabriel. 2020. "Making Love and Putting on Obscene Plays and Poetry Outside the Empty Former Prisons." In *We Want it All*, edited by A. Abi-Karam and K. Gabriel, 1–7. New York.

Adorno, T. W. 1997. *Aesthetic Theory*. Minneapolis.

Agamben, G. 1998. *Homo Sacer*. Stanford.

Agamben, G. 2016. *The Use of Bodies*. Stanford.

Ahmed, S. 2006. *Queer Phenomenology*. Durham, NC.

Aizura, A. Z. et al. 2020. "Thinking with Trans Now." *Social Text* 38: 125–47.

Alderson, D. 2016. *Sex, Needs, and Queer Culture*. London.

Alfonzo, B. D. 2021. "El fratricidio: antecedentes épicos y derivaciones trágicas de un tópico resemantizado en la figura del exilio edípico en *Fenicias* de Eurípides." *Nova Tellus* 39: 45–70.

Allan, W. 2000. *The* Andromache *and Euripidean Tragedy*. Oxford.

Allan, W., ed. 2008. *Euripides: Helen*. Cambridge.

Amin, K. 2017. *Disturbing Attachments*. Durham, NC.

Amin, K. 2018. "Glands, Eugenics, and Rejuvenation in *Man into Woman*." *TSQ* 5: 589–605.

Amin, K., A. J. Musser, and R. Pérez. 2017. "Queer Form: Aesthetics, Race, and the Violences of the Social." *ASAP / Journal* 2: 227–39.

Anker, E. S., and R. Felski. 2017. "Introduction." In *Critique and Postcritique*, edited by E. S. Anker and R. Felski, 1–30. Durham, NC.

Appiah, K. A. 2014. *Lines of Descent*. Cambridge, MA.

Arthur, M. 1977. "The Curse of Civilization: the Choral Odes of *Phoenissae*." *HSCP* 81: 163–85.

Atack, C. 2020. "Plato's Queer Time: Dialogic Moments in the Life and Death of Socrates." *Classical Receptions Journal* 12: 10–31.

Bagg, R., ed. 1973. *Euripides: Hippolytos*. Oxford.

Bailey, C. 2015. "Love Multiplied." *Quarterly Review of Film and Video* 32: 38–57.

Barthes, R. 1992. *Michelet*. Berkeley.

Barthes, R. 2002. *The Neutral*. New York.

Bassi, K. 2017. "Mimesis and Mortality: Reperformance and the Dead among the Living in *Hecuba* and *Hamlet*." In *Imagining Reperformance in Ancient Culture*, edited by R. Hunter and A. Uhlig, 138–59. Cambridge.

Bassi, K. forthcoming. "The Posthumous Future in Sophocles' *Oedipus at Colonus*." In *Doing the Psychology of the Ancient World*, edited by L. Huitink, V. Glaveanu, and I. Sluiter. Leiden.

Battezzato, L. 1999–2000. "Dorian Dress in Greek Tragedy." *ICS* 24–5: 343–62.

Battezzato, L. 2000. "The Thracian Camp and the Fourth Actor at *Rhesus* 565–691." *CQ* 50: 367–73.

Battezzato, L. 2005. "The New Music of the *Trojan Women*." *Lexis* 23: 1–31.

Beckett, S. 2010. *The Unnamable*. London.

Bending, L. 2002. "From Stunted Child to 'New Woman.'" *The Yearbook of English Studies* 32: 205–16.

Benjamin, H. S. 1966. *The Transsexual Phenomenon*. New York.

Benjamin, W. 1969a. "The Image of Proust." In *Illuminations*, 201–16. New York.

Benjamin, W. 1969b. "Theses on the Philosophy of History." In *Illuminations*, 253–64. New York.

Benjamin, W. 1999. "Dream Kitsch." In *Selected Writings*, 2.1 (1927–1930), 3–5. Cambridge, MA.

Berlant, L. 1998. "Intimacy: A Special Issue." *Critical Inquiry* 24: 281–8.

Berlant, L. 2011. *Cruel Optimism*. Durham, NC.

Berlant, L. 2012. *Desire/Love*. Brooklyn, NY.

Berlant, L., and L. Edelman. 2014. *Sex, or the Unbearable*. Durham, NC.

Berlant, L., and L. Edelman. 2019. "What Survives." In *Reading Sedgwick*, edited by L. Berlant, 37–62. Durham, NC.

Berlant, L., and M. Warner. 1998. "Sex in Public." *Critical Inquiry* 24: 547–66.

Bersani, L. 1976. *A Future for Astyanax*. Boston.

Bersani, L. 1995. *Homos*. Cambridge, MA.

Bersani, L. 2015. *Thoughts and Things*. Chicago.

Bersani, L., and A. Phillips. 2008. *Intimacies*. Chicago.

Best, S. 2018. *None Like Us*. Durham, NC.

Bey, M. 2017. "The Trans*-Ness of Blackness, the Blackness of Trans*-Ness." *TSQ* 4: 275–95.

Bey, M. 2020. *The Problem of the Negro as a Problem for Gender*. Minneapolis.

Bierl, A. 2009. *Ritual and Performativity*. Cambridge, MA.

Billington, M. 2007. "*The Bacchae*." Published August 13, 2007. Last visited August 21, 2021. *The Guardian*. https://www.theguardian.com/culture/2007/aug/13/edinburghfestival2007. edinburghfestival3

Billotte, K. 2015. "The Power of Medea's Sisterhood." In *The Oxford Handbook of Greek Drama in the Americas*, edited by K. Bosher, F. Macintosh, J. McConnell, and P. D. Rankine, 514–24. Oxford.

Boedeker, D. 1997. "Becoming Medea" In *Medea*, edited by J. J. Clauss and S. I. Johnston, 127–48. Princeton, NJ.

Bond, G. W., ed. 1988. *Euripides: Heracles*. Oxford.

Bos, A. P. 2007. "Aristotle on Dissection of Plants and Animals and his Concept of the Instrumental Soul-Body." *Ancient Philosophy* 27: 95–106.

Bowlby, R. 2013. *A Child of One's Own*. Oxford.

Bremmer, J. N. 2004. "Attis." *Mnemosyne* 57: 534–73.

Brilmyer, P., F. Trentin, and Z. Xiang. 2019. "The Ontology of the Couple, or, What Queer Theory Knows about Numbers." *GLQ* 25: 223–55.

Brim, M. 2020. *Poor Queer Studies*. Durham, NC.

Brody, J. D. 2008. *Punctuation*. Durham, NC.

Bromley, J. 2011. *Intimacy and Sexuality in the Age of Shakespeare*. Cambridge.

Bruno, R., and A. Carson. 2021. *Euripides: The Trojan Women. A Comic*. London.

Budin, S. 2016. *Artemis*. Oxford.

Burian, P. 1977. "Euripides' *Heraclidae*: An Interpretation." *CP* 72: 1–21.

Burlando, A. 1997. Reso: *i problemi, la scena*. Genoa.

Burnett, A. P. 1985. "*Rhesus*: Are Smiles Allowed?" In *Directions in Euripidean Criticism*, edited by P. Burian, 13–51. Durham, NC.

Burns, C., ed. 2019. *Trans Britain*. London.

Bussy, D. 1949. *Olivia*. Hoboken, NJ.

Butler, J. 1993a. "Critically Queer." *GLQ* 1: 17–32.

Butler, J. 1993b. *Bodies That Matter*. New York.

Butler, J. 2000. *Antigone's Claim*. New York.

Butler, J. 2003. "Afterword: After Loss, What Then?" In *Loss*, edited by D. L. Eng and D. Kazanjian, 467–73. Berkeley.

Butler, J. 2004. *Precarious Life*. London.

Butler, J. 2011. "Remarks on 'Queer Bonds'." *GLQ* 17: 381–7.

Butler, J. 2018. "Solidarity/Susceptibility." *Social Text* 36: 1–20.

Byrd, J. A. 2020. "What's Normative Got to Do with It?" *Social Text* 38: 105–23.

Bibliography

Cairns, D. 2014. "Medea: Feminism or Misogyny?" In *Looking at Medea*, edited by D. Stuttard, 111–23. London.

Calame, C. 1997. *Choruses of Young Women in Ancient Greece*. Lanham, MD.

Capers, B. 2011. "Real Rape Too." *California Law Review* 99: 1259–307.

Carlà-Uhink, F. 2017. "'Between the Human and the Divine': Cross-Dressing and Transgender Dynamics in the Graeco-Roman World." In *TransAntiquity*, edited by D. Campanile et al., 3–37. New York.

Carson, A. 1986. *Eros the Bittersweet*. Princeton, NJ.

Carson, A. 1990. "Putting Her in Her Place: Woman, Dirt, and Desire." In *Before Sexuality*, edited by D. M. Halperin, J. J. Winkler, and F. I. Zeitlin, 135–70. Princeton, NJ.

Carson, A. 1998. *Autobiography of Red*. New York.

Carson, A. 2004. "The Art of Poetry." *Paris Review* 171: 191–226.

Carson, A. 2006. *Grief Lessons*. New York.

Carson, A. 2009. *An Oresteia: Agamemnon by Aiskhylos, Elektra by Sophokles, Orestes by Euripides*. New York.

Carson, A. 2014. *The Albertine Workout*. New York.

Carson, A. 2021. *H of H Playbook*. New York.

Carter, D. M. 2020. "*Children of Heracles*." In *Brill's Companion to Euripides*, edited by A. Markantonatos, 96–120. Leiden.

Castle, T. 2009. "Some Notes on 'Notes on Camp'." In *The Scandal of Susan Sontag*, edited by B. Ching and J. Wagner-Lawlor, 21–31. New York.

Cavarero, A. 2008. *Horrorism*. New York.

Chambers, C. M. 2017. "From 'Awe' to 'Awww'." In *The Retro-Futurism of Cuteness*, edited by J. Boyle and W.-C. Kao, 66–86. Goleta, CA.

Chen, M. 2012. *Animacies*. Durham, NC.

Chen, M. 2013. "Animals Without Genitals" In *The Transgender Studies Reader 2*, edited by S. Stryker and A. Z. Aizura, 168–77. New York.

Chinn, S. E. 2003. "Feeling Her Way." *GLQ* 9: 181–204.

Chiovenda, M. K. 2020. "Derrida's Unconditional Hospitality as the Improbable." *Social Science Quarterly* 101: 2437–49.

Chitty, C. 2020. *Sexual Hegemony*. Durham, NC.

Chong-Gossard, J. H. K. O. 2015. "*Andromache*." In *Brill's Companion to the Reception of Euripides*, edited by R. Lauriola and K. N. Demetriou, 143–73. Leiden.

Chu, A. L. 2018. "Extreme Pregnancy." In *Once and Future Feminist*, edited by M. Emre, *Boston Review* Forum 7 (43.3): 66–9.

Chu, A. L. 2019. *Females*. New York.

Chu, A. L., and E. H. Drager. 2019. "After Trans Studies." *TSQ* 6: 103–16.

Chuang, H. T., and D. Addington. 1988. "Homosexual Panic: A Review of its Concept." *Canadian Journal of Psychiatry* 33: 613–17.

Churchill, C., and D. Lan. 1986. *Mouthful of Birds*. London.

Clay, D. 1975. "The Tragic and Comic Poet of the *Symposium*." *Arion* 2: 238–61.

Cleto, F. 2002. "Introduction: Queering the Camp." In *Camp*, edited by F. Cleto, 1–42. Ann Arbor, MI.

Cochran, J. M. 2017. "What's Cute Got To Do With It?: Early Modern Proto-Cuteness in *King Lear*." In *The Retro-Futurism of Cuteness*, edited by J. Boyle and W.-C. Kao, 175–94. Goleta, CA.

Cohen, C. 2005. "Punks, Bulldaggers, and Welfare Queens." In *Black Queer Studies*, edited by E. P. Johnson and M. G. Henderson, 21–51. Durham, NC.

Cole, E. 2019. *Postdramatic Tragedies*. Oxford.

Colebrook, C. 2009. "On the Very Possibility of Queer Theory." In *Deleuze and Queer Theory*, edited by C. Nigianni and M. Storr, 11–23. Edinburgh.

Collard, C., and M. Cropp, eds. 2008. *Euripides: Fragments*. Cambridge, MA.

Collard, C., and J. Morwood, eds. 2017. *Euripides: Iphigenia at Aulis*. Liverpool.

Collier, P., trans. 2002. *Marcel Proust: The Fugitive*. London.

Corfman, S. B. 2020. "Melting Muscles: Cassils's *Tiresias* at the Intersection of Affect and Gendered Embodiment." *TSQ* 7: 5–19.

Corrigan, K., and E. Glazov-Corrigan. 2004. *Plato's Dialectic at Play*. University Park, PA.

Coviello, P. 2019. *Make Yourselves Gods*. Chicago.

Craik, E. M., ed. 1988. *Euripides: Phoenician Women*. Warminster.

Crawford, L. 2017. "Slender Trouble." *GLQ* 23: 447–72.

Cribiore, R. 2001. "The Grammarian's Choice: The Popularity of Euripides' *Phoenissae* in Hellenistic and Roman Education." In *Education in Greek and Roman Antiquity*, edited by Y. L. Too, 241–59. Leiden.

Cropp, M. J., ed. 2000. *Euripides: Iphigenia in Tauris*. Warminster.

Currah, P., and T. Mulqueen. 2011. "Securitizing Gender." *Social Research* 78: 557–82.

Dasen, V., and S. Ducaté-Paarmann. 2006. "Hysteria and Metaphors of the Uterus in Classical Antiquity." In *Images and Gender: Contributions to the Hermeneutics of Reading Ancient Art*, edited by S. Schroer, 239–61. Zurich.

Davidson, J. 2001. "Dover, Foucault, and Greek Homosexuality." *Past and Present* 170: 3–51.

Davies, R. B. 2018. *Troy, Carthage, and the Victorians*. Cambridge.

Dean, T. 2019. "Afterword: The Raw and the Fucked." In *Raw*, edited by R. Varghese, 257–81. Regina.

Dean, T. 2020. "Genre Blindness in the New Descriptivism." *MLQ* 81: 527–52.

de Lauretis, T. 1994. *The Practice of Love: Lesbian Sexuality and Perverse Desire*. Bloomington, IN.

de Lauretis, T. 2011. "Queer Texts, Bad Habits, and the Issue of a Future." *GLQ* 17: 243–63.

Deleuze, G., and F. Guattari. 1983. *Anti-Oedipus*. Minneapolis.

Deleuze, G., and F. Guattari. 1986. *Kafka: Toward a Minor Literature*. Minneapolis.

De Man, P. 1996. *Aesthetic Ideology*. Minneapolis.

D'Emilio, J. 1983. "Capitalism and Gay Identity." In *Powers of Desire,* edited by C. Stansell, A. Snitow, and S. Thompson, 100–13. New York.

Derrida, J. 1980. "The Law of Genre." *Critical Inquiry* 7: 55–81.

Derrida, J. 1994. *Specters of Marx*. New York.

Derrida, J. 1996. *Archive Fever: A Freudian Impression*. Chicago.

Derrida, J. 2000. *Of Hospitality*. Stanford.

Derrida, J. 2005. "The Principle of Hospitality." *Parallax* 11: 6–9.

Detienne, M., and J.-P. Vernant. 1989. *The Cuisine of Sacrifice among the Greeks*. Chicago.

Deutscher, P. 2017. *Foucault's Futures*. New York.

Diggle, J., ed. 1994. *Euripidis Fabulae*, vol. 3. Oxford.

Dinshaw, C. 1999. *Getting Medieval*. Durham, NC.

Dinshaw, C. 2012. *How Soon is Now?* Durham, NC.

Dover, K. J. 1978. *Greek Homosexuality*. Cambridge.

Dowling, L. 1994. *Hellenism and Homosexuality in Victorian Oxford*. Ithaca, NY.

Doyle, J. 2007. "Between Friends." In *A Companion to Lesbian, Gay, Bisexual, Transgender, and Queer Studies*, edited by G. E. Haggerty and M. McGarry, 325–40. Malden, MA.

Doyle, J., and D. J. Getsy. 2013. "Queer Formalisms." *Art Journal* 72: 58–71.

DuBois, P. 2002. *Trojan Horses: Saving the Classics from Conservatives*. New York.

Duggan, L. 2002. "The New Homonormativity." In *Materializing Democracy*, edited by R. Castronovo, D. D. Nelson, and D. E. Pease, 175–94. Durham, NC.

Dunn, F. M. 1996. *Tragedy's End*. Oxford.

Edelman, L. 2004. *No Future*. Durham, NC.

Edelman, L. 2011. "Against Survival." *Shakespeare Quarterly* 62: 148–69.

Edelman, L. 2017. "Learning Nothing: *Bad Education*." *differences* 28: 124–73.

Bibliography

Edelman, L. 2022. "Solidarity." In *Proximities: Reading with Judith*, edited by D. Sanyal, M. Telò, and D. Young. *Representations.*

Edelman, L., and J. Litvak. 2019. "TWO MUCH: Excess, Enjoyment, and Estrangement in Hitchcock's *Strangers on a Train.*" *GLQ* 25: 297–314.

Eng, D. L., and J. K. Puar. 2020. "Introduction: Left of Queer." *Social Text* 38: 1–23.

Eng, D. L., J. Halberstam, and J. E. Muñoz. 2005. "Introduction: What's Queer about Queer Studies Now?" *Social Text* 23: 1–18.

Falkner, T. M. 1995. "Euripides and the Tragedy of Old Age." In *The Poetics of Old Age in Greek Epic, Lyric, and Tragedy*, edited by T. M. Falkner, 169–210. Norman, OK.

Fantuzzi, M. 2006. "La Dolonia del *Reso* come luogo dell'errore e dell' incertezza." In *I luoghi e la poesia nella Grecia antica*, edited by M. Vetta and C. Catenacci, 241–62. Alessandria.

Fantuzzi, M. 2018. "On the Alleged Bastardy of *Rhesus.*" In *Marginality, Canonicity, Passion,* edited by M. Formisano and C. S. Kraus, 177–202. Oxford.

Fassino, M. 2003. "Avventure del testo di Euripide nei papiri tolemaici." In *I viaggi dei testi*, edited by L. Battezzato, 33–56. Amsterdam.

Federici, S. 2009. *Caliban and the Witch*. Brooklyn, NY.

Ferguson, R. 2003. *Aberrations in Black*. Minneapolis.

Ferris, B. G. 1854. *Utah and the Mormons*. New York.

Fiereck, K., N. Hoad, and D. S. Mupotsa., eds. 2020. *Time Out of Joint: The Queer and the Customary in Africa. GLQ* 26: 3.

Fitton, J. W. 1961. "*The Suppliant Women* and the *Herakleidai* of Euripides." *Hermes* 89: 430–61.

Foley, H. 1982. "Marriage and Sacrifice in Euripides' *Iphigenia in Aulis.*" *Arethusa* 15: 159–80.

Foley, H. 1985. *Ritual Irony*. Ithaca, NY.

Foley, H. 1989. "Medea's Divided Self." *CA* 8: 61–85.

Ford, A. 2002. *The Origins of Criticism*. Princeton, NJ.

Foster, E. 2010. *Thucydides, Pericles, and Periclean Imperialism.* Cambridge.

Foucault, M. 1978. *The History of Sexuality: An Introduction.* New York.

Foucault, M. 1990. *The History of Sexuality: The Use of Pleasure.* New York.

Foucault, M. 1998. *Ethics: Subjectivity and Truth.* New York.

Foucault, M. 2010. *The Government of Self and Others.* New York.

Freccero, C. 2006. *Queer/Early/Modern.* Durham, NC.

Freccero, C. 2007. "Queer Times." *SAQ* 106: 485–94.

Freccero, C. 2013a. "Queer Spectrality." In *The Spectralities Reader*, edited by M. del Pilar Blanco and E. Peeren, 335–60. London.

Freccero, C. 2013b. "Historicism and Unhistoricism in Queer Studies." *PMLA* 128: 781–86.

Freccero, C. 2015. "Tangents (of Desire)." *The Journal for Early Modern Cultural Studies* 16: 91–105.

Freeman, E. 2007a. "Queer Belongings." In *A Companion to Lesbian, Gay, Bisexual, Transgender, and Queer Studies*, edited by G. E. Haggerty and M. McGarry, 295–314. Malden, MA.

Freeman, E. 2007b. "Introduction." *GLQ* 13: 159–76.

Freeman, E. et al. 2007. "Theorizing Queer Temporalities." *GLQ* 13: 177–95.

Freeman, E. 2010. *Time Binds.* Durham, NC.

Freeman, E. 2019. *Beside You in Time.* Durham, NC.

Friedman, D. 2019. *Before Queer Theory.* Baltimore.

Fries, A., ed. 2014. *Pseudo-Euripides: Rhesus.* Berlin.

Frye, M. 1992. *Willful Virgin.* Freedom, CA.

Gabriel, K. 2016. "Gender as Accumulation Strategy." *Invert Journal* https://invertjournal.org.uk/posts?view=articles&post=7106265#gender-as-accumulation-strategy

Gabriel, K. 2018. "Specters of Dying Empire: The Case of Carson's *Bacchae.*" *Tripwire* 14: 315–23.

Gabriel, K. 2021. "The 'Antipoet Of The Greeks,' Or, How Euripides Became a Modernist." *Classical Receptions Journal* 13.

Gantz, T. 1993. *Early Greek Myth*. Baltimore.

Garber, M. 1993. *Vested Interests*. New York.

Garrison, E. P. 1995. *Groaning Tears*. Leiden.

Gleeson, J. J., and E. O'Rourke. 2021. "Introduction." In *Transgender Marxism*, edited by J. J. Gleeson and E. O'Rourke, 1–32. London.

Goldberg, J., and M. Menon. 2005. "Queering History." *PMLA* 120: 1608–17.

Goldhill, S. 1986. *Reading Greek Tragedy*. Cambridge.

Goldhill, S. 2021. "Freud, Archaeology, and Egypt." *Arion* 28: 75–104.

Gould, J. 1973. "Hiketeia." *JHS* 93: 74–103.

Gould, J. 1980. "Law, Custom and Myth: Aspects of the Social Position of Women in Classical Athens." *JHS* 100: 38–59.

Goux, J.-J. 1992. "The Phallus: Masculine Identity and the 'Exchange of Women.'" *differences* 4: 40–75.

Greenberg, C. 1961. "Avant-Garde and Kitsch." In *Art and Culture*, 3–21. Boston, MA.

Gregory, J., ed. 1999. *Euripides: Hecuba*. Atlanta.

Gregory, J. 1999–2000. "Comic Elements in Euripides." *ICS* 24–5: 59–74.

Griffith, M. 2006. "Horsepower and Donkeywork: Equids and the Ancient Greek Imagination." *CP* 101: 307–48.

Griffith, M. 2009. "Orestes and the In-Laws." In *Bound by the City*, edited by D. E. McCoskey and E. Zakin, 275–330. Albany, NY.

Griffith, M. 2015. *Greek Satyr Play*. Berkeley.

Grube, G. M. A. 1961. *The Drama of Euripides*. New York.

Gunderson, E. 2021. "Theology's Shadow." In *Classical Philology and Theology*, edited by C. Conybeare and S. Goldhill, 199–224. Cambridge.

Gurd, S. 2005. *Iphigenias at Aulis: Textual Multiplicity, Radical Philology*. Ithaca, NY.

Gurd, S. 2007. "Cicero and Editorial Revision." *CA* 26: 49–80.

Gurd, S., and M. Telò, eds. 2022. *The Before and the After: Archê and Avenir in a Time of Crisis*. Goleta, CA.

Halberstam, J. 2005. *In a Queer Time and Place*. New York.

Halberstam, J. 2011. *The Queer Art of Failure*. Durham, NC.

Halberstam, J. 2012. *Gaga Feminism*. Boston, MA.

Halberstam, J. 2015. "Straight Eye for the Queer Theorist." https://bullybloggers.wordpress.com/2015/09/12/straight-eye-for-the-queer-theorist-a-review-of-queer-theory-without-antinormativity-by-jack-halberstam/

Halberstam, J. 2018. *Trans**. Oakland, CA.

Halberstam, J. 2020a. *Wild Things*. Durham, NC.

Halberstam, J. 2020b. "Nice Trannies." *TSQ* 7: 321–31.

Hale, J. 1997. "Suggested Rules for Non-Transsexuals Writing about Transsexuals, Transsexuality, or Transsexualism, or Trans." https://sandystone.com/hale.rules.html

Haley, S. P. 1995. "Self-Definition, Community, and Resistance: Euripides' *Medea* and Toni Morrison's *Beloved*." *Thamyris* 2: 177–206.

Hall, E. 1990. *Inventing the Barbarian*. Oxford.

Hall, E. 2013. *Adventures with Iphigenia in Tauris*. Oxford.

Hall, E. 2014. "Divine and Human in Euripides' *Medea*." In *Looking at Medea*, edited by D. Stuttard, 124–37. London.

Hall, E. 2018. "Materialism Old and New." In *The Materialities of Greek Tragedy*, edited by M. Telò and M. Mueller, 203–17. London.

Halperin, D. M. 1989. "Is There a History of Sexuality?" *History and Theory* 28: 257–74.

Halperin, D. M. 1990. *One Hundred Years of Homosexuality and Other Essays on Greek Love*. New York.

Halperin, D. M. 1995. *Saint Foucault*. Oxford.

Bibliography

Halperin, D. M. 2002. *How to Do the History of Homosexuality*. Chicago.

Halperin, D. M. 2015. "Not Fade Away." In *Ancient Sex*, edited by R. Blondell and K. Ormand, 308–28. Columbus, OH.

Halperin, D. M. 2019. "Queer Love." *Critical Inquiry* 45: 396–419.

Hamacher, W. 2010. *Minima Philologica*. New York.

Handy, A. B., and T. W. Johnson. 2015. "Eunuchs Online." *TSQ* 2: 710–16.

Hannah, D. 2010. "Queer Hospitality in Herman Melville's 'Benito Cereno.'" *Studies in American Fiction* 37: 181–201.

Hanson, A. 2007. "The Hippocratic *parthenos* in Sickness and Health." In *Virginity Revisited*, edited by B. MacLachlan and J. Fletcher, 40–65. Toronto.

Hanson, E. 2011. "The Future's Eve: Reparative Reading after Sedgwick." *SAQ* 110: 101–19.

Harney, S., and F. Moten. 2013. *The Undercommons*. New York.

Harris, D. 2000. *Cute, Quaint, Hungry, and Romantic*. New York.

Heddon, D., and J. Milling. 2005. *Devising Performance*. London.

Heller, D. 2013. "In Defence of the Catfight." *I.B. Tauris Blog*, June 20, 2013. Last visited October 8, 2020. https://theibtaurisblog.com/2013/06/20/in-defence-of-the-catfight/

Heller, D. 2017. "Catfight! Camp and Queer Visibility in *Orange is the New Black*." In *Television for Women*, edited by R. Moseley, H. Wheatley, and H. Wood, 73–89. London.

Herdt, G., ed. 1996. *Third Sex/Third Gender*. New York.

Hirschfeld, M. 1910. *Die Transvestiten*. Berlin.

Holland M., and R. Hart-Davis, eds. 2000. *The Complete Letters of Oscar Wilde*. New York.

Honig, B. 2013. *Antigone, Interrupted*. Cambridge.

Honig, B. 2021. *A Feminist Theory of Refusal*. Cambridge, MA.

Hopman, M. 2008. "Revenge and Mythopoiesis in Euripides' *Medea*." *TAPA* 138: 155–83.

Humphrey, D. 2020. *Archaic Modernism*. Detroit.

Jackson, L. C. M. M. 2020. *The Chorus of Drama in the Fourth Century BCE*. Oxford.

Jansen, M. C. 2012. "Exchange and the Eidolon: Analyzing Forgiveness in Euripides's *Helen*." *Comparative Literature Studies* 49: 327–47.

Jendza, C. 2020. *Paracomedy*. Oxford.

Johnson, E. P. 2005. "'Quare Studies', or (Almost) Everything I Know about Queer Studies I Learned from My Grandmother." In *Black Queer Studies*, edited by E. P. Johnson and M. G. Henderson, 124–57. Durham, NC.

Johnson, T. 1976. *Failing*. New York.

Jones, J. 1971. *On Aristotle and Greek Tragedy*. London.

Juffras, D. M. 1993. "Helen and Other Victims in Euripides' *Helen*." *Hermes* 121: 45–57.

Kahil, L. 1990. "Iphigenia." In *Lexicon Iconographicum Mythologiae Classicae*, 5.1, 706–34. Zurich.

Kaimio, M. 1988. *Physical Contact in Greek Tragedy*. Helsinki.

Kao, W.-C., and J. Boyle. 2017. "Introduction." In *The Retro-Futurism of Cuteness*, edited by J. Boyle and W.-C. Kao, 13–28. Goleta, CA.

Kasimis, D. 2012. "The Tragedy of Blood-Based Membership: Secrecy and the Politics of Immigration in Euripides's *Ion*." *Political Theory* 41: 231–56.

Kasimis, D. 2020. "Medea the Refugee." *The Review of Politics* 82: 393–415.

Kasmani, O. 2019. "Thin Attachments" *Capacious* 1.4: 34–53.

Kavoulaki, A. 2008. "The Last Word: Ritual, Power, and Performance in Euripides' *Hiketides*." In *Performance, Iconography, Reception*, edited by M. Revermann and P. Wilson, 291–317. Oxford.

Keegan, C. M. 2020a. "Transgender Studies, or How to Do Things with Trans*." In *The Cambridge Companion to Queer Studies*, edited by S. Somerville, 66–75. Cambridge.

Keegan, C. 2020b. "Against Queer Theory." *TSQ* 7: 349–53.

Keegan, C. 2020c. "Getting Disciplined: What's Trans* About Queer Studies Now?" *Journal of Homosexuality* 67: 384–97.

Keeling, K. 2019. *Queer Times, Black Futures*. New York.

Kempf, E. J. 1920. *Psychopathology*. St. Louis.

Kidd, M. 2002. "Queer Myth and the Fallacy of Heterosexual Desire: Luis Riaza's *Medea es un buen chico* (1981)." In *Medeas*, edited by A. López and A. Pociña, 1059–71. Granada.

Kierkegaard, S. 1989. *The Concept of Irony, with Continual Reference to Socrates*. Princeton, NJ.

Kitto, H. D. F. 1977. "The *Rhesus* and Related Matters." *YCS* 25: 317–50.

Knox, B. M. W. 1977. "The *Medea* of Euripides." *YCS* 25: 193–225.

Konstan, D. 2007. "Medea: A Hint of Divinity?" *CW* 101: 93–4.

Kovacs, D., ed. 1999. *Euripides: Trojan Women, Iphigenia among the Taurians, Ion*. Cambridge, MA.

Kovacs, D., ed. 2002a. *Euripides: Bacchae, Iphigenia at Aulis, Rhesus*. Cambridge, MA.

Kovacs, D., ed. 2002b. *Euripides: Helen, Phoenician Women, Orestes*. Cambridge, MA.

Kovacs, D. 2003. "Toward a Reconstruction of *Iphigenia Aulidensis*." *JHS* 123: 77–103.

Kraus, C. S. 1998. "Dangerous Supplements: Etymology and Genealogy in Euripides' *Heracles*." *PCPhS* 44: 137–57.

Kruse, M. 2019. "Sedgwick's Perverse Close Reading and the Question of an Erotic Ethics." In *Reading Sedgwick*, edited by L. Berlant, 132–40. Durham, NC.

Kyriakou, P. 1997. "All in the Family: Present and Past in Euripides' *Andromache*." *Mnemosyne* 50: 7–26.

Ladenson, E. 1999. *Proust's Lesbianism*. Ithaca, NY.

Larson, J. 2017. "Venison for Artemis? The Problem of Deer Sacrifice." In *Animal Sacrifice in the Ancient Greek World*, edited by S. Hitch and I. Rutherford, 48–62. Cambridge.

Lavery, G. 2016. "The *Mikado*'s Queer Realism." *Novel* 49: 219–35.

Lavery, G. 2019. "The King's Two Anuses: Trans Feminism and Free Speech." *differences* 30: 119–51.

Lavery, G. 2020. "Egg Theory's Early Style." *TSQ* 7: 383–98.

Lawrence, S. 1997. "Audience Uncertainty and Euripides' *Medea*." *Hermes* 125: 49–55.

Le Guin, U. K. 2019. *The Carrier Bag Theory of Fiction*. London.

Lenfant, D. 2013. "Des eunuques dans la tragédie grecque." *Erga Logoi* 2: 7–30.

Lesjak, C. 2013. "Reading Dialectically." *Criticism* 55: 233–77.

Lesser, R. H. 2018. "Homeric Studies, Feminism, and Queer Theory." *Cloelia*, June 19, 2018. Last visited July 2, 2020. https://medium.com/cloelia-wcc/homeric-studies-feminism-and-queer-theory-interpreting-helen-and-penelope-ac63b5970628

Lévi-Strauss, C. 1955. "The Structural Study of Myth." *Journal of American Folklore* 68: 428–44.

Lewis, S. 2019. *Full Surrogacy Now*. New York.

Liapis, V. 2009. "*Rhesus* Revisited." *JHS* 129: 71–88.

Liapis, V., ed. 2012. *A Commentary on the* Rhesus *Attributed to Euripides*. Oxford.

Liapis, V. 2013. "Staging *Rhesus*." In *Performance in Greek and Roman Theatre* edited by G. W. M. Harrison and V. Liapis, 235–53. Leiden.

Liu, P. 2020. "Queer Theory and the Specter of Materialism." *Social Text* 38: 25–47.

López Saiz, B. 2017. "Ares y Dionisos: discurso político y poesía trágica en *Fenicias* de Eurípides." *Synthesis* 24, e019.

Loraux, N. 1987. *Tragic Ways of Killing a Woman*. Cambridge, MA.

Loraux, N. 1993. *The Children of Athena*. Princeton, NJ.

Loraux, N. 1995. *The Experiences of Tiresias*. Princeton, NJ.

Loraux, N. 1998. *Mothers in Mourning*. Ithaca, NY.

Love, H. 2007. *Feeling Backward*. Cambridge, MA.

Love, H. 2010. "Truth and Consequences: On Paranoid Reading and Reparative Reading." *Criticism* 52: 235–41.

Love, H. 2011. "Milk." In *Shakesqueer: A Queer Companion to the Complete Works of Shakespeare*, edited by M. Menon, 201–8. Durham, NC.

Bibliography

Love, H. 2013. "Close Reading and Thin Description." *Public Culture* 25: 401–34.

Love, H. 2014. "Queer." *TSQ* 1: 172–5.

MacCormack, P. 2012. "The Queer Ethics of Monstrosity." In *Speaking of Monsters*, edited by C. J. S. Picart and J. E. Browning, 255–65. New York.

Macintosh, F. 2011. "Review of *Orestes Terrorist.*" *Didaskalia* 8. https://www.didaskalia.net/issues/8/14/

Maffi, A. 2005. "Family and Property Law." In *The Cambridge Companion to Ancient Greek Law*, edited by M. Gagarin and D. Cohen, 254–66. Cambridge.

Marcuse, H. 2011. "The Ideology of Death." In *Philosophy, Psychoanalysis, and Emancipation*, vol. 5, edited by D. Kellner and C. Pierce, 122–31. New York.

Marshall, C. W. 2014. *The Structure and Performance of Euripides'* Helen. Cambridge.

Mastronarde, D. J., ed. 1994. *Euripides: Phoenissae.* Cambridge.

Mastronarde, D. J. 1999–2000a. "Introduction." *ICS* 24–5: 17–21.

Mastronarde, D. J. 1999–2000b. "Euripidean Tragedy and Genre." *ICS* 24–5: 23–39.

Mastronarde, D., ed. 2002. *Euripides: Medea.* Cambridge.

Mastronarde, D. J. 2010. *The Art of Euripides.* Cambridge.

Mastronarde, D. J., and J. M. Bremer. 1982. *The Textual Tradition of Euripides'* Phoinissai. Berkeley.

Matzner, S. 2016. "Queer Unhistoricism." In *Deep Classics*, edited by S. Butler, 179–201. London.

McCallum, E. L., and M. Tuhkanen. 2011. "Becoming Unbecoming: Untimely Mediations." In *Queer Times, Queer Becomings*, edited by E. L. McCallum and M. Tuhkanen, 1–24. Albany, NY.

McDermott, E. A. 1989. *Euripides'* Medea: *The Incarnation of Disorder.* University Park, PA.

McDermott, E. 2000. "Euripides' Second Thoughts." *TAPA* 130: 239–59.

McFarland, J., V. Slothouber, and A. Taylor. 2018. "Tempo-rarily Fat: A Queer Exploration of Fat Time." *Fat Studies* 7: 135–46.

McHugh, H., and D. Konstan, eds. 2001. *Euripides: Cyclops.* New York.

Medda, E. 2017. " 'O saffron robe, to what pass have you brought me!': Cross-dressing and Theatrical Illusion in Aristophanes' *Thesmophoriazusae.*" In *TransAntiquity*, edited by D. Campanile et al., 137–51. New York.

Mendelsohn, D. 2002. *Gender and the City in Euripides' Political Plays.* Oxford.

Menninghaus, W. 2009. "On the 'Vital Significance' of Kitsch: Walter Benjamin's Politics of 'Bad Taste.'" In *Walter Benjamin and the Architecture of Modernity*, edited by A. Benjamin and C. Rice, 39–58. Melbourne.

Menon, M. 2008. *Unhistorical Shakespeare.* London.

Menon, M. 2011. "Queer Shakes." In *Shakesqueer: A Queer Companion to the Complete Works of Shakespeare*, edited by M. Menon, 1–27. Durham, NC.

Mercier, T. C. 2021. "Re/pro/ductions: Ça déborde." *Poetics Today* 42: 23–47.

Meyer, M. 1994. "Introduction: Reclaiming the Discourse of Camp." In *The Politics and Poetics of Camp*, edited by M. Meyer, 1–22. London.

Michelini, A. 1987. *Euripides and the Tragic Tradition.* Madison, WI.

Michelini, A. 2009. "The 'Packed-Full' Drama in Late Euripides: *Phoenissae.*" In *The Play of Texts and Fragments*, edited by J. R. C. Cousland and J. R. Hume, 169–82. Leiden.

Miller, D. A. 2021. *Second Time Around.* New York.

Mills, S. 2014. "'It Wouldn't Happen Here . . . Could It?'—Chorus and Collusion in Euripides' *Medea.*" In *Looking at Medea*, edited by D. Stuttard, 92–100. London.

Mirto, M. S. 1984. "Il lutto e la cultura delle madri: le *Supplici* di Euripide." *QUCC* 18: 55–88.

Mirto, M. S. 2012. "La figura di Teti e la crisi del gamos eroico nell'*Andromaca* di Euripide." *MD* 69: 45–69.

Morrison, T. 1992. *Playing in the Dark: Whiteness and the Literary Imagination.* Cambridge, MA.

Morwood, J., ed. 2008. *Euripides: Bacchae and Other Plays.* Oxford.

Mossman, J., ed. 2011. *Euripides: Medea.* Liverpool.

Mueller, M. 2001. "The Language of Reciprocity in Euripides' *Medea*." *AJP* 122: 471–504.

Mueller, M. 2016. *Objects as Actors*. Chicago.

Muñoz, J. E. 1999. *Disidentifications*. Minneapolis.

Muñoz, J. E. 2009. *Cruising Utopia*. New York.

Murray, G., ed. 1913. *The Rhesus of Euripides*. New York.

Murray, G. 1946. *Greek Studies*. Oxford.

Musser, A. J. 2016. "Re-membering Audre." In *No Tea, No Shade*, edited by E. P. Johnson, 346–61. Durham, NC.

Musser, A. J. 2018. *Sensual Excess*. New York.

Namaste, V. 2000. *Invisible Lives*. Chicago.

Nelson, M. 2015. *The Argonauts*. Minneapolis.

Nero, C. 2005. "Why Are the Gay Ghettoes White." In *Black Queer Studies*, edited by E. P. Johnson and M. Henderson, 228–45. Durham, NC.

Ngai, S. 2012. *Our Aesthetic Categories: Zany, Cute, Interesting*. Cambridge, MA.

Nirta, C. 2018. *Marginal Bodies, Trans Utopias*. New York.

Oddey, A. 1994. *Devising Theatre*. Abingdon.

Ohi, K. 2015. *Dead Letters Sent: Queer Literary Transmission*. Minneapolis.

Olsen, S. 2012. "Maculate Conception: Sexual Ideology and Creative Authority in Heliodorus' *Aethiopica*." *AJPh* 133: 301–22.

Olsen, S. 2022. "Embracing Thetis in Euripides' *Andromache*." *CA*.

Ormand, K. 2009. "Electra in Exile." In *Bound by the City*, edited by D. E. McCoskey and E. Zakin, 247–73. Albany, NY.

Ormand, K., and R. Blondell. 2015. "One Hundred and Twenty-Five Years of Homosexuality." In *Ancient Sex*, edited by R. Blondell and K. Ormand, 1–22. Columbus, OH.

Orrells, D. 2011. *Classical Culture and Modern Masculinity*. Oxford.

Orrells, D. 2015. *Sex: Antiquity and Its Legacy*. London.

Østermark-Johansen, L. 2014. "Introduction." In Pater 2014, 1–66.

Østermark-Johansen, L. 2017. "Pater's 'Hippolytus Veiled': A Study from Euripides?" In *Pater the Classicist: Classical Scholarship, Reception, and Aestheticism*, edited by C. Martindale, S. Evangelista, and E. Prettejohn, 183–99. Oxford.

Papadimitropoulos, L. 2006. "Marriage and Strife in Euripides' *Andromache*." *GRBS* 46: 147–58.

Parsons, P. 1971. "A Greek Satyricon?" *BICS* 18: 53–68.

Pater, W. 2014. *Imaginary Portraits*, edited by L. Østermark-Johansen. London.

Pater, W. 2020. *The Collected Works of Walter Pater: Classical Studies*, vol. 8 (edited by M. Potolsky). Oxford.

Patterson, R. 1982. "The Platonic Art of Comedy and Tragedy." *Philosophy and Literature* 6: 76–93.

Pellegrini, A. 2007. "After Sontag: Future Notes on Camp." In *A Companion to Lesbian, Gay, Bisexual, Transgender, and Queer Studies*, edited by G. E. Haggerty and M. McGarry, 168–93. Malden, MA.

Pickard-Cambridge, A. W., J. Gould, and D. M. Lewis. 1988. *The Dramatic Festivals of Athens*. Oxford.

Pippen, A. 1960. "Euripides' *Helen*: A Comedy of Ideas." *CJ* 55: 151–63.

Poe, J. P. 2004. "Unconventional Procedures in *Rhesus*." *Philologus* 148: 21–33.

Poole, W. 1990. "Male Homosexuality in Euripides." In *Euripides, Women, and Sexuality*, edited by A. Powell, 108–50. New York.

The Postclassicisms Collective. 2020. *Postclassicisms*. Chicago.

Potolsky, M. 2020. "Critical Introduction." In *The Collected Works of Walter Pater*, vol. 8 (*Classical Studies*), 1–43. Oxford.

Powers, M. 2018. *Diversifying Greek Tragedy on the Contemporary US Stage*. Oxford.

Bibliography

Prauscello, L. 2006. *Singing Alexandria*. Leiden.

Preciado, P. 2018. *Countersexual Manifesto*. New York.

Preciado, P. 2021. *Can the Monster Speak?* Boston, MA.

Prins, Y. 1999. *Victorian Sappho*. Princeton, NJ.

Prins, Y. 2017. *Ladies' Greek*. Princeton, NJ.

Prosser, J. 1998. *Second Skins*. New York.

Proust, M. 2003. *In Search of Lost Time*. Translated by C. K. Scott-Moncrieff and T. Kilmartin and revised by D. J. Enright. New York.

Puar, J. K. 2007. *Terrorist Assemblages*. Durham, NC.

Puar, J. K. 2015. "Bodies with New Organs: Becoming Trans, Becoming Disabled." *Social Text* 33: 45–73.

Puar, J. K. 2017. *The Right to Maim*. Durham, NC.

Pucci, P. 1980. *The Violence of Pity in Euripides' Medea*. Ithaca, NY.

Pucci, P. 2012. "Helen's Many Faces." *QUCC* 100: 49–65.

Pugliese, J. 2004. "The Incommensurability of Law to Justice." *Law and Literature* 16: 285–311.

Purves, A. 2018. "What and Where is Touch?" In *Touch and the Ancient Senses*, edited by A. Purves, 1–20. London.

Rabinowitz, N. S. 1984. "Proliferating Triangles: Euripides' *Andromache* and the Traffic in Women." *Mosaic* 17: 111–25.

Rabinowitz, N. S. 1993. *Anxiety Veiled*. Ithaca, NY.

Rabinowitz, N. S. 2002. "Excavating Women's Homoeroticism in Ancient Greece." In *Among Women*, edited by L. Auanger and N. S. Rabinowitz, 106–66. Austin, TX.

Rabinowitz, N. S. 2015. "Melancholy Becomes Electra." In *Sex in Antiquity*, edited by M. Masterson, N. S. Rabinowitz, and J. Robson, 214–30. London.

Rabinowitz, N. S. 2020. "*Iphigenia among the Taurians*." In *Brill's Companion to Euripides*, edited by A. Markantonatos, 299–319. Leiden.

Racine, J. 1962. *Tragédies choisies de Racine*. Garden City, NY.

Rao, R. 2020. *Out of Time*. Oxford.

Relihan, J. C. 1993. *Ancient Menippean Satire*. Baltimore.

Rich, A. 1980. "Compulsory Heterosexuality and Lesbian Existence." *Signs* 5: 631–60.

Rich, A. 1986. *Of Woman Born*. New York.

Riley, K. 2008. *The Reception and Performance of Euripides'* Heracles: *Reasoning Madness*. Oxford.

Riley, K. 2018. "'All the Terrible Beauty of a Greek Tragedy': Wilde's 'Epistola' and the Euripidean Christ." In *Oscar Wilde and Classical Antiquity*, edited by K. Riley, A. J. L. Blanshard, and I. Manny, 175–94. Oxford.

Ritchie, W. 1964. *The Authenticity of the* Rhesus *of Euripides*. Cambridge.

Rivier, A. 1944. *Essai sur le tragique d'Euripide*. Lausanne.

Roisman, H. 2014. "Medea's Vengeance." In *Looking at Medea*, edited by D. Stuttard, 101–10. London.

Roisman, H. 2018. "The *Rhesus*–a Pro-Satyric Play?" *Hermes* 146: 432–46.

Rose, J. 2018. *Mothers: An Essay on Love and Cruelty*. New York.

Roselli, D. K. 2007. "Gender, Class and Ideology: The Social Function of Virgin Sacrifice in Euripides' *Children of Heracles*." *CA* 26: 81–169.

Rosenberg, J. 2014. "The Molecularization of Sexuality." *Theory & Event* 17 n.p.

Ross, I. 2013. *Oscar Wilde and Ancient Greece*. Cambridge.

Rubin, G. 2011. "Thinking Sex." In *Deviations: A Gayle Rubin Reader*, 137–81. Durham, NC.

Ruffell, I. 2011. *Politics and Anti-Realism in Athenian Old Comedy*. Oxford.

Ruffell, I. 2013. "Humiliation? Voyeurism, Violence, and Humor in Old Comedy." *Helios* 40: 247–77.

Ruffell, I. 2014. "Utopianism." In *The Cambridge Companion to Greek Comedy*, edited by M. Revermann, 206–21. Cambridge.

Ruffell, I. 2020. "Poetics, Perversions, and Passing: Approaching the Transgender Narratives of Aristophanes' *Thesmophoriazousai*" *Illinois Classical Studies* 45: 333–67.

Rutherford, R. 2014. "The Final Scene." In *Looking at Medea*, edited by D. Stuttard, 84–91. London.

Ruti, M. 2017. *The Ethics of Opting Out*. New York.

Said, E. 1979. *Orientalism*. New York.

Said, E. 2006. *On Late Style*. New York.

Salah, T. 2017. "What Does Tiresias Want?" *TSQ* 4: 632–38.

Samuels, E., and E. Freeman. 2021. "Introduction: Crip Temporalities." *SAQ* 120: 245–54.

Sanyal, D., M. Telò, and D. R. Young, eds. 2022. *Proximities: Reading with Judith*. Representations.

Schlosser, J. A. 2012. " 'Hope, Danger's Comforter': Thucydides, Hope, Politics." *The Journal of Politics* 75: 169–82.

Schor, N. 2001. "Male Lesbianism." *GLQ* 7: 391–9.

Scodel, R. 1997. "Teichoscopia, Catalogue, and the Female Spectator in Euripides." *Colby Quarterly* 33: 76–93.

Scott, J. 2005. *Electra after Freud*. Ithaca, NY.

Scott, J. C. 1985. *Weapons of the Weak*. New Haven, CT.

Seaford, R. 1987. "The Tragic Wedding." *JHS* 107: 106–30.

Seaford, R., ed. 1988. *Euripides: Cyclops*. Oxford.

Sebo, H. 2014. "Strife and Starvation: Euripides' *Helen*." *Arethusa* 47: 145–68.

Sedgwick, E. K. 1985. *Between Men*. New York.

Sedgwick, E. K. 1990. *Epistemology of the Closet*. Berkeley.

Sedgwick, E. K. 1993. *Tendencies*. Durham, NC.

Sedgwick, E. K. 2003. *Touching Feeling*. Durham, NC.

Sedgwick, E. K. 2011. "The Weather in Proust." In *The Weather in Proust*, 1–41. Durham, NC.

Segal, C. 1971. "The Two Worlds of Euripides' *Helen*." *TAPA* 102: 553–614.

Segal, C. 1996. "Euripides' *Medea*: Vengeance, Reversal, and Closure." *Pallas* 45: 15–44.

Shahani, N. 2013. "The Future is Queer Stuff." *GLQ* 19: 545–58.

Shapiro, J. 2015. "Pederasty and Popular Audience." In *Ancient Sex*, edited by R. Blondell and K. Ormand, 177–207. Columbus, OH.

Sheldon, R. 2016. *The Child to Come*. Minneapolis.

Shuttleworth, S. 2010. *The Mind of the Child: Child Development in Literature, Science, and Medicine, 1840–1900*. Oxford.

Smith-Prei, C., and M. Stehle. 2016. *# Awkward Politics*. Montreal & Kingston.

Soares Brandão, A., and R. Lira de Sousa. 2013. "Hitchcock's Queer Doubles." *Ilha do Desterro* 65: 17–28.

Sontag, S. 1964. "Notes on 'Camp'." In *Against Interpretation*, 275–92. New York.

Sourvinou-Inwood, C. 1997. "Medea at a Shifting Distance." In *Medea*, edited by J. J. Clauss and S. I. Johnston, 253–96. Princeton, NJ.

Spade, D. 2015. *Normal Life: Administrative Violence, Critical Trans Politics, and the Limits of Law*. Durham, NC.

Spaeth, B. S. 2014. "From Goddess to Hag." In *Daughters of Hecate*, edited by K. Stratton and D. S. Kalleres, 41–58. Oxford.

Stanley, E. A. 2011. "Near Life, Queer Death." *Social Text* 29: 1–19.

Stanley, E. A. 2015. "Introduction: Fugitive Flesh." In *Captive Genders*, edited by E. A. Stanley and N. Smith, 7–20. Oakland, CA.

Stavrinou, A. S. 2014. "Inside and Out: The Dynamics of Domestic Space in Euripides' *Andromache*." *Hermes* 142: 385–403.

Stavrinou, A. S. 2016. "Hermione's Spartan Costume: The Tragic *skeue* in Euripides's *Andromache*." *ICS* 41: 1–20.

Steiner, D. T. 2021. *Choral Constructions in Greek Culture*. Cambridge.

Stockert, W., ed. 1992. *Euripides, Iphigenie in Aulis*. Vienna.

Bibliography

Storey, I. C. 1989. "Domestic Disharmony in Euripides' *Andromache*." *G&R* 36: 16–27.

Stryker, S. 2004. "Transgender Studies: Queer Theory's Evil Twin." *GLQ* 10: 212–15.

Stryker, S. 2008. *Transgender History*. Berkeley.

Stryker, S. 2020. "Introduction: Trans* Studies Now." *TSQ* 7: 299–305.

Stryker, S., and P. Currah. 2018. "General Editors' Introduction." *TSQ* 5: 161–3.

Stryker S., et al. 2008. "Introduction: Trans-, Trans, or Transgender?" *WSQ* 36: 11–22.

Stuelke, P. 2021. *The Ruse of Repair*. Durham, NC.

Symonds, J. A. 1873. *Studies of the Greek Poets*. First Series. London.

Swift, L. A. 2009. "Sexual and Familial Distortion in Euripides' *Phoenissae*." *TAPA* 139: 53–87.

Tanner, T. 1979. *Adultery in the Novel*. Baltimore.

Taplin, O. 1977. *The Stagecraft of Aeschylus*. Oxford.

Taplin, O. 2003. *Greek Tragedy in Action*. London.

Tavernise, S. 2021. "The U.S. Birthrate Has Dropped Again." *The New York Times* (May 5).

Telò, M. 2002. "Per una grammatica dei gesti nella tragedia greca (II): la supplica." *MD* 49: 9–51.

Telò, M. 2018. "The Boon and the Woe." In *The Materialities of Greek Tragedy*, edited by M. Telò and M. Mueller, 133–52. London.

Telò, M. 2020. *Archive Feelings*. Columbus, OH.

Telò, M. 2022a. *Resistant Formalisms*. Goleta, CA.

Telò, M. 2022b. "Blanchot, Derrida, and the Gimmick." In *The Before and the After: Archê and Avenir in a Time of Crisis*, edited by S. Gurd and M. Telò. Goleta, CA.

Telò, M. forthcoming. "Queer (A)edi-(m)ology: On Callimachus's *Aetia* Prologue." *Ramus*.

Thalmann, G. 1993. "Euripides and Aeschylus: The Case of the *Hekabe*." *CA* 12: 126–59.

Tilleman, M. 2010. "(Trans)Forming the Provocation Defense." *Journal of Criminal Law and Criminology* 100: 1659–88.

Tompkins, A. 2014. "Asterisk." *TSQ* 1: 26–7.

Torrance, I. 2013. *Metapoetry in Euripides*. Oxford.

Tyrrell, W. B. 1984. *Amazons*. Baltimore.

Umachandran, M. Forthcoming. "Fungal Methods, Queering the Carrier Bag, and Black Lesbian Speculative Fiction." In *Routledge Handbook of Classics and Queer Theory*, edited by E. Haselswerdt, S. Lindheim, and K. Ormand.

Usher, M. D. 2002. "Satyr Play in Plato's *Symposium*." *AJP* 123: 205–28.

Vaccaro, J. 2011. "Felt Matters." *Women and Performance* 20: 253–66.

Vaccaro, J. 2015. "Feelings and Fractals." *GLQ* 21: 273–93.

Van Zyl Smit, B. 2014. "Black Medeas." In *Looking at Medea*, edited by D. Stuttard, 138–45. London.

Walton, M. J. 2009. *Euripides Our Contemporary*. London.

Ward, M. 2019. "Assemblage Theory and the Uses of Classical Reception: the Case of Aristotle Knowsley's *Oedipus*." *Classical Receptions Journal* 11: 508–23.

Warner, M. 1993. "Introduction." In *Fear of a Queer Planet*, edited by M. Warner, vii–xxxi. Minneapolis.

Wasdin, K. 2020. "Concealed Kypris in the *Iphigenia at Aulis*." *CQ* 70: 43–50.

Weil, S. 2005. "The *Iliad* or the Poem of Force." In *An Anthology*, edited by S. Miles, 162–95. London.

Weiner, J., and D. Young. 2011. "Queer Bonds." *GLQ* 17: 223–41.

Weiss, N. A. 2018. *The Music of Tragedy*. Oakland, CA.

West, M. L., ed. 1987. *Euripides: Orestes*. Warminster.

West, M. L. 1999. "Ancestral Curses." In *Sophocles Revisited*, edited by J. Griffin, 31–46. Oxford.

Westengard, L. 2019. *Gothic Queer Culture*. Lincoln, NE.

Weston, K. 1991. *Families We Choose: Lesbians, Gays, Kinship*. New York.

Wiegman, R., and E. A. Wilson, eds. 2015. *Queer Theory Without Antinormativity. differences* 26.1

Willink, C. W., ed. 1986. *Euripides: Orestes*. Oxford.

Wittig, M. 1992. *The Straight Mind and Other Essays*. Boston, MA.

Wohl, V. 2002. *Love among the Ruins*. Princeton, NJ.

Wohl, V. 2005. "Beyond Sexual Difference: Becoming-Woman in Euripides' *Bacchae*." In *The Soul of Tragedy*, edited by V. Pedrick and S. Oberhelman, 137–54. Chicago.

Wohl, V. 2011. "The Politics of Enmity in Euripides' *Orestes*." In *Greek Drama IV*, edited by D. Rosenbloom and J. Davidson, 244–69. Oxford.

Wohl, V. 2014. "Play of the Improbable: Euripides' Unlikely *Helen*." In *Probabilities, Hypotheticals, and Counterfactuals in Ancient Greek Thought*, edited by V. Wohl, 142–59. Cambridge.

Wohl, V. 2015. *Euripides and the Politics of Form*. Princeton, NJ.

Wohl, V. 2018. "Stone into Smoke: Metaphor and Materiality in Euripides' *Troades*." In *The Materialities of Greek Tragedy*, edited by M. Telò and M. Mueller, 17–33. London.

Worman, N. 1999. "The Ties that Bind: Transformations of Costume and Connection in Euripides' *Heracles*." *Ramus* 28: 89–107.

Worman, N. 2020. "Euripides and the Aesthetics of Embodiment." In *Brill's Companion to Euripides*, edited by A. Markantonatos, 749–74. Leiden.

Worman, N. 2021. *Tragic Bodies*. London.

Wright, M. 2006. "*Orestes*, a Euripidean Sequel." *CQ* 56: 33–47.

Wright, M. 2008. *Euripides: Orestes*. London.

Wyles, R. 2013. "Heracles' Costume from Euripides' *Heracles* to Pantomime Performance." In *Performance in Greek and Roman Theatre*, edited by G. Harrison and V. Liapis, 181–98. Leiden.

Yeargeau, M. 2018. *Authoring Autism*. Durham, NC.

Young, D. R. 2014. "Queer Seriousness." *World Picture 9* ("Serious").

Young, D. R. 2016. "Queer Love." In *Gender: Love*, edited by J. C. Nash, 197–210. Farmington Hills, MI.

Young, D. R. 2019a. "Ironies of Web 2.0." *Post45* https://post45.org/2019/05/ironies-of-web-2-0

Young, D. R. 2019b. "A Man with a Mother: *Tarnation* and the Subject of Confession." In *I Confess!*, edited by T. Waugh and B. Arroyo, 436–51. Montreal & Kingston.

Zeitlin, F. I. 1970. "The Argive Festival of Hera and Euripides' *Electra*." *TAPA* 101: 645–69.

Zeitlin, F. I. 1980. "The Closet of Masks: Role-playing and Myth-making in the *Orestes* of Euripides." *Ramus* 9: 51–77.

Zeitlin, F. I. 1981. "Travesties of Gender and Genre in Aristophanes' *Thesmophoriazusae*." *Critical Inquiry* 8: 301–27.

Zeitlin, F. I. 1996. *Playing the Other*. Chicago.

Zuntz, G. 1955. *The Political Plays of Euripides*. Manchester.

INDEX

Index

Index

Index

Index

Index